ROMAN YORKSHIRE

Roman
YORKSHIRE

People, Culture and Landscape

PATRICK OTTAWAY

BLACKTHORN PRESS

Blackthorn Press, Blackthorn House
Middleton Rd, Pickering YO18 8AL
United Kingdom

www.blackthornpress.com

ISBN 978 1 906259 33 4

Designed and typeset by Carnegie Book Production, Lancaster
Printed and bound in Malta by Gutenberg Press

To Ned and Barty, two young Yorkshiremen
beginning to learn about the Romans

Filiis optimis et carissimis

Contents

List of illustrations

List of tables

Preface

T HE ROMANS continue to exert a profound and persistent hold on our imagination. Whether we think of the personalities and events that shaped an empire or of the huge diversity of material culture from the monumental public buildings to the most delicate of jewellery and even the humble cooking pots, there is something both familiar and exciting about one of the world's great civilisations. It is no wonder, therefore, that so many of us look around at our own locality and ask what happened here in Roman times and why? What did the Romans do for *us*? This book tries to answer these questions for a region of Britain corresponding to the county of Yorkshire before the reorganisation of county boundaries in 1974.

The last history of Yorkshire in Roman times was published in 1936 by F. R. Pearson, a Bridlington schoolmaster, although there have been other works since then which have dealt with parts of the region, notably two titles in the *Peoples of Roman Britain* series: *The Parisi* by Herman Ramm (1978) and *The Brigantes* by Brian Hartley and Leon Fitts (1988). Since Pearson's time relevant documentary sources for the region which originate in the Roman period itself have been added to only by the remarkable wooden letters from the fort at Vindolanda in Northumberland which contain a few, if important, references to places in Yorkshire. However, the amount of archaeological information, even since Ramm and Hartley and Fitts were writing, has increased enormously, not only from well-known Roman sites like York or Catterick, but from all over the region. Whereas Pearson had to rely a good deal on what was known about York itself, and about the region's Roman forts and roads, we now know about settlements inhabited by people of all sorts and conditions, from the landed elite to the humblest toilers on the land. In recognition of this, another of my aims has been to refer to as many different places as possible where Roman archaeology has been found. Although there may still, even so, be many significant omissions, I hope I have, none the less, shown that in Roman times there were people living all over the Yorkshire region; only the really high ground in the Pennines and North York Moors was not settled at all. There were, one might say, Romans around every corner from the River Tees in the north to the River Don in the south, and from Ribblehead in the west to Spurn Head in the east. The vast majority of these people were subsistence farmers who lived on what they could grow and on the animals they could keep. Most of the others did hard manual work in quarries, mines and workshops. With the development of new methods of investigation, it has been the lives of the mass of the population which archaeology has been particularly successful in revealing in recent years. Although we shall never know their names, as we do of a few of their overlords, it is these anonymous working people who dug the ditches and pits, built the walls and roads, and made the pots, and often lived very brief lives for their pains, who are the real heroes and heroines of my story.

After an introductory chapter there are two chapters which set the scene for the history which follows, one of these concerns the natural environment of the Yorkshire region and the other reviews both the sources of evidence for the Roman period and the way that research has used those sources over the centuries. There is then a chapter on Yorkshire in the immediate pre-Roman period which introduces seven themes: settlement and landscape, agriculture, manufacturing, exchange and trade, the visual arts, religion and the treatment of the dead. After a chapter on the military conquest of the Yorkshire region, I return to each of these themes in four chapters structured around broad chronological divisions of the Roman period from the late first century to the early fifth. After the first two of these there is a short chapter concerned with York at the time of the visit of the Emperor Septimius Severus. I have not wanted York to appear too dominant in the story of Roman Yorkshire, but I felt it only right to give due weight to a dramatic episode in the history not only of the city itself, but of Roman Britain as a whole. The final chapter briefly takes the story of Yorkshire beyond the end of the Roman period and looks at the legacy of Rome in the region.

This has been a hard book to write and has taken much longer than I anticipated. However, anyone who has small children will know that if one is trying to make a living, one's free time for other projects is very limited. A good deal of what follows has therefore been written at the dead of night when the house was quiet except for occasions when a wakeful child required comfort or a drink of milk. The book is dedicated to my very dear sons, Ned and Barty, but I must add my gratitude to Alan Avery of the Blackthorn Press for continuing to believe that the book would eventually see the light of day.

For their assistance with my work on the book I am very happy to acknowledge the generous assistance of a number of friends and colleagues. First of all, there are those who have made unpublished reports available in the region's Sites and Monuments Records: Jason Dodds (West Yorkshire), Louisa Matthews (North Yorkshire and South Yorkshire), Jim McNeil (South Yorkshire), and Dave Evans and Ruth Atkinson (Humber Archaeology Partnership, East Riding). In addition, Dave Aspden of ArcHeritage sent a draft report on the important early Roman cemetery at Waterdale, Doncaster in advance of publication. Trevor Brigham and Ken Steedman sent me unpublished reports on work by Humber Field Archaeology and images from their archive. John Cruse gave advice on the use and manufacture of querns. Alan King discussed aspects of his work in the Dales and suggested suitable images. Rodney Mackey discussed his excavations at Welton Wold with me and generously allowed the use of images of the site. Karl Noble kindly allowed me to photograph items of sculpture on display in Clifton House Museum, Rotherham. Ian Roberts of West Yorkshire Archaeological Services sent some of the text on Wattle Syke in advance of publication and allowed the use of images from WYAS archive. Peter Robinson of Doncaster Museum Service, Doncaster Metropolitan Borough Council showed me images of the pottery kilns from the museum archives and took photographs of vessels in the collections specifically for the book for which I am most grateful. Pete Wilson (English Heritage) sent me unpublished reports on Cawthorn and Staxton.

The images in the book are acknowledged individually, but in addition to those thanked above, I am grateful to the following for making images available: Anthony Crawshaw, Gareth Edwards (Manor House Museum, Ilkley), Gail Falkingham (North Yorkshire County Council Heritage Unit), Andrew Fleming, Javis Gurr (English Heritage), Peter Halkon (Hull University), Elizabeth Hartley, Gwen Jones, Miles Johnson (Yorkshire Dales National Park), Christine Kyriacou (York Archaeological Trust), Steve Moorhouse, Martin Millett (Cambridge University), Andrew Morrison (York Museums Trust), Nick Pearson (On Site Archaeology), Peter Rowe (Tees Archaeology), Terry Suthers, Paula Ware (MAP), and Stuart Wrathmell (ASWYAS).

Finally I owe a very special debt of gratitude to Lesley Collett (York Archaeological Trust) for preparing many of the plans in the volume with her usual skill and keen eye for good presentation.

Patrick Ottaway, February the first, 2013 – St Bride's Day

Roman names and places

There are a number of places in Yorkshire for which we know a Latin name, but I refer to them in the text by their modern name only. The Latin names and their meanings – usually based on Romanisation of a native name – are given in the list below, based largely on Rivet and Smith (1979). For the Roman name of Malton, about which there is some debate, reference may also be made to Creighton (1988).

Aldborough	*Isurium Brigantum* – 'place in the region on this side of the River *Uria*'
Bowes	*Lavatris* or *Lavatrae* – 'river bed'
Bainbridge	*Virosidum* – 'seat'
Brough on Humber	*Petuaria* – 'fourth'
Castleford	*Lagentium* – 'fort of the swordsmen'
Catterick	*Cataractonium* – 'battle ramparts'
Doncaster	*Danum* – 'rapidly flowing river'
Elslack	*Olenacum* or *Olicana* – 'place of a man whose name was Olen'
Greta Bridge	*Maglona* – 'high' or 'noble place'
Ilkley	*Verbeia* – 'winding river' or *Olicana*
Malton	*Derventio?* – 'river in the oak wood'
Slack	*Camulodunum* – 'fort of the war god'
Stamford Bridge	*Delgovicia?* – 'place of spear fighters'
Tadcaster	*Calcaria* – 'limestone quarries'
York	*Eboracum* – 'place of yew trees'

Dates

All dates are AD unless BC is specifically stated.

1 | Introduction to Roman Yorkshire

'In the abundance and variety of its Roman antiquities, Yorkshire stands second to no other county'

Frank and Harriet Wragg Elgee (1933)

The Yorkshire region

A Roman army first entered what we now know as Yorkshire in about the year AD 48, according to the Roman author Cornelius Tacitus.[1] This was some five years after the invasion of Britain itself ordered by the Emperor Claudius. The soldiers' first task in the region was to assist in the suppression of a rebellion against a Roman ally, Queen Cartimandua of the Brigantes, a native people who occupied most of northern England. The Roman army returned to the north in about the years 51–2, once again to support Cartimandua who was, Tacitus tells us, now under attack by her former consort, a man named Venutius.[2] In 69 a further dispute between Cartimandua and Venutius, for which Tacitus is again the (only) source, may have provided a pretext for the Roman army to begin the conquest of the whole of northern Britain.[3] England south of Hadrian's Wall, including Yorkshire, was to remain part of the Roman empire for about 340 years.

The region which is the principal subject of this book is Yorkshire as it was defined before local government reorganisation in 1974. There was no political entity corresponding to the county in Roman times. It was, according to the second-century Greek geographer Ptolemy, split between the Brigantes and the Parisi, a people who lived in what is now (after a brief period as Humberside) the East Riding. The county of Yorkshire with its three parts – the ridings – is first known to history in the late Anglo-Saxon era some 600 years after Britain had ceased to be part of the Roman Empire. One might be forgiven, therefore, for asking whether it is legitimate to write a history of Roman Yorkshire other than to satisfy the requirements of a series in which most of the other volumes are concerned with periods when the county name had real meaning.

There are probably two main reasons for an answer in the affirmative. The first is that regional studies of Roman Britain are useful because they allow a clearer look at particular problems and themes than is usually possible in studies of the province of *Britannia* as a whole. There is such a vast amount of data, especially archaeological, for the study of Roman Britain that a province-wide account can only treat regional issues superficially. Secondly,

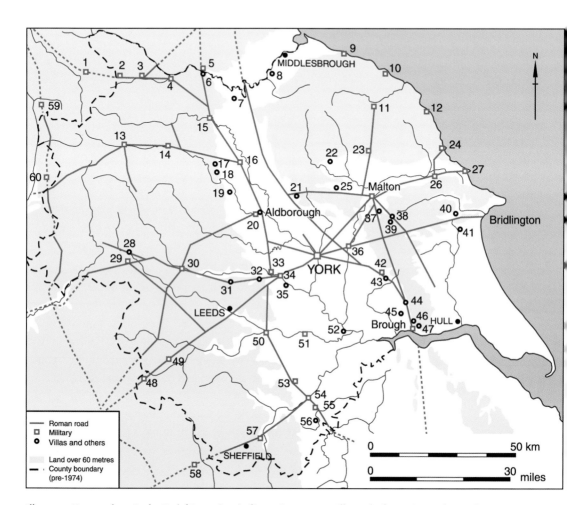

Illus. 1.1   Roman places in the Yorkshire region (military sites, towns, villas and other major settlements)

Key: 1, Brough under Stainmore (Cumbria); 2, Rey Cross; 3, Bowes; 4, Carkin Moor; 5, Piercebridge (Co. Durham); 6, Manfield (Holme House); 7, Dalton on Tees; 8, Ingleby Barwick; 9, Huntcliff; 10, Goldsborough; 11, Lease Rigg; 12, Ravenscar; 13, Bainbridge; 14, Wensley; 15, Catterick; 16, Healam Bridge; 17, Snape; 18, Well; 19, Castle Dykes, North Stainley; 20, Roecliffe; 21, Oulston; 22, Beadlam; 23, Cawthorn; 24, Scarborough; 25, Hovingham; 26, Staxton; 27, Filey; 28, Kirk Sink, Gargrave; 29, Elslack; 30, Ilkley; 31, Adel; 32, Dalton Parlours; 33, Newton Kyme; 34, Tadcaster; 35, Kirkby Wharfe; 36, Stamford Bridge; 37, Langton; 38, Wharram-le-Street; 39, Wharram Grange and Wharram Percy; 40, Rudston; 41, Harpham; 42, Hayton; 43, Shiptonthorpe; 44, North and South Newbald; 45, North and South Cave; 46, Brantingham; 47, Welton Wold; 48, Castleshaw; 49, Slack; 50, Castleford; 51, Roall Manor Farm; 52, Drax; 53, Burghwallis; 54, Doncaster; 55, Rossington Bridge; 56, Stancil; 57, Templeborough; 58, Brough-on-Noe (Derbys.); 59, Over Burrow Bridge (Cumbria); 60, Burrow in Lonsdale (Lancs.).

if Roman Britain is to be divided up, then the historic county of Yorkshire is as good as any other region of comparable size – c.1.5 million hectares – for study because it includes such a great variety of landscape types and environmental conditions. There are the relatively dry and temperate lowlands of the Vale of York and Holderness at one extreme and the wetter, colder uplands of the Pennines and North York Moors at the other. It is, to some extent at least, as a result of this diversity that not only military sites, but more or less the whole spectrum of traditionally recognised types of Roman settlement in Britain, from native farmsteads and villas to towns, can be found in the region. Yorkshire therefore provides us with an excellent opportunity to examine the relationship between, on the one hand, landscape and environment and, on the other, settlements and their cultural, economic and social characteristics.

Furthermore, pre-1974 Yorkshire has a certain geographical integrity being defined by clear natural boundaries on almost all sides. To the north is the River Tees, to the east lies the North Sea coast which runs south to the Humber Estuary, a cultural and political, as well as physical boundary from prehistoric times to the present day. In the immediate pre-Roman period, for example, the Humber divided the Parisi from the Corieltauvi of Lincolnshire and Nottinghamshire, a division confirmed in Roman arrangements for local government after the conquest. On the west side of Yorkshire the former county boundary is at one point no more than 15km from the Irish Sea, but for the most part it corresponded to the Pennine watershed from which rivers like the Swale and the Aire flow east into Yorkshire and others, like the Ribble, flow west into Lancashire.

Yorkshire in the Roman world

How should we regard the role and significance of our region in Roman Britain and in the Roman world as a whole? Roman Britain is often portrayed as a remote place, an outpost on the periphery of an empire the centre of which lay if not exactly on the banks of the Tiber then certainly in the Mediterranean littoral. Seen in this way Roman Britain becomes rather like a distant possession of the British empire – a Solomon Islands or a St Helena – somehow inherently backward and unsophisticated, if not barbarous, merely by virtue of its physical distance from the mother country. An inevitable inference drawn from this way of looking at Roman Britain is that its history must be one of things done *to* the Britons *by* the Romans – a historical process of Romanisation, making Britons into Romans, revealed by changes in material culture: buildings, roads, pottery, metalwork and so forth.

It cannot be denied, of course, that the impact of the Roman Empire on Britain was substantial, although much greater in some areas than others. One can readily contrast south central and south-eastern Britain with lands north of the Humber which in respect of, for example, towns and villas remained underdeveloped. However, the process of change in the Roman period, a process with which this book is very much concerned, can no longer be seen as involving the imposition of a pre-existing template of 'Romanity', or 'Romanness' on the Britons which takes no account either of differences in the Britons themselves and their particular environmental and geographical circumstances, or of the diversity of the Roman empire as a whole.

One good reason why we can look at the relationship between Roman and native in a way that gives the latter a voice, barely audible before the mid-twentieth century, is that since then archaeologists have begun to discover evidence for the native population of Roman Britain on a scale never previously thought possible. This will be discussed in more detail later in the book, but suffice it to say here that where once it seems to have been assumed that the unsophisticated Britons had left little trace, new techniques of prospection, survey and excavation give us their settlements and material culture allowing them to make their own distinctive contribution to the history of the period.

For most people in Roman Britain, whether in Yorkshire or elsewhere, their farmsteads, fields, pastures and woodlands were at the centre of the known world. In an era of poor communications very few people would have travelled, at least on a regular basis, more than a day's walk or, for the fortunate, a day's ride from home. Only a small elite in the military, governmental or commercial ranks of Roman society would have had much conception of how their own patch related to the rest of Britain, let alone the Roman Empire as a whole. Having said this, in the Yorkshire region, as in others, the Romans encountered people with a vibrant and resilient culture, if at a less advanced level of development than their own, people who were equal to making some sort of choice about what they did and did not like from what the Roman Empire had to offer. We should therefore consider the process of change after AD 69 in our region within the context of the interaction between Roman and native which created a culture peculiar to its region – one more variation on the theme of what it meant to be Roman.

It will be clear from the references cited in this volume that there are documentary sources of evidence for Britain surviving from the Roman period and some which bear in particular on the north, but, as I shall discuss in more detail in Chapter 3, they are very limited in the topics they cover. The principal body of evidence for the story of Roman Yorkshire is archaeological and so in contrast to other volumes in the History of Yorkshire series this volume must of necessity deal less with personalities and politics, and more with such themes as settlement, society, economy, religion and burial customs. First of all, however, we must look at what the landscape of the region looked like in the Roman period and what natural resources were available for its management and exploitation.

2 | The Environment and Landscape of the Yorkshire Region

Introduction

In this chapter I will try to give an overview of the geographical, geological and environmental characteristics of the Yorkshire region. Even more than today, perhaps, they had a considerable influence on economic and social development in Roman times and their interaction created the landscape with which people had to come to terms in order to make a living.

Physical geography

The physical geography, or physiography, of the Yorkshire region can be characterised in simple terms. There is a central lowland zone running from the River Tees in the north to the Humber Basin in the south, flanked by major uplands to the east and west which on the east are broken up by two smaller lowland zones: the Vale of Pickering and the Plain of Holderness.

One gets a very good sense of the physical geography of Yorkshire by following some of the principal Roman roads in the county, themselves testimony to the conquerors' engineering capabilities in taming the landscape. For example, let us begin at York and head for Carlisle (Roman *Luguvalium*), close to the northern frontier of Roman Britain, first of all travelling west and then north, and then north-westwards. We can take the modern A59 and B6265 which run on or close to the line of a Roman road almost as far as the former Roman town at Aldborough, following a ridge of high ground through the low-lying Vale of York. The modern road deviates from the ancient line to pass through Boroughbridge, the medieval successor to Roman Aldborough as a crossing point over the River Ure, before reaching the A1. From Marton-le-Moor (3km north of Boroughbridge) the A1 follows more or less the line of Dere Street, the name by which the main Roman road to the north is now known. We are in the Vale of Mowbray by the time we reach the next major Roman site at Catterick at the crossing over the River Swale.

From Catterick it is 8km to Scotch Corner where we turn off onto the A66 which follows the line of another Roman road. After Scotch Corner the A66 very gradually begins to rise more than it falls until at Greta Bridge, where there was a Roman fort at the crossing of the River Greta, we are *c*.150m above sea level. After Greta Bridge the road rises again over the next 9km to Bowes where the fort sits above the valley of the Greta at close to 300m above sea level. Bowes is at the eastern end of the Stainmore pass which crosses the Pennines into Cumbria. At the highest point of the pass, about halfway between Bowes and the Roman fort at Brough (in Cumbria), at the county boundary between Yorkshire and Cumberland as it was before 1974, lies the Roman camp at Rey Cross which is 447m above sea level. Much of the land to the north and south of Rey Cross is moorland, 300m or more above sea level. Fifteen kilometres to the north-west, in the north-western corner of Yorkshire is the county's highest point at Mickle Fell which rises to 790m above sea level. Other high points in the Yorkshire Pennines include Ingleborough at 724m above sea level.

Illus. 2.1 The principal geographical regions and rivers of Yorkshire.

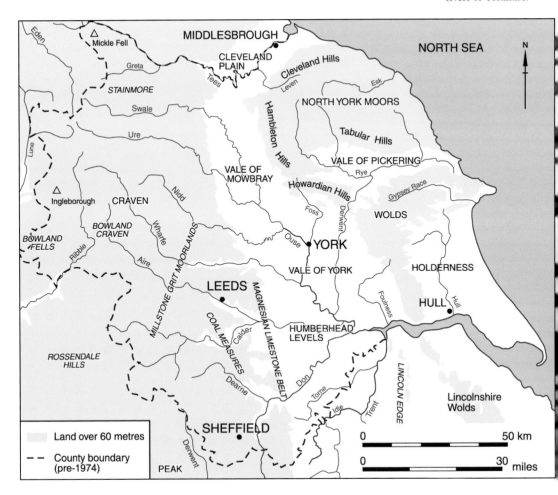

Illus. 2.2 Greta Bridge Roman fort: the defences (ditch, and rampart beyond it) seen from outside the south-east corner looking towards the south gate. (Photo: P. Ottaway)

Cutting through the Pennines at intervals are valleys – the Yorkshire Dales – which have served as communication routes from earliest times and were controlled by the Romans with strategically placed forts. From the Pennine watershed the only major river to flow west for any appreciable distance through Yorkshire is the Ribble. All of Yorkshire's other rivers flow east or south-east towards the lowlands. The northernmost of these is the Tees which still forms part of the boundary with County Durham until it reaches the new county of Cleveland. Before reaching the North Sea, near Middlesborough, the Tees was crossed by Dere Street at Piercebridge, west of Darlington, where there was a Roman bridge. Some remains of it can be seen today on the Yorkshire side, marooned by the shifting river bed. The other rivers in the Dales flow into the Humber Basin. The most northerly of these is the Swale which we crossed at Catterick on our journey to Carlisle. Near Aldborough the Swale meets the Ure which then joins the Ouse at Nun Monkton before flowing through York to the Humber. The Ure itself flows south-eastwards through Wensleydale in which there was a Roman road which passed by Bainbridge fort on its way across the Pennines to Lancaster.

To the south of Wensleydale is Wharfedale. The River Wharfe rises high in the Pennines near Ribblehead and flows south-eastwards passing Grassington, site of a well-preserved prehistoric, Roman and later landscape of enclosures and settlements.[1] From Grassington the Wharfe flows on to Ilkley where there was a fort known to the Romans either as *Olicana* or *Verbeia*, the latter name probably being that of a river goddess.[2] The Wharfe reaches the Ouse at Tadcaster, another probable fort site. South of Wharfedale is Airedale in which, from its source near Malham, the River Aire flows south-east through Skipton, and passes near to the Roman fort at Elslack. Also known as Burwen Castle, the fort lies on a Roman road heading west from Ilkley towards the valley of the Ribble and the fort at Ribchester in Lancashire. Finally, there is Calderdale; the Calder rises near Burnley in Lancashire, crosses the county boundary into Yorkshire near Todmorden and then near Mytholmroyd it was crossed by a Roman road from Ilkley to Manchester. The Calder then flows east towards Castleford, site of a Roman fort, where it meets the River Aire.

In Yorkshire's central lowland zone, the Tees Basin runs into the Vale of Mowbray which extends to a southern limit at around Northallerton from where it gives way to the Vale of York. South of York, between Selby, Doncaster and Goole there lies a large area usually referred to as the Humberhead Levels or the Humber Basin. Much of the area would have been poorly drained in Roman times and settlement tends to be on islands of relatively high ground. Yorkshire's central lowlands are up to *c.*60km wide and the land rarely rises higher than 30m above sea level until one reaches the Magnesian Limestone belt on the west side or the Yorkshire or Lincolnshire Wolds on the east. Ridges of higher ground within the lowlands are, however, provided by the York and Escrick moraines, composed of debris left behind by retreating glaciers at the end of the last Ice Age (*c.*8000 BC). The two moraines cross the Vale of York, looping south and east from near Aldborough to pass either through York or to the south of Tadcaster and York (through the village of Escrick) to meet again at Stamford Bridge on the River Derwent. The York moraine was a route for travellers in prehistoric times and York itself was at an important point on this route as it is here that the moraine is cut by the River Ouse, then easily navigable from the Humber estuary. These simple facts of local geography go a long way to explaining why the Romans were to choose York as a base for an army of conquest.

The River Derwent, which may have formed a boundary between the Brigantes and the Parisi, rises at the eastern end of the Vale of Pickering, near Scarborough, and then flows westwards before turning to go south through Malton, a Roman fort site, and Stamford Bridge, famous for the battle in 1066, but in origin also a Roman fort. South of Stamford Bridge, at Kexby, the Derwent is crossed by the Roman road from Brough on Humber to York before reaching its confluence with the Ouse at Drax, the site of a villa. East of the Derwent there is a low lying zone known as the Walling Fen, drained by the River Foulness (pronounced 'Foona'). In the Iron Age and Roman times it was composed of islands, some suitable for settlement, between marshes and waterways. Archaeologist Peter Halkon considers the

Foulness to have been at the heart of 'The valley of the first iron masters', where an important resource was iron-bearing deposits created by precipitation in water – 'bog ore'. Halkon's archaeological excavations have shown that the iron production took place on a substantial scale here in the late pre-Roman Iron Age.[3]

On the east side of Yorkshire there are two distinct areas of upland. To the south of the Tees Basin and east of the Vale of Mowbray lies a bloc composed of the Cleveland Hills, the Hambleton Hills, the North York Moors and the Tabular Hills. The highest point is 454m above sea level near Urra on the north side; the land then falls away slightly to the east, but is still c.300m above sea level on Fylingdales Moor above Ravenscar on the east coast. These uplands are penetrated by small rivers and becks which run mostly from north to south into the Vale of Pickering, although the Esk, the only substantial river between the Tees and the Humber runs due east to the sea at Whitby. Continuing the line of the Hambleton Hills to the south-east and closing off the western end of the Vale of Pickering are the Howardian Hills. At Kirkham Abbey the River Derwent runs through a gorge which divides the Howardians from the second upland zone in the east of the county, the Yorkshire Wolds. The Romans were apparently unable to get their road from York to the fort at Malton through the gorge and so, as one can see on the A64 today, which follows the Roman line, the road, after dipping down to cross the Cram Beck, near the site of important late Roman potteries, rises sharply up Barton Hill on to the eastern edge of the Howardians before descending equally sharply down Golden Hill into Malton itself.

The more northerly of the smaller lowland zones on the east side of Yorkshire is the Vale of Pickering which extends from near Malton, in the west, to the east coast between Reighton, south of Filey, and Scarborough. It was originally a lake after the last glaciation and its perimeter was extremely fertile and attractive to prehistoric populations. Famous sites on the southern edge of the Vale include Star Carr and Seamer Carr. After drying out, however, the Vale became rather poor land for farming being clayey and prone to flooding.

The scarp slope of the Wolds runs along the south side of the Vale of Pickering to Flamborough Head on the east coast and along the west side of an arm which extends south almost as far as Brough on Humber. The Wolds do not reach the height of the North York Moors, let alone the Pennines, not rising more than 150m above sea level for the most part. However, there is a high point of 240m at the top of Garrowby Hill, 11km east of Stamford Bridge, and the Wolds presented a formidable barrier between the Vale of York and Holderness. One can get a good sense of this on what is now the A166 which probably follows a Roman road line from York to the coast at Bridlington. At Garrowby Hill the road rises very sharply, but at the top one has the most wonderful views over the Vale of York and Humber Estuary, views which at sunset can be truly magical. The Wolds are punctuated by glacially formed dry valleys ('slacks') and water sources are limited, although running from

Illus. 2.3   The Carr Naze, Filey, the site of the late Roman signal station (centre) which has almost completely eroded into the North Sea. (Photo: Blackthorn Press)

west to east is the Gypsey Race stream in the Great Wold Valley, famous for its prehistoric monuments.

The south-east corner of Yorkshire is occupied by the Plain of Holderness, a gently undulating landscape divided in two by the River Hull which rises near Driffield and flows due south for *c*.30km, being tidal for much of its length. The Hull separates the claylands to the east from the dip slope of the Wolds to the west before reaching the Humber at Kingston upon Hull. On the coast of Holderness, and around Scarborough, north of Flamborough Head, erosion has been ongoing since Roman times and as much as a kilometer of land has been lost to the sea.

Geology

Both the physiography and landscape of Yorkshire have been substantially determined by its geology. A good introduction, on which much of the following is based, was published in 2003 by Paul Buckland and Geoff Gaunt.[4] They show how very varied the region is geologically with a wide range of solid rocks and succeeding them in much of the county diverse Quaternary, or 'drift', deposits largely formed in and after the last Ice Age.

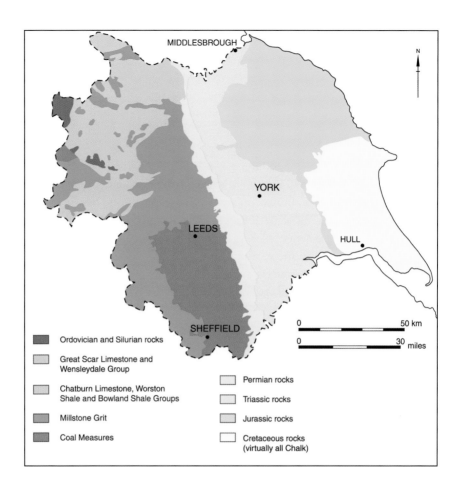

Illus. 2.4 The Yorkshire region: map of solid geology (after Buckland and Gaunt 2003).

Ordovician and Silurian rocks

Great Scar Limestone and Wensleydale Group

Chatburn Limestone, Worston Shale and Bowland Shale Groups

Millstone Grit

Coal Measures

Permian rocks

Triassic rocks

Jurassic rocks

Cretaceous rocks (virtually all Chalk)

Illus. 2.5 The Yorkshire region: map of drift geology (after Buckland and Gaunt 2003).

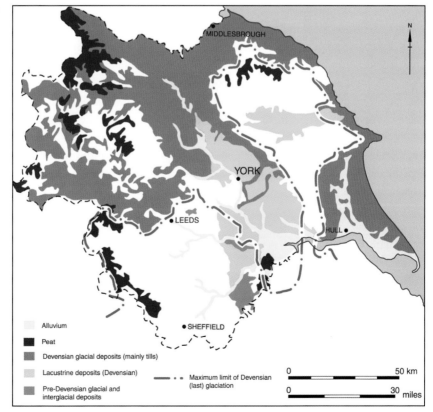

Alluvium

Peat

Devensian glacial deposits (mainly tills)

Lacustrine deposits (Devensian)

Pre-Devensian glacial and interglacial deposits

Maximum limit of Devensian (last) glaciation

Once again it makes sense to work from west to east looking at the oldest rocks first. Apart from a few small outcrops of the Ordovician and Silurian eras near Ingleton, north of Settle, the oldest belong to the Carboniferous series which forms most of the northern Pennines. In the north-westernmost part of Yorkshire this is represented by the Lower Carboniferous series comprising the Great Scar Limestone (seen, for example, at Kilnsey Crag in Wharfedale) and the overlying Wensleydale Group consisting of interbedded limestones, mudstones and sandstones. The Wensleydale Group produces galena, lead ore, which was mined in Roman times. Drainage on the limestone creates a range of distinctive landscape features, including pot holes, rock shelters and caves, some of the latter, such as Victoria Cave in Langcliffe Scar near Settle – discovered in 1837 the year of the queen's coronation, hence the name – have produced Roman artefacts and may have been the scene of religious rituals demanding a dark and quiet venue.[5] The Quaternary deposits above the Carboniferous include blanket peat (decomposed vegetable matter) and clay (often referred to as 'till'), and on the valley floors gravel and alluvium. The soil on the high ground is a thin acidic clay loam which has been subject to considerable degradation, but in the valleys there is usually good soil which has been suitable for agriculture since prehistoric times. In much of the Craven plateau, a rough triangle between Skipton, Settle and Grassington, the Lower Carboniferous (successively Chatburn Limestone, Worston Shale and Bowland Shale) is covered by a clayey till which created the sort of heavy soils usually thought difficult to work with the simple cultivation tools of early farmers.

Elsewhere in the Pennines, in a zone running south from near Richmond across the lower parts of the Dales to just north of Leeds, and then south to Derbyshire, the solid geology is Millstone Grit. There is also Millstone Grit west of Settle in part of the Forest of Bowland. As the name implies, this is a rock which has been used for millstones since Roman times and also for the smaller quern stones used for grinding grain by hand. Millstone Grit can also be an excellent building stone as it has good load-bearing properties. It was extensively used in the Roman period at York, for example in the great sewer serving the legionary fortress baths and for the aisle columns standing 7m high in the main hall of the fortress headquarters.[6] One source of Millstone Grit for York was probably a quarry in Bramham Park near Wetherby from where the stone was shipped down the River Wharfe. Its robust qualities also recommended Millstone Grit to the monumental masons of Roman Yorkshire for tombstones and sarcophagi. Quaternary deposits in Millstone Grit regions are usually a clayey till, but on the moors in the south-western fringes of Yorkshire there is peat.

In the central southern part of Yorkshire the Carboniferous is represented by the Coal Measures. Here there are deposits of shale, mudstone and fine-grained sandstone with coal and ironstone seams. Coal was mined in Roman times, but only on a small scale from surface deposits; on occasions it had a specialist use for cremating the dead and in religious rituals involving sacred fires. In an area south of Bradford, around Elland, there occurs a micaceous sandstone which can be quarried as thin slabs. Elland Flag, known more commonly as York Stone, was commonly used in Roman times for floors and roofing.[7] Quaternary deposits on the Coal Measures often created heavy clay soils and so prehistoric and Roman settlement tends to be concentrated on sandstone outcrops or on the gravels and sands in the valleys of the Rivers Aire and Calder.

We may now move forward in geological time to the Permian era, represented principally by Magnesian Limestone. This runs in a narrow belt south from the Tees to Doncaster before it crosses the county boundary just west of Worksop in Nottinghamshire. Over much of this belt the land rises as a ridge well above the lowlands to the east; for example, east of Castleford it reaches 78m above sea level and at Pontefract as much as 84m. In building their main road north from Doncaster as far as Tadcaster, the Romans took advantage of the elevation and drainage properties of this ridge. The Permian is largely covered by till and other Quaternary deposits as far south as the Wetherby area beyond which it supported light, calcareous loamy soils ideal for early agriculture.

Magnesian Limestone has been regarded as a top quality building stone since the Roman period and has the advantage of being a freestone, meaning it has no distinct bedding plane and can be cut in any direction. Magnesian Limestone was extensively used in Roman York, probably sourced in quarries near Tadcaster 15km to the south-west.[8] In the facing of Roman walls it usually occurs as small blocks (*saxa quadrata*), and these can still be seen in surviving stretches of the fortress defences, principally in the Museum Gardens. A mineral found in the Permian at, for example at Sherburn in Elmet, *c.*20km west of York, is calcium sulphate known in hydrated form as gypsum or Plaster of Paris. In Roman times a deposit of gypsum was, on occasions, included in the stone or lead sarcophagi of certain high status individuals, especially at York.

East of the Permian in the Vales of York and Mowbray, including the southern Tees Basin, we move forward again in geological time to the Triassic period. The solid geology here is sandstone and above this Mercia Mudstone (formerly Keuper Marl) on the east side of the Vale of York. In places sandstone is near the surface providing usable building material. At Aldborough, for example, there is a quarry just to the south-west of the Roman town, thought to be on the site of a Roman predecessor which produced the distinctive, if rather poor, red sandstone used for the town defences and other buildings. However, for the most part the Triassic sandstone is covered by thick Quaternary deposits. They include extensive clays on which drainage was usually poor, but there are also sands and gravels which give rise to light soils suitable for arable agriculture. They may be found, for example, on the York moraine and at Heslington, *c.*3km east of York, late Iron Age and Roman farmsteads and field systems have been found on the south-facing slope. Although the clays were not ideal for agriculture, they could be used as a resource for tile and pottery manufacture as at York where kilns were probably located immediately east

Illus. 2.6   Victoria Cave near Settle. The large entrance was created for the British Association in 1870 by a substantial quarrying of the rock face, although chambers and galleries at the rear still conjour up a mysterious atmosphere. The original entrance was only 1.1m wide and 0.9m high.
(Photo: P. Ottaway)

of the fortress on the banks of the River Foss.[9] Peat, used as fuel in Roman York and other places,[10] occurs in the Vale of York, at Askham Bog south of the city, and in the Humberhead Levels at Thorne Moor between Goole and Thorne, and at nearby Hatfield Moor, east of Doncaster.

Our journey through geological time now brings us to the Jurassic period represented by a solid geology of limestone, sandstone and clay mudstones which cover the north-eastern part of Yorkshire including the North York Moors and Vale of Pickering.[11] In addition, the narrow 'Jurassic bench' runs south between the Triassic of the Vale of York to the west and the chalk of the Wolds, reaching the Humber at Brough. Used extensively for building in Roman Malton and also in York, to which it was probably transported via the Derwent and the Ouse, was the Oolitic Limestone of the Jurassic which occurs both north of the Vale of Pickering in the Tabular Hills and in a restricted zone to the south of the Vale. Another resource in the Jurassic was the clay found at Crambeck (between York and Malton) used for making pottery. There is peat on the high ground of the moors, but otherwise the Quaternary deposits above the Jurassic are largely clayey tills, although there is a sand and gravel ridge on the north side of the Vale of Pickering near Wykeham. In the Vale itself clay was formed in the lake of the immediate post-Glacial period and, as in the prehistoric period, Roman settlement tends to be concentrated on areas of well-drained soil on the Vale edges.

The youngest rocks in Yorkshire are those of the Cretaceous period represented by chalk which forms the Yorkshire Wolds. Chalk is not really suitable as a building stone unless it can be protected from the weather, but an important resource abundant in the chalk is flint used to make tools in prehistoric times and also, on occasions, in Roman and later times. The soils on chalk are light and well drained rendering them eminently suitable for early agriculture, although water sources on the Wolds are scarce and it is not surprising that Roman villa owners considered it worth digging wells up to 30m deep at Rudston and Welton. Chalk also underlies the plain of Holderness where the Quaternary deposits are principally clayey till with some islands of sand and gravel whilst stretches of alluvium flank the River Hull and the Humber estuary. Soils are generally heavy and clayey and drainage was poor until recent times hence there were extensive marshes adjacent to the Hull, peaty on the upper reaches and salty near the estuary. Now largely lost, were a number of lakes, or meres – Skipsea Mere is a surviving example – which attracted early agriculture and settlement.

Climate

Both physiography and geology had an important bearing on what sort of agriculture was possible in Roman Yorkshire, and hence on settlement patterns, but another factor to consider is climate. Classical sources refer to Britain as a foggy, wet island. For example the Greek geographer Strabo notes:

> The weather tends to rain rather than snow and on days when there are no clouds fog persists for a long time with the result that throughout the whole day the sun can be seen only for about three or four hours about noon.[12]

Although they may have emphasised the less agreeable aspects of British weather, what Strabo and other Classical authors recognised was that Britain had a temperate, maritime climate without the great extremes of precipitation or temperature which were found in other parts of the Roman world.

It is not easy to gain accurate information on climate in the past and compare it with what prevails today. We live in a period of rapid climate change and there have been similar periods in the past so we cannot expect the climate of Roman Britain to have been any more static than our own. One way of learning about past climate is by examination of well-dated buried deposits which contain pollen. This gives an indication of vegetation which can be correlated with climatic variables. Borehole columns from sediment basins, principally peat bogs, usually provide suitable pollen data and they seem to suggest that the climate in Britain became warmer and drier in the middle of the first millennium BC. This encouraged agriculture and a rise of population.[13] Climate in the Roman period itself does not, on the whole, appear to have been much different from what it is today, although summers may have been warmer.[14] In a well found in the legionary fortress at York certain species of bug were found outside their present range in Britain suggesting a climate with a mean July temperature at least 1°C higher than in the city today.[15] This well was filled in the late second century, but it is thought that from the mid-third century onwards there was an episode of global warming. The evidence from coastal and low-lying areas in Yorkshire and elsewhere suggests a gradual rise in sea levels, often referred to as a marine transgression, due to melting of the polar ice cap.[16] This may have had the effect of making settlement and agriculture in low-lying parts of the Humberhead Levels, for example, unviable due to persistent flooding and warping, i.e. the deposition of silt on the land.

In addition to a climate not that different in general terms in the Roman period from what it is today, the extent of climatic variability across the Yorkshire region was probably similar to what we experience. We can, therefore, get some understanding of this variability and its effects on agriculture and settlement from the data available for recent years from the Meteorological Office. As far as rainfall is concerned, these data tell us that the Pennine zone on the western side of the county receives a great deal more than the lowlands and Wolds to the east. Average rainfall at Malham Tarn (381m above sea level) in the years 1971–2000 was c.1518mm per annum. Sheffield at 131m above sea level, on the eastern edge of the Pennines, received an average of 824mm whilst High Mowthorpe on the Wolds, a little higher than Sheffield at 175m above sea level, but on the east of the county received only 729mm, less than half the Malham figure. York received, on average, no more than about 600mm of rain.

Mean annual temperature in England today at low altitudes is c.8.5°–11°C and declines by c.0.5°C for each rise in 100m above sea level. At Malham Tarn between 1971 and 2000 the mean annual temperature, month by month, was between 10.1°C maximum and 4°C minimum. At Sheffield the corresponding figures were 13.1°C and 6.4°C and at High Mowthorpe 11.6°C and 5.1°C. Although temperature is clearly related to elevation, it also changes as one moves from south to north in England and at Durham, c.32km north of the Tees, the figures are 12.5° and 5.2°C, slightly less than Sheffield. The warmest months in 1971–2000 were, as one would expect, July and August and the coldest January and February. However, the length of the growing season for crops and vegetation depends both on variations in mean temperature over the year and the number of hours of sunshine. On the south coast of England there is an average of about 1,750 hours of sunshine per annum, but Malham Tarn only averaged 1,149 hours in 1971–2000 whilst Sheffield received an average of 1,381 hours and High Mowthorpe 1,398 hours.

What the data quoted above would mean, if transferred to the Roman period, is that the uplands of the Pennines and North York Moors, with their largely thin and acid soils, were wetter, colder and had less sunshine than the lowland zones. All other things being equal, the uplands were a good deal less suitable for arable agriculture and, therefore, did not have the capacity to support as dense a population. One can still get a good impression of a difference in the agricultural regime between lowland and upland areas in our region on the route I described between York and Stainmore. As far as Greta Bridge arable fields prevail, but by the time one reaches Bowes there is far less arable and beyond Bowes one sees only sheep.

Within the region there were evidently differences in the arable regime in Roman times which were probably related to environmental factors. For example, based on the study of cereal grains from archaeological sites, preserved by charring or waterlogging, wheat appears to have been grown all over Yorkshire, but in the northern part of the county, and over the boundary in Durham, barley, being more tolerant of cold and poor light, assumed a greater importance. In deposits of cereal sampled at Catterick barley was the dominant crop whereas in those from Castleford or York it formed a much smaller proportion.[17]

Flora and fauna

Flora

The evidence for Yorkshire's flora in the past comes from two principal sources. Firstly, there are the pollen sequences already referred to. They show how the clearance of woodland and its replacement by arable cultivation or pasture, which began in the late Neolithic or early Bronze Age in some areas, picked up pace in the mid- or late Iron Age and continued into the early Roman period. This was shown, for example, at Ellerton Moor in Swaledale where two clearance periods 510–380 BC and 1 BC–AD 80 were identified.[18] Further south, in the Pennines, at Thornton Mire and Rishworth Moor, the expansion of cultivation and pasture also seems to have occurred in the mid- to late Iron Age.[19] In the North York Moors at Harwood Dale Bog and Fen Bogs the evidence is for massive clearance in the late Iron Age.[20] One consequence of conversion to arable agriculture on poor upland soil in the Pennines and on the North York Moors was that it soon became exhausted and unsuitable for cereals as early as the Iron Age, the land becoming the heath it remains today.[21] In the lowland zones, such as the Humberhead Levels and Holderness, woodland clearance, as much for pasture as arable, was clearly well advanced by the beginning of the Iron Age and continued in the Roman period.[22]

There is also evidence for flora from settlement sites where plant remains survive either in charred form, principally as pips, seeds and stones, or as a result of the inhibition of decay due to the waterlogging of deposits in a few favoured, largely riverside, locales such as Castleford and York.[23] A very wide range of species has been recorded, largely indigenous to Britain with the exception of obvious imports, such as grapes, olives and figs. There is little archaeological evidence for any Roman introductions to Britain, although they are supposed to have included the sweet chestnut and wild garlic. The species recorded divide primarily into food plants and wild plants. Deliberately cultivated food plants, for which there is good evidence, are principally cereals (largely represented by charred grain) rather than vegetables of which remains do not survive well in the ground. Also clearly consumed in quantity were various fruits, whether cultivated or gathered opportunistically, including elderberry (represented by seeds) and cherry (by stones).

At Dalton Parlours villa (near Wetherby) the wild plant remains suggested a mosaic of surrounding ecological zones, probably typical of many parts of the lowland zone in Roman times, including arable land, grassland, disturbed and waste places, heathland, woodland, and damp or wet places.[24] In the Roman town south-west of the Ouse at York wild plants not only derived from local ecological zones, but from further afield indicating aspects of trade connections. Some plant species had clearly travelled a considerable distance, perhaps in the guts of cattle brought in for sale or slaughter from their grazing lands. For example, there are species which are usually confined to salt marshes, the nearest being c.40km away in the lower reaches of the River Hull.[25]

The trees known in the region in Roman times, for which the evidence is not only pollen and seeds, but also wooden objects, were again largely indigenous. One must imagine a world without the horse chestnuts, sycamores and numerous exotic trees which have flooded into Britain in the last two hundred years or so. The principal species varied a little from region to region according to ground conditions. On Magnesian Limestone, for example, lime was dominant, on clay it was likely to be oak which prevailed, and birch and pine were to be found on poor sandy soils. Other common trees were alder, ash, hazel and field maple, in addition to the fruit trees, notably apple, cherry and plum.

Fauna

Evidence for the fauna of Roman Yorkshire comes largely from animal bones found in archaeological deposits. Collections are dominated by those of cattle, sheep and pig which were the principal sources of food. In addition, dog and horse bones occur quite frequently; they would have been working animals, although some of smaller dogs may have been treated as pets. In addition to the bones of wild mammal species which still live in the region today others, now extinct, which have been found on Roman sites include wild boar (York), bear (Catterick)[26] and black rat (York and Dalton Parlours).[27] There may have been beavers and wolves in Roman Yorkshire, but no good evidence for them has yet come to light. The skull of a Barbary ape from Catterick presumably belonged to an animal imported as a pet.[28]

Collections of Roman bird bones are dominated by fowl which formed a small but persistent accompaniment to diet throughout the Roman period; eggs were presumably eaten in quantity, but their shells rarely survive. The bones of other bird species largely divide into those which were eaten and those which scavenged around human settlements. In small numbers York has produced evidence for the likes of goose, mallard, golden plover and woodcock, which were probably food, and for the scavengers sparrow, jackdaw and raven.[29] At Filey the garrison diet in the late Roman signal station evidently included cormorant and guillemot as bones with knife cuts suggesting deliberate removal of flesh were found.[30] A golden eagle bone from Catterick is hard to explain, but may have been from a bird kept for hunting.[31]

The bones of amphibians have been only rarely recorded, but those of frog come from Roman wells at Dalton Parlours and Rudston villas, and of toad from Rudston and York. Filey Roman signal station is unusual in producing the bones not only of frog and toad but also of lizard and snake, creatures which are thought to have formed the diet of owls living in the central tower.

There were, of course, fish in the sea off Yorkshire in Roman times and in its rivers and streams, but our knowledge of them is largely the result of selection for food and it is not possible to give a complete picture of what was swimming around. Deep sea fishing was rare in Roman times and so most of the marine fish whose bones survive are from those like herring which were probably found in the Humber Estuary. Amongst the species of fresh water fish from York the bones of members of the carp family were dominant, and eels and perch were also common.[32]

In the same waterlogged deposits which preserve plant remains there may also be those of insects and other invertebrates. Deposits in the Roman town at York have produced remains of over 400 insect taxa[33] whilst the late Roman well at Dalton Parlours produced over a hundred.[34] Insects are usually very specific to certain types of environment and so, like the plant remains, give a good indication of past ecological conditions in and around the sites where they were found. These conditions may vary, for example from open grassland, to waste and disturbed ground to the sort of middens of rotting matter often found in densely settled places.

The study of the material relating to the region's fauna and flora summarised here is a relatively new branch of archaeological research which has come to maturity since the 1970s. However, so-called 'environmental archaeology' is only one aspect of the archaeological investigations which have given us an in-depth and sophisticated insight into the history of Roman Yorkshire. A review of how the region's Roman archaeology has been investigated, and a comparison of archaeological and written sources as evidence follow in the next chapter.

The Search for Roman Yorkshire

3

Introduction

In the two previous chapters I have attempted to set the scene for the history of the Roman period in Yorkshire. In doing this I have alluded to some of the primary sources of evidence for the period, but in this chapter I shall look at these sources, both written and archaeological, in more detail and say something about the sort of information they give us. I shall then move on to an outline history of the investigation of Roman Yorkshire from the time when serious interest in the subject began some 400 years ago.

Literary sources

The contemporary literary sources which refer to, or are relevant for, studying the history of Roman Britain are very varied in terms of their character, date and reliability. However, no Roman author can really be said to have written history in the sense that we understand it today, an objective account based on the careful and balanced consideration of a range of sources and types of evidence. We must therefore evaluate the context in which authors were writing and consider the audiences and objectives they had in mind. Amongst those who have something to say about our region or who are, at least, able to give us some useful background we may begin with Julius Caesar. His brief campaigns in the south-east of England in 55 and 54 BC are described in *On the Gallic War* (*De Bello Gallico*), but Caesar evidently had the whole of the British Isles surveyed and gives us a brief description. However, a good deal of what he has to say is more in the nature of a traveller's tale intended to appeal to the imagination of readers in Rome rather than provide factual information. For example, Caesar is responsible for the famous, or infamous, reference, to the Britons dyeing themselves blue with woad. This was further embellished by Herodian in the third century who tells us that the Britons were tattooed. Between them they have contributed to a popular image of all 'ancient Britons' and 'Celtic' people, from Boudicca to Braveheart, which is very hard to dislodge.

Writing in either the late first century BC or early first century AD, was the Greek geographer Strabo. He not only commented on the British weather, but, in a well-known passage, described Britain as the source of grain, cattle, gold, silver and iron along with hides, slaves and dogs bred specifically for hunting.[1] Whilst there may have been little gold in Yorkshire, we know that all the other commodities listed would have been readily available for exploitation in the region after the conquest.

Perhaps the most important Roman historian to write about Britain, who, moreover, tells us something specifically relevant to Yorkshire, is Cornelius Tacitus (c.55–120). Tacitus's principal historical works include *The Annals* (of Ancient Rome) which cover the years 14–68. Here he refers to the campaign of the year 48 in which the Roman army first entered the region.[2] *The Annals* also have the first of his two references to Cartimandua, Queen of the Brigantes, and her consort, Venutius.[3] The second reference occurs in *The Histories* in which Tacitus covers events in the 'Year of the Four Emperors' (68 – 69) from the end of the Emperor Nero's reign to the beginning of Vespasian's.[4] The north of Britain as a whole appears in *The Agricola*, a biography of Tacitus's father-in-law, Gnaeus Agricola, governor of Britain c.78–84.

Although Tacitus has often been treated as a cornerstone of the late first-century history of Britain, we must be cautious of accepting what he has to say uncritically. It is difficult to assess the factual accuracy of, for example, what he says on the subject of Cartimandua for whom he is the only ancient source. Tacitus did not visit Britain himself but probably relied a good deal on what he was told by his father-in-law. He was writing with a particular audience in mind and one of his aims was to denigrate the Emperor Domitian (81–96) whom he blamed for the abandonment of Agricola's conquests in Scotland. Tacitus's approach is very much focused on illustrating the merits and failings in the behaviour and character of 'great men' when put under the stress of war and conflict. Agricola, not surprisingly, comes through with flying colours.

Tacitus, like Caesar, was happy to titillate his audience in Rome with the unusual and exotic as we can see in his description of Cartimandua – her name, incidentally, is thought to mean 'sleek or shiny pony,' indicative of the way horses were regarded as status symbols in native society. At one point we hear of the armour bearer Vellocatus for whom Cartimandua has left Venutius, being 'bolstered by the lust and savagery of the queen'; this no doubt created the intended frisson in a largely male audience in Rome which liked its barbarians to be barbarous – as long as they were a good distance away – and if they were women as well, so much the better.

For most of the second century Britain is not well served by Roman authors, although the Greek-speaking Egyptian, Ptolemy, active in the years c.140–60, compiled a geography of the Roman empire which includes Britain.[5] Ptolemy provides a list of place-names in Britain, including *Eboracum* (York), *Isurium* (Aldborough) and *Olicana* (Elslack or Ilkley), and geographical features such as *Gabrantovicum Sinus* (bay of the Gabrantovices) which may be Bridlington Bay. Ptolemy is also one of the principal sources for the names and location of the native territories of Britain, including those of the Brigantes and Parisi – indeed for the latter he is the only contemporary source.

Also of a geographical character are itineraries or 'road books' intended for use by, amongst others, the imperial post, the *cursus publicus*. The most comprehensive as far as Britain is concerned is the Antonine Itinerary (named after the Emperor Antoninus – usually known as 'Caracalla') of the early third century which contains lists of place-names in the empire arranged along the main roads and gives distances between them. For Britain there are fifteen itineraries and over one hundred place-names, many in the Yorkshire region.[6]

Of the third-century Roman historians who refer to Britain, Cassius Dio Cocceianus (*c.*150–235), a Greek speaker of senatorial rank from Bithynia (now Turkey) is the most important. He wrote a history of Rome from its foundation to 229, although much of his work is lost and we rely largely on an eleventh-century epitome (abstract) of his text. Dio's work becomes a contemporary account in the late second century, and although he never visited Britain, as far as we know, he has important things to tell us about the British campaign of the Emperor Septimius Severus which ended with his death in York in 211 (see Chapter 8).[7] Belonging to a similar period as Dio is another Greek speaker, Herodian, who wrote a history of the Roman empire for the years 180–238, i.e. from the death of the Emperor Marcus Aurelius to the reign of Gordian I. Like Dio, Herodian did not know Britain at first hand but makes some references to events here. For example, he refers briefly to a barbarian attack on Britain in the early third century which may have led to Severus coming to the province in person.

Whilst the reliability of Dio and Herodian from a purely factual point of view is difficult to assess, they do create a very compelling picture of the violent and unpredictable atmosphere in the imperial court, especially under Septimius Severus and his immediate successors. Considered even less reliable by scholars is the Augustan History (*Scriptores Historiae Augustae*), probably written in the fourth century and structured as biographies of all the Roman emperors from Hadrian to Numerian (117–284). The Augustan History refers briefly to the visits of Hadrian and Severus to Britain and to a few other military events including campaigns in the north in the 160s and 170s, but is perhaps most valuable for the impression it gives of the preoccupations and vices of the Roman ruling class.

For the later Roman period the principal contemporary account relevant to Britain is that of Ammianus Marcellinus, a native of Syria. The surviving part of his work deals with the years 354–78, the reigns of the Emperors Constantius II, Julian and Valentinian I. Once again this tells us a lot about the character of imperial politics and military affairs but there are also a few important references to events involving Britain, including attacks by hostile forces in 360, 364 and 367 which may well have affected the Yorkshire region.

Epigraphy

Epigraphy is the study of inscriptions, that is to say texts, usually quite brief, or even just a few letters and / or numbers which were written – or 'inscribed' – on to objects made in a wide variety of media including stone, metal, bone and wood. The letters to be found in inscriptions are usually Roman capitals, although on wooden writing tablets, often written in ink, they may be in cursive – Roman hand writing.

Inscriptions on stone

Illus. 3.1   Ilkley: tombstone of woman with an inscription referring to her origin as a member of the Cornovii, a people whose homeland lay in the west Midlands. Found in 1884 near the fort.
(© Olicana Museum)

Inscriptions on stone appear most commonly on public monuments. In Britain they come principally from military sites and are usually dated to between the late first and early third centuries. First of all, there are commemorations, announcements or notices which may refer to specific events, but in the Yorkshire region usually refer to building work. Another well-known type of inscribed stone monument is the milestone of which there are eleven from Yorkshire. They usually exist as stone cylinders up to c.2m high and 0.3m thick which were set up along the line of main roads to mark the miles between the principal towns. Milestones do not usually give distances as such and named places are rare, although 'Eburacum [York] 22 miles' appears on one from Castleford.[8] However, milestones usually bear an imperial dedication which on those from Yorkshire allows them all to be dated to the years 251–53 or 276–83, perhaps indicating two third-century campaigns of road maintenance.

In addition to secular commemorations on stone, there are also religious dedications. In our region they are mostly to be found on free-standing altars. These exist as stone blocks, usually standing c.0.30m–1.5m high, with a plinth at the base and a cornice at the head (Illus. 7.10). On the top is a dished area, the focus, used for burning sweet-smelling substances or for pouring libations. The focus is often flanked by what is intended to represent a bundle of rods, the *fasces*, a traditional symbol of authority in the Roman world. Any inscription, highly standardised in form, may give the name of the god to whom the dedication was made, the name and status of the person making it, and some version of a set formula to say it is in fulfilment of a vow made in return for a favour the god has granted to the donor. For example, an altar to the *matres* (mother goddesses) from Doncaster carries the common formula VSLM '*votum soluit libens merito*' – 'willingly and deservedly fulfilled his vow'.[9] The majority of the twenty or so inscribed Yorkshire altars come from places with a military presence. Soldiers were accustomed to addressing the gods with a public statement and had the means to pay for it. On occasions, wealthy people might go even further and pay for, or contribute towards, the construction of a temple. For example, an inscribed tablet from York names the merchant Lucius Viducius Placidus who sponsored what is thought to have been an arch and passage in a temple.[10] The motivation for such a gift, like that involved in setting up an altar, was partly to demonstrate piety, one of the admired virtues in the Roman world and approved of by the gods, but also the donor's wealth and status.

Finally, there are inscriptions on funerary monuments – tombstones and, more rarely, sarcophagi. These inscriptions can be seen as both commemorations, in this case of an individual and his or her family, and religious dedications in the sense that the deceased is usually commended to the spirits of the departed, worshipped as gods known as the *manes*. In addition to the name of the deceased, his or her age may be given as well as some indication of status as, for example, a soldier or merchant, and finally the name of the person(s) responsible for setting up the stone. A small number of Yorkshire tombstones, mostly from York (14), but also from Elmswell (1), Ilkley (2) and Templeborough (4), have or had a representation in relief of the deceased and sometimes other members of his or her family to accompany the inscription. As far as inscribed sarcophagi are concerned, there are relatively few from Britain as a whole, but ten are known from York[11] and there are regional examples from rural sites at East Ness[12] and Sutton-under-Whitestonecliff, both in Ryedale.[13]

Writing tablets

Papyrus rolls were in general use for writing in much of the Roman world. A papyrus roll is probably what is shown on Julia Velva's tombstone from York in the hand of a male figure, probably the Aurelius Mercurialis named in the inscription (Illus. 8.6).[14] It may be seen as a demonstration of his status as an educated and literate person at a time when these attributes were largely confined to the elite. Whilst there may be no surviving papyrus rolls from Britain, as they are only preserved in the sort of dry conditions prevailing in desert areas, there are numerous examples of wooden writing tablets which have survived in waterlogged ground.

Wax tablets exist as flat rectangles of wood with one face hollowed out to make a reservoir for the wax on which one wrote with a metal stylus. A pair of wax tablets is probably what is represented in the left hand of the standard bearer Lucius Duccius Rufinus on his tombstone from York, another man proud of his literacy (Illus. 3.5).[15] Styli are not common finds in our region, but it is noticeable that they are mostly found in and around forts, such as Catterick, or in towns, like York, rather than on rural settlements including villas where one might expect a literate elite; a fine fourth-century stylus from Beadlam villa is a rather exceptional find.[16] The tablets were usually used in pairs, held together with a cord, which were folded for despatch and then sealed with wax, often stamped by the sender's seal ring. Examples of wax tablets from Yorkshire are few, although there are fragments of four or more from Castleford[17] and two from Shiptonthorpe,[18] but sadly none of them bears a decipherable text.

One wrote on the second type of wooden writing tablet in ink as is exemplified by a large number found at the northern frontier fort at Vindolanda, Northumberland (principally dated c.AD 95–105).[19] They are usually post-card sized and were stitched together in pairs, although multiples are known. A few are known from Carlisle, but none has yet been recognised in Yorkshire, although it is surely only a matter of time before examples are found at York. The Vindolanda writing tablets provide a vivid picture of frontier life in a typical auxiliary fort and are therefore relevant for the study of forts in the Yorkshire region, garrisoned in the late first to early second centuries. The tablets comprise a range of different types of document including muster rolls, accounts of supplies, official requests for favour, and personal letters between friends and mess mates. Three places in Yorkshire are mentioned: York (the earliest written reference – in the form *Eburacum* instead of the more common *Eboracum*),[20] Aldborough, a place to stop for *faex*, or wine-lees, a cheap refreshment[21] and Catterick, from where hides were transported to the frontier zone.[22]

What the Vindolanda tablets bring home very forcibly is that the Romans were great bureaucrats whose skills in literacy and numeracy were put at the service of almost obsessive record keeping. We often hear about the Roman army's abilities as a ruthless killing machine, but the principal reason why Rome was able to hold on to a vast empire for so long may have had less to do with its soldiers' martial capabilities than with their ability to keep records of supplies, troop strengths and movements, and to send instructions and requests based on this information. The Roman pen, one might say, was as mighty, if not mightier, than the Roman sword. In a civilian context there was also a tradition of record keeping, for example relating to taxation and legal matters. As we still see today, in circumstances where most people are illiterate, a governing class which can read and write and do sums has an enormous advantage in controlling and subjugating them.

Inscriptions on other media

In addition to inscriptions on stone and on the writing tablets, Yorkshire has produced quite a wide range of inscriptions on other media with texts which range from the sophisticated products of the imperial bureaucracy to owner's or maker's marks. They are quite typical of what is found in Britain as a whole and the information of historical relevance is fairly limited except, perhaps, for the subject of names. As in the case of those on stone, inscribed objects, with a few exceptions, come from military sites and the larger settlements, which is probably a good indication that any facility in writing in Latin was restricted to the region's elite, usually in government or the military.

A brief survey may begin with official inscriptions. Little need, perhaps, be said about inscriptions on Roman coins which are extensively discussed elsewhere. However, also in the state-sponsored category of inscription are military diplomas and there are two from Yorkshire, both incomplete, of the Hadrianic period (early second century). A diploma, inscribed on small sheets of metal, usually copper alloy, was a copy of a tablet in Rome, or some other important centre, which gave grants of Roman citizenship, with all the legal privileges they entailed, to groups of auxiliary soldiers who had completed their military service – often lasting up to twenty-five years. The diploma from Stannington near Sheffield had been presented in the year 124 to a man of the First Cohort of Sunici, from the banks of the Rhine in Lower Germany, and refers to grants to soldiers in six cavalry regiments and twenty-one cohorts of infantry.[23] The second diploma found at Brompton, north-east of Malton, in 2007 was copied from an original in *Brigetio*, Pannonia (Komarom/Szony in Hungary) and had been given to a soldier of the Fifth Cohort of Raetians (from what is now Switzerland). In addition, it probably refers to thirteen cavalry regiments and thirty-seven infantry cohorts serving in Britain.[24]

Another class of official inscription, of which there are Yorkshire examples, relates to military production. They include the stamps of the Ninth and Sixth legions which occur on tiles made at York.[25] There are also stamps found on so-called 'pigs' or blocks of lead, of which there are four recorded from mining areas in the Pennines.[26] They feature the reigning emperor's name and examples are known of Domitian, Trajan and Hadrian. In addition, two of them bore the stamp BRIG(ANTICVM) meaning from the territory of the Brigantes. Also relating to economic activity of an official nature are small lead seals used on consignments of goods, one referring in abbreviated form to a military unit C II AST (Second Cohort of Asturians) comes from Bainbridge fort[27] and another from York refers to PBI, the Province of *Britannia Inferior*, of which it was the capital after *c.*213 – on the opposing face is a bull, emblem of the Sixth Legion.[28]

From civilian contexts makers' and owners' inscriptions occur on objects in a number of different media. There are, for example, makers' inscriptions on three *trullae*, saucepan-like vessels which were used in religious ceremonies. One from Malton reads ALPICVS F (= 'fecit', made) and the two others from High Stittenham, found with three others uninscribed, close to the Roman road between York and Malton, are inscribed P CIPI POLIB/POLVIBI = Publius Cipus Polibius, thought to be a manufacturer in Campania, Italy.[29] By way of another example, there are the distinctive makers' marks found on small, flat stone tablets used for preparing medicines, especially eye ointment. From York there is one of these so-called 'oculist's stamps' on a tablet of green soapstone, inscribed 'Julius Alexander's salve for irritations'.[30]

The most familiar medium for the Roman maker's mark is probably pottery. There are, first of all, the well-known stamps on imported vessels in the red, shiny earthenware known as samian. In our region, however, local potters might also use a stamp bearing their names. For example, a man named Sarrius was active at the Doncaster kilns c.135–70 and regularly stamped his mortaria (plural) – a mortarium (singular) was a mixing bowl with a thick rim and an inner surface roughened with grit (Illus. 7.20–21).[31] Rather rarer in our region are maker's inscriptions on other materials, but there is an example on a glass bottle from York with the name FR = Frontinus, and the base of a flask bears the word PATRIMON(I)I suggesting it was the product of an imperially owned workshop, perhaps in York itself.[32]

Owners' marks include those on a bronze camp kettle from York, rendered in punched dots, referring to the two centuries to whom it successively belonged – the first that of Attius Severus and the second that of Aprilis.[33] Items of kit bought by soldiers were, apparently, often sold on by their owners once a tour of duty was over. Many owners' marks fall into the category of informal inscriptions, usually referred to as 'graffiti', which occur widely on objects of all sorts. Some exist as single names and others may be abbreviated to one or two letters. Pottery vessels commonly bear graffiti scratched on with a sharp implement, but of particular local interest is the name of the Sixth Legion centurion Sollius Iulianus scratched on a fragment of a leather tent from York.[34] The same man is also known on a building stone from Hadrian's Wall commemorating construction work by his men.

Archaeology

Introduction

Written sources can provide elements of a chronological framework for the history of even a remote region of the Roman Empire like Yorkshire. They refer to datable events, even if the details are often obscure, and to particular individuals who capture our imagination and bring history to life. The sources also give us a general background to the political, military and social environment of the Roman world. However, the detailed history of Roman Yorkshire is, of necessity, largely based on archaeological evidence, that is to say the material remains of the period.

These remains can be conveniently divided into two broad categories: on the one hand, there are artefacts and ecofacts, and, on the other, sites and landscapes. To look at it another way, we may think of remains which are portable and those which, in most circumstances, are not. As we have seen, the written sources are limited in what they tell us and great care must be taken in their interpretation, but the same can also be said of the archaeological.

Artefacts and ecofacts

Artefacts recovered from archaeological sites of the Roman period fall into a number of different categories. Amongst the more bulky are building materials, such as stone and tiles, craft and industrial debris, notably from pottery manufacture and metalworking. Then there is the pottery itself, made in vast quantities, and there are also objects made in a great range of other materials including iron and non-ferrous metals, glass, stone, bone and antler, leather, wood and textile. The rather unlovely term ecofact refers to biological material including animal bones – food debris for the most part – plant remains, usually carbonised seeds, and, in certain circumstances, insects and even micro-organisms such as the eggs of intestinal parasites found in human or animal stools.

Most artefacts of the Roman period derive from activity in and around settlements, but the mechanisms by which they reached the ground were varied. Some items were simply lost by accident. Most were discarded as refuse, on the ground around buildings, in deliberately dug pits or in disused ditches, wells or other holes in the ground. However, unlike today when we are pretty casual about discard of material no longer of immediate use, in the Roman world any re-usable material would have been carefully recycled – unless we realise this, assessments of the prosperity or otherwise of the population based on archaeological finds can be dangerously false. In addition to refuse, there are items which were deliberately buried, whether in graves to accompany the dead ('grave goods') or for ritual purposes. Watery places were favoured in this latter respect and the High Stittenham *trullae*, for example, may have been buried as an offering to a water spirit in the boggy ground where they were found. Finally, there are coin hoards, of which at least 120 from Yorkshire, ranging in size from just four pieces to over ten thousand, were recorded in a survey published in 2000 by Anne Robertson.[35] More examples have been found since as metal detector use has increased. Hoards are usually thought to represent wealth buried on a particular occasion for future recovery, but there are also hoards which accumulated over a period of time, for example in sacred wells, which may have been offerings to the gods.

Ecofacts usually reached the ground as refuse, but, on occasions, items such as joints of meat were deliberately buried as grave goods, and dead animals might be placed in particular locations for ritual purposes.

Illus. 3.2 Cropmarks of enclosures on the Magnesian Limestone at Wattle Syke near Wetherby, July 1976. The view is to the north-west with the A1 on the right and the A659 on the left. (© English Heritage, Derrick Riley collection)

Sites and landscapes

At its simplest, the term 'site' to an archaeologist means a place where activity of some sort took place in the past. A site may be a relatively restricted part of a settlement or the whole of it – a single excavation trench in York and the whole of Roman York can, in different contexts, be described as 'a site'. However, there are also very extensive zones containing the remains of past activities, such as agriculture, which are usually better described as landscapes.

We know about ancient sites and landscapes in a number of different ways. Some former settlements have never been entirely forgotten, being referred to in written sources over the centuries or represented by upstanding structural remains, such as the fortress wall in York or the fort earthworks at Cawthorn, near Pickering. Most Roman sites, especially in rural areas,

are, however, known to us today from scatters of building materials, pottery and other artefacts on the ground surface where they have been redeposited after disturbance by ploughing and other agencies. In addition, sites and their surrounding landscapes have been located by aerial photography which can detect cropmarks formed by the differential growth of crops over buried features. These may be ditches and pits in which the soil retains higher moisture levels than the surrounding ground and therefore appears darker, or walls and other structures over which the soil is thinner and dryer causing it to appear lighter. Aerial photography is a particularly useful means of prospection on ground with shallow soils above well-drained materials such as sand, gravel or limestone on which cropmarks may be very clearly visible. The other routine means of prospection used by archaeologists is geophysical survey which detects magnetic or electrical resistence anomalies in the ground, interpretation of which can allow identification of buried man-made features.

The impact of the past

Archaeological sites contain the evidence in material form for a great range of human activities in the past. On occasions there may also be evidence for natural processes like erosion or flooding. These activities or processes will leave what we may conveniently call either a negative or a positive impact on the ground. A negative impact is the result of the removal of material as in, for example, the digging of a ditch, a pit or a drain. A positive impact can mean, on the one hand, erection of a structure, the throwing up of a rampart or a burial mound, or, on the other, the deposit of such things as building rubble, garden soil or refuse. Deposits may accumulate either on the ground

Illus. 3.3   Heslington near York: a typical late Iron Age field ditch under excavation. (Photo: P. Ottaway)

surface or make up the infilling of negative features, the ditches, pits, etc. A deposit can also result from natural accumulation in the silting up of a ditch, for example, or as the sediment ('warp') left behind after a flood.

Over time, as structures are created and demolished, and deposits build up, we get what archaeologists call stratification, that is to say superimposed layers of material which represent a sequence of activities and processes. A site which has been occupied over a long period of time may have a considerable build up of stratification. In parts of York, for example, there is over 5m above the original undisturbed ground level. This represents some 2000 years of history beginning with the Roman period. In rural areas, where human activity has been far less intense over the years than in a place like York, we may find very little stratification or even just features cut into the natural bedrock. As far as the Roman period is concerned, they will usually be the ditches which defined trackways, fields and other enclosures as well as pits for refuse and storage, and the circular gullies which, in many areas, are the principal trace left by the typical prehistoric and Roman rural dwelling, the roundhouse.

Archaeology and history

In excavation an archaeologist's task is to carefully define each separate deposit, structure and feature – or 'context' as they are called generically – and remove them as far as possible in the reverse sequence in which they were created, the latest back to the earliest – excavation is rather like running a film backwards, but very slowly. At the same time a detailed record must be made of each context, and the artefacts and ecofacts collected and kept separate from those from other contexts. The stratigraphic method of excavation and the accompanying techniques of detailed recording are fundamental to an understanding the past of any period through archaeology. However, for history to be written the contexts must be placed in sequence and given real dates so that phases of activity in the past can be established and characterised. Certain categories of excavated material are of particular value to archaeologists for dating these phases. For the Roman period a coin is that rare commodity, the artefact of which the date of manufacture can be readily determined (if it is reasonably uncorroded) because each one bears the image and titles of the emperor in whose reign it was minted. Details of these titles may allow some coins to be dated to a single year. There are also artefacts whose date of manufacture can be determined – if not to a single year – on typological grounds, i.e. on the basis of the study of how their form, decoration and composition changed through time.

Roman pottery lends itself very well to typological study. The plastic nature of clay means that there is an enormous diversity in terms of fabric, form and decoration. Change over time in all three respects can be calibrated. Imported samian ware has traditionally been the best known and most extensively studied Roman pottery, but many types of local wares are now well researched and can also be dated with a reasonable degree of accuracy. To pottery as a datable artefact one may add glass, a material whose properties are in many ways similar to those of pottery and so also subject to considerable formal and decorative variability. Glass was initially imported to Britain in Roman times, but, in due course, was made locally – even in Yorkshire – and occurs, usually heavily fragmented, in considerable quantities. Artefacts in non-ferrous metal, especially brooches and other jewellery, may also be datable on typological grounds.

Archaeological typology is now increasingly supplemented by various scientific dating techniques which have achieved a considerable degree of sophistication in the last twenty to thirty years. They include radiocarbon dating which is based on calibrating the extent of decay of the radioactive isotope of carbon in organic material such as wood or bone. There is also archaeomagnetism which is based on measuring changes in the earth's magnetic field. It is suitable for dating fired clay in hearths and the like as the effect of firing is to fossilise the alignment of iron atoms in the clay on the magnetic north of the day.

In spite of the techniques which archaeologists have at their disposal, dating phases and, therefore, sequences of activity is not straightforward. Most archaeological deposits contain material older, sometimes considerably older, than the date at which they themselves were created. This is due to the continual process of ground disturbance which takes place on any settlement occupied for a long period of time. Disturbance leads to the redeposition of artefacts after their initial deposition in earlier periods. Furthermore, people in the past, just as they do today, might have cherished an artefact, a favourite pot or brooch, for many years before it was eventually lost or thrown away. Taken together, the uncertainties and problems of dating mean that even for the Roman period, for which there is a considerable amount of suitable material, giving a date to a particular building, road, ditch etc is often not possible to less than about a fifty year span unless it can be – and this is rare – directly associated with a documented event. For example, at York we believe, on the basis of Tacitus's *Agricola*, that the Roman army arrived in about the year 71 – the earliest structures found in the legionary fortress must therefore be of about this time also.

In this book I have tried to evaluate the accuracy of statements on dating given in the source material, but there comes a point at which, unless one is going to re-examine all the finds and records from a site, one has to take what is published at face value. One does not always do this with confidence, however, as the study of pottery dating, in particular, has developed steadily over the years such that many reports, some published, perhaps, no more than ten years ago, may not be entirely reliable. Furthermore, even today excavators are not always very systematic about associating finds with the deposits from which they came, and finally some sites have just not produced much datable pottery or other material.

Survival of archaeological remains

The extent of its material remains and, therefore, their capacity for telling us about the Roman period in the Yorkshire region varies from place to place. There are a number of factors governing what survives in the ground today. First of all, there is simply the variation in intensity and diversity of what happened in the past in different places. For example, throughout the Roman period there was a much greater range of activities taking place in York, which had a larger and denser population than anywhere else in the region and so it is not surprising that there is a lot of Roman archaeology in the city. In rural areas, by contrast, where the population was relatively small there may be very little.

Aside from the character of what happened in the Roman period itself and the way its material remains were generated, we must also consider the impact on those remains of what happened afterwards. For example, Roman stone buildings in York, and more or less every other Roman settlement in Yorkshire, were extensively demolished – or 'robbed' to use the archaeologist's term – in the late Anglo-Saxon and medieval periods so that the stone could be reused. The Roman buildings became, in effect, quarries and so very little Roman masonry now survives above ground unless it retained some purpose. The Multangular Tower at York has survived because after being part of the Roman fortress, it was refurbished for the city's medieval defences (Illus. 5.16).

There has also, since Roman times, been a continual process of digging ditches, pits, cellars, service trenches and foundations etc, especially in towns, which has had an impact on earlier remains. In rural areas where there may have been relatively little or no deposition of material in later times to protect them, Roman remains are particularly vulnerable to the destructive effect of ploughing. Since World War II new forms of deep ploughing have become widespread and can bite down into the natural limestone, clay etc thereby destroying any archaeological deposits on the original ground surface and, moreover, the upper parts of features cut into the natural material. What may, for example, survive today as quite a shallow ditch may, in fact, have been much more substantial in the past and accompanied by a bank which is now completely lost. In some areas, such as the Pennines, we know that enclosures of Roman date were defined by stoney banks rather than ditches, but their original extent must have been much greater before repeated ploughing and related clearance.

The impact of these so-called 'post-depositional' factors on the survival of archaeological remains should be seen alongside the effects due to the chemistry of the ground in which remains are buried, effects which are themselves often related to the extent to which the ground has been drained and aerated since Roman times. An acid burial environment, such as is found in some sandy or clayey areas, is usually inimical to the good preservation of either organic materials such as bone, leather, and wood, or non-organics including metal and even, on occasions, pottery. An alkaline burial environment, such as is

Illus. 3.4   York: wall of a timber building at Tanner Row in the Roman town south-west of the Ouse. (© York Archaeological Trust)

found on the Wolds, for example, is often less aggressive to organics, especially bone, and to non-organic materials including metalwork.

If ground has been poorly drained or remained completely waterlogged over time, as a result, perhaps, of a rise in the water table, then little oxygen may have been able to get into it and organic material may be very well preserved because the usual decay processes have not taken place. At York certain parts of the Roman town south-west of the River Ouse are below a water table which has risen considerably since Roman times. As a result, timber structures and organic artefacts are well preserved. The fort area at Castleford, close to the River Aire, has similar ground conditions. Waterlogged deposits in rural areas are rare as Roman farmers tended to stick to well-drained land, but pasture might lie on marginal land which flooded intermittently as at Balby Carr near Doncaster where late Iron Age/early Roman ditches preserved unusual evidence for accompanying hedges in the form of clippings in the ditch fills.[36] By contrast, if archaeological remains lie in well-drained and highly aerated conditions as on Magnesian Limestone and Chalk the survival of organic materials, other than bone, may be poor.

In summary, what we know about Roman Yorkshire from archaeology is very much dependent, firstly, on the extent of the impact of later activity and, secondly, on the character of the burial environment. There is considerable variation in both respects across the county. In spite of the advances in archaeological techniques it is, therefore, impossible to give an entirely balanced picture of what happened everywhere in the Roman period, because the evidence may have simply not survived. None the less, the topics archaeology is able to address are wide-ranging taking in, for example, environment, agriculture, settlement, technology, trade, the visual arts, religion and burial customs. For Roman Britain, at least, if not necessarily for the empire as a whole, the written sources are almost completely silent on all of these. Furthermore, through the study of stratified sites, in particular, archaeology is also good at revealing the processes of change through time even if the stages at which change took place cannot always be very accurately dated.

Reconstructing the past

What then do archaeologists do with all the data they gather concerning those (and other) topics listed in the previous paragraph? In brief, one might say they are used to reconstruct the past and thereby further its understanding. At one level this will involve reconstruction of an individual object or structure to show what it once looked like. Comparison with other examples of similar type and date which have survived in a more complete condition will be fundamental and for structures the archaeologist will need some knowledge of the properties and load-bearing capacity of construction materials. For example, the villa reconstruction drawings in Illus 7.15 and 9.11 are based on the excavated ground plans combined with an estimate of the likely height of the walls, based on the thickness of the foundations, and of the likely roof pitches based on Roman buildings (elsewhere in the empire) where roofs still survive. Two vexed questions which often arise in attempts at reconstruction are, first, whether Roman buildings in Britain had more than one storey and, second, in the case of a building with stone in the lower courses of its walls, whether it had been in stone throughout or had a timber superstructure. These are both difficult to resolve as what usually survives (in Britain at least) is just the base of the walls or even just the foundations, although occasionally a collapsed wall has survived to tell us more. For example, at Carsington (Derbys.) part of a stone gable wall was found 0.6m thick on foundations 0.8m deep which had once stood c.10.5m high which would have easily allowed a building of two storeys with an attic.[37] However, there is no way of knowing whether this was typical; the two reconstructions show single storey buildings, but second floors are perfectly possible.

At a more general level archaeologists try to reconstruct the culture of people in the past and their economic and social systems. For the Roman period written sources provide a good deal of background information, but an important part of the process involves analysing patterns in the archaeological data and relating them to human behaviour. For example, a good deal of discussion about Roman Britain is concerned with its economic development. In the absence of contemporary statistics this is a somewhat inexact science as we must rely on data for, for example, the expansion or otherwise of settlements, episodes of new building (especially public building), the level of production of manufactured goods, primarily pottery, and the extent of trade, especially of imports from outside Britain, again primarily pottery. These data can be looked at chronologically to identify periods of growth and decline, and also geographically to show, for example, the role that towns played in economic development. Geographical data are expressed in one of the fundamental tools of archaeological research, the so-called 'distribution map' which might, for example, show at a glance where imported Roman pottery was found in Yorkshire within a particular time frame. As another example we might study the impact of Roman ideas on funerary customs in Yorkshire based on a distribution of cremation burials – hardly known in the late pre-Roman Iron Age. We find that these burials, which do not usually occur before the mid-second to early third century, are mostly found at or near the forts and towns suggesting that the impact of Roman ideas on treatment of the dead in the region was not immediate following the conquest.

A more ambitious use of archaeological data has been the classification and characterisation of human societies in the past, especially important for the prehistoric or protohistoric periods for which there is little or no contemporary written evidence. Classification has usually been based on the association in a particular region of distinctive features in material culture such as types of pottery, styles in art, methods of building construction, burial customs etc. These features have then been related to a chronological framework so as to define particular 'cultures' and write their history. These archaeological cultures have often taken their modern names either from the place where the distinctive material features were first identified in association (the 'type site') or from people referred to in the ancient sources. In the first case we might note that in Yorkshire we have the 'Arras Culture' of the east Yorkshire Iron Age, named after a cemetery discovered in 1815–17 at Arras near Market Weighton. It is defined primarily by the custom of placing burials under a mound, or barrow, within a square or rectangular space surrounded by a ditch (a 'square-ditched barrow').[38] A small number of these burials, of high status individuals, were accompanied by a wheeled vehicle, usually referred to as a 'chariot'. The Arras Culture cemeteries are largely fourth to second century BC and sometimes seen as a defining feature of the culture of the Parisi some considerable time before they were named by Ptolemy, but whether tribal identity had any great continuity in prehistoric times is uncertain.

Another Iron Age culture is named after La Tène, a lakeside site in Switzerland. La Tène was once used almost interchangeably with the term 'late Iron Age' in Britain, although now it tends to be largely confined to the definition of art styles. La Tène culture has also been treated as an aspect of a larger cultural entity, that of the Celts. Defining who the Celts were has been the subject of considerable debate,[39] but one which is relevant to this book because it raises the question of the ethnic identity of the native people encountered by the Romans in Britain. The Celts first appear in history in Greek texts of c.500 BC as people on the northern fringes of the Classical world. Archaeologists have often described as Celts the Iron Age populations across large swathes of central and western Europe, including the British Isles. It was thought that they had sufficient in common in their material culture to suggest that they must have been a fairly coherent people in other ways, sharing such things as language, social organisation, religious beliefs and customs in respect of marriage, child rearing etc not visible archaeologically.

One can still find plenty of references in current historical works to the people encountered by the armies of Caesar and Claudius in Britain as Celts. For example, at the time of writing the term is used on the City of York website in its historical introduction pages. Terms such as 'Celtic field' and 'Celtic shorthorn' (a type of native cattle) are still in common usage. However, many scholars now question the validity of the 'culture history' approach to studying the past and doubt whether it is, for example, really justifiable to think of the indigenous Iron Age population of Britain as having all that much in common with contemporary populations in the rest of Europe. Furthermore, an idea, once much in vogue, of successive changes in the Iron Age culture of Britain being caused by waves of invasions or migrations from the Continent is now considerably downplayed. Julius Caesar, writing in the mid-first century BC, makes a well-known reference to a people he calls the Belgae who, he implies, had once been raiders seeking plunder and were now immigrants living in the south-east of Britain.[40] Acceptance of Caesar's statement at face value led to the identification of a culture known as 'Belgic' defined in the archaeological literature by such features as 'oppida' (the word is Caesar's), i.e. proto-towns such as *Camulodunum* (Colchester) and *Verulamium* (St Albans), and richly furnished burials, often containing wine jars ('amphorae') and other imported luxury goods. Today it is generally thought that Caesar may not be that reliable a witness and greater emphasis in explaining change in the British Iron Age is given to indigenous developments and the influence of trade and other forms of contact rather than invasions. The rather more neutral term 'Briton' tends to be used more often than 'Celt' to describe the people of Roman Britain who are now considered to be very largely descendants of indigenous forebears going back to the Bronze Age and before. However 'Celtic' is still accepted as a term to describe the art styles and language of the native Britons. This was not a written language, but some elements can be detected in Latinised form in inscriptions. For example, many names appear to have a native origin including the Velva in Julia Velva and Barita in Candida Barita, both from York.[41]

'Roman' is, of course, another term which defines a culture as well as a period of history. This brings us back to the debate about Romanisation and whether it is those aspects of Roman Britain which show it sharing in an empire-wide culture or the distinct aspects of Britain and its local regions which are the key to understanding the 'Romano-British' period. There are types of buildings such as fora, temples, villas etc and artefacts including not only the obvious militaria, but types of pottery, glassware, jewellery etc, all of which were introduced to Britain after the conquest. Their occurrence can be plotted in a chronological and spatial sense, but the question still remains as to how far the distribution of 'Roman' buildings and artefacts in a region like Yorkshire means that the Britons accepted other aspects of Roman culture – did they all speak Latin and wear togas? In any event, was there really that much of a homogeneous Roman culture, rather than a mixture of many different cultures, to accept or otherwise? This debate about how 'Roman' Roman Britain was and what did 'Roman' mean anyway has its origins more or less at the time that research into the subject began. We shall now go back to those origins and briefly review the history of research with particular reference to the Yorkshire region.

Roman Yorkshire discovered

The antiquarian era

Although one cannot say that knowledge of the Roman past was ever really lost in this country, the sort of academic research into Roman Britain, and the Roman world in general, based on both Classical written sources and material remains is really a product of the European Renaissance. The scholars who studied the early history of Britain from the sixteenth to the nineteenth century are often designated 'antiquarians', a term which has acquired a certain pejorative flavour in the era of the archaeologist

Illus. 3.5 York: tombstone of the Ninth Legion standard bearer Lucius Duccius Rufinus (height: 1.9m). (© York Museums Trust)

which is not really justified. It would have to be said, however, that what initially attracted antiquarian interest were, for the most part, those categories of artefacts such as coins, bronzes, tomb monuments and sculpture, thought to be representative of Roman civilisation known from its literature. The same might be said of structures, and there was a clear antiquarian preference for studying fortifications, roads, public buildings and villas. None the less, whilst we might now belittle their methods, without our early scholars many important remains of the Roman period would not have been preserved and there would be none of the pioneering academic publications which have laid the foundations for modern scholarship.

Illus. 3.6 Part of John Warburton's map of Yorkshire, published in 1720, showing the line of Wade's Causeway, the Roman road across the North York Moors taken as far as Whitby on the coast. (City of York Council Archives ©)

One of the earliest, widely available publications to include descriptions of the antiquities of Roman Britain is William Camden's *Britannia* of which the first edition, in Latin, appeared in 1586. This was the result of Camden's many journeys through Britain to gather information first hand about Roman roads and the places referred to in surviving documents such as the Antonine Itinerary. Many of these places were in Yorkshire, including, for example, Bainbridge described (in English) in the 1637 edition:

> At the very place where these Rivers [Ure and Bain] meete, and where there stand a few small Cotages which of the first Bridge made over the Ure, they

call Baintbrig, there lay in old time a Garison of the Romanes: whereof the very Reliques are at this day remaining.

One might say that, after Camden, the search for Roman Yorkshire began in earnest. The collection and recording of Roman antiquities attracted the attention of scholars from many different walks of life, although their discoveries were often accidental. Early examples include the Roman tilery stumbled across in woodland at Grimescar near Huddersfield by charcoal burners in 1590,[42] and the discovery by workmen, in 1597, of a Roman altar behind a house at Greetland, near Halifax, first noted in the 1600 edition of Camden.[43] Amongst seventeenth-century discoveries of note were the inscribed coffin at East Ness, near Helmsley, found in ploughing in 1619, and two altars found at Catterick in 1620 and 1622 – both subsequently lost.[44] Still on display, however, in York, is the tombstone of the standard bearer Lucius Duccius Rufinus found in the wall of the churchyard of Holy Trinity, Micklegate in 1686.

Whilst these and other early finds aroused the interest of a fairly small elite of cognoscenti, it was the establishment of learned societies and museums in the eighteenth and early nineteenth centuries which really put the study of the Roman period on its feet. In 1707 the founders of the Society of Antiquaries of London had their first meeting and they would soon receive communications from all over the country. For example, on 12 February 1735/6:

Mr Lethiullier sent a drawing of part of a Roman tessellated pavement discovered at Well in the North ryding of Yorkshire with an account in writing of the situation, and divers other particulars relating to it …[45]

In 1793 The Society's journal *Archaeologia* would posthumously publish General William Roy's *Military Antiquities of the Romans in Great Britain* which included surveys of sites in Yorkshire including the fortifications at Cawthorn.[46]

In Yorkshire itself one of the most prominent antiquaries was Ralph Thoresby (1658–1725), a wool merchant from Leeds, who published numerous papers on Roman antiquities in the years 1685–1705 and created his own museum for which a catalogue dates to 1712. In his diary he noted, amongst other things, the discovery and destruction of Roman remains at Adel, north of Leeds.[47] Another scholar of the same period, Martin Lister (1638–1712), the eminent doctor and zoologist, lived for a while in York and, strange though it may seem to us now, was apparently the first person to recognise that the Multangular Tower in Museum Gardens was Roman. An early attempt to map Roman roads in Yorkshire appears on John Warburton's county map of 1720.

Well-known scholars of national reputation, including William Stukeley (1687–1765) and John Horsley, author of *Britannia Romana* (1732), made reference to Roman discoveries in Yorkshire. However, a local landmark publication was *Eburacum*, published in 1736 by Francis Drake (1698–1771), a York surgeon. This is a great compendium of information about the history of York, much of it taken from earlier sources to which Drake added his

Illus. 3.7 York: the
Multangular Tower in
1807 looking north-east
towards Bootham Bar,
etching by J. Halfpenny.

own observations and assertions, some fanciful, such as the likelihood of the
Emperor Constantine's birth in the city. Drake also discusses Roman roads and
other Roman sites in the region including Cawthorn (to whose fortifications
he gave the letters A–D, still used today) and mosaics found in the 1730s in
Aldborough.

By the mid-eighteenth century the era of the private museum was beginning
to give way to one in which access was given to the general public. In 1759
the British Museum opened its doors for the first time and would in due
course acquire, *inter alia*, material of the prehistoric and Roman periods
from Yorkshire, including the great hoard of mid-first-century AD metalwork
found near the late Iron Age enclosure at Stanwick, near Richmond, in 1843.[48]
Interest in the Roman period clearly quickened in the later eighteenth and early
nineteenth centuries. New discoveries in York included, in 1770, an inscribed
tablet referring to the foundation of a temple of Serapis.[49] In Aldborough, more
mosaics came to light as well as building remains, including what was part of
the forum near St Andrew's church, also in 1770.[50] The important Ravenscar
inscription taken to refer to the construction of one of the late Roman signal
stations on the east coast was found in 1774 (Illus. 10.2).[51] In 1817 Lease Rigg
fort on the North York Moors was recognised as a Roman 'camp' by the
prominent local historian Rev. George Young.[52]

Fig. 1.

Fig. 2.

DEO·SANCTO
SERAPI
TEMPLVM·ASO
LO·FECIT
CL·HIERONY
MIANVS·LEG
LEG·VI·VIC

Illus. 3.8   York: a Mithraic relief showing the ritual bull-slaying, and an inscribed tablet commemorating the construction of a temple of Serapis (from Wellbeloved 1842).

Illus. 3.9   Dragonesque brooch with enamel inlay from Malton exhibited at the York meeting of the Royal Archaeological Institute in 1846 (length c.40mm).

Following the example of the British Museum, both collectors of antiquities and learned societies began to feel it incumbent on them to make their collections available to the public for their edification and improvement. In our region the Stone Age artefacts found in Kirkdale Cave in 1821 led to the creation of the Yorkshire Philosophical Society which was to establish the Yorkshire Museum in York, the earliest purpose-built museum in England. It was opened in 1830 with one of its principal objectives being to display Roman artefacts from the city. Similar learned societies emerged elsewhere in the county, at Leeds, for example, which also had a museum, and Whitby where the Literary and Philosophical Society, founded in 1823, remains one of the few societies which still runs its own museum – in which one can see the Ravenscar inscription.

Amongst new academic studies of the Roman remains of Yorkshire was a map of Roman roads and other remains on the Yorkshire Wolds and North

York Moors presented to the Society of Antiquaries in 1836 by John Walker of Malton.[53] In 1842 Charles Wellbeloved (1769–1858), a Unitarian minister and one of the founders of the Yorkshire Philosophical Society, published his own *Eburacum*, the first comprehensive survey of the history and remains of Roman York since Drake over a hundred years previously. It included first hand observations such as the fortress wall revealed and destroyed in the construction of St Leonard's Place and remains disturbed in the construction of the city's first railway station in 1839–40. Twelve years later, in 1852, Henry Ecroyd Smith published *Reliquiae Isurianae*, a lavish account of Roman remains found at Aldborough. As a pratical contribution to conservation of

Illus. 3.10   Well: part of a mosaic pavement (probably late second-century) from the villa, found in 1859 now in the village church. (Photo: Blackthorn Press)

the Roman past at this time one may cite restoration of a section of the town wall at Catterick by the landowner, Sir William Lawson.

Archaeology: the early years

In 1846 the recently formed Royal Archaeological Institute met in York for its third congress under the presidency of Earl Fitzwilliam.[54] In the proceedings of the meeting maps presented included one of Roman Yorkshire by Sir Charles Newton along with a number of more detailed maps of the Stanwick 'entrenchments' and the Roman fort at Castleshaw. Amongst the antiquities displayed at the meeting was the Stanwick metalwork hoard along with two lions carved in stone from Catterick and clay moulds for making counterfeit Roman coins from Lofthouse between Leeds and Wakefield. As a result of the meeting Henry McLauchlan was appointed to carry out a survey of 'antiquities', including Stanwick and Catterick, between the Swale and the Tees.[55]

A landmark in the study of Yorkshire's antiquities and history was the foundation of the Yorkshire Archaeological Society (YAS) in 1863. The use of the word 'archaeological' rather than antiquarian is significant because archaeology was only just beginning to take shape as the academic discipline which we would recognise today. Research objectives in these early years of Roman archaeology were very much under the influence of Classical studies which meant, first of all, military history, hence the excavation in our region of, for example, the fort baths at Slack, near Huddersfield (1865–66)[56] – a hypocaust had been removed from the site in 1824 – and the baths and granaries at Templeborough near Rotherham (1877–78).[57] The Roman civilian sphere was represented by villa excavations at Dalton Parlours, Collingham (1855),[58] Castle Dykes, North Stainley (1866 and 1874),[59] and Langton, near Malton (1863 and 1899).[60] In addition, the idea of what we would now call 'rescue archaeology', that is recording remains in advance of redevelopment has its real genesis in the late nineteenth century. This was prompted by the increasing scale of ground works required for construction projects including, for example, those related to the railways. In 1865–66 a cutting for the Malton – Thirsk railway shaved off the north-east corner of the fort at Malton bringing Roman artefacts and burials to light of which a record was made by Charles Monkman, a dedicated local antiquary.[61] On a much bigger scale, construction of the present railway station at York in 1877 was accompanied by recording of an extensive Roman cemetery by Revd James Raine, Chancellor of York Minster.[62]

In 1906 an important development for Roman archaeology in Yorkshire was the foundation by the YAS of the Yorkshire Roman Archaeological Committee (YRAC), the direct forebear of the YAS Roman Antiquities Section of today. The work sponsored by the YRAC before and after, and even during, World War I still reflected the desire of the more educated class in society to stand where Agricola, Hadrian and Severus and their cohorts had stood.

The investigation of military sites took centre stage with excavations at forts including Castleshaw, Elslack, Newton Kyme and Slack, and at the late Roman signal station at Huntcliff, on the coast near Saltburn. At Templeborough the work of a former tax inspector turned archaeologist, Thomas May, has some claim to be Britain's first 'rescue' excavation on any scale, taking place in 1916 in advance of construction of the Steel, Peach and Tozer steel works.[63]

Archaeology between the wars

After World War I research priorities for Roman archaeology in the Yorkshire region were little changed; military and political history continued to dictate the agenda. However, methodology, in terms of the application of the principles of stratigraphy, began to improve markedly. Publications included not only accurate measured plans but also detailed cross-sections which formed the basis for illustrating sequences of construction, demolition etc which could be dated by the finds associated with each layer. At York in 1925–28 Professor Stuart Miller, working for the York Excavations Committee, confirmed the extent of the legionary fortress and studied its history, largely by means of carefully dug and recorded sections through the defences – his excavation at the east corner is still open for public inspection.[64] At Malton one of Yorkshire's most prolific excavators, Philip Corder, worked at the north-east gate of the fort in 1927[65] and then with Thomas Romans and Ian Richmond, led an important series of excavations at Brough on Humber in 1933–37, establishing the sequence of a fort followed by a major civilian settlement.[66] Roman forts excavated between the wars also included Bainbridge,[67] Ilkley,[68] and those at Cawthorn.[69] In addition, the signal stations at Filey and Scarborough were investigated by one of the leading Romanists of his day, F.G. Simpson.[70] At Catterick an excavation within what is now thought to be the fort annexe took place in 1938,[71] the first in advance of a new bypass which would take the A1 around the village; work would resume after World War II. Non-military sites received rather less attention from excavators, although at the Roman town of Aldborough work took place on the defences in 1937–38[72] and important excavations at Langton villa, led by Corder and Dr John Kirk, were undertaken in 1926 and 1930.[73] As in previous eras, lesser rural settlements were largely overlooked, although a harbinger of things to come was the extensive investigation, led latterly by Corder, at Elmswell, to the north of the present village, in 1935–38.[74] Specialised research into Roman pottery in the region was promoted by Corder's work at the kiln site at Throlam, near Holme-on-Spalding Moor.[75]

The 1930s saw publication of three important summaries of the Roman archaeology of Yorkshire. In 1933 the Roman period occupied a chapter in the *Archaeology of Yorkshire* by Frank Elgee, curator of the Dorman Museum in Middlesbrough, and his wife Harriet Wragg Elgee. Two years later came the still indispensable *Gazetteer of Roman Remains in East Yorkshire* by Mary Kitson Clark with its compendium of references to Roman roads, forts, burials and other finds. Thirdly, in 1936 F.R. Pearson, Senior History Master at

Bridlington School, published his *Roman Yorkshire* which remains useful today because of its author's keen eye for the Yorkshire landscape and the way the Romans managed it with their roads and military fortifications.

Although one might say that archaeology came of age in the interwar period, it was, none the less, still an era of a rather more relaxed attitude to the recovery of antiquities and study of archaeological sites than would be conceivable today. For example, in the report of 1946 on the Roman shrines on Scargill Moor we read:

> The exposed top of the altar was first observed about 1936 by Mr William Wilkinson and Mr John Hilary ... On clearing away the soil they saw that the altar was inscribed. Little significance was first attached to the discovery [!], and interest in it was revived only towards the end of the war ...[76]

Archaeology in the post-war period: 1945–1972

Although a few discoveries were made during World War II, such as the site of Brantingham villa near Brough on Humber in 1941,[77] archaeological research was largely suspended. In the immediate post-war period and into the 1960s Roman military sites and related civilian settlements continued to exercise their grip on the interests of excavators. In York archaeological work in 1950s and 1960s took place, for the most part, in the legionary fortress, especially on the defences. In 1962 the study of Roman York stepped up a gear with the publication of *Eboracum*, the first volume of the Royal Commission on Historical Monuments for England's great inventory of the city – one hundred and twenty years after Wellbeloved, this was well over due. The RCHME followed this up by sponsoring a great campaign of excavations under York Minster in 1966–71 in advance of the reinforcement of the medieval foundations; extensive remains of barracks and the fortress headquarters were encountered.[78] Forts explored included Bainbridge,[79] used over ten seasons as a training dig for Leeds University students, Bowes,[80] Castleshaw,[81] Doncaster,[82] Lease Rigg[83] and Slack.[84] At Brough on Humber a campaign of excavations by John Wacher, re-examining the fort and later town, took place in 1958–61,[85] and Wacher also worked at Catterick in advance of the long-delayed bypass in 1958–59.[86] At Malton attention was turned to the *vicus* outside the fort by Mitchelson in 1949–52 and Wenham in 1968–70.[87]

A technique of investigation which has its origin in the interwar period, but has really revolutionised our knowledge of the archaeological resource of Britain as a whole since World War II, is aerial photography. Yorkshire had a small pioneering role as one of the first aerial archaeological surveys was undertaken in 1932 by O.G.S. Crawford on the prehistoric and Roman landscape at Grassington in Wharfedale. After the war much of Britain was photographed from the air and large numbers of new sites were revealed through the work of such pioneers as J. K. St Joseph and Derrick Riley, both of whom worked in the Yorkshire region.[88] Not only were new military sites

Illus. 3.11   Beadlam villa: remains of the main house (Building 1 on Illus. 9.10) looking north-east. (Photo: Blackthorn Press)

such as the fortress at Rossington Bridge discovered, but also rural landscapes divided up by great ditch systems such as those on the sandstone of south Yorkshire and north Nottinghamshire. The detection and mapping of these landscapes accompanied a new interest in Roman rural settlement and led to a number of important excavations in the 1960s and 1970s. One of these took place on a great expanse of the Wolds in advance of quarrying at Garton and Wetwang Slacks, near Driffield, in 1965–75.[89] The work revealed a history of settlement from the Neolithic to the Roman period and demonstrated the value of working on a very large area (c.40ha) in order to understand the development and organisation of landscape in the past. Rural settlement in Yorkshire was also investigated in this period, if not on the scale of Garton –Wetwang, by Raymond Hayes, one of the most dedicated fieldworkers in our region, on sites in the North York Moors and Vale of Pickering.[90] The era in which the countryside was represented almost exclusively by the Roman villa had come to an end, although there was important work in the 1960s and 1970s on villas at Rudston,[91] Beadlam,[92] Dalton Parlours[93] and Kirk Sink near Gargrave.[94]

Archaeology in the modern era: rescue and beyond

The early 1970s were a real watershed in the history of British archaeology in terms of its organisation and resources. The scale of threats to archaeological sites of all periods due to such agencies as farming, quarrying and urban development had reached a level at which far more in the way of an archaeological response was needed than was available from the mix of amateur archaeologists, universities and public bodies, such as RCHME, whose resources were strictly limited. Following a well-organised campaign, the rescue crisis came to the notice of both central and local government, and there was to be a great increase in the public funding for work on archaeological sites under threat all over the country. A good deal of this was channelled into the new professional archaeological units which, as far as our region is concerned, were set up in York (1972) and in Humberside and West Yorkshire (both 1975). The early work of the Humberside and West Yorkshire units involved production of comprehensive archaeological surveys which still form the basis for the study of the Roman period (and other periods) in these regions.[95]

Alongside the establishment of the units there was a growing acceptance of archaeology as a material consideration in the planning process – meaning that before planning permission was granted to a developer, provision had to be made for an archaeological investigation. County councils began to establish Sites and Monuments Records which now form the basis for development control in respect of archaeology. The status of archaeology in the planning process was formalised in 1990 by a statement of government policy in the Department of the Environment's Planning Policy Guidance Note 16 (PPG16) *Archaeology and Planning* the result of which was to require access and resources to be made available by developers to evaluate sites of potential archaeological interest before planning permission was granted. Similar provisions now form part of the National Planning Policy Framework (2012).

Official recognition of the importance of archaeology has meant that since the mid-1970s the scale and scope of investigation in Yorkshire has increased enormously. The number of recorded sites and related landscapes of all periods has grown very rapidly and they have appeared in areas previously more or less blank in the records. Increased resources and opportunities have gone hand in hand with a greater ambition in both fieldwork and in the analysis of data. This ambition has led to a number of very important methodological advances in such areas as geophysical survey, environmental archaeology, scientific dating, and artefact conservation and analysis.

On the ground, rural settlement has come to loom much larger than hitherto in the Roman archaeology of our region, but sites capable of throwing light on the Roman conquest and other military matters have not been ignored either. There has been a major review and survey of the Stanwick earthworks, accompanied by further excavation on the defences and in the interior which has led to the revision of many of the conclusions made by Sir Mortimer Wheeler following his excavations in 1951–52.[96] Important work has also taken place at many of the region's Roman forts, sometimes in advance of impending development as at Castleford[97] or in rather less pressured circumstances as at Castleshaw,[98] Hayton,[99] and Lease Rigg.[100] A reconsideration of Cawthorn, as part of the development of a site management strategy by the North York Moors National Park, was followed by a new excavation programme in 2000–01.[101] Aerial photography has led to the discovery of new fort sites at Burghwallis (Robin Hood's Well)[102] and Roall Manor Farm,[103] both near Doncaster, and at Roecliffe, near Boroughbridge[104] and Wensley in the Dales.[105]

It would be impossible to sum up all the work in Roman archaeology in Yorkshire since the early 1970s but there are, perhaps, two big stories. The first concerns Roman York. For such an important centre it is fair to say that the RCHME *Eburacum* volume of 1962 showed that its history and topography were poorly understood when compared to many major Roman centres. Since then, however, driven largely by rescue considerations as a result of new development, further work has taken place in the fortress, not only on the headquarters, but also on the bath house, including the sewer system,[106] the barracks and the defences.[107] Even more important has been the investigation of the civilian settlement south-west of the Ouse,[108] complemented by further work in the cemeteries and environs.[109] Unfortunately much of the fieldwork remains unpublished, but the potential now exists for a fully rounded picture of the Roman military and civilian sites to emerge and put York at the heart of Romano-British studies.

The second big story of Roman Yorkshire – even bigger than York – in the last thirty years or so has been the discovery of its rural settlement and landscape and, based on this, the study of the native population and its economic and social relationship with the Roman elite. A good deal of the work has taken place in advance of new developments, facilitated by archaeology's status in the planning system. Some of it has been on a very considerable scale, particularly where undertaken before construction of new road schemes and pipelines for gas, oil or water which have often led to the investigation of great linear tranches through the landscape. Good examples of road scheme projects include the A1 – M1 link road (1992–98) between Tingley junction on the M62 and Bramham Crossroads on the A1,[110] and the Darrington–Dishforth A1 (M) upgrade (2003–06),[111] both funded by the Highways Agency and partners.

Alongside the development-led work there have been projects run purely for research purposes, usually with a strong amateur and local community input. Three in particular stand out for their scope and ambition, to say nothing of their longevity. Two of them have been supported by English Heritage of which the longest running was Wharram Percy (1948–90) on the Wolds, *c.*10km south-east of Malton. The project began as a search for the deserted medieval village, but then widened out into the study of the landscape in earlier periods including the Roman.[112] The second project, at West Heslerton, led by Dominic Powlesland, began with prehistoric sites threatened by sand quarrying, but has now expanded to concern itself with the archaeology of the whole parish and neighbouring parishes in the Vale of Pickering.[113] Thirdly, and largely unsupported by public money, there is the Foulness Valley project, led by Peter Halkon, supported by East Riding Archaeological Society. Work began in 1980 by taking a 8km square around Holme-on-Spalding Moor in east Yorkshire with a view to establishing the relationship between agriculture and industry in the Iron Age and Roman periods and assessing the impact of environmental factors such as soils and watercourses on settlement patterns.[114] Subsequently, the project scope has expanded to encompass work at Hayton and Shiptonthorpe on the main Roman road from York to Brough. All three projects have been able to work themselves into the grain of the landscapes with which they are concerned, over a long period, and thereby trace the intimate details of their relationship with the people of the past in a way which brings them vividly to life. In addition to these excavation-based projects, one should also note two other important long-running projects relating to the Roman period. Firstly there is the Yorkshire Quern Survey, sponsored by the YAS, which studies an important, if often unregarded, aspect of material culture. Secondly, one must note the work on Roman roads in West Yorkshire led by Donald Haigh, supported by pupils at Bradford Grammar School, which has added new detail to the great nationwide survey of Britain's Roman roads by Ivan Margary.[115]

For a historian of the Roman period in the Yorkshire region writing in 2013 the last thirty years, with their ever-increasing quantities of high quality data from excavation and survey, has been an exciting time for research. One gets a sense, for the first time since serious interest was aroused some 400 years ago, that we are starting to get an overview of how the whole of Yorkshire and its region in the Roman period developed, an overview not based purely on York, the forts, the roads and the villas. We are now able not only to put a considerable amount of new flesh onto the bones of the military and political history provided by the written sources, but to produce narratives concerned with settlement, population, agriculture, trade and other topics based on evidence from a great range of different places. Moreover, these are narratives which do not have to treat the Roman period as a homogeneous whole, but one in which change can be clearly detected and analysed. I hope to reflect this in the following chapters.

4 Romans and Natives before the Conquest

Introduction

In this chapter I shall be discussing the Yorkshire region, principally, from about the beginning of the first century AD until the years 69–71 when, following the ascent of the Emperor Vespasian to the throne, the Roman conquest of the north began in earnest.

The first direct encounter between the Romans and the Britons had taken place in the south-east of Britain when, as a result of his campaigns in Gaul in 55 and 54 BC, Julius Caesar had occasion to cross the Channel, apparently in pursuit of fugitives. However, it was to be Claudius (AD 41–54), who settled on Britain as the place to gain the military success he needed to secure his legitimacy as emperor. He despatched an army of conquest numbering some 40,000 men in the year 43. In 51–52, less than ten years after the invasion, a unit of auxiliary soldiers found themselves on the south bank of the River Rother at Templeborough, near the deserted Iron Age hill-fort at Wincobank. Little did they know it, but Templeborough was the first Roman fort in what was to become Yorkshire about one thousand years later. To the east, 21km away, another body of soldiers, this time a detachment of legionaries – a *vexillum* – may have set up a rather larger encampment – a vexillation fortress – on the banks of the River Torne at Rossington Bridge, just south of Doncaster.[1] Templeborough and Rossington Bridge, along with other bases in Nottinghamshire and north Derbyshire, were probably built as part of the campaign led by the Roman governor of Britain, Didius Gallus, to support Queen Cartimandua of the Brigantes. According to Tacitus, she was under attack from her former consort Venutius, probably as a result of his opposition to her handing over the fugitive Caratacus to the Romans.[2] The son of Cunobelinus, a great king in the south-east of England just before the conquest, Caratacus had made his name as a leader of anti-Roman forces, first in the south-east of England and then in Wales before his final defeat. In addition, Cartimandua had had the temerity to eject Venutius from her bed and replace him with his armour-bearer, Vellocatus.

In the years 51–52 southern Yorkshire was frontier territory; to the south lay the new Roman province of *Britannia* and to the north the independent territory of native British people. As we understand it, most of northern England was occupied by the Brigantes, a people described by Tacitus as 'the most numerous' in Britain.[3] The term Brigantes – plural of *Brigans* – has often been translated as 'the high ones' which may mean 'the overlords' or simply 'the hill dwellers'.[4] Rather than being in any sense a cohesive political unit, they were probably a loose confederation of numerous smaller groups with leadership shifting from one to another.

Whilst it is impossible to define actual frontier lines in the late Iron Age, and in any case they would have been constantly moving about, by the first century AD the northern limit of the Brigantes' territory appears to have lain in the southern lowlands of Scotland. The southern limit ran roughly from the Humber in the east to the Mersey in the west.[5] Whilst this may have been, in general, poorly defined, it has been suggested that in South Yorkshire (east of Sheffield) the River Don formed a boundary between the Brigantes and the Corieltauvi who occupied much of the east Midlands and Lincolnshire. By the year 51 their land lay inside the Roman Empire. Templeborough and Rossington Bridge (both south of the Don) may, therefore, have been on the edge of Corieltauvian territory as the Romans would, perhaps, have been reluctant to place fortifications in Brigantian territory itself while it was still nominally independent.

According to Ptolemy the only part of the north not under Brigantian control corresponded roughly to the East Riding of Yorkshire. This was the home of the Parisi. It has been suggested, based on the distribution of the distinctive square-ditched barrow burials of the Iron Age Arras culture, that the northern boundary of the Parisi lay on the northern scarp of the limestone hills north of the Vale of Pickering whilst the western boundary was formed, south of Malton, by the River Derwent, although Iron Age barrows have been found near York, west of the Derwent at Skipwith and Thorganby.[6]

The principal literary source for the immediate pre-Roman period in Britain as a whole is Tacitus, although, as we have seen, there are only three short, if important, references to events in the Yorkshire region itself. Otherwise we must rely on archaeological remains. In the near absence of closely datable arte-facts, however, a detailed historical account is difficult to write. The Brigantes and Parisi minted no coins, although some datable coins of the Corieltauvi and other British tribes have been found in Yorkshire. Native pottery was simple in form and changed in a relatively slow and unpredictable manner.[7] Only a few sites received datable imported pottery from other parts of Britain or very occasionally from sources further afield including northern Gaul (Roman *Gallia Belgica*) where 'Gallo-Belgic' ware was made from the later first century BC until c.AD 70–80.[8] It usually occurs as platters, bowls and other vessels for the table. 'Gallo-Belgic' ware is rare as far north as Yorkshire, but it is, none the less, important evidence for early trade contacts with the Roman Empire.

Queen Cartimandua is often referred to as a 'client' of the Romans, a ruler in a frontier area trusted to keep the peace in return for protection against attack from other parties. Creating the conditions for the easy absorption of a client's lands into the Roman Empire, after his or her death, has a long history. On occasions, however, things could go badly wrong as they did in Britain in the years 60–61. Tacitus again is a contemporary source for events which followed the death of the East Anglian client king Prasutagus of the Iceni.[9] His daughter Boudicca, outraged by the rough treatment meted out to her and to her people, and prompted by discontent at the loss of land to Roman colonists around Colchester, led a native revolt against Rome. Her armies succeeded in burning Colchester, London and *Verulamium* (Roman St Albans) before being defeated by the Roman army under Petilius Cerialis with the loss, so Tacitus tells us, of 80,000 of her followers!

Understandably, the Roman advance through Britain was halted for a few years during what remained of the troubled reign of the Emperor Nero while the province recovered from the revolt. In the year 68, however, Nero committed suicide and after a brief interregnum of three different emperors in 69, Vespasian, the commander of legions in Syria, gained the imperial crown.

Settlement and landscape in the late Iron Age: an age of enclosure

Had the soldiers at Templeborough ventured across the Rother they would have found a world of small farmsteads surrounded by small fields interspersed with pasture and managed woodlands. Analysis of pollen from borehole samples, the increased presence of grain in archaeological deposits and the distribution of quern stones suggest increasing cereal production and growth of population in many parts of the Yorkshire region in the mid-late Iron Age. In the same period we find the gradual emergence of enclosed landscapes in which large tracts of land were divided up to form what are usually described as 'field systems'. The enclosures, or fields, were defined by ditches and earthen banks (although the latter rarely survive) and, in certain upland areas, by stone walls or banks of earth and stones. Hedged boundaries may have been more common than is apparent because evidence for them rarely survives.The pattern of land division was often structured around major pre-existing boundaries going back to the Bronze Age or early Iron Age such as Grim's Ditch *c.*6km east of Leeds and the dykes, or 'entrenchments' on the Wolds. These boundaries were followed and re-stated by trackways or droveways, defined by a ditch on each side, which sometimes extend over several kilometres. Enclosed landscapes would seem to mark the establishment of more permanent, less peripatetic communities than had existed hitherto, communities who were prepared to make a substantial investment in land management and improved farming methods. In addition, formal land division may have served to prevent disputes over access to land caused by a rising population and, at the same time, may

Illus. 4.1
Reconstruction of an
Iron Age roundhouse
within a ditched
enclosure at Heslington
near York, looking
north-east towards the
York moraine.
(© P. Ottaway)

also have been an accompaniment to the emergence of a more hierarchical society in which the elite found it convenient to divide up their land with a view to making it easier to assess for extraction of some of the fruits of agricultural production from their people.

Considerable effort has gone into mapping these enclosed landscapes, using the cropmarks visible on aerial photographs, supplemented by survey and excavation on the ground.[10] In an attempt to refine their dating, establish regional characteristics and understand the agricultural regime implied by them, attempts have been made at classification of their morphology. In summary, it now appears that during the late Iron Age/early Roman period in Yorkshire there were complex processes of change at work in the landscape and what we are looking at, whether on an aerial photograph or on the ground, may be the product of several stages of modification and expansion.

Throughout the region there are enclosures which are curvilinear or irregular in form, perhaps reflecting either the local topography or the ad hoc clearance of woodland which preceded their setting out. Whilst such enclosures may often be early in the process of land division, they were also formed in the Roman period as well. None the less, by the late Iron Age some regularity in the pattern of land division can be found in large areas of the countryside. In many parts of Yorkshire one can identify so called 'co-axial' field systems composed of elongated boundaries defining strips of land on a common alignment which may extend over great distances. Shorter divisions go across these strips creating enclosures of various sizes, but usually *c.*0.5–1ha. In other areas, particularly in the uplands, single enclosures or small groups of enclosures appear to be more typical. A particular feature of enclosures extending up hillsides, often clearly visible today as a sort of terrace, is the lynchet bank created over a period of time as the soil in the enclosure above slipped down the slope, coming to rest at the boundary.

There is some debate over the function of enclosures of the various forms and sizes, but, on the whole, it is agreed that they were probably fields for both arable cultivation and keeping stock whilst the trackways gave stock access through the fields to unenclosed pasture. Some enclosures of distinct form may have had specialised functions. For example, it has been suggested that circular or subcircular enclosures may have been used for breaking and training horses. There are also D-shaped enclosures, although their special function, if any, cannot yet be determined.

Dispersed through these enclosed landscapes were settlements, principally represented by roundhouses, either singly or clustered in small groups, often in their own small enclosures taken out of the corner of a larger one. It is not always clear, however, whether all the roundhouses in a group were occupied at the same time and excavation sometimes suggests that an individual house was rebuilt on successive occasions, each time on a slightly different site.

A brief review of the evidence for the enclosed landscapes of late Iron Age/early Roman Yorkshire may begin in the northern Pennines. In central Swaledale Andrew Fleming and Tim Laurie have identified several large areas of coaxial land division on moorland above present-day villages of Healaugh, Reeth, Grinton, Marrick and Marske.[11] Divisions are defined by the remains of low stone banks of dump construction which may orginally have supported hedges thereby allowing effective stock control. The banks largely survive on high ground over 300m above sea level, but may originally have run down to the bottom of the valley of the Swale where they have been removed by medieval and later ploughing. Fleming suggests that enclosure began in *c.*300 BC following a major forest clearance episode. A rise in population appears to have continued unbroken by the Roman conquest and new settlements were fitted into the earlier pattern. Platforms terraced into the valley side were the location of roundhouses of both pre-Roman and Roman date.

South of Swaledale in the Craven uplands, in an exhaustive survey undertaken before World War II, Arthur Raistrick identified as many as 500 sites that he thought might have been occupied in the Iron Age.[12] They lay principally on terraces in the valleys of the Wharfe, Skirfare and upper Ribble, and on the limestone plateau by Ingleborough, all areas where good quality pasture would have been available. For the most part, the sites existed as small oval or roughly rectangular enclosures defined by mounds of boulders, gravel and turf or as what are known as 'orthostat' walls which have an earth and rubble core flanked by large upright stone slabs set on edge ('orthostats' see Illus. 7.14). Enclosures often contained a 'hut' in one corner surviving as a

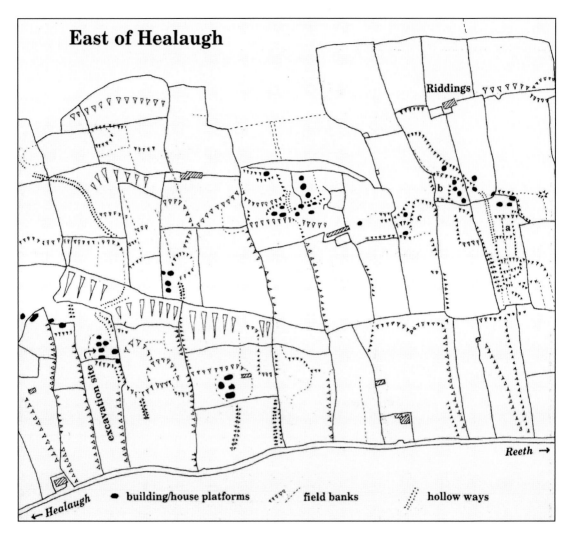

East of Healaugh

Riddings

excavation site

Reeth →

← Healaugh

● building/house platforms   field banks   hollow ways

Illus. 4.2   Swaledale, between Riddings (near Reeth) and Healaugh, plan showing field banks for co-axial fields, trackways and building/house platforms. Scale *c*. 1:5500. (reproduced courtesy of Andrew Fleming ©)

circular bank *c*.2.5m–4.9m in diameter. Near to the enclosures Raistrick found low balks defining small fields.

A large block of early fields in an area *c*.100ha in extent north of Grassington, in Wharfedale, survives as part of a multi-period landscape on land rising to 300m above sea level.[13] The fields are roughly rectangular and vary in size, but *c*.0.25ha is typical. They are defined today by lynchets and low banks with stoney cores. Within the field system are numerous smaller closes within which there are circular huts, although this is not a village in the sense we usually understand it and it is difficult to know how many might have been occupied at any one time. Small scale excavations at Park Stile and Lea Green, as early as 1893–94, and other work subsequently have produced Roman pottery, probably arising from use of domestic refuse as manure on the fields. This does not prove the system has a Roman origin, but an expansion of it probably occurred during the Roman period; it was suggested by Frere and St

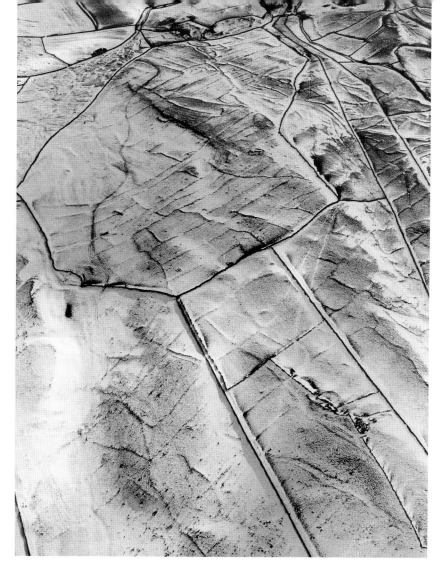

Illus. 4.3 Aerial photograph of early field systems and settlements at High Close, Grassington overlain by field walls of post-medieval times, looking south-west towards the village. (© Anthony Crawshaw)

Joseph that this was due to the demands of the Roman army for agricultural products. New details of the area are currently being revealed at High Close by the Yorkshire Dales Landscape Research Trust.[14]

Elsewhere in Craven, at its western limit, the Ingleborough Archaeological Group has surveyed and sample excavated an enclosure 72m × 60m at Thornton in Lonsdale near Ingleton.[15] The site had a favourable location on a sheltered, south- facing slope with a little river valley to the east. It is representative of a number of similar enclosures on the western side of the Pennines, defined by surviving banks, which have a rectilinear plan with internal divisions, perhaps serving as stock pounds, as well as structural remains. The excavation established that the enclosing bank and outer ditch probably dated to the immediate pre-Roman period. Internally a drystone wall was thought to represent a building but its form was not entirely clear. Although finds were scarce, sufficient pottery survived, supported by

Illus. 4.4   Aerial view north of enclosures at Ingman Lodge Shaw Pasture below limestone terraces (left), *c*.1.5km south of Ribblehead Station. The field boundaries and trackway seen on the right run towards the River Ribble to the east. (Photograph by J.K. St Joseph © Cambridge University)

radiocarbon dates, to suggest occupation continued until the early third century AD if not for a longer time.

On the valley terraces around the Ingleborough massif, in the valleys of the Chapel-le-Dale Beck (on the west side) and the River Ribble (on the east), Alan King has recorded well-preserved farmsteads with the remains of roundhouses and associated droveways and enclosures thought to represent garden plots, stock pens and fields.[16] For example, at Ribblehead sites lie on the northern slopes of Ingleborough just below the uppermost terrace of Gordale Scar limestone at *c*.300m above sea level. Other groups of enclosures lie at regular intervals along the west side of the Ribble valley as far as Horton in Ribblesdale and, more intermittently, as far as Settle. A mixed farming regime may have prevailed on these uplands even where there is little arable today, although crop yields might not have been as good as in the fertile lowlands. Some fifteen kilometres to the east of the Ribble valley enclosures have been

Illus. 4.5 (*opposite*) Earthwork complex at Thornsber Barn, Arncliffe, Littondale. A co-axial field system forms the core of this landscape with its origins, perhaps, in the Iron Age which was in use until the Middle Ages. The unusual circular enclosure (see Leak and Leak 1970) is now thought to be post-Roman. (© Steve Moorhouse) found at Malham and others, probably related primarily to pastoral agriculture, lie at up to 550m above sea level between Malham Tarn and Littondale. On a limestone terrace at Middle House, *c.*1km north of Malham Tarn, a settlement of stone-built roundhouses has been identified.[17] In Littondale, on the south side of the River Skirfare, Steve Moorhouse has recorded an extensive coaxial field system at the heart of a multi-period landscape at Thornsber Barn, Arncliffe.[18]

There have been few excavations of the extensive late prehistoric and Roman settlements in Swaledale and Craven, but their material culture (or at least what survives) appears to have been quite limited until the later Roman period. On

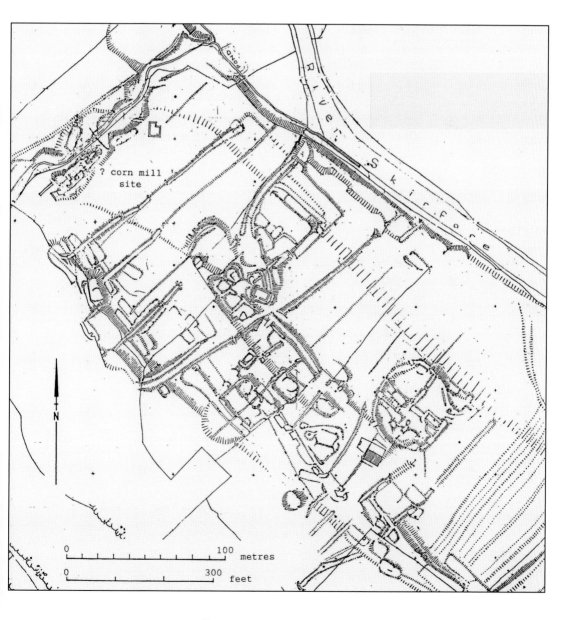

the basis of what he knew of from Craven, Raistrick characterised its people as 'poverty-stricken', and he thought they had been only too happy to get hold of '... cultural fragments which could be bartered or plundered from the adjacent Roman stations ...' However, he went on, being a 'proud people' they had rejected the temptations of the Roman world and chosen 'freedom with poverty'. This is, however, very much a twentieth-century view of a people who had, after all, adapted to environmental conditions in the area over many generations and achieved a perfectly sustainable life style.

In the southern Pennines, on the moorland east of the Don as it runs south towards Sheffield, there are, as in the uplands further north, enclosures defined by stoney banks which may be of pre-Roman origin, although they only produce Roman pottery.[19] Similar enclosures are found elsewhere on the Coal Measures in South Yorkshire, preserved in a few surviving areas of ancient woodland which have never been ploughed, for example in Canklow Woods, south-east of Rotherham.[20] Cropmarks in the Coal Measures are easier to see on the sandstone outcrops than on the shale and mudstone, but there may, in any event, have been a preference for the former with their well-drained subsoil. At Wombwell, for example, in a large area on an east-facing slope rising to 144m above sea level,[21] trenching revealed a sequence of enclosures, possibly of Iron Age origin, at the southern end of a north–south trackway defined by ditches. Further east at Shafton, 7km north-east of Barnsley, on elevated ground above the River Dearne to the south, two sites were excavated in 2002–03 revealing an enclosed landscape in an area where previously no settlement of the Roman period was known.[22] West of Shafton High Street an east–west trackway defined by ditches met a substantial north–south ditch up to 3m wide and 1.10m deep, a primary land boundary, to west side of which an enclosure with subdivisions was attached. An Iron Age origin is likely, although, as is often the case in South Yorkshire, there was no pottery other than Roman. On the Shafton bypass, c.1km to the south-east of High Street, part of a large (c.600m²) subcircular ditched enclosure with a western entrance was probably late Iron Age in origin before its redefinition in the Roman period.

On the eastern side of the Coal Measures enclosed landscapes, similar to those on the adjoining Magnesian Limestone further east, have been identified, for example, in the Methley area, south-east of Leeds where cropmarks have been identified on the gravel terraces of the Aire-Calder confluence. Excavations at Moss Carr, Methley, adjacent to a trackway, revealed a rectangular enclosure within which there were, perhaps, four successive roundhouses, and in a second possible enclosure there were three phases of another roundhouse.[23] At Normanton Golf Course on heavy clay, the site – a shallow bowl of marginal land – lay adjacent to the junction of two streams in its south-west corner. A late Iron Age enclosure with a central roundhouse lay within a larger enclosed area. In the Roman period the roundhouse enclosure fell out of use to be replaced by ditches defining three wide strips, aligned north-east / south-west, up to c.160m wide, parallel to one of the streams and at 90° to the other.[24] The replacement, in the Roman period, of earlier arrangements by formal coaxial land divison is a sequence similar to that found elsewhere in South Yorkshire. Finally for the Coal Measures, at the western end of the A1–M1 Link road (on the east side of Leeds) there have been extensive investigations at Stile Hill, Colton and Swillington Common of the northernmost elements of an extensive cropmark landscape in which a developing regime of land division began in the mid-late Iron Age, based on a north–south trackway.[25]

On much of the Magnesian Limestone cropmarks of late Iron Age and Roman field systems are very extensive, reflecting its suitability for arable agriculture.[26] Amongst the best examples to be studied by excavation are those at Wattle Syke, near Wetherby (Illus. 3.2),[27] at sites on the line of the A1–M1 Link road (eastern end)[28] and at Ferrybridge (in advance of construction of the A1–M62 link).[29] At Ferrybridge a regular pattern of land division was established south and south-west of the banks of the Neolithic henge monument which would have probably been a prominent feature of the landscape. Several land units were organised around trackways and defined by ditches (Illus. 4.7, Phase 3). In the corners of these units there were small ditched enclosures containing roundhouses, a very typical arrangement in this part of Yorkshire. South of Doncaster field systems and settlement sites seem to be less easily detected because of a greater use of stone walls and banks – now ploughed away – rather than ditches; some examples probably have a Roman rather than earlier origin.[30]

In the northern part of the Yorkshire region in the Tees lowlands aerial photography has identified numerous groups of subrectangular enclosures which were clearly characteristic of the late prehistoric/early Roman period.[31] There is something of a concentration in the Piercebridge area, around where Roman Dere Street would cross the Tees. This suggests development of the landscape in the Roman period, although both the crossing point and surrounding enclosures probably have pre-Roman origins. At Holme House, Manfield, excavations revealed a ditched enclosure with a roundhouse in the centre; subsequently this was the site of a Roman villa which may suggest it was the residence of an important person in earlier times.[32] Other enclosure sites in the Tees lowlands have been excavated at, for example, Ingleby Barwick[33] and Potto.[34] On the edge of the Moors at Street House (near Loftus), close to the sea, there was an Iron Age/early Roman enclosure in which there was evidence for the production of salt, a most valuable commodity probably traded over some considerable distance.[35] To the south-west, in the Vale of Mowbray, at Scorton, immediately north-east of Catterick (Illus. 5.6) an enclosed landscape has been revealed into which the Roman military would carefully insert itself with an early camp adopting the alignment of the Iron Age ditches.[36]

On the edge of the Vale of York, below the Howardian Hills, excavations on the line of the Easingwold bypass revealed part of an enclosed landscape

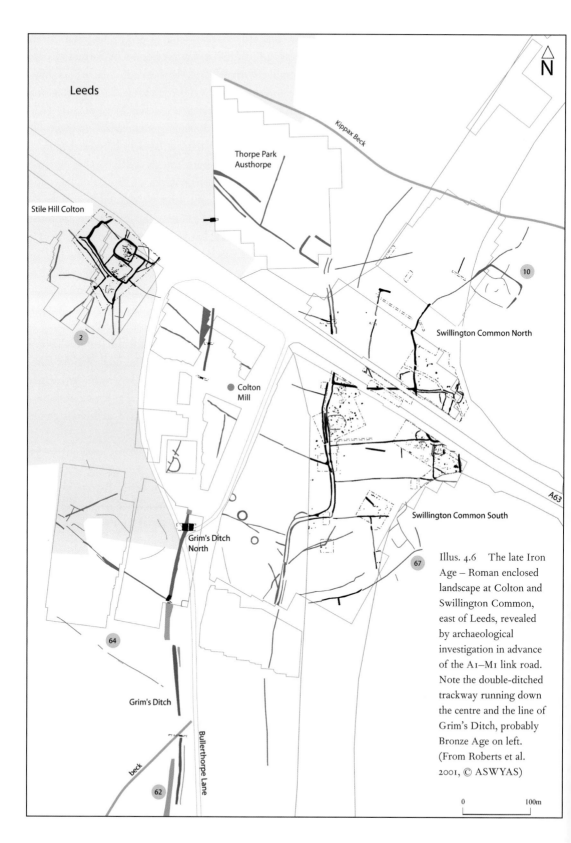

Leeds

Thorpe Park
Austhorpe

Kippax Beck

Stile Hill Colton

2

10

Swillington Common North

Colton
Mill

A63

Swillington Common South

Grim's Ditch
North

67

64

Grim's Ditch

Bullerthorpe Lane

beck

62

Illus. 4.6   The late Iron
Age – Roman enclosed
landscape at Colton and
Swillington Common,
east of Leeds, revealed
by archaeological
investigation in advance
of the A1–M1 link road.
Note the double-ditched
trackway running down
the centre and the line of
Grim's Ditch, probably
Bronze Age on left.
(From Roberts et al.
2001, © ASWYAS)

0   100m

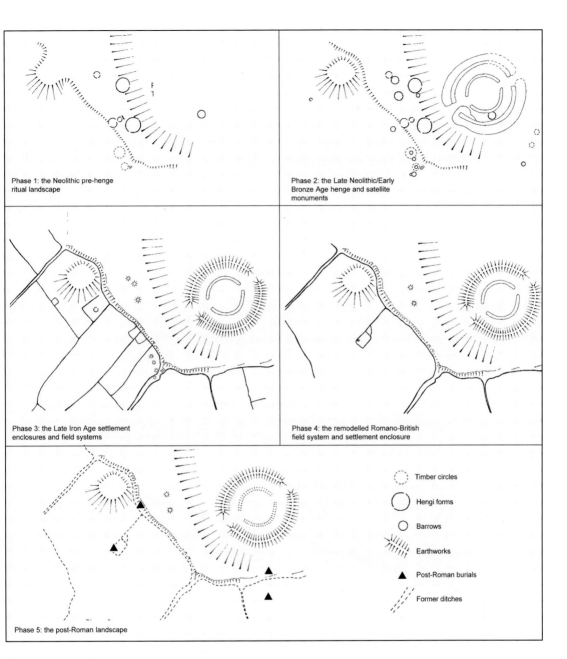

Phase 1: the Neolithic pre-henge
ritual landscape

Phase 2: the Late Neolithic/Early
Bronze Age henge and satellite
monuments

Phase 3: the Late Iron Age settlement
enclosures and field systems

Phase 4: the remodelled Romano-British
field system and settlement enclosure

Phase 5: the post-Roman landscape

Timber circles

Hengi forms

Barrows

Earthworks

Post-Roman burials

Former ditches

Illus. 4.7   Ferrybridge: simplified plan showing development of the site examined in advance of the A1–M62 link road. (From Roberts 2005, © ASWYAS)

with, in its latest phase a small group of roundhouses, probably abandoned at about the time of the Roman conquest.[37] Elsewhere in the Vale extensive coaxial field systems, defined by ditches, have been identified from aerial photography, usually on areas of free-draining sand and gravel rather than clay. Good examples exist at Elvington, c.11km south-east of York,[38] and at Naburn, 3km south of York. At the latter an area of enclosures c.3ha in extent, some containing roundhouses, has been mapped and selectively excavated.[39] The houses did not survive into the Roman period, although the enclosures continued in use. At Heslington, c.3km east of York, on the south face of the York moraine c.4ha of an extensive and regularly laid out field system of the mid-late Iron Age has been revealed by excavation (it was not visible from the air) within which there were a number of roundhouses; a large one stood at the centre of a substantial ditched enclosure, perhaps housing members of the local elite (Illus. 4.10).[40] Although not thought suitable for early arable agriculture, the clay lands around York were not entirely deserted as was shown by traces of roundhouses and ditches at Rawcliffe Moor, c.4km north of the city.[41]

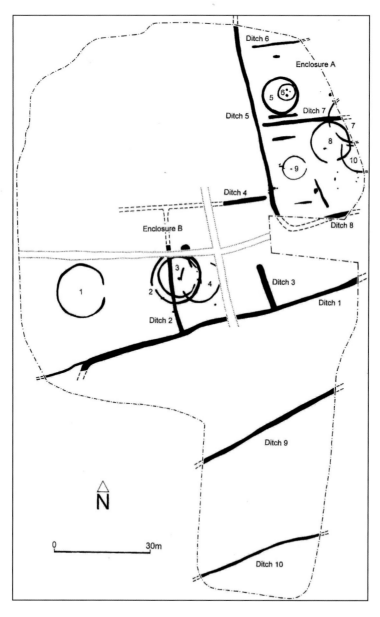

Illus. 4.8 Topham Farm, Sykehouse: site plan showing the location of roundhouses and enclosure ditches (from Roberts 2003, © ASWYAS).

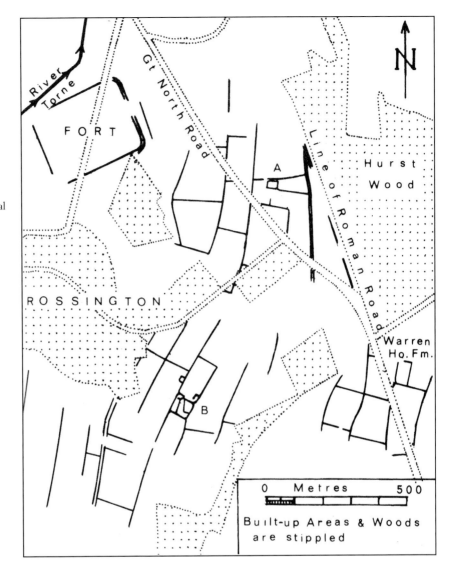

South of York lie the Humberhead Levels which encompass the flat,
low-lying land around the Rivers Aire, Derwent, Don and Ouse. In the
eastern part, east of the Derwent, the landscape has been studied intensively
in the Foulness Valley project.[42] Once again areas of enclosure are common on
sandy soils; a particularly dense cropmark landscape lies in Holme-on-Spalding
Moor and Hotham parishes. Excavation, for example, at Bursea Grange, 4 km
south of Holme-on-Spalding- Moor, indicates the enclosures are likely to have
had an Iron Age origin. Further south, in a zone not otherwise much studied
between the Rivers Aire and Don, a sequence of linear ditched boundaries and
rectilinear enclosures, probably of Iron Age origin was recorded at Sykehouse,
10 km north of Doncaster.[43] As many as ten roundhouses were defined by ring
gullies, but, except for two, they can be grouped as three houses rebuilt on

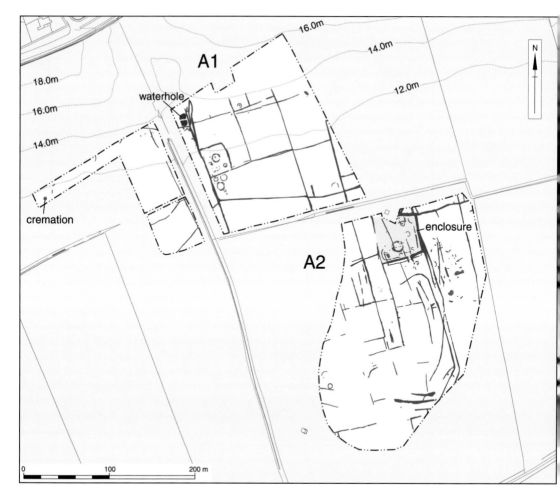

two or three occasions on the same site. This sort of picture is quite common in the region and may either have been due to the irreparable deterioration of a structure from time to time or a wish to start anew on certain significant occasions, perhaps after the death of an important resident.

Great interest has been focused on what aerial photography has revealed south of the Don. In what are now South Yorkshire and north Nottinghamshire a number of areas, largely on sandstone outcrops, have produced a very regular version of the coaxial field system defined by ditches, in which land appears to have been laid out in elongated strips of rectangular enclosures often referred to as 'brickwork fields'.[44] The strips, often slightly curving, appear to be c.50m–100m wide and short cross divisions create enclosures of c.0.5–3ha. Ditches, where excavated, have often been shown to be quite substantial with widths of 2m and depths of 1m or more. What excavation also shows is that the fairly regular pattern revealed on the aerial photographs may, on occasions, hide a landscape of several phases of land division. The relationship of the Roman road from Lincoln to Doncaster to the brickwork

Illus. 4.10   Heslington East near York: plan of the lattice pattern of late Iron Age – early Roman ditched enclosures. The possible elite enclosure is at the north end of Area A2; also shown is the location of a water hole of prehistoric origin. © York Archaeological Trust)

fields around Rossington, south of Doncaster, suggests that the road is later and so the fields here, at least, are probably Iron Age in origin.[45] Elsewhere in South Yorkshire good examples of brickwork fields are known near Armthorpe and Edenthorpe, north-east of Doncaster and excavations at Far Field Road, Edenthorpe in 1993 and 1995 appeared to reveal a continual process of land division between the late Iron Age and the second century AD.[46] However, at Gunhills, Armthorpe brickwork fields were shown to have a Roman rather than pre-Roman origin.[47] A little to the north-east of Armthorpe, on gravel at Dunsville, undated ditches of regular land division were recorded along with a D-shaped enclosure which appeared to be Roman.[48]

Immediately south-east of the centre of Doncaster, on the western edge of the Humberhead Levels at Balby Carr, is an area of low-lying alluvium which appears to have attracted settlement beginning in the mid-late Iron Age inspite of a propensity to flood. A series of excavations in an area c.3.5ha in extent has found a sequence which, as at Normanton (see above), once again illustrates a trend from irregularity to regularity of land division. The sequence began with an unenclosed settlement of five roundhouses.[49] Ninety metres to the north-east was a circular enclosure within which there was another roundhouse.[50] Next came a group of irregularly shaped, ditched enclosures with associated trackways of the late Iron Age to early Roman period to the eastern side of which a more regular brickwork system of fields was subsequently attached.[51] Palaeoenvironmental analysis suggests heavily shaded areas of swamp dominated by alder carr. The brickwork fields were probably pasture bordered by water-filled ditches with hedgerows beside them, the predominant species of preserved roundwood being alder, willow, hazel and hawthorn.

From some of the lowest of the lowlands we may return now to an upland area of the county, the North York Moors. The high moors were no more suitable for farming in Roman times than today, but in a number of sheltered areas peripheral to them, small groups of rectilinear enclosures, as well as isolated examples, defined by banks and ditches, have been identified. For example, at Roxby (c.5km south of the seaside village of Staithes) a late Iron Age/early Roman ditched enclosure containing two roundhouses was excavated along with a group of six unenclosed roundhouses c.300m to the north.[52] In the Kildale area, c.16km south-west of Roxby and c.4km south of Guisborough, several settlements have been identified in the valley of the River Leven which is part of a route through the moors eastwards to Eskdale.[53] At Crag Bank (c.200m above sea level) a lynchet aligned north-west/south-east, thought to be of Iron Age origin, was identified and south-west of it, down the slope, three plots of land were examined. In one there were remains of a roundhouse with a paved floor and hearths associated with second-century Roman pottery. Further settlement sites, with remains of buildings represented largely as paved areas, occupied throughout the Roman period, have been identified in the valley of the Lounsdale Beck (which feeds the River Leven) and at the head of Kildale.

On Levisham Moor, c.9km north of Pickering, at c.200m above sea level, groups of enclosures of c.0.25ha were defined by banks and ditches laid out adjacent to and respecting earlier boundaries; some enclosures contained roundhouses.[54] Further south, on the Jurassic limestone on the southern edge of the Moors, a classic example of a field system of late Iron Age origin has been recorded at Newbridge Quarry, 5km north of Pickering.[55] This would have been a landscape very well suited to early arable farming. A north–south trackway defined by ditches, presumably heading for grazing grounds on higher ground, was the focus for a network of ditched enclosures appended primarily to its eastern side which clearly developed further in the Roman period.

In east Yorkshire, largely on the Wolds, a distinctive phenomenon is the so-called 'ladder' pattern of very regular land division in which small rectilinear enclosures extend in bands across the landscape often respecting an earlier trackway.[56] Good examples are known, for example, in Burton Fleming and Kilham parishes and between Wharram le Street and Duggleby on the north side of the Gypsey Race. At Garton and Wetwang Slacks there was a complex of ditched enclosures of ladder type set in an Iron Age/early Roman landscape, accompanied by other settlement features.[57] Running east to west for c.1.8km on the south side of the slack (a local word for valley) was a trackway, defined, as is usual, by a ditch on each side, which probably connected settlements on the Wolds to a water source at Elmswell to the east, above the plain of Holderness. In the Iron Age the trackway was a focus for burials in square-ditched barrows of Arras culture type, but it remained in continuous use into the Roman period. Further up the valley to the west the trackway met another which approached from the north-east and survives as a green lane to this day.[58] On the northern edge of the Wolds in West Heslerton, East Heslerton and Sherburn parishes another, very extensive, ladder has been identified by Dominic Powlesland on sand and gravel deposits, running along the south side of the Vale of Pickering, centred on the 30m contour.[59]

At the junction of the Wolds and the plain of Holderness, on boulder clay just north of Bridlington, two adjacent sites, one at High Wold, Bempton Lane[60] and the other, immediately to the east, at Sewerby Cottage Farm[61] have examined parts of another extensive enclosed landscape known from aerial photography. At High Wold the sequence began in the late Iron Age with a range of unenclosed structures (Phase 1), followed by a typical late Iron Age ditched rectangular enclosure (53m × 48m internally), with a roundhouse in the centre, adjacent to a trackway and other smaller enclosures (Phase 2); the complex would continue to evolve in the Roman period (Phases 3–4). At Sewerby Cottage Farm the sequence began with a late Iron Age burial in a square-ditched barrow followed, still in the Iron Age, by creation of large ditched enclosures.

At the southern tip of the Wolds chalk, at Melton, 3km east of Brough on the Humber estuary, a large excavation 13.2ha in area, in advance of road

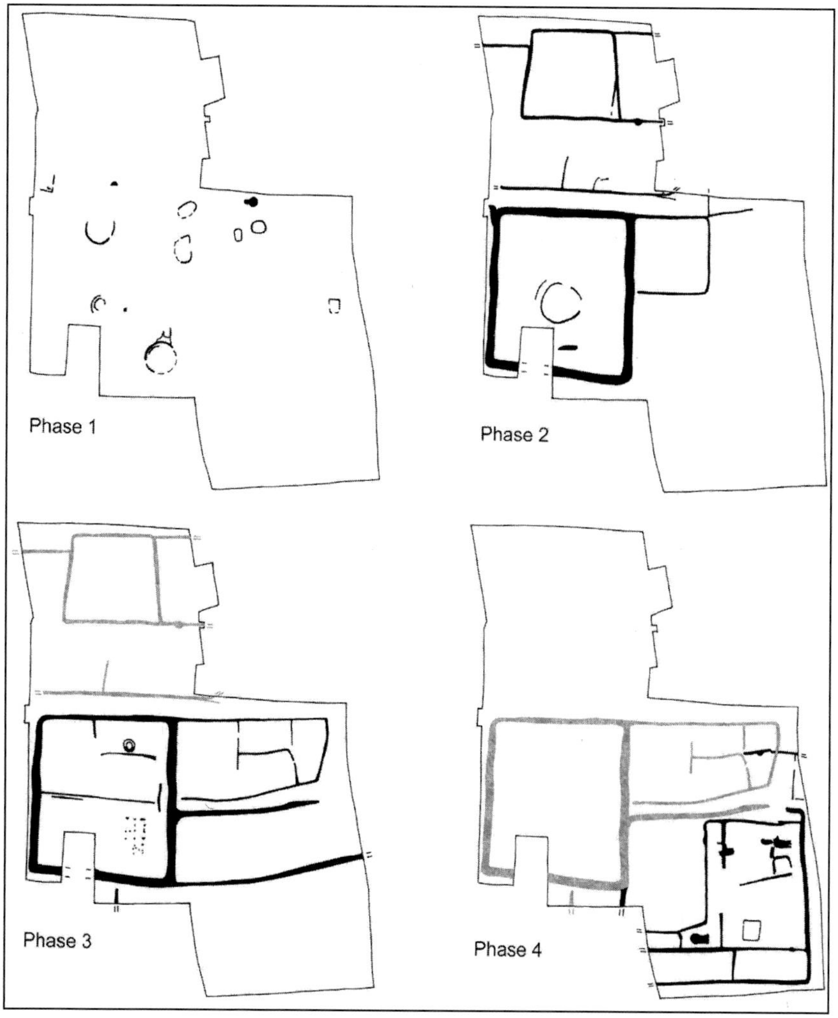

Illus. 4.11 High
Wold, Bempton Lane,
Bridlington: phased
development of the site,
late Iron Age to Roman
(from Roberts 2009, ©
ASWYAS).

improvement, has revealed another story of long term landscape use from the
Bronze Age onwards.[62] By the late Iron Age two trackways, defined by ditches,
crossed the site, the earlier running north–south crossed by another running
east–west. Use of the former had created a hollow way worn into the chalk
and it had probably been part of an important route linking the Wolds to the
Humber. North-east of the junction of the trackways lay three roundhouses,
defined by post-holes, two more lay to the south-east of it. An Arras-type
grave was found and in the ditch around it was a Late Iron Age coin of the
Corieltauvi, one of a number found in this area, close to the landing place at
Redcliffe (see below). Imported Gallo-Belgic pottery and some South Gaulish
samian also hints at trade connections beyond the purely local.[63]

Late Iron Age/early Roman enclosed landscapes have, until recently, proved
more elusive on the clay of Holderness than on the chalk of the Wolds,
although on soils suitable for agriculture west of the Hull valley extensive

cropmarks have been recorded in the Cottingham and Woodmansey areas. Excavations at Low Farm, Cottingham, for example, revealed a late Iron Age settlement of enclosures and roundhouses.[64] East of the River Hull evidence for settlement, probably of late Iron Age origin, has been identified in the lower part of the valley. For example, at Saltshouse Road, Sutton, there were two ditched enclosures, each c.90m × 60m, and a small group of roundhouses (Illus. 7.17). The site was located at the interface of the silts of the river valley and the clay of Holderness, allowing a certain environmental diversity favourable for both arable and pastoral agriculture.[65] On the east coast of Holderness at Aldbrough yet another typical late Iron Age landscape has been discovered which continued to develop in the Roman period. Two trackways defined by ditches met at a right angle and other enclosures were attached to them, one with a large central roundhouse and traces of two other subsidiaries.[66] An unusual hint of the proximity of the sea was a fragment of a dolphin skull found in a pit.

The roundhouse

Typical of the Iron Age and still in use as a building type throughout the Roman period in our region was the roundhouse. Roundhouses were usually 10m–14m in diameter and their remains can be represented in the ground in a number of ways. Reconstructing the superstructure of a roundhouse on the basis of these remains is a matter of debate and has been the subject of a number of experimental projects.[67] However, there were probably a number of architectural traditions in Yorkshire, as in other regions. In the lowlands where ploughing has often been very destructive of structural remains, one often finds just a circular gully with a break at one point marking the doorway. These gullies are usually interpreted as eavesdrips for draining away the rainwater running off the roof of a building of which no other remains survive. In some instances, post-holes or stake-holes survive, sometimes set in a trench which formed a circle defining the perimeter of the building. In other instances, as at Dalton Parlours near Wetherby,[68] post-holes clustered in a square pattern in the centre of the building; the posts are thought to have given the roof additional support and also allowed for an attic floor. In other instances post-holes are only found where they supported a porch at the doorway. At Roxby on the North York Moors the relatively well-preserved remains of two of the roundhouses showed that their external walls were essentially a screen based on vertical stakes with the weight of the roof being taken on an internal ring of posts.[69]

External walls would usually have been made from wattles – rods made from hazel or willow – intertwined with stakes or posts, and covered with daub, i.e. clay mixed with straw, and sometimes, perhaps, with animal dung. The remains of the Roxby buildings and those of the late Iron Age roundhouses at Kildale and Percy Rigg, also on the North York Moors, included stone rubble which was probably used as additional walling infill. In the Pennines, where suitable timber was in short supply, roundhouses may have had an entirely dry stone construction for their walls, although timber beams and rafters would have been needed for the roofs.[70]

The location of what was usually a single doorway in a roundhouse varies, but there was a clear preference for the east or south-east. This may indicate no more than a desire to avoid the prevailing wind from the south-west and/or to be greeted in the morning by the rising sun. Alternatively, or in addition, the location may have had some religious significance, connected with worship of a sun deity.

Roundhouse roofs would have been conical with rafters probably running from a ring beam around the top of the walls to the point of the cone, braced perhaps with an additional ring beam near the top. The roof covering would have been a thatch of reeds, rushes or sedge, according to what was available

Illus. 4.12   Stanwick: site plan (by Adrian Bury & Associates, © North Yorkshire County Council).

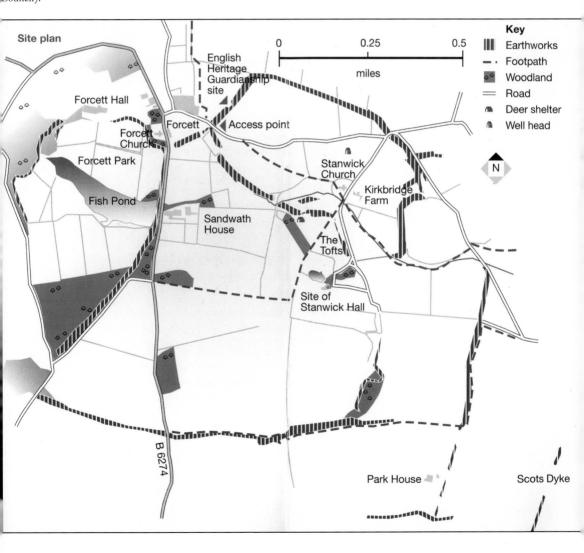

Site plan

Key

▊▊▊	Earthworks
-·-	Footpath
ᏑᏑ	Woodland
═	Road
🛖	Deer shelter
🛖	Well head

0   0.25   0.5

miles

N

English Heritage Guardianship site

Forcett Hall

Forcett Church

Forcett   Access point

Forcett Park

Fish Pond

Sandwath House

Stanwick Church

Kirkbridge Farm

The Tofts

Site of Stanwick Hall

B 6274

Park House

Scots Dyke

locally. There were no chimneys and smoke from the hearth made its way gradually through the roof, in the process, perhaps, killing off unwelcome insects. Roundhouse floors rarely survive, although there are examples in the region of spreads of rough stones and cobbles. In the centre of the floor the remains of the hearth may survive, although this is a feature which is especially vulnerable to the plough.

What all attempted reconstructions have shown is that, although an apparently simple structure, relatively easy to erect, the roundhouse can be very durable and robust. It was, moreover, suitable for a number of different purposes being used as dwelling, byre, store house and even for metalworking as at Levisham Moor and Roxby. Perhaps the principal drawback in our eyes, and in the eyes of any Romans used to more sophisticated accommodation, would be that roundhouses did not usually have any substantial internal partitions and so there was no real privacy for the residents.

Stanwick

There may have been differences in the size and architectural form of round-houses which, up to a point at least, reflected the status of their inhabitants. However, there is little evidence in the late Iron Age of the Yorkshire region for a settlement hierarchy headed by places from which power was exercised and where economic, social or religious functions were concentrated, except for the great enclosure at Stanwick. This is the nearest we get to the oppida in the south of England, places which not only accommodated aristocratic residences and their accompanying cemeteries, but were also centres for manufacturing and commercial activities, including the minting of coins.

Stanwick lies on the west side of the Vale of Mowbray, c.10km north of Richmond and 3.75km south of the River Tees, between the fertile lowlands and the Pennine foothills.[71] Excavations by Sir Mortimer Wheeler in 1951–52[72] and Durham University in 1986 and 1988–89[73] suggest the Stanwick site has a long history, but the most important episode in that history came at the end. At about the time the Claudian invasion had reached the coast of Kent in the year 43 an area c.300ha in extent was enclosed by a great ditch and, made from the material dug out of it, a substantial bank, or rampart, which ran for c.8km. As one can still see at Cat Wood on the north side of the enclosure (English Heritage Guardianship site on Illus. 4.12), where one of Wheeler's excavations has been left open, the distance from the base of the rock cut ditch to the top of the rampart is c.5m. The outer face of the rampart was faced with stone giving the later village its name; Stanwick is derived from Old English Steinwegges = 'stone walls'. Although this is monumental architecture in a rudimentary form compared to what the Romans could achieve, it is, none the less, a remarkable testament to the amount of labour an Iron Age ruler – possibly Cartimandua or Venutius – could muster and organise on certain occasions.

There were several entrances into the Stanwick enclosure, but the principal entrance was apparently on the north-west side where the visitor approached

Illus. 4.13 Stanwick,
Cat Wood. Sir Mortimer
Wheeler's excavation
of 1951–52 showing the
ditch and bank with
surviving stone facing.
On the right a layer of
debris from the collapsed
bank has been left in
place. (Reproduced
courtesy of the Society
of Antiquaries of
London ©)

through a passage guarded to the east by an internal bank and ditch (just to
the left of 'access point' on Illus. 4.12. At the point where one passed the inner
end of this bank Wheeler found a sword and a human skull damaged by deep
cuts from a sharp implement, perhaps the sword itself. Originally both skull
and sword may have been prominently displayed (with other trophies) such as
to make a statement, on the one hand, about the status of the enclosure and
its rulers, and, on the other, about the fate awaiting their enemies.

There are a number of internal earthworks at Stanwick, apparently focused
on the Mary Wild Beck which runs more or less from west to east through the
northern part of the enclosed area. Framed by earthworks is The Tofts, an area
named after the house platforms of a deserted medieval village. Excavations
in The Tofts revealed a long sequence of pre-Roman occupation with the
remains of small enclosures and roundhouses. Although they do not occur
in the earliest phases, the finds from the later provide remarkable evidence
for contact with the Roman world at about the time the ramparts were built.
This evidence takes the form, first of all, of pottery, including samian and
Gallo-Belgic ware for the table whilst amphora sherds suggest there was wine
to drink at feasting time.[74] In addition, there are fragments of Roman tile and

window glass suggesting buildings, in addition to the traditional roundhouses, which were, up to a point at least, constructed in a Roman style. It is tempting to use these finds as confirmation that Stanwick was indeed the residence of the Brigantian royal house enjoying the benefits of their client status. The acquisition of Roman luxury goods on favourable terms which could then be dispensed to loyal supporters may have been a crucial factor underpinning Cartimandua's long reign as queen.

In some respects the function of Stanwick remains unclear. Defence cannot really have been a consideration as the ramparts are far too long to defend effectively and just outside their eastern perimeter the enclosed area is overlooked by a low hill (Henah Hill). What the great bank and ditch may have done, however, is mark out a special area within which intercommunal rivalries were put aside. Here, perhaps, the Brigantes came together at certain times for religious festivals which may have taken place by the Mary Wild Beck, given the sacred character given to watery places in native religion. In addition, Stanwick may also have served as a market place where exchange of goods took place amongst the Brigantes themselves as well as with a Roman army seeking to acquire foodstuffs, especially grain and livestock. There is, after all, plenty of room at Stanwick for flocks of sheep and herds of cattle.

On the basis of what Tacitus tells us, in the year 69 Cartimandua's reign apparently came to an abrupt end.[75] Whether, as Wheeler suggested, Venutius,

Illus. 4.14 Stanwick: the inner face of the rampart on the north-east side of the enclosure. (Photo: P. Ottaway)

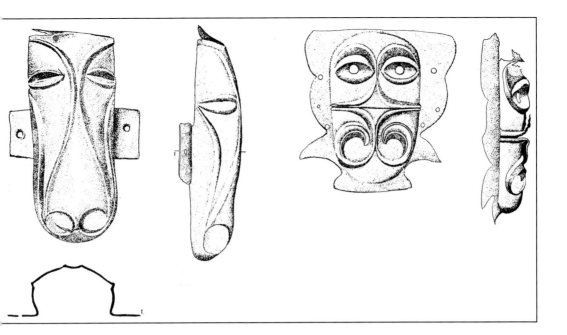

having ousted the queen, made a last stand against the Romans at Stanwick we may never know, but it is certain that the great enclosure did not outlast the Roman conquest and no fort or city was built here. Instead Stanwick was simply bypassed by the two main Roman roads in the area.

On the basis of their unusual finds assemblages it may be suggested that other settlements in the vicinity of Stanwick had some particular relationship with it, belonging, perhaps, to leading supporters of the ruling house. In 1843 a hoard of late Iron Age metalwork was found c.1km east of Stanwick at Langdale Farm, Melsonby.[76] It consisted of c.146 objects including chariot fittings and horse trappings appropriate to elite ownership. In an attempt to discover more about the Stanwick area around the time of the Roman conquest and about the hoard, excavations were undertaken in 1994–95 on the supposed site where it was discovered.[77] Two phases of occupation were identified: the first consisting of two Iron Age roundhouses and the second a network of gullies and ditches. Most remarkable, however, is that the pottery assemblage from the second phase, of the mid-first century AD (c.55–75/80), was similar to that from Stanwick, and completely different from what one would expect on a rural settlement of this period. Sherds of Roman pottery, including flagons, samian and amphorae, greatly exceeded in number those of native pottery. There were also fragments of glass and of briquetage, the large vessels used for brine from which salt was extracted; its distribution may have been strictly controlled by the elite. A similar, if smaller, suite of pottery and more briquetage, was found at Scotch Corner, c.7km south of Stanwick in association with the later part of a sequence of ditches and two roundhouses.[78] Like Stanwick, neither the Melsonby nor the Scotch Corner settlements survived into the Roman period and they may have been subject to deliberate destruction by the conquerors when they overthrew the old regime.

The social order

The lack of differentiation in settlement type in the late Iron Age (except for Stanwick) might suggest a social structure without a complex hierarchy. However, whilst the extensive and disciplined organisation of the landscape one can see in many parts of the Yorkshire region may, to some extent, be the result of co-operation between community members, the maintenance of that organisation over long periods of time suggests the existence of an elite capable of exerting considerable control over the population. The chariot burials of the Arras culture appear to be archaeological confirmation of the existence of a privileged elite in east Yorkshire at least, but there is no reason to suppose that it did not exist elsewhere in the region. It has also been inferred from Caesar's description of Gaul in the mid-first century BC that contemporary society in Britain was not without hierarchical divisions.[79] He tells us that 'there are only two classes of men who are of any account'. These were the 'druids' – a priestly caste – and the 'knights', members of the warrior aristocracy whose status depended on birth, wealth and the number of retainers they could muster for warfare. The 'common people' were in Caesar's view, 'treated almost as slaves …'

The high rank of Cartimandua and Venutius was probably inherited from their families of the previous generation, although successful warriors of humbler origin, such as Vellocatus, the armour-bearer, presumably had opportunities for upward social mobility whilst women might rise socially through marriage. In addition to the ownership and control of landed estates, high rank would also have been expressed in a number of other ways including the bearing of arms and other regalia, and the possession of horses, herds of cattle and flocks of sheep. Certain specialist occupations, such as metalworkers, especially weaponsmiths, might also have enjoyed a distinct status which set them apart from the majority of the population, but at the bottom of the heap there was probably a slave caste. Numerous iron slave chains – neck-shackles, fetters and manacles – of Iron Age date, have been found in Britain, although not as yet in Yorkshire.[80]

Agriculture: down on the farm

The economy of late Iron Age Yorkshire was intimately bound up with agriculture; almost everyone who lived in the region, slave or free, would have been involved – only the very privileged few could avoid toiling on the land for most of the year. Once it was thought that much of the north of England in the Iron Age and the Roman period, especially the upland areas, had an agricultural regime which was largely pastoral. Little evidence had been found for the grain storage pits so common in the south. Furthermore, excavators were not geared up for looking for cereal grains in deposit samples until quite recently. Some flavour of the old view can be found in Sir Mortimer Wheeler's musings on Cartimandua, whom he saw as a Belgic princess from the south-east of England who had married a 'cattle rancher' and got '... thoroughly tired of unmitigated mutton'.[81]

There is now considerable evidence in the form of both charred grain and storage pits for cereal growing in the Yorkshire region, and the rest of the north. Even in the upland regions the presence of quernstones for grinding grain suggests that there was a mixed farming regime in which crops were grown. Only the high moors, above about 300m above sea level, where climate and soil were unsuitable for arable, would have been largely pastoral.

Types of cereal crop and methods of production employed in the Iron Age were to remain largely unchanged in Yorkshire until the end of the Roman period and beyond. Ploughing usually employed a simple ard, a wooden implement drawn by oxen which had an iron-shod 'share' which broke the ground, but did not turn it over like a plough of later times.[82] In some places, such as the Craven uplands, the small size of fields has suggested the use of a spade to break up the soil rather than a plough.[83] The principal cereal crops in our region were spelt wheat (*triticum spelta*) and barley (*hordeum vulgare*). Evidence from late Iron Age sites at Rock Castle and Scotch Corner (both near Stanwick), and from Roman Catterick[84] suggest that barley was grown to a greater extent than wheat in the uplands and more northerly areas of the county.

Spelt wheat is rather different from the wheat we have become familiar with in recent times. For a start it stood higher in a field than modern wheat which has been designed to suit the combine harvester.[85] In addition, the result of selective cultivation over the centuries has, amongst other things, made wheat easier to thresh, that is to say it is easier to extract the grain from its hull; modern wheat is what is often known as 'free-threshing'. However, the tough hull of spelt protects the grain from insects and disease. Spelt will tolerate a wide range of soil types, not just the light and well drained, but also heavy clays, and it copes well with the cold; it is therefore suited to winter sowing.[86] Spelt has good storage capabilities both in the type of deep pit used in the late Iron Age and in Roman granaries. Although it gives poorer yields per hectare than modern wheat, experimental farming at Butser Iron Age Farm in Hampshire suggests, none the less, that about 1ha of spelt, grown in the traditional manner without weed-killers, would feed a family of eight for a year.[87] Furthermore, by the late Iron Age yields were probably improving as a result of regular manuring of the land, a great step forward in ensuring its fertility.

Wheat and barley, as well as oats for which there is also some evidence, would have fed both humans and animals. For humans, wheat implies consumption of risen loaves of bread as it contains the right proteins to form the gluten which allows the dough to form an open texture, whilst barley, without those proteins, would have been made into flat, griddle cakes.[88] Barley, wheat and oats may have also been used in brewing, although barley is much the most commonly used cereal today. There is no evidence for hops so the product would, strictly speaking, have been ale rather than beer.

What is known of the sowing, harvesting and processing of cereals in Iron Age and Roman times is based largely on the evidence of charred grains, chaff and other seeds, usually from field weeds, found in excavations.[89] We know that each stage was extremely labour intensive, and its success or otherwise had a profound influence on the fortunes of the economy as a whole from year to year. The cycle for spelt wheat, for example, began, after autumn ploughing, with sowing in autumn-winter with a view to a harvest the following summer. Harvesting involved mobilising large numbers of people in a short period. It was back-breaking work; occurrence of seeds from low-growing plants and twining weeds in the grain indicates that the culms (stalks) were cut fairly low down with a sickle or simply uprooted. The grain, encased at this stage in what are known as 'spikelets' in the ears at the head of the stalks, and what would become straw were thereby gathered in one operation. Threshing involved separating the ears from the straw usually by beating the stalks on the ground with flails. The result was a pile of debris ('chaff') to be sorted. Coarser weed seeds and any remaining straw were removed by raking and hand picking. What was left was winnowed – thrown in the air during a light breeze to remove the finer chaff – and then sieved. In England, with its damp climate, it was sometimes necessary to dry or parch the spikelets to render the

Illus. 4.16 Beehive quern upper stones (a–b) and lower stone (c) of Millstone Grit from Dalton Parlours villa (height: 180, 216 and 250mm) (from Wrathmell and Nicholson 1990, © ASWYAS).

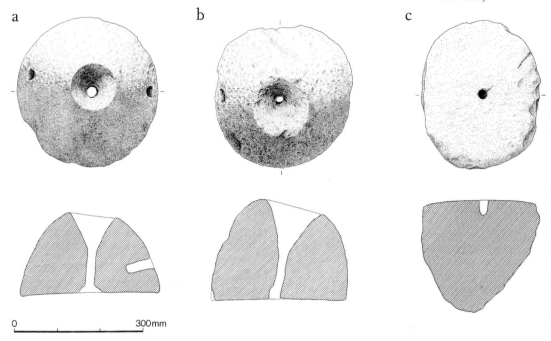

a   b   c

0   300mm

hulls brittle enough to allow the grain to be removed by pounding. Drying might involve spreading the crop out on an enclosed floor surface or holding it over an open hearth. Further sieving and winnowing removed more chaff and produced cereal grain suitable for food, although some weed seeds might still survive, especially if the same size as the grain. Unfortunately they included those of the corncockle which were poisonous.

Grinding the grain to make meal involved the use of a quern. In early prehistoric times the saddle quern was used which consisted of two stones which were rubbed against each other, but an introduction of the Iron Age was the beehive quern. It consisted of two components, c.300–350mm in diameter. The lower one, a tapering stone with a socket in the centre, was set in the ground and the domed upper stone (akin to a traditional beehive, hence the name) was placed above it. The upper stone had a 'feed pipe' running down the centre in which was placed a wooden spindle; its base fitted into the socket of the lower stone. Grain was introduced into a 'hopper' at the head of the feed pipe and ran down to the surface of the lower stone. The upper stone was agitated or rotated by means of one or two handles set in a socket or sockets in the side. The grain was crushed by friction between the stones and the weight of the upper on the lower, causing the meal to emerge from the gap between

Illus. 4.17 Modern Dexter cattle of a similar size and conformation to Roman cattle.
(Photo: P. Ottaway)

them into a receptacle for collection. Because the quern was apparently set at ground level the user presumably had to sit or kneel on the ground, often for long periods, which cannot have been particularly comfortable. In both the Iron Age and Roman period in the Yorkshire region beehive querns were usually made of Millstone Grit and other sandstones which have good wearing properties,[90] although the meal would have had a certain amount of fine grit in it – good for the digestion but not the teeth.

An understanding of animal husbandry, and of the production and consumption of meat in the late Iron Age and the Roman period depends largely on the study of bones, especially those of the three principal meat producers: cattle, sheep and pig. The numbers of bones of each animal from a site can give some impression of their relative importance in local agricultural and dietary regimes. However, it must be borne in mind when converting numbers of bones to weight of meat that the carcase size of a cow is roughly equivalent to eleven sheep or six pigs. In one of the very few Iron Age bone assemblages, and a small one at that, from our region, at Dalton Parlours, cattle bones accounted for only c.24% of those of the principal meat animals, much lower than in some Roman assemblages (see below and Table 1), although cattle would still have been the principal meat source by weight.[91]

Their bones tell us that the Iron Age animals in the Yorkshire region were small compared to what one would expect to see today and much closer to their undomesticated forebears; little was to change in the Roman period. Aspects of husbandry are revealed by age at death patterns worked out from the extent of wear on teeth. They differ markedly from today when, for example, beef cattle are usually killed before they reach eighteen months. In the Iron Age and the Roman period the majority of cattle were slaughtered when mature (4–5 years old) or elderly. They were multi-purpose animals not raised specifically either for meat or milk, although, if female, used as a source of both. Cattle were also used for ploughing and haulage. Their dung could be used as manure or as a component of the daub on house walls. When it finally met its end, no part of an animal was wasted: hide, hair, hooves, bones and blood all had a use. As far as sheep are concerned, age at death data from the bones found in the Roman forts at Castleford suggest a major kill-off episode at two-three years for eating, but 25–33% reached maturity at four years. Sheep may be seen, like cattle, as multi-purpose, in their case a source of both milk and wool, before slaughter for consumption. Pigs were kept primarily for meat, blood and lard and so they would be killed at their prime eating age of c.2 years.

Manufacturing: hot metal!

Of all the manufacturing crafts practiced in the Iron Age, the one which required the greatest technological knowledge and organisational ability was metalworking. In pre-Roman Britain there was a long-lived tradition of great skill in working non-ferrous metals, primarily copper and its alloys, but also gold and silver. High quality copper alloy artefacts from the Yorkshire region include, for example, the chariot fittings and horse trappings from the Arras culture graves[92] and the Stanwick hoard.

Copper was extracted from ore found, as far as the Yorkshire region is concerned, only in the Richmond area, but otherwise largely in west Wales and Scotland. After smelting, copper was usually alloyed with tin (c.10%) to make bronze, a harder metal. Manufacturing bronze and other non-ferrous metal objects either involved casting in a mould, usually of stone, or forging directly from an ingot, itself cast in a mould. Casting an object employed the lost wax method which has a long history lasting through Roman times up to the present day. First of all, a wax model of the desired object was made and then it was covered in clay to make a mould. This was heated to melt the wax which was poured away to leave an impression of the object in the fired clay. Molten metal was taken in a crucible from the hearth, poured into the mould and once the metal had cooled down the mould was opened and the completed object was taken out. Some objects then had to be worked by hand, especially if they needed a decorative finish. A craft practiced alongside non-ferrous metalworking in the Iron Age and Roman period to further enhance the appearance of certain items was enamelling. This involved taking ground glass and heating it to create a material with a hard, smooth finish. Enamel was usually used to fill small panels in sword hilts, horse trappings, brooches and the like.

In addition to non-ferrous metalworking, the extraction, smelting and smithing of iron was widespread in the Iron Age.[93] Although production was on nothing like the scale that would be achieved in the Roman period, the technology was well understood and changed little after the conquest. The craft required great skill in managing heat as well as in gathering raw materials and in preparing the charcoal used as fuel. Late prehistoric iron smelting in east Yorkshire has, as already noted, been studied in some detail by Peter Halkon in the valley of the River Foulness.[94] Rather than ironstone as is more usual, the source of iron here was probably so-called 'bog ore', deposits of iron oxide which are formed where iron-bearing surface water meets organic material such as turf. On sand ridges along the banks of the Foulness some nineteen smelting sites have been found. Elsewhere in the region ironstone was used and an important ore source was Rosedale in the North York Moors.

The ore was first roasted to remove any water and then smelted in what is usually known as the direct or bloomery process which involved heating it to temperatures in excess of 800°C in a reducing atmosphere (i.e. without oxygen), rich in carbon monoxide derived from charcoal. This could have been done in a pit known as a 'bowl furnace', but in the Foulness valley it is thought that shaft furnaces, which allow a stronger updraught of air, were used; they probably stood up to c.2m high and were made of thick clay formed around a wicker framework. It was not possible to get the iron itself molten in the direct process, although some of the impurities could be tapped off in liquid form. The end product was a 'bloom' which could be forged into bars for supply to smiths. The metal still contained slag which was removed, up to a point, by hammering, but a little usually survived as thin strings, giving iron objects made in the direct process a slightly fibrous appearance.

Halkon reports experimental work that suggests that each kilogram of iron bloom needed 100kg of charcoal which in turn required one tonne of wood as well as twenty-five person days of labour. Testimony to the level of production at Welham Bridge, on the River Foulness, was a heap of 5338kg of smelting slag representing, according to one estimate, the production of c.2000kg of iron bloom. The period of time over which this accumulated is not known, but the impression we get from archaeological investigations in the area is of a specialist operation requiring a considerable labour force.

Smelting probably took place in relatively few places in the late Iron Age, usually close to the ore sources themselves. On the North York Moors at Roxby, for example, a bowl furnace for smelting was found in one of the roundhouses[95] and there was another in a small structure amongst the Levisham Moor enclosures.[96] However, smithing was a craft practiced on a small scale in many settlements, usually witnessed by the occurrence of slag lumps arising from accumulation in the smith's hearth. This would have been at ground-level rather than being a structure at waist-level; the latter was known in the Roman world, if not to any great extent in Britain. Certain smiths presumably had particular skills above the normal, especially in the forging of steel blades on swords and edged tools such as knives and shears. Steel was iron with a carbon content of in excess of c.0.5% which was usually introduced into the metal by carburisation. This involved either heating an iron strip which was then welded on to the knife etc, or heating the blade edge itself, in charcoal over a prolonged period.

Surprisingly perhaps, in view of the skill employed in managing heat for metalworking, there is little sophistication in the pottery of late Iron Age Yorkshire. Many parts of the region used little pottery, but there was a common tradition of pottery production on the east side of the county from the Humber to the Tees, although some locally distinctive features, whether in fabric, form or decoration, have also been identified. This tradition continued to flourish well into the Roman period.[97] For example, at Newbridge Quarry, Pickering where the enclosures were clearly in use until the late second century AD, as much as 90% of the pottery was in the Iron Age tradition rather than of Roman type.[98] Even in east Yorkshire, however, pottery was produced in relatively small quantities in the Iron Age, compared to the Roman period, and was almost exclusively in the form of jars used for cooking in an open hearth. Vessels were formed by hand rather than on the wheel. Firing would usually have involved a simple bonfire or 'clamp' kiln, in the centre of which were the vessels to be fired, surrounded by the fuel – charcoal – covered by a mound of clay or turf. This created a reducing atmosphere which led to the universally dark colour of the vessels. That the more sophisticated updraft kiln used by the Romans was known, although rare, in the pre-Roman period was demonstrated by the unexpected discovery of an example at Crossgates, Seamer (near Scarborough). An archaeomagnetic date for the last firing was 20 BC–AD 40.[99]

Other technologies of the Iron Age in Yorkshire are less visible to archaeology than those described above partly because they did not require facilities like hearths or kilns and partly because they were based on organic materials such as bone, textile and wood which have not survived in any quantity. Because they are more or less indestructible, we do, however, know something of the manufacture of querns. Surveys have located a number of production sites in upland regions with suitable stone, usually betrayed by discarded rough-outs. Finishing may have been effected at the places where the querns were actually used.[100] Regional styles of quern have been identified which probably emerged in the Iron Age and changed little in the Roman period. For example, the normal height of a beehive quern is c.100–250mm, but in lower Airedale and Wharfedale they are usually taller, over 250mm, and in the Wolds around Driffield by contrast they are usually more 'bun shaped', at a height of 100mm or less.

Exchange and trade

Evidence for exchange, or trade, over any distance is scarce in Yorkshire's Iron Age, although most commodities are very likely to have originated close to the place where they were consumed or used. However, there are some which may have travelled a fair distance from their source. If this source can be located, then distribution maps can be used to identify the networks along which trade took place. Querns, for example, can often be sourced by their geology to a fairly restricted area. A study of querns in North Yorkshire and southern Durham has indicated the existence of intraregional links which were to be maintained unbroken after the Roman conquest.[101] There are querns – or part-made querns – made of Millstone Grit which are found not only in the Dales, near their sources in the Pennines, but all over the lowlands to the east and beyond. By contrast, there are also querns made of inferior stone, such as the Jurassic sandstone of the North York Moors, which travelled shorter distances from their source.

The word 'trade' as applied in the study of antiquity, Roman or pre-Roman, may refer to a number of different mechanisms by which commodities were passed from hand to hand. However, unlike today, commercial transactions based on prices set by the interplay of demand and supply, and reckoned in money as a means of exchange usually played quite a small part, at least in somewhere like Britain. Ancient trade is sometimes described as 'socially embedded' meaning that the motivation of the parties involved was not geared to making a profit in the sense which we understand it today, but rather to achieving other objectives such as ensuring an adequate level of subsistence for all or establishing good relations between communities and the prevention of conflict. Observation by anthropologists of non-industrial and simple societies of recent times can give us something of an insight into how these trade mechanisms worked in the past.

What is often referred to as 'reciprocity', of which the most obvious form is the barter of one commodity for another, deemed of more or less equal value, probably remained the principal mechanism for small scale exchange of food, clothing and other necessities throughout the Iron Age and the Roman period. In addition, gifts passed from one individual or one community to another on a regular basis. In societies where gift exchange plays an important part in social relations, each gift is made in the expectation of a reciprocal gesture. The commodities exchanged might not necessarily have great intrinsic value, but are invested with considerable symbolic significance for maintaining good relations between the parties.

Another common form of exchange in antiquity was the redistribution of commodities which usually operated in the context of an unequal relationship between the donor and recipient. At its simplest a ruler would appropriate commodities, such as grain or livestock, from his subjects in the form of tax or tribute. These commodities were then redistributed by him to elite followers such as to reward or secure their loyalty. Amongst the commodities involved in redistributive processes in the ancient world were not only agricultural products but also so-called 'prestige goods', such as gold or certain types of weapon, which may have had considerable scarcity value and to which access was closely controlled so as to ensure their desirability. Possession of prestige goods conferred a privileged status on both the donor and recipient. One might imagine, for example, that a commodity from the Continent, such as wine, for which there is evidence at Stanwick, had been given by the Romans to the ruling house of the Brigantes and was then redistributed to its leading supporters.

In addition to trade based on reciprocity and redistribution, there was probably some commercial trade, especially in commodities not available locally, even in the Iron Age, in which the terms of trade were determined by supply and demand. Neither the Brigantes nor the Parisi minted coins which probably meant bullion often served as a medium of exchange. However, the number of players in the market would have been extremely limited so that there was little in the way of free competition. Trade of this sort may have taken place in a variety of institutional environments, including, for example, what a study of trade in Africa has called a 'peripheral market' because of its location on the boundary between territories or on coastal sites.[102] Access to these markets is restricted to a small class of middle men under elite control – hence the sort of trade taking place there is often described as 'administered'.

An example of a late Iron Age peripheral market in the Yorkshire region may have existed near North Ferriby on the north bank of the Humber estuary.[103] The site at Redcliffe lies on the highest ground in the immediate area, just above the flood limit, although it has suffered badly from erosion. Pottery recovered from the cliff face from 1932 onwards and in a small scale excavation in 1986 includes mid-first-century samian, Gallo-Belgic ware and amphorae, otherwise scarce in Yorkshire before the conquest, as well as mid-first-century brooches. There may have been a landing place at Redcliffe, controlled by the Parisian elite, where commodities such as tin (for making bronze), high-quality pottery and glass ware were imported, and agricultural products and ironwork, the latter produced in the nearby Foulness Valley region, were exported to the Roman world. As a result, perhaps, of trade based on Redcliffe, there is a concentration of Corieltauvian coin finds in the immediate area.[104]

Whatever the exact role of Redcliffe, some form of trade probably accounts for a good deal of the Iron Age coinage found in Yorkshire. Excluding those in hoards (see below), some one hundred and seventeen Iron Age coins from the county had been recorded by 1992. In addition to those from around Redcliffe, another group comes from a zone in the south of the region which probably lay close to the land frontier between the Brigantes and Corieltauvi. Within this zone lies Ferrybridge where, in excavations adjacent to the Neolithic henge site, no coins were found, but there was a small quantity of mid-first-century pottery imported from what was then Roman Britain.[105] This hint of contacts more than simply local, suggests the henge may have played a role as a site where the exchange of prestige goods took place, perhaps associated with religious ceremonies at what was already an ancient monument.

In Yorkshire the practice of hoarding coins, perhaps resulting from trade and kept as savings or for some other purpose, began in the immediate pre-Roman period with hoards known from Lightcliffe near Bradford (57 coins) of c.AD 40, Castle Hill, Almondbury near Huddersfield (over 200 coins), of perhaps about the same date, and Honley, also near Huddersfield (24 coins) of c.72–73 (just after the time of the Roman advance north). All three hoards had a predominance of Roman coins with the rest being issues of the Corieltauvi.[106]

The visual arts: a world of abstraction

There is a great range of artistic expression of the people of Iron Age and Roman Britain about which we know little; for example, their music, dance and much of their drama are all more or less completely lost. However, we do have numerous artefacts which exhibit aspects of the decorative styles employed in the visual arts. In this section I consider some examples from Yorkshire's late Iron Age which suggest that innovations from the Roman world were making themselves felt even before the conquest.

A part of the Oxford English Dictionary's definition of art refers to '… innovative and imaginative skill applied to design, as in painting, architecture etc'. The basis of the skill in design of the artist working in Iron Age Britain, in what is still referred to as the 'Celtic' tradition, was abstract patterns with

Illus. 4.18   The Elmswell plaque (length: 240mm; from Corder and Hawkes 1940, © Society of Antiquaries of London).

bold eccentric curves. They can be seen on metalwork, for example, inscribed in low relief on flat surfaces such as mirror backs, or incorporated into low relief moulding on items like the Arras Culture chariot fittings. From Yorkshire, one of the finest pieces of metalwork of the mid-first century AD is a plaque found at Elmswell (near Driffield, East Riding) made of a thin sheet of bronze on an iron base, thought to have been fitted to a casket.[107] It has a design of flowing curves garnished with rosettes in low relief but in its symmetrical character it is thought to indicate Roman influence. On the upper edge is a strip decorated with champlevé enamel. The casket it adorned may have been an item imported from elsewhere in Britain, perhaps lost on its way from Redcliffe to a rich customer. In a romantic flight of fancy the archaeologist Christopher Hawkes concluded his report on the plaque by commenting that

Illus. 4.19   Copper alloy terret from Aldborough in the form of human head (height: c.94mm; drawn by D.M. Waterman, from Richmond 1954 © Cambridge University Press).

YOKE

the Roman influence would have been to the taste of Cartimandua and that the casket '... may well have been one of the love gifts that passed between the adulterous armour-bearer [Vellocatus] and the guilty queen' [!].

Anthropomorphic representation is rare in pre-Roman art of the Yorkshire region and, when it occurs, is highly stylized, as shown by small masks representing a moustachioed face and a horse's head in the Stanwick hoard (Illus. 4.15) or two small ox heads on the handle of a mirror probably found at Ingleton (in the British Museum).[108] These objects are also dated to mid-first century AD and may be further examples of a growing acceptance in northern England of the art styles of the Roman empire in which sophisticated representations of the human figure, animals and other natural phenomena were commonplace. Of much the same date from Aldborough is a copper alloy terret once fixed to a yoke of a native aristocrat's chariot to hold the reins.[109] It features a head on each 'shoulder' of which there is a scroll once

Illus. 4.20   Chalk figurines from east Yorkshire (height: 25–97mm; 38–110mm) (© British Museum).

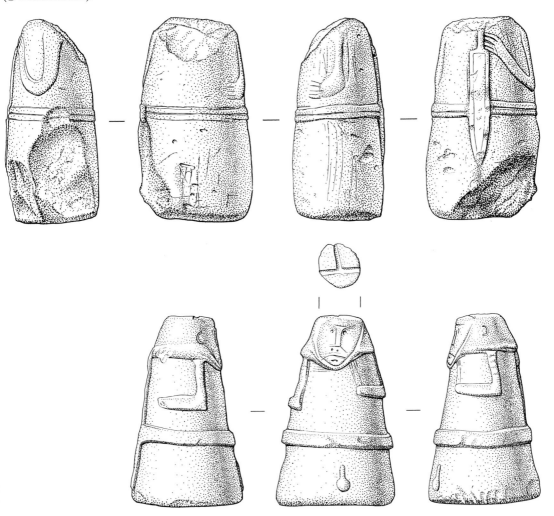

surrounding an enamel boss. The face, surely intended as divine rather than strictly human, has a moustache and large staring eyes. From the sides of the head emerge horns whose core was once formed by an iron ring. Sir Ian Richmond commented that 'it bears the hallmark of an immensely rich aristocracy, favoured children of Cerunnos' – a horned fertility god of native origin who was also worshipped in the Roman period.[110]

The rendering of a god in human form may reflect the growing influence of the Roman world on religious as well as artistic ideas. This brings us to a very distinctive group of figurines, carved in chalk, which occur in late Iron Age and early Roman contexts in east Yorkshire.[111] Over forty are now known and they come from sites immediately north and south of the Wolds, including Malton and neighbouring Norton-on-Derwent. The figurines range in (original) height from 70mm to 200mm, although their heads are often missing. Over half of these figures clearly represent warriors as they have swords which are often shown running vertically down the centre of their backs. Another distinctive feature, found in some cases, is the suspension from the figure's belt of the sword scabbard near its central point. This was evidently a local custom as scabbards in the Iron Age were usually suspended from the top. The warrior may have been a divine and mythical hero and what often appears to have been deliberate decapitation may indicate the figurines had a role in some form of cult practice.

Religion: the mysterious gods

Religion in antiquity, whether based on a sophisticated theology, which might involve the profound contemplation of cosmic phenomena, or at the level of what we would call superstition and magic, was a powerful and persuasive force engaging the attention, intellect and passions of all members of society. To quote Robin Lane Fox referring to the Roman world in the first–third centuries AD: 'atheism, in our sense, was not an option.'[112]

Whilst evidence for religion in the Roman world in general, including Yorkshire, is, as we shall see, extensive, deriving from both written and archaeological material, for the native British world of the late Iron Age there is relatively little. What there is can be highly enigmatic in the complete absence of inscriptions, and near absence of either representations of deities or structures dedicated to worship. Contemporary references from the Roman world to the religion of the native Britons are few. As we have already seen, Caesar mentions the priestly caste of the druids as one of the privileged classes in Gaul and in his opinion they originated in Britain.[113] We may also note Tacitus's comments on the religion of the German tribes whom the Romans encountered. This was probably similar to that of the Britons in that gods were not represented in human form and were worshipped in sacred groves rather than buildings.[114] In addition to such literary references, archaeological evidence from the Continent, as well as a retrospective view from the Roman period and from post-Roman Irish and Welsh literary sources, allow some further inferences to be made about religion in the late Iron Age.[115]

In the Yorkshire region, as in Britain as a whole, religious ideas were probably centred on a belief in the existence of a pantheon of gods and in their power, should they wish, to intervene in human affairs. The power these gods possessed inspired awe and fear, and thus they required obedience and worship. At the same time, however, the gods could be appealed to for assistance by means of sacrifices or offerings. Sacrifice often involved blood letting, but, for the most part, of an animal rather than a human being, although we are led to believe by Roman authors, such as Pliny the Elder, that human sacrifice did take place amongst barbarians, including the Britons.[116] A body found in Lindow Moss, Cheshire, thought to have been deliberately killed in the mid-first century AD, may bear this out.[117] He had been garroted, struck hard on the skull and had his throat cut in a manner which suggests ritual murder to some scholars.

In addition to blood sacrifice, we can identify material offerings to the gods in a number of different contexts. In both the late Iron Age and the Roman period the deliberate collection, arrangement and deposition of items in the ground, whether in specially dug pits or in pre-existing wells, ditches etc, seems to have been quite common. Rivers and other watery places were also favoured. The generic term often used for this phenomenon is 'structured deposition' meaning that some form of choice of an item (or items) had been made before it played a part in a prescribed sequence of behaviour, probably related for the most part to a symbolic role in cult practice. Structured deposits can include a range of different man-made objects, often, like iron tools, in themselves apparently quite mundane, as well as plants and animals. However, highly prestigious objects were chosen on occasions and a spectacular example of what may be interpreted as a structured deposit is the cache of weapons found at South Cave, c.5km north of Brough on Humber at the foot of the southern arm of the Wolds.[118] It was buried in a pit dug into the ditch of an earlier enclosure, probably at about the time of the Roman conquest of east Yorkshire. There were five iron swords in their decorated copper alloy scabbards and a bundle of thirty-three iron spearheads tied together with leather bindings. The context in which the hoard was buried is unknown, but it may have been a ritual offering to a local war god who had to be appeased at a time when the Romans were aggressively disarming the local warriors.

Identifying particular deities and their powers in Iron Age Britain is not easy but it seems that some of them were identified with the heavenly bodies. In addition, whether conceived as gods or not, a particular sacred quality was given to a great range of other natural phenomena. Certain animals, such as the stag and the boar, clearly possessed this quality. For example, a few of the Arras Culture graves contained pig's heads.[119] They may have been intended to symbolise the participation of the dead in a funeral meal, but might also have served to associate them with the strength and speed of the boar which, it was hoped, they would inherit in their life in the next world. Features in the landscape were also seen as sacred, especially water sources, rivers and streams because of the obvious connection of water with fertility. I have already suggested that the Brigantes gathered at Stanwick for religious ceremonies focused on the Mary Wild Beck. Such ceremonies in the native world would have formed part of a prescribed cycle of festivals through the year which coincided with important, cosmic and seasonal events. They were, no doubt, the opportunity for feasting and sacrifice.

Treatment of the dead: burial, the exception not the rule?

In societies for which burial in the ground is the preferred mode of treating the dead, a body may be cremated first or laid in the ground unburnt as what archaeologists usually call an inhumation. Whether as a cremation or an inhumation, both the burial itself and burials grouped together in cemeteries may allow clues to be gathered on a society's beliefs about the great mystery of the next life. Burial practice can also provide a window on secular aspects of society in terms of its structure and ranking, and on such topics as ethnicity and the relationship between the sexes.

Any discussion of Iron Age burials in Yorkshire usually centres on the well-documented east Yorkshire Arras Culture tradition of inhumation in cemeteries on the Wolds at, for example, Garton Slack, Burton Fleming and Kirkburn.[120] The bodies were usually placed in a crouched position (with legs drawn up under the chin) or with the knees bent in a 'flexed' position; both positions would remain a persistent, if minority, feature of burial practice in the region until the end of the Roman period. An imitation of the foetus presumably had some significance in representing the cyclical character of human life.

Some evidence for burial practice at the end of the Iron Age in east Yorkshire was found at Garton and Wetwang Slack, following the abandonment of the region's great Arras Culture cemeteries.[121] There were isolated single graves and small groups of graves. In one group, radiocarbon dated to the first century BC, there were seventeen burials of which three were in ditched barrows. Nine skeletons were flexed, seven crouched and only one extended and supine. Grave goods were scarce but in one of the barrows the burial was accompanied by an iron mirror. In another area there were seven late Iron Age graves containing thirteen individuals, one of which was accompanied by thirty-five glass beads. In yet another group there were twenty-nine infants, two thirds of whom were laid out in the foetal position. Adjacent were the burials of a sheep and two calves which probably had some cult significance.

Elsewhere in Yorkshire, outside the Arras Culture region, burials of the late Iron Age are rare suggesting, perhaps, that only certain members of the community were buried after death. Raistrick refers to burials associated with the settlement at Grassington and with other settlements in Craven, although it is not clear whether they are late Iron Age or earlier.[122] He describes multiple burials under mounds and isolated burials under piles of stones as well as burials thought to be Iron Age in the limestone caves of the area. Where recorded in any detail, the skeletons were usually crouched and, on occasions, accompanied by an iron knife. However, in the absence of closely datable artefacts radiocarbon dating would be needed to establish an accurate date for these burials. This has recently been done for a group of six inhumations from Gargrave in Craven which were dated to the late Iron Age or immediate post-Roman conquest period.[123] They were buried either crouched or flexed but without artefacts. Sufficient bone survived of two adult females in the group to show that they had been only 1.53m tall, although whether this was typical of the British population in the locality is not known in the absence of comparable studies.

At Stanwick two inhumation burials found in excavations of earthworks adjacent to the Tofts in 1986 were probably late Iron Age,[124] but if there was a cemetery for the Brigantian royal house it is yet to be found. In the lowlands of West Yorkshire mid-late Iron Age burials have been found in pits which were probably first used for grain storage. Examples come from Micklefield[125] and Ledston[126] between Leeds and York. All the bodies in these pit burials were crouched on their left sides. At Ferrybridge, burials radiocarbon dated to the first century AD, some of which may belong to the early Roman period rather than the late Iron Age, were found in a pit alignment which appears to mark off the sacred area of the henge.[127]

Cremation of the dead is not entirely unknown in Yorkshire in the late Iron Age, although it was nothing like as common as in parts of central and southern England. Barrows found near York on Skipwith Common and nearby at Thorganby, excavated in the nineteenth century, apparently produced burnt human bone.[128] A single cremation burial, with mid-first-century pottery, has been found at Redcliffe, perhaps of someone of southern origin involved in trade.[129] Further east, six cremation deposits, some in native-style pottery vessels, which may be late Iron Age or early Roman, come from Easington, near Spurn Head.[130] They are curious because they only consist of a token 30g or so of burnt bone whereas a cremated human body may be expected to produce in excess of 2000g. Of a similar date, alongside a trackway at Moor Lane, Stamford Bridge, five small pits were found containing cremated bone, largely of animals, but also including a few fragments of human bone.[131]

Whilst late Iron Age burials may be a little more common in Yorkshire than had appeared until very recently, we are still left with the problem of what happened to most of the dead — and to the rest of the bodies in those token cremations. Perhaps many more burials are still waiting to be discovered scattered in pits and ditches. At present, however, we must conclude that some method of disposal was adopted which leaves little trace in the ground.[132] One possibility is excarnation which involves exposing a corpse to the elements to be gradually consumed by insects, rodents and birds before, perhaps, what was left was scattered to the four winds. At present we cannot be sure, but the problem of how the dead were treated remains with us in the early Roman period. There is no evidence that the conquest had much immediate impact on one of the most important of human social customs.

5 | From Vespasian to Hadrian

The Roman Conquest of the Yorkshire region

Introduction

In about the year AD 71 the Roman army advanced into northern England, crossing both the Humber Estuary and the River Don into what is now Yorkshire, this time to take permanent control. In the nearly fifty years between 71 and 117 – the year Hadrian became emperor – the Yorkshire region was subject to military conquest and witnessed the construction of a great fortress at York and numerous forts linked by a system of roads.

Until about the year 85 Tacitus provides a framework for the political and military history of Britain as a whole including the north. Archaeological remains of this early Roman period in our region are dominated by those of the military sites. They produce buildings, usually of timber, but occasionally in stone, of types hitherto unknown, and a mass of pottery and other artefacts in a wide range of materials. By contrast, native settlements and their associated field systems produce very little other than pottery and even that can be scarce. The conclusion is inescapable that the Roman army represented a culture far more productive and technologically sophisticated in almost every respect than that which it found in northern England.

Dating of archaeological deposits on military sites themselves and, to an extent, on native sites in this period benefits from the appearance of new types of pottery made in military kilns at York and elsewhere or imported, either from other parts of Britain or from the Continent. Dominating the continental material is samian, largely from southern Gaul, which was imported to Britain until *c*.110 when it was replaced by the products of workshops around Clermont Ferrand in central Gaul. Although pottery allows us a new accuracy in dating archaeological contexts, the other class of artefact which is particularly valuable for dating, coinage, is quite scarce even on military sites. Soldiers' wages, paid in coin, represented the principal mechanism by which Roman currency reached Britain, but in these early days of imperial rule, even the lowest denominations had a purchasing power greater than the small change of later Roman times and the men were clearly careful with their money.

Vespasian became emperor in the year 69. His family name was Flavius hence he is the first of the so-called 'Flavian' emperors – the last being Hadrian (died 138). Vespasian was also the first emperor to be created outside Rome thereby setting a precedent which would, in due course, cause considerable problems for the empire, encouraging any army commander who felt he was powerful enough to try his hand at seizing the throne. However, in 69 Vespasian restored much needed stability to an empire recovering from the reign of Nero. In order to secure his position and impose his authority on the leading citizens of Rome, Vespasian, like Claudius before him, saw that there were advantages to be had in extending the empire. Britain, as well as Germany, appeared to be the easiest options. New campaigns allowed opportunities for the emperor's supporters to enrich themselves and conquest still provided the dynamic which assured the political stability of the Roman Empire and prevented competition for power becoming civil strife.

The dispute between Cartimandua and Venutius made a good story for Tacitus's readers in Rome and, if true, can be seen as a pretext for the invasion of the north, but there can surely be no question that the Romans had always intended to conquer the whole island of Britain. After Venutius had defeated Cartimandua, the Roman army moved in and Tacitus tells us that '... after a number of indecisive engagements our cohorts and cavalry squadrons [i.e. auxiliary troops and not legions, who were held in reserve] managed to extricate the queen from her dangerous situation. ... Venutius inherited the kingdom and we the fighting'.[1] If she were still alive, Cartimandua was probably sent off into an honourable retirement by the Romans. Having ruled for at least twenty years she was probably in her forties by now and so already fairly old by the standards of the day.

The preliminaries to the conquest of the north, including the defeat of Venutius, were probably the task of Vettius Bolanus, Governor of Britain in the years 68–71. This may be the historical context for a Roman presence at York which appears to slightly pre-date the fortress founded by the next governor, Petilius Cerialis. Appointed in 71 Cerialis had previously been a legionary legate (commander) in Britain at the time of Boudicca.[2] In the year 70, as legate of Lower Germany, Cerialis had suppressed a revolt in the Rhineland. However, according to Tacitus, it was only 'by luck', meaning, presumably, that he was Vespasian's son-in-law, that Cerialis succeeded to the governorship of Britain where he was to serve for two years.

Vespasian's army

Before looking further at the Roman military campaigns in the Yorkshire region we should take a closer look at the army commanded by Petilius Cerialis and other generals of the time. There were two types of Roman soldier in the late first century: the legionaries and the auxiliaries (from the word *auxilia* meaning helpers). The legionaries were usually based in fortresses whilst the auxiliaries were largely based in forts or, if only part units, in smaller fortlets. Whilst on campaign, the army employed temporary camps.

The invasion in the year 43 brought four legions to this country, but after the year 87 there were only three forming the permanent garrison in Britain. These men all enjoyed the privileges of Roman citizens and might aspire to reach the highest ranks in the imperial social hierarchy. The invasion also brought about 20,000 men in auxiliary regiments to Britain, some of whom were infantry and some cavalry, raised from subject peoples throughout the empire. Their names reflect their origins such as, for example, the Fourth Cohort of Gauls based at Templeborough and then Castleford. For the most part the auxiliary soldiers were not citizens, but could expect to be granted citizenship on discharge after 20–25 years' service.

There were some similarities in the organisation of the legions and auxiliary infantry regiments. The basic unit was the *contubernium* of eight men who would share a tent on campaign and two rooms in a barrack block when back at base. Ten *contubernia* made a century of eighty men commanded by a centurion. Six centuries made up a legionary cohort of 480 men. A legion consisted of ten cohorts, and as the first cohort was of double strength there were, in theory at least, 5200 men to which a small unit of cavalry was added. The commoner type of auxiliary infantry unit (*cohors quingenaria peditata*) was made up of about 500 men but there were also units about 1000 strong (*cohors milliaria peditata*). In a mounted auxiliary unit the basic unit was six men who shared their accommodation with their horses; a *turma* consisted of thirty men plus the two decurions who commanded them. Sixteen *turmae* made up a cavalry unit of 480 men known as an *ala* (wing in Latin). A third type of auxiliary unit was the *cohors equitata* – a unit which was part mounted consisting of six centuries of infantry and four *turmae* of cavalry.

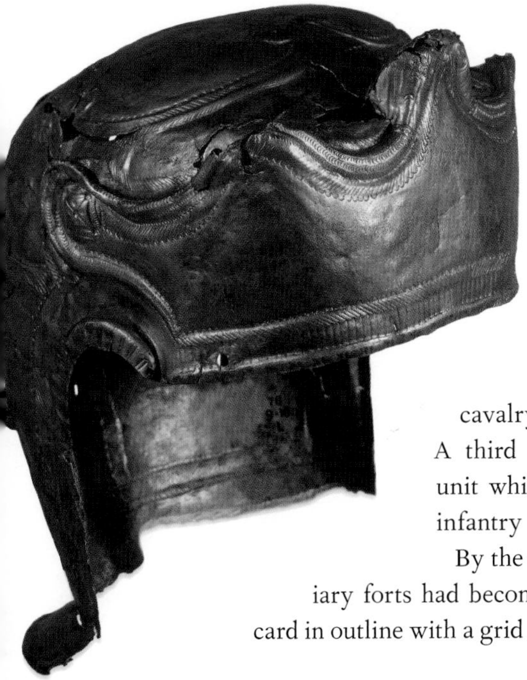

By the late first century both legionary fortresses and auxiliary forts had become fairly standardised in plan, resembling a playing card in outline with a grid of streets usually laid out by military surveyors using

Illus. 5.1   The Guisborough helmet. (© British Museum)

units of the Roman foot (0.296m). The principal streets were the *via praetoria* which led from the headquarters building (*principia*) in the centre of the site to the main gate (*porta praetoria*) and the *via principalis* which ran between the two main side gates across the front of the headquarters. That part of the fortress which lay in front of the headquarters was known as the *praetentura*, and the part behind it was known as the *retentura*. In the spaces between the streets there was a suite of buildings which varied little from site to site.

The size of a base was related, to a large extent, to the type and size of unit it was intended for. The fortress at York was *c.*26ha in extent, quite typical for a fortress of the late first century, housing a full legion, whilst the legionary vexillation fortress at Rossington Bridge was only *c.*9.3ha. The internal areas of auxiliary forts in Yorkshire region usually range from *c.*1ha to 4ha (the average football pitch is 0.75ha). Those at the smaller end of the scale, like Slack, housed units about 500 strong whilst the larger forts like Doncaster and Malton would have had space for 1000 men.

The command structure of a legion was closely integrated with the career paths of men in the upper echelons of imperial society who would expect to progress to senior posts in the government of the empire. A legionary commander, the legate (*legatus*), was usually in his 30s and a man from the senatorial order, the highest rank in the empire. If he was fortunate, as Vespasian had been, a legate might aspire to become emperor. The legate was supported by his tribunes; the second in command, the *tribunus laticlavius*, would also have been from the senatorial order, but in his twenties. The other five tribunes, *tribuni angusticlavii*, were from the next highest rank, the equestrian order or knights. Senior officers usually served for no more than three years in a post before moving on. The highest ranking officer in a more permanent position in the legion was the camp prefect (*praefectus castrorum*) who took charge of the organisation of the fortress, and of the soldiers' training and equipment. From an inscription, originally on a stone coffin, we know of a man named Antonius Gargilianus who fulfilled this role at York, perhaps in the early third century.[3] The camp prefect was supported by the centurions who were responsible for their men on a day to day basis. Other legionaries with specific tasks included a *tessararius* who was responsible for the daily passwords – a tombstone of a *tessararius* of the Second Legion, named Pudens, comes from Ilkley.[4] Usually based in Caerleon in south Wales, he was perhaps in a detachment on special assignment when he died.

An auxiliary infantry unit was commanded by a tribune, if 500 strong, or by a prefect if 1000 strong. Whilst their men were usually non-citizens, the commanders were citizens and often came from the ranks of the governing class in the province in which the unit had been raised. A prefect who, presumably on retirement, had come to live in York was a man named Publius Aelius Marcianus, known from an altar he dedicated to Jupiter and 'the gods and goddesses of hospitality and home.'[5] This may seem a rather odd combination, but one wonders whether it is a clever reference to Virgil's

Aeneid in which Dido says, welcoming Aeneas to Carthage, 'Jupiter, you who are said to have created the laws of hospitality ...' Is Marcianus showing off his literary knowledge here?

Soldiers' clothing, equipment and weaponry in Yorkshire of the conquest period was pretty much what one would have found elsewhere in the Roman world. On his tombstone Lucius Duccius Rufinus, a Ninth Legion standard bearer from York, wears what is probably supposed to be armour made of metal scales which would have been sewn onto a leather jerkin worn over a short tunic (Illus. 3.5).[6] Over his armour he wears a type of military cloak known as a *sagum*. Archaeological finds of equipment in Yorkshire are largely from auxiliary units. Amongst a few examples which can be noted here, pride of place probably goes to an unusual brass parade helmet found at Guisborough in 1864 (now in the British Museum). It is made of brass ornamented in repoussé with figures of Mars, Minerva and Victory.[7] In addition, there are binding fragments from both helmets and shields from Castleford[8] whilst found on the defences of the fort at Doncaster were the remains of a complete auxiliary shield of which the central boss, hand grip and bindings were well preserved.[9] Worn by both auxiliaries and legionaries in the conquest period was a type of armour known as *lorica segmentata* in which interlocking strips of metal were sewn onto a leather base – there are fragments from Castleford.[10] As for weaponry, a legionary typically had a javelin (*pilum*) and a short sword (*gladius*) used for close combat fighting. Auxiliary infantrymen also had a *gladius* along with a spear. A *gladius* was found in Sewell's Cave, near Settle, perhaps an offering to a native deity by a local man following a successful skirmish with the Romans.[11] Castleford fort has produced three iron spearheads.[12] Auxiliary cavalrymen had a longer sword (*spatha*) for slashing while mounted. All soldiers carried a dagger and there is a suspension loop from a dagger sheath from Castleford.

Representing the trappings from a cavalryman's horse in our region is the unusual find from Fremington Hagg, near Reeth in Swaledale, of a more or less complete set of silvered bronze fittings from a bridle.[13] As far as the horses themselves are concerned, Roman cavalrymen's tombstones show the rider's feet quite close to the ground and the evidence of horse bones, for example from Castleford,[14] suggests that they were probably equivalent of a sturdy Welsh Mountain pony standing about 14–15½ hands to the withers (a Grand National winner today stands at least 16 hands; a hand = 4 inches/*c.*100mm).

The tasks that soldiers, whether legionaries or auxiliaries, were expected to perform, in addition to fighting, were very varied. Some of them would be more appropriate today to civil servants and policemen. However, as regularly paid agents of the empire the army had a wide remit, at least until conquered territory could be handed over to a competent and compliant local authority. This included not only keeping the peace and disarming the native people, but also administering justice and collecting taxes. Soldiers would also have supervised road maintenance and the extraction of minerals, including

lead and ironstone, probably by prisoners and slaves. The Pennine forts at
Bainbridge and Ilkley may have had a particular role in organising lead mining.
Exploitation of Yorkshire's lead by the Romans appears to have begun fairly
quickly after the conquest, although it may have earlier origins. Excavations
at Victoria Camp (above Victoria Cave) near Settle revealed a clay-lined
bowl, thought to be a furnace for smelting lead, unfortunately undated, but
possibly pre-Roman.[15] Two lead blocks, or 'pigs', one bearing an inscription
dating it to the year 81, in the reign of the Emperor Domitian, were found in
the 1730s about 3km south of Pateley Bridge.[16] A third, now lost, from near
Appletreewick, apparently bore an inscription of Trajan dated to the year
98 and a fourth, also lost, from Marrick, was Hadrianic.[17] Any workings of
Roman date have probably been destroyed by later mining.

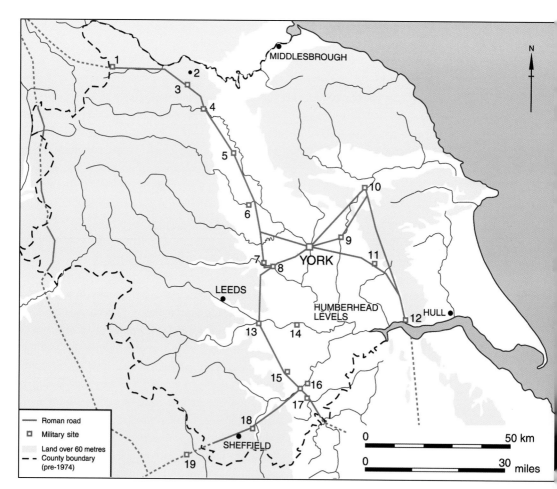

Illus. 5.2   Plan showing military sites (and Stanwick) in Yorkshire of the conquest period (up to c.AD78). Key: 1, Rey
Cross; 2, Stanwick ; 3, Carkin Moor; 4, Catterick; 5, Healam Bridge; 6, Roecliffe; 7, Newton Kyme; 8, Tadcaster; 9, Stamford
Bridge; 10, Malton; 11, Hayton; 12, Brough on Humber; 13, Castleford; 14, Roall Manor Farm; 15, Burghwallis; 16, Long
Sandall; 17, Rossington Bridge; 18, Templeborough.

The Roman army on campaign

From Cerialis to Agricola

The course of events in the conquest of the north cannot be reconstructed in detail, although Tacitus refers to battles, 'some bloody'.[18] To judge by one of the Vindolanda tablets, the Romans were rather dismissive of the Britons in the north calling them *'Brittunculi'* – 'wretched little Brits'[19] – but as the revolt of Boudicca had shown, the Britons could, on occasions, give the Romans a hard fight. However, the difference between the two sides was essentially one between warriors and soldiers. The former were brave, even reckless, but intent on personal glory as much as victory, whilst the latter were well-armed and trained professionals able to submit personal ambition to the common cause.

By the end of the first season's campaigning Petilius Cerialis, at the head of the Ninth Legion, formerly based in the fortress at Lincoln, had probably chosen the site of his northern command base at York. When one sees how York lies in the middle of the lowland zone north of the Humber in a place where a navigable river, tidal in Roman times but fordable at low tide, meets a pre-existing land route, it is clear that it was chosen, in the first instance, for strategic reasons to make a good starting point for conquest. However, by choosing York, not previously a place of much importance, Cerialis, would at a stroke, change the political and economic geography of the region for ever.

Roman military strategy when occupying new territory was to break up the native population into small, manageable groups. This was done by creating a network of roads with forts at the critical junctions between them. In addition, forts were often close to important river crossings which prevented the rivers themselves being used by hostile forces. Other features which the Romans preferred for their fort sites included level ground and a slightly elevated, but not inaccessible, position such as to ensure reasonably good surveillance of the immediate surroundings. Sites adjacent to springs for providing a water supply were also preferred.

The location of early Roman forts and roads shows us that there were two routes taken to reach York from Lincoln. The most direct was the Roman road, now known as Ermine Street, and followed by the A15, which reaches the Humber at Wintringham. The estuary would, however, have been a serious obstacle not being easily navigable with its shifting shoals and banks, and high current speeds.[20] Today the window of opportunity for rowing or sailing a boat safely across from Wintringham to Brough Haven on the north bank is brief, being only about two hours after high tide. Although the character of the estuary may have been a little different in Roman times, it is unlikely to have allowed a much easier passage. The extent to which a Humber crossing was used in the invasion is therefore likely to have been limited. However, on the north bank, the army established a fort at Brough on Humber (successor to an earlier camp) adjacent to a pre-existing native settlement. From Brough a route which would, in due course, become a major Roman road, ran north-westwards to York along the north-eastern edge of the Humberhead Levels and below the Wolds scarp. A fort was established at Hayton, more or less equidistant between Brough and York in an area where archaeological investigation suggests there was a substantial native population which required supervision.[21]

The second route north, which probably brought the bulk of Cerialis's army, ran north-west from Lincoln and crossed the River Trent at Littleborough (Notts.) where there was a fort of the Cerialian period. It then crossed the River Idle at Bawtry before making for the valley of the River Don, carefully sticking to elevated ground at c.15m above sea level, only going below 7.5m at the crossing of the River Torne.[22] The route then approached the Don at the first convenient crossing to the east of a gorge through the Magnesian Limestone belt.[23] Within what is now Doncaster the road took a line which is closely followed today by Hall Gate, High Street and Frenchgate. Excavations at 8–10 High Street, Silver Street/Hall Gate and 10–14a Hall Gate have located the road immediately north of the modern streets.[24] The fort lay a little to the north-east of the road overlooking the river on a small level outcrop of gravelly alluvium a few metres above the floodplain. The parish church stands in the middle of the fort site allowing the prominent position chosen by the

Romans to be easily appreciated today. Another fort on the Don apparently lay at Long Sandall c.5km north-east of Doncaster, but the site has largely been destroyed and little is known of its date, although it may have been a temporary establishment pre-dating Doncaster itself.[25]

After crossing the Don the army would have headed north to a crossing over the River Aire at Castleford. The fort sits on a low ridge overlooking the south bank of the river, just below its confluence with the Calder and enjoyed a view over the flood plain to the north. Excavations between 1974 and 1991 found considerable traces of timber buildings dated to c.71–86 (referred to as Fort I), although there was no obviously regular plan and no defences were located earlier than those of the rebuilt fort of c.86 (Fort II).[26] It is likely, therefore, that Fort I was either rather larger than Fort II or was not a fort of the usual type. In addition to the buildings, a very important discovery in Fort I was a midden which, rather like one of similar date at Catterick, contained a vast quantity of artefacts including leather and wooden items well preserved in the waterlogged ground.

Two other forts in the Castleford–Doncaster area, both unexcavated, may also belong to the Cerialian period. The first lies at Burghwallis (Robin Hood's Well), c.10km north of Donacaster and a little to the east of the route to Castleford.[27] The second is at Roall Manor Farm, c.13km east of the route north.[28] It sits on a sandstone outcrop above an old course of the River Aire, faces north-east, and may have been intended to control movement along the waterway.

The army's march north from Castleford largely followed the Magnesian Limestone belt, subsequently the line of a major trunk road. The Britons may have attempted to oppose the Romans at the Aberford Dykes, c.7km south-west of Tadcaster. The dykes seem designed to control movement northwards, although not necessarily by the Romans.[29] There are three substantial linear earthworks (each a bank and ditch) apparently built to control an important ford over a stream known as the Cock Beck. The principal element is the Becca Banks, c.5.5km long and measuring up to 7.6m from the base of the ditch to the top of the bank. The earthwork lies on the north side of the valley of the beck, taking advantage of the natural scarp. Shorter earthworks, South Dyke and the Rein, lie on the south side of the valley. Excavations at Becca Banks and South Dyke for the A1–M1 link road suggested a late Iron Age date for construction with the ditches filling up in the Roman period.

After Aberford and just before Tadcaster the route to York swings away to the north-east. It is presumed that there was a fort at Tadcaster at a crossing over the River Wharfe, but nothing is known of it. It is possible that a part of Cerialis's army did not go straight to York, but continued due north to another crossing over the Wharfe at Long Brough, Newton Kyme, preparatory to continuing the campaign through the lowlands of the Vale of York.[30] This may well be the context for two temporary camps at Newton Kyme, the earliest elements in a sequence of Roman fortifications on the south bank of the river. Post-dating one of the camps is a small fort identified from aerial photography, but not dated. From Tadcaster the route to York leaves the Magnesian Limestone for a raised ridge of boulder clay which is followed today, if not exactly on the Roman line, by the A64 trunk road.

Having established himself in York, Cerialis clearly wasted no time in pressing on northwards to Carlisle, following the route to Scotch Corner and then across Stainmore described in Chapter 2. The first fort at Carlisle was probably established in about 72–73. However, the only fort in Yorkshire north of York which can be ascribed with a degree of certainty to Cerialis is one which came to light in 1993 during widening of the A1, at Roecliffe on the south bank of the River Ure.[31] It is 28km, or a day's march, from York, and 21km from Newton Kyme. There may also have been a fort at Aldborough at

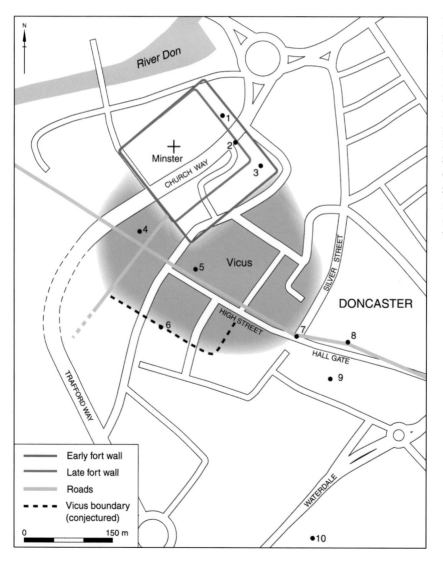

Illus. 5.4 Doncaster: plan of the fort and vicus showing Roman sites referred to in the text. Key: 1, Askew's Print Shop, Church Street; 2, Church Way (1971); 3, High Fishergate; 4, Frenchgate; 5, 8–10 High Street; 6, St Sepulchre Gate; 7, Hall Gate / Silver Street (1960); 8, 10–14a Hall Gate; 9, 53–54 Hall Gate; 10, Waterdale.

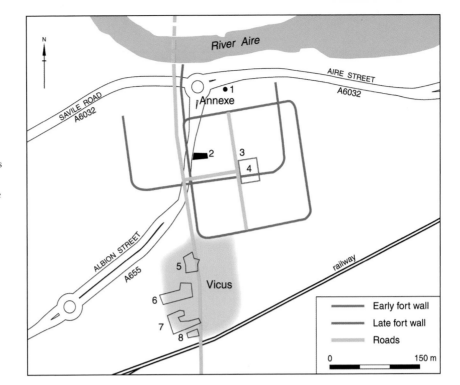

Illus. 5.5 Castleford: plan of the fort and vicus showing Roman sites referred to in the text. Key: 1, baths; 2, midden; 3, granary; 4, headquarters building; 5, Vicus Site I; 6, Vicus Site 10; 7, Vicus Sites 44–45/51; 8, Vicus Site 42.

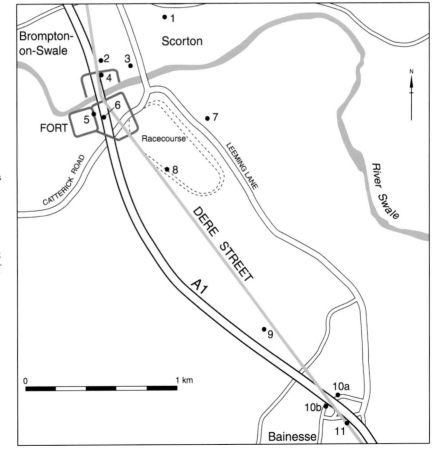

Illus. 5.6 Catterick: plan showing Roman sites referred to in the text. Key: 1, Scorton (Hollow Banks); 2, Brompton-on-Swale (NAA excavation); 3, Catterick Bridge; 4, Catterick 1972 (defences of 'stores depot'); 5, Thornborough Farm (fort defences); 6, Bypass site; 7, Site of camp; 8, Racecourse (burials); 9, Catterick Triangle; 10a–b, Bainesse Farm (east and west of Dere Street); 11, site of camps south of Bainesse.

the point where Dere Street crossed the Ure, but Roecliffe, just west of Dere Street, would presumably have been its predecessor.

The fort itself at Roecliffe is largely known from aerial photographs and geophysical survey, but excavations in the settlement (*vicus*) to the east of it (see below) show it can only have been occupied for a short period of up to about ten years. With an area of *c*.3.8ha the fort could have accommodated 1000 men who, from time to time, may have included both auxiliaries and legionaries. Amongst military equipment found in the excavations there was the head of a legionary *pilum*. An unusual feature of Roecliffe is a curving outwork ditch and bank on its east side which gave extra protection to the fort and *vicus*, but perhaps initially put in place to protect the soldiers while they were constructing the fort.

About 16km north of Roecliffe (and *c*.5km south of Leeming) is a Roman fort at Healam Bridge. Archaeological work in advance of widening the A1 had not been fully published at the time of writing, but geophysical survey suggests that the road to the north, Dere Street, ran through the middle of the fort which would go against the usual Roman practice in the region of setting forts a little to one side of major roads.[32] The implication may be that the fort – or perhaps it was just a camp – is earlier than the road. However, only excavation can confirm a Cerialian date. The next day's march would have brought the army to an important crossing over the Swale at Catterick. Here there is a long sequence of Roman occupation, although it is currently thought that the first fort dates to the 80s.[33] It is likely, however, that a temporary camp east of Catterick racecourse,[34] two camps south of Bainesse which appear to predate Dere Street,[35] and another at Scorton, *c*.3km north-east of Catterick,[36] were the work of Cerialis's forces. Another camp at Breckenbrough in lower Swaledale, near Thirsk, may be of the same period.[37]

North-west of Catterick Cerialis may have been responsible for a small fort at Carkin Moor (unexcavated) immediately south-east of Stanwick, perhaps used to supervise the suppression of a hostile Brigantian elite. The Roman road from Scotch Corner to Carlisle, now under the A66, passed through the middle of the fort which was probably only briefly occupied. Further to the north-west, a camp (8.3ha in area) at Cow Close, 1km north-east of Bowes may also belong to Cerialis's campaign,[38] but more likely to be his is the camp at Rey Cross at the highest point on Stainmore.[39] The camp defences – still visible today – consist of a bank and ditch with eleven surviving entrances each guarded by a *titulus*, a low mound sited just outside a gate to prevent an enemy's frontal assault. The Roman road passed through the camp, but it changed alignment after an entrance on the eastern side in a manner suggesting that the roadline was adjusted to take account of a camp already in existence.

Another camp in the Pennines which, although undated, may belong to Cerialis lies on Malham Moor, on a route from Wharfedale to the Ribble.[40] With an area of 8.2ha (similar to Cow Close) it could have accommodated a legion on campaign in an area of considerable native settlement. The camp has

so-called *claviculae* at the four entrances, short curving outward extensions of the defences which had the same purpose as the *tituli* at Rey Cross in blocking a frontal assault on the gates and could also be used to trap unwary attackers attempting to retreat (also at Cawthorn, see Illus. 5.9).

Two other undated camps at strategic locations may have been part of the Roman army's move north-east from York towards the area around Malton where a Cerialian base is a possibility. At Buttercrambe, c.1km north of Stamford Bridge, a small camp of 1.74ha overlooked the River Derwent.[41] A larger camp at Wath (4.9ha) suitable for a legionary detachment lies 11km west of Malton on the north side of the Howardian Hills and has good views northwards over the Vale of Pickering.[42]

Finally, mention should be made of the first major Roman road to the north which ran up the west side of the Pennines. This is also likely to be the work of Cerialis's governorship.[43] It ran north from a fort at Ribchester (Lancs.) and then passed west of Slaidburn through the Forest of Bowland (in Yorkshire pre-1974), left Yorkshire briefly before passing back into the county immediately to the west of Low Bentham and continued up the valley of the River Lune to a fort at Burrow in Lonsdale (Lancs.). The road then passed briefly through Yorkshire (pre-1974) again west of Sedbergh before heading north towards a fort at Low Burrow Bridge (Cumbria) and then on to Carlisle; at the fort at Brougham (Cumbria) it met the road which crossed the Stainmore from Bowes.

The governorship of Agricola

In 73 Petilius Cerialis was replaced as Governor of Britain by Sextus Julius Frontinus whose principal focus of attention was the conquest of Wales. In 77 or 78 Frontinus was succeeded by Gnaeus Julius Agricola who, unusually, did a double stint of six years as governor. He is the subject of the well-known biography by his son-in-law Tacitus and he is also the first governor of Britain to be referred to by name in an inscription from the province – on water pipes in the fortress at Chester which he founded in about 78. As a result of Tacitus's account, Agricola may have been credited with achievements which belong rightly to Frontinus or to others, but archaeology does seem to suggest that many of the forts in the north of Britain were founded during Agricola's governorship following campaigns which completed the conquest of Wales and took him as far as the north of Scotland.

In Yorkshire some forts of the conquest period were abandoned by Agricola, including Brough on Humber and Hayton, perhaps suggesting the Parisi were no longer a threat to peace. Roecliffe was decommissioned by c.79–80, and may have been replaced by a fort at Aldborough. About 37km north of Aldborough at Catterick the fort is thought to be Agricolan. It lies on a slightly elevated plateau above the River Swale. Excavations have examined the eastern defences and, in advance of the Catterick bypass, a large area east of the fort, at least part of which was in an annexe (for extent of the excavated area see Illus. 9.5).[44] The route north continued to the River Tees which was crossed at Piercebridge where there must surely have been an Agricolan fort, probably on the County Durham side, although it has not been found in spite of extensive archaeological fieldwork.[45]

On the Roman road from Scotch Corner to Carlisle there was a series of what are thought to be Agricolan forts. Greta Bridge, c.20km from Catterick, is located at a point where the Roman road makes its major first bend to allow it to cross the River Greta. The fort lies a little to the south-west of the road line on a low plateau overlooking the Greta to the east. There has been very little excavation here, but earthworks of the defences are well preserved on the south side of the fort (Illus. 2.2). The next fort, and the last on the road in Yorkshire, is at Bowes at the eastern end of the Stainmore pass.[46] Bowes fort is marked today by a twelfth-century keep in the north-west corner showing that the strategic eye of the Romans could not be bettered over one thousand years later. The site lies on a promontory which slopes down to the south and has spectacular views over the valley of the Greta and the moorland beyond. The Roman road, now followed by the village street, bypassed the northern defences.

Illus. 5.8 Bainbridge: the fort site (centre) seen from the west. (Photo: P. Ottaway)

To the south of the road to Carlisle another major route across the Pennines ran through Wensleydale, although it cannot be traced with certainty east of a fort at Wensley.[47] This fort is unexcavated, but may be of the Agricolan period. 14km further west was a fort at Bainbridge. It is situated on a drumlin, or hill (the Brough), composed of glacial clay and gravel, overlooking the confluence of the Rivers Bain and Ure. The Brough is 248m above sea level, allowing extensive views up and down Wensleydale. Although water could be a problem for a fort on high ground, here there were springs. The road west of Bainbridge can still be followed on the ground as far as Ribblehead and Ingleton, but is not so clear after that, although the Roman fort at Lancaster was presumably the destination.

Moving south again brings us to a road through Wharfedale which originated in York and led through the Aire Gap to Ribchester (Lancs.). A fort at Adel, north of Leeds, on this road has long been suspected on the basis of numerous Roman finds in the area, including three altars, one dedicated to the goddess Brigantia.[48] Geophysical survey seems to show a fort of 1.25ha lies just south of the junction of King Lane and Eccup Lane, although in the absence of excavation this cannot be demonstrated conclusively. Nor can much be said of the fort's history, although an Agricolan foundation is likely. From Adel the road headed north-westwards. An archaeological investigation west of Eccup Lane showed that the Roman road builders had the skill to cope with unstable peaty ground by laying down tightly packed timbers capped with clay to make a stable base; above this were laid the cobbles of the road itself.[49] The road probably ran along the ridge known as the Chevin to Burley in Wharfedale and then on to the fort at Ilkley. Another road approached Ilkley from the north-east, originating in Aldborough, which crossed the River Nidd near Hampsthwaite Church. It is then followed by the Knaresborough–Skipton road for c.3km after which it ran across Blubberhouses Moor where the line can still be traced. At Ilkley the Wharfe was probably crossed at a ford still shown on nineteenth-century maps and the road then passes west of the fort which lies on a knoll overlooking the river.[50] On either side of this knoll there were once brooks which flowed down to the Wharfe giving the fort added protection. From Ilkley the road from York runs west to Addingham and then to Burwen Castle, Elslack where a fort was excavated in 1909.[51] Elslack occupies a commanding position in a pass which links the valleys of the Aire, Wharfe, Ribble and Calder.

Another road headed south-west from Ilkley towards Manchester, but the next major route across the Pennines ran from York via Tadcaster to Manchester. Two Agricolan forts lie on the line as it passes through the high ground in Yorkshire: at Slack and Castleshaw. The fort at Slack is at Outlane, c.7km west of Huddersfield, at c.250m above sea level.[52] The fort has its corners at the cardinal points; to the north-east and north-west the land rises gently towards what are now the M62 and the Huddersfield–Oldham road, but on the south-west side it falls away sharply and to the south-east more gradually towards streams which meet near the south corner of the fort. The line of the road running south-west from Slack to the fort at Castleshaw, a distance of c.12km, has recently been accurately plotted for the first time by the Huddersfield and District Archaeological Society.[53] Castleshaw guarded the road as it climbed to a pass across the Pennines.[54]

East of York a road ran along the York moraine for c.11km to a fort at Stamford Bridge which commanded an important crossing over the River Derwent.[55] Also on the eastern side of the county there was a new fort at Malton, perhaps replacing an earlier base.[56] Malton is c.26km north-east of York and overlooks the valley of the Derwent which was fordable at this point in antiquity. A fort at Malton would have had great strategic value as it controlled routes into the Vale of Pickering and the Wolds to the east and into the Howardian Hills to the west. Prominent earthworks representing the defences of a large fort of c.3.45ha can still be seen in Orchard Field, south-east of the road to Old Malton. Further east on the road to the coast, on the south side of the Vale of Pickering, just 8km from the sea at Scarborough, a fort has recently been discovered by geophysical survey at Staxton. The fort is quite likely to be Agricolan, although this is not certain.[57]

North of Malton, at a distance of c.17km, is Cawthorn where there are well-preserved fortifications identified by Sir Ian Richmond in the 1930s as 'practice

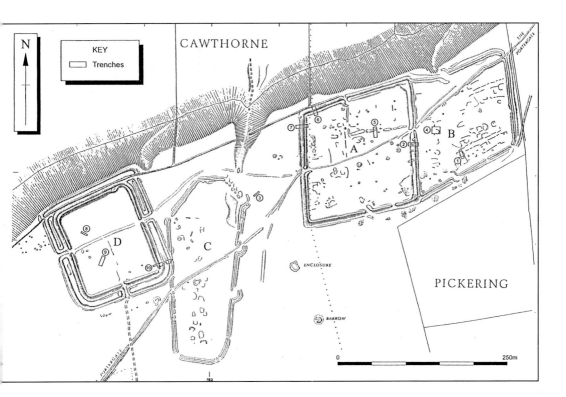

CAWTHORNE

KEY

Trenches

PICKERING

ENCLOSURE

BARROW

0   250m

Illus. 5.9   Plan of
the fortifications at
Cawthorn showing
location of trenches
and internal features
identified in 1999–2000
(from YAS Roman
Antiquities Section
Bulletin, 18, 2001, ©
English Heritage)

camps' but now thought to be a camp and two forts.[58] The original character
of the area is rather difficult to appreciate today because of extensive modern
plantations, but in Roman times it would have been open moorland. The site
lies on the northern scarp of the Tabular Hills, high ground which slopes gently
down towards the Vale of Pickering to the south but drops quite sharply to the
Sutherland Beck to the north. The sequence began with Fort A extending over
c.3ha which, in a second period of occupation, had a defended annexe of c.2.4ha
added to the east (B). Excavations in the fort in 1999 and 2000 identified a street
flanked by buildings probably with timber frames, but with turf walls. Another
turf-walled building was found in the annexe. These buildings were, perhaps,
rapidly erected temporary accommodation for the garrison. No other turf-built
military structures are known in Britain, although they may have been used
more frequently than is now apparent. Fort A was probably followed by Fort D,
initially with a single defensive ditch; the road to the north would have entered
through the south gate and exited through the east gate. The camp (C) was
then constructed curiously close to Fort A, although it avoids blocking the fort's
north-east gate. Partly as a result of this proximity the camp has a very unusual
plan, with no parallels elsewhere in Britain; it is shaped rather like a coffin with
claviculae at its three entrances on the east side. The defences of Fort D were
then re-established with a double ditch system, the outer cutting into the camp.

The Cawthorn fortifications are of an uncertain date as very little material
culture has been found in the excavations, presumably because occupation was

brief or at least either intermittent or seasonal when the road was passable. They have previously been thought to belong to around the year 100, but archaeomagnetic dates on hearths found in the recent excavations in Fort A would not contradict an Agricolan date, as for Lease Rigg fort to the north. This would make sense as it is difficult to see what a later historical context would be for new fortifications in a sparsely populated area which one would have thought had been pacified by the end of the first century. However, there is a small amount of pottery from the recent excavations which seems to suggest some sort of activity continued until the early Hadrianic period.

From Cawthorn a Roman road, now known as Wade's Causeway, continued to the north; on Wheeldale Moor one can see a stretch of stony material c.2km long which is taken to be remains of the road.[59] It runs to a fort which is thought to be an Agricolan foundation at Lease Rigg near Grosmont, 12km from the coast at Whitby.[60] The fort stands on a narrow ridge overlooking the lower Esk valley with its unusual elongated plan determined by the constrained site. As the fort was only 1ha internally, it was probably garrisoned by part of an auxiliary unit; an annexe of 0.65ha lies on the west side.

Agricola would have been replaced after his second term as Governor of Britain as a matter of course but he also appears to have fallen foul of the Emperor Domitian (81–96) whom Tacitus blamed for not recognising his achievements sufficiently. In 87 a crisis in the Rhineland led to the withdrawal of the Second Legion *Adiutrix*, one the four legions then in Britain. As a result it was not possible for the Romans to keep control of their recent conquests in Scotland. Agricola's fortress at Inchtuthil on the banks of the Tay was abandoned along with almost all the forts north of a line from the Tyne to the Solway, a line in due course to be adopted by Hadrian's Wall. As Tacitus commented acidly: 'Britain was conquered and immediately abandoned'.[61]

After the departure of Agricola and withdrawal of the Second Legion *Adiutrix* some further reorganisation of the British garrison took place as can be seen in changes to the forts in the Yorkshire region. At Bainbridge in Wensleydale Brian Hartley, its most recent excavator, found that the fort of which earthwork remains are still visible, 1.16ha internally, had its origins in about the year 85.[62] Also in the Pennines, but further south on the road from York to Manchester the Agricolan fort at Castleshaw was abandoned in c.95, although a smaller fortlet was built on the same site ten years later.

At Castleford the fort is thought to have been rebuilt in c.85–86 (Fort II), apparently, at c.3.37ha, rather smaller than Fort I, although one of the larger forts in the region. The defences of Fort II have been located and shown to be of the conventional type with a ditch and rampart. The fort faced west towards the main Doncaster–York road which passed close by. The headquarters site can be identified in the centre, as expected, and amongst other known buildings was a granary (Illus 5.5).

Roman fortifications and their buildings

Whilst on campaign, the Roman army built camps (sometimes called 'marching camps'), temporary fortifications, some of which may have been occupied for only a few days, although their bank and ditch defences can still be found. Camps vary considerably in size depending on the unit to be accommodated. Within the camps accommodation was in tents. Permanent fortifications, represented by fortresses for legions, and forts and fortlets for auxiliaries, had as their principal purpose accommodation of the men and their equipment. Although they had defences which might prevent sudden attacks by hostile forces and even the intrusion of wild animals, they were not like a medieval castle which was primarily designed for defence. The Roman army expected to go out into the field to fight where its superior discipline and weaponry could be brought to bear on the enemy.

Timber buildings

The buildings to be found in Roman fortifications of the late first and early second centuries were largely of timber, although there were a few stone buildings, notably bath houses. Whether in timber or stone, Roman buildings were very different from anything which was known in Britain before the conquest. For a start, they usually had a rectilinear rather than a round plan and were often considerably larger and more architecturally ambitious.

Timber buildings were constructed not just with the axe and adze, known in the Iron Age, but also a new tool for cutting timber, the saw with a cross-cut blade, a Roman innovation in Britain. The mortice and tenon joint and the scarf joint were amongst new ways of fitting timbers together. Iron nails and other structural fittings were used in large quantities for the first time.

The simpler military timber buildings employed rows of posts, usually driven straight into the ground. More sophisticated buildings, which might enclose an internal space of up to 2000m^2 in the case, for example, of a military headquarters, employed some form of frame to ensure rigidity and provide support for a heavy roof. Walls usually had posts morticed into a sill beam either laid flat, directly onto the ground, or supported on a low wall of clay or stone. Between the posts there was usually horizontal planking or wattle coated with daub. Both internal and external surfaces might be given a protective coating of plaster or lime wash.

The roofs of timber buildings are the parts about which least is known, but a wall plate probably connected the tops of the posts and into this A-frame roof trusses were set at intervals corresponding to the post locations. The trusses supported boards given a waterproof cladding usually in the form of clay tiles or stone slabs. Rows of rectangular tiles, known as *tegulae*, with flanges along their sides, were arranged such that each row overlapped the one below. The junctions between a *tegula* and the next one on either side were covered by tiles of semicircular cross-section known as *imbrices* (plural of *imbrex*). At the eaves of military buildings there were sometimes small vertical tiles called antefixes which closed off the lowest *imbrices*. On occasions antefixes bore military emblems in relief, although York examples mostly bear stylised female faces, perhaps of protective deities.[63] In the absence of gutters and drain pipes, roofs would have had a wide overhang to ensure rainwater did not run down the walls. Thatch, turf or shingle may also have been used for roofs on occasions, but little trace of these materials survives.

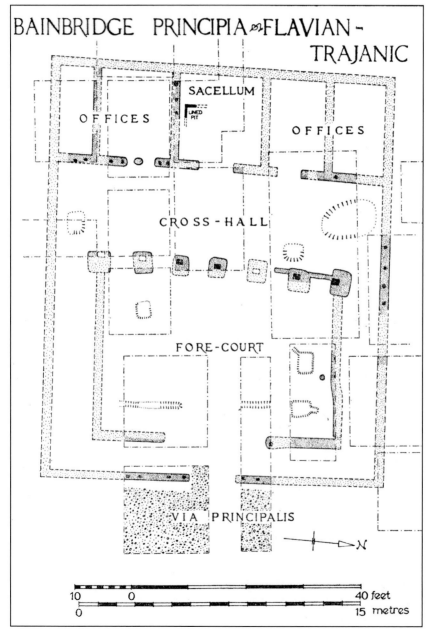

Illus. 5.10 Bainbridge: plan of the late first-century fort headquarters building (drawn by Brian Hartley, from Wilson, D. R. 1969. © Cambridge University Press)

Construction of a timber fort required the organisation of a huge quantity of labour and materials in a relatively short time. Depending on certain assumptions about the size of the fort structures, it has been calculated that some 184m³ of timber, primarily oak, would have been needed for the palisades, gates and towers on the defences of a fort of 1.6ha.[64] Another 440m³ would have been needed for the internal buildings. Construction would have involved felling trees in an area of woodland of *c.*6.5–12ha in extent. In addition, more wood was needed for cladding and wall infill.

In the centre of a fort or fortress was the headquarters building with its central courtyard. A typical example of the late first century was excavated at Bainbridge.[65] It was built using the post-in-trench method and measured *c.*21m × 18.4m. On three sides there were rooms used as offices, stores and the like, whilst on the fourth side was a large hall. At Bainbridge this had no aisles, although in other examples there might be either one or two aisles flanking a central space. A hall with two aisles is often described as a 'basilica'. At one end of the hall was the tribunal, a platform from which the commanding officer addressed his troops. As was usual, behind the hall at Bainbridge there was a row of five rooms which served as offices except for the one in the centre. This was the *sacellum*, the shrine, in which sacred cult statues were kept along with the unit's standards when the men were not out on campaign. Below the *sacellum* there was often a cellar or pit used for storage of unit funds and the soldiers' pay and savings. The idea was that the valuables enjoyed not only temporal, but also divine protection – so woe betide any intruder as he might face the retribution of both men and gods! Across the courtyard the main door of the hall faced the *via praetoria*, leading to the main gate which in turn faced in the direction of an expected attack. An enemy arriving at the main gate would therefore be invited to look straight into the *sacellum*. Upon seeing the mighty gods of Rome he would then abandon all hope and retreat in disorder – at least that was the theory!

The largest and most sophisticated headquarters building in Yorkshire was in the fortress at York.[66] Parts have been excavated under York Minster where they can still be seen. This was a stone structure of about the year 100 and it is worth stressing here that the mortared stone wall was introduced to Britain by the Romans. It allowed the construction of buildings of far greater architectural ambition than anything seen hitherto. The space for the York headquarters was a square of sides *c.*78.5m long. The aisled hall (basilica) on the north-east side of the courtyard measured *c.*68m × 32.5m. The height of the hall is difficult to estimate, but 20m or more to the top of a gabled roof is not impossible. By way of comparison the height of the nave vault in the Minster today is about 30m. In the hall there were sixteen free-standing columns, a row of eight on each side, supporting the walls of the central nave. The lower part of one column (the north-westernmost on the south-west side of the nave) can still be seen in its original position in the Minster Foundations. A more or less complete column (the north-westernmost on the north-east

Illus. 5.11   York: reconstruction of the fortress headquarters, looking east.

side of the nave) was found in excavation where it had fallen, perhaps in the late ninth century. It stands *c*.7.7m high with a shaft 0.88m in diameter. The column, the only complete example from a Roman aisled hall in Britain, has been re-erected outside the south door of the Minster and gives some hint of the grandeur of the building from which it comes.

The character of the accommodation in a fortress or fort was closely related to the organisation of the Roman army with a strict hierarchy of space descending from the large house occupied by the commanding officer down to the cramped pair of barrack rooms occupied by the eight men of the *contubernium*. The commanding officer's house (*praetorium*) usually stood next to the headquarters, to one side or behind it. It was a large and luxurious establishment built around a courtyard in Mediterranean style with private baths and heated rooms. One gets the impression that to attract suitable high-ranking individuals to command the auxiliary regiments in remote provinces like Britain it was necessary, at the very least, to give them and their families a nice house to live in. Excavated CO's houses known at Yorkshire's forts are of various periods. The most complete plans belong to a second- third-century example from Templeborough[67] and to an early fourth-century example at Ilkley.[68]

The men were accommodated in barracks, long low buildings usually divided up into ten pairs of rooms for a century of eighty men, although practice varied. The pairs of rooms were used for sleeping, storage of kit and for eating meals as there was no communal mess hall. Cooking was done on hearths in the rooms and in ovens set into the ramparts. At the end of each barrack block, nearest the defences, there was a small suite of rooms for the centurion and his family.

No complete plans of barracks are known from the York fortress, but their remains in the form of beam slots and post-holes for vanished timbers have been found at several sites.[69] It is possible to estimate that each barrack was 78.5m long and a pair, including the alley between them, was 25m wide; each group of eight men had about 28m^2 of accommodation. From demolition debris we know that barrack walls were usually plastered and given simple painted designs based on red stripes. Many forts in the Yorkshire region have also produced evidence for conquest period barracks. For example, at Slack as many as six timber barracks were excavated in 1913–15.[70] There was also a pair of stone-walled barracks, built back to back, with evidence for the verandah in front of the men's rooms, a very characteristic feature of these buildings. Doorways to the rooms were identified on the basis of worn thresholds, but it was not possible to say that there were the standard ten pairs. At Brough on Humber fort there were probably rooms of the standard number and type in the barracks,[71] but at Hayton, where most of a barrack block was excavated, there seem to have been only seven pairs of rooms,[72] a small indication that within apparent uniformity one can often find peculiarities which make each fort slightly different from the others.

In addition to the troops' accommodation, other military buildings included workshops, for making and repairing equipment, and the granaries which were designed to hold the large quantities of food needed by a unit of soldiers. It has been calculated that an auxiliary soldier needed a minimum of 0.9kg of grain per day for bread, porridge etc and so a cohort of 480 men needed 432kg per day.[73] In addition, for each horse in a cavalry unit 1.5kg dry weight of barley was needed per day and in winter also 4.5kg of hay. The Roman granary was a great improvement on the Iron Age storage pit as a means of keeping food both fresh and accessible. A granary was constructed with thick walls and a heavy roof so as to provide insulation against excessive heat; this was also facilitated by a floor raised off the ground to allow circulation of air below it. In addition, the raised floor was an obstacle to invasion by vermin. Timber granaries are known in late first- and early second-century forts in Yorkshire, for example at Castleford (Fort II) where the building was immediately north of the headquarters and faced the *via principalis*.[74] It measured at least 21m long by c.10m wide and the floor was raised on posts set into slots running across the width of the building. By the end of the first century the building was replaced by one of stone which provided more effective insulation and fire prevention; this was one of the few pre-Hadrianic stone buildings in the region apart from the military bath houses. Probably the same size as its predecessor, the stone granary seems to have had a

Illus. 5.12 York:
the sewer serving the
legionary fortress baths.
(© York Archaeological
Trust)

gabled entrance of some pretension supported on four columns resting on large blocks.

That Roman military granaries were not always successful in keeping their contents in good condition was shown by discoveries at Coney Street, York, just outside the fortress.[75] On the basis of surviving slots into which beams supporting the walls had once been set, it was evident that there had been two successive late first- to early second-century timber structures standing on the north-east bank of the River Ouse. In deposits associated with the earlier building remains there was cereal grain, but more remarkable was the large quantity of well-preserved grain beetles. An uncontrollable infestation had probably led to demolition of the building after which the ground was sealed with a thick layer of clay before a new granary was erected in its place. In the beam slots of the second building a large amount of charred grain was found which is thought to have resulted from an accidental fire, a hazard to which timber structures were always prone.

Finally in this survey we must visit the bath house which of all Roman buildings, whether in a military or civilian context, can be said to epitomise traditional Roman culture and ways of life. They were not only used for washing, but also for a range of games, sports and other social activities; one might think of the baths as 'leisure centres' in modern terms. Fortresses had sufficient space to accommodate the baths within the defences, but fort bath houses were usually placed outside the gates. Because of the problems of managing heat and water in a timber building, bath houses were usually built in stone.

In the York fortress the bath house occupied a large plot of $c.9100m^2$ on the south-east side of the *praetentura*. Little is known in detail about the structures within it, although the earliest are pre-Hadrianic. What has been studied, however, and, remarkably, still survives is the main sewer, located today below the north side of Church Street.[76] The principal channel, fed by a number of side channels, was found running for some 44m on a north-west / south-east line. Constructed from massive blocks of Millstone Grit and limestone, the sewer is just large enough for a person to crawl along – in Roman times slaves would have been sent down through man holes to clean it out. The sewer's function was to remove dirty water and other waste from the baths and latrines, and then discharge them in the river. A possible source of the water used in the baths was suggested by examination of the silt deposited in the sewer which, surprisingly perhaps, produced the seeds and pollen of plants which prefer limestone to the clay of York.[77] This suggests the existence of a system of pipes and siphons to bring water by force of gravity from the nearest limestone country, either in the Tadcaster area some 20km away to the south-west or perhaps somewhere near Malton, 26km to the north-east.

Fort baths were supplied with water piped from local springs and they were usually sited near to a river or stream which served as a natural sewer. For example, at Slack, the baths lay immediately east of the fort above a stream to the south-east. At Catterick the bath house lay in the annexe east of the fort and near to the River Swale. The baths at Templeborough lay outside the north-west gate near the River Rother. At Castleford the bath house lay in an annexe to the north of the fort, close to the Aire. The early Roman bath houses at Catterick,[78] Castleford[79] and Templeborough[80] were built on a simple plan in which bathers proceeded from one end of the building to the other. First of all, they removed their clothes in the changing room (*apodyterium*) and left their slaves to look after them. They then worked up a sweat, perhaps, by exercise such as weight lifting or wrestling, or by sitting in a heated room, the *caldarium*. Templeborough appears to have had an additional, and

Illus. 5.13 Castleford: the baths in the fort annexe looking north-west with the caldarium centre and tepidarium above. (© ASWYAS)

unusual, circular *caldarium* detached from the main baths block. A furnace, stoked by slaves, provided the hot air which circulated under the floor of the *caldarium* in what is known as a hypocaust. Sweating opened up the pores in the skin and brought the dirt to the surface. After oiling themselves our bathers would scrape the sweat and dirt off with a metal tool called a strigil. They might then go and have a warm bath in the *tepidarium* or plunge into a cold bath in the *frigidarium*. The cold water closed up the pores again, got the blood circulating and imparted a pleasant glow to the skin. Finally, our bathers rubbed themselves down with nice smelling oils and scents or perhaps employed a professional masseur to do it for them.

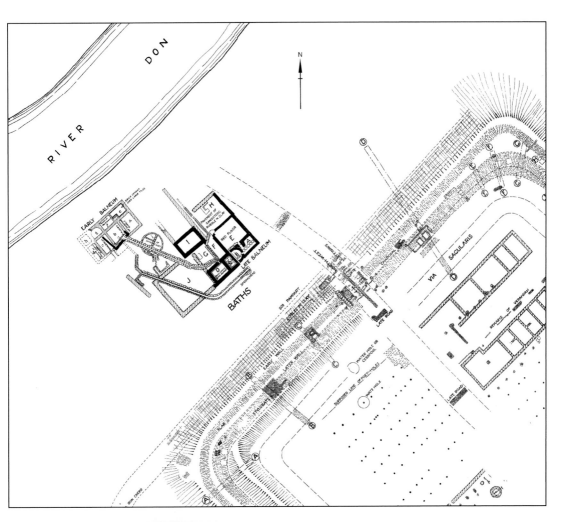

Illus. 5.14 Plan of the early and later Roman baths ('balnea') at Templeborough between the River Don and the north-west defences of the fort (after May 1922).

Illus. 5.15 Cawthorn: cross-section through the inner rampart of Fort D showing stacked turves. (Photo: P. Ottaway)

The defences

Around the perimeter of a fort or fortress ran the defences. In the late first century they usually consisted of a ditch, or ditches, and on the inside a rampart largely composed of material dug out of the ditch. The York fortress rampart was built up to a height of about 3m and was approximately 6m wide, dimensions which are typical of the fort ramparts as well.[81] The York rampart also had a stable base of oak logs, and above this it was strengthened with timber strapping and bands of turf; it was also faced with turf. A similar approach to construction was taken elsewhere. At Templeborough, the earliest fort defences in Yorkshire had a rampart base of 'hard clay and cobbles' below turves to a surviving height of c.3m at the time of May's excavations.[82] At Ilkley the clay rampart rested on a base of flat stones whilst at Slack the rampart is reported to have been composed of 'piled sods' resting on a stone base.[83]

At Cawthorn, the two forts have some of the best-preserved earthen defences in the Roman Empire and it is still possible to get a good impression of what they originally looked like.[84] Fort A has a single ditch c.4.25m wide and 2m deep, and Fort D as seen today has a double ditch, except on the north side where no ditch was needed as there is a steep drop. In the event of attack, the platform between the two ditches served as a killing ground for anyone who had negotiated the outer ditch. The ditches of Fort D had a so-called 'Punic' profile in which the outer face is steeper than the inner. This meant it was relatively easy for an attacker to jump into, but if he then wished to beat a hasty retreat, it was much more difficult to get out of. Although not clearly present at Cawthorn, another common feature in fort ditches is a narrow slot dug along the bottom which made it easier to clean with a spade. In addition an attacker turning quickly to retreat risked getting his foot stuck in the slot and twisting his ankle – hence it is often known as an 'ankle-breaker'. Excavations at Fort D at Cawthorn in 2000 revealed the inner rampart constructed largely of stacked turves and it is a testimony to how good a job the Romans did that it still stands to a height of 1.5m and width of 5m after nearly 2000 years.

At the rear, the base of a rampart was usually vertical for about 1m. Steps were placed at intervals to allow access to a timber walkway along the top which was protected by a timber palisade. At Brough on Humber it was shown that to ensure solidity of the structure the principal posts supporting the palisade were set in a ground beam before the rampart was built up around them.[85] A fort usually had four gates, one on each side, opening on to the main streets. There would have been a tower on each side of the gate and the rampart walkway continued through the towers and across the top of the gate. At intervals around the circuit there were timber observation towers.

Any replacement of timber structures in stone in the forts, whether on the defences or internally, usually began to take place in the second half of the second century. At Malton, Corder thought a stone wall had been added to the fort defences in the reign of Trajan (98–117), but the sequence of structures found in his excavations at the north-east gate and its dating is hard to make sense of from the published report.[86] However, the early addition of a wall to the defences at Malton is not quite so unusual as it would once have seemed in light of recent evidence from York.

The stone defences of the fortress at York

The question of when the timber structures on the defences of the York fortress were replaced in stone is one of the more taxing in Romano-British archaeology, but its resolution shows us that even well-known historic monuments can still provide us with surprises.

The fortress walls and their associated interval towers exhibit two principal styles of construction. The first, which primarily concerns us here, existed in the walls and towers on the south-west and north-west sides of the fortress, and also on the north-east side between the north corner and the north-east gate and in a short stretch south-west of the south-east gate. Fine stretches of wall standing to near its full original height (c.5m) can be seen today in the Museum Gardens. There is no distinct plinth at the base and at the rear the wall face has been left roughly finished as it would have been entirely obscured by the earthen rampart piled up behind it. At a height of about 2.3m the outer facing stones are interrupted by a horizontal band of five tile courses. At the top of the wall, below the (missing) parapet, there was a cornice of tiles, a few fragments of which still survive, stepped out, one above the other.

On the north-west, north-east and (though none has been seen) probably south-east sides of the defences the stone towers were about 6m square, and set wholly behind the wall; they were like those in more or less every first- and second-century fort in Britain. On the south-west side of the fortress, however, the towers represent a much higher level of architectural ambition. Projecting outwards from the fortress wall line, there were great polygonal towers at the west and south corners – the former still visible as the Multangular Tower – and between the corners there were six projecting interval towers; similar towers may have flanked the south-west gate, but have not been seen. These towers are massive structures; the interval towers measured c.21m × 10.5m and the corner towers were c.25m long and c.15m wide. In every respect, the south-west front of the fortress seems intended to impress all who saw it, whether visitors arriving in York by river or residents in the settlement on the south-west bank. What then was the historical context?

It was once thought that the walling and towers just described belonged to the late third or early fourth century and they were often designated 'Constantinian', thereby associating them with an emperor whose reign began in York in 306. The basis for this date was primarily the resemblance between the towers on the south-west front and projecting towers – albeit much smaller – on late Roman fort defences elsewhere in the empire including in Britain at Cardiff Castle, for example. A review by the present author, based on the limited amounts of pottery and coins from various excavations of the ditches and rampart on the fortress defences, suggested a late second- or early third-century date.[87] However, this would still imply that the original clay, turf and timber defences were maintained for at least a hundred years after Cerialis's time since there was no earlier circuit of walls which had been demolished as was also once thought.

There is some work in stone on the York fortress defences which can be dated, by pottery associated with construction, to the early second century, probably the reign of Trajan (98–117). This includes an interval tower near the east corner and the east corner tower itself (the remains of both are still visible), and possibly the south-east gate. A large (but incomplete) inscribed tablet dated to 107–08, found in King's Square near the gate site may have commemorated its construction.[88] What has (until recently) seemed curious, however, is that the Roman army should have chosen to begin reconstruction in stone in one of the least prominent parts of the fortress instead of on the highly visible south-west side where the main gate stood.

In an attempt to resolve the question of the date of the Multangular Tower, excavations in 2002–04 as part of York Archaeological Trust's St Leonard's Hospital project, opened a trench inside it. In the course the work two timber

Illus. 5.16   York: the Multangular Tower, the west corner of the legionary fortress. (Photo: P. Ottaway)

Illus. 5.17   York: the fortress wall, detail of the exterior face with the cornice of tiles originally below the parapet which does not now survive. (Photo: P. Ottaway)

piles from under the Roman concrete foundations were recovered. In spite of the uncertainty over the dates previously claimed for the tower, it came as quite a shock when radiocarbon determinations on these piles suggested the trees (alder) from which they had been made were felled sometime between the years 80 and 110.[89] It looks now as though reconstruction in stone on the fortress defences did begin, as one would logically think it would have done, on the south-west front before, presumably, taking in other areas, although the work was apparently left incomplete until the mid- to late second century. The important question which remains is what was the model for the towers which appear to be unlike any others in a Roman military fortification in the western empire for another 150 years or so? Projecting towers are known at town gates in Gaul and Italy, although the polygonal form seen at York is highly unusual. York, it seems, may have been something of an outpost of the empire, but it could still find itself a place where new ideas on military architecture were pioneered. A place where, moreover, a new technique of construction using small stone facing blocks with intervening tile courses was adopted, a technique which even in Gaul, which one might have thought more advanced than Britain, seems to have appeared no earlier than c.100.[90]

The question of the historical context of the Multangular Tower and contemporary walling on the fortress defences has now taken us to a time span different from any previously considered, but York does now fall more or less into line with the other permanent fortresses in Britain, at Caerleon and Chester, where work in stone on the defences was undertaken in the early second century. One possible date for reconstruction at York might lie in about the year 105, following the abandonment of most of Agricola's forts in

Scotland and Roman withdrawal to the Tyne–Solway line. As part of a new strategy for the garrisoning of Britain one can envisage a decision being made to keep York as the legionary base in the north-east rather than somewhere further north, a decision set in stone, as it were, by the new construction work on the defences. This may well have included the south-east gate, perhaps commemorated by the King's Square tablet, and, within the fortress, the construction of the headquarters building. The reason that the work in stone on the defences was apparently left incomplete may have been the withdrawal of the Ninth Legion from York at some time between 107–08 (the date of the King's Square tablet) and Hadrian's visit to Britain in 120.

Outside the base: annexes, *canabae* and *vici*

Attached to the defences of a Roman fort there was often what is described as an annexe which was itself provided with defences, although perhaps not quite of the same standard as the base itself. In addition to housing the baths, as at Castleford, annexes were probably used for such things as lodging troops in transit, storage of equipment, stabling horses and accommodation of animals destined for the dinner table. The annexe might be quite substantial; that attached to the east side of Fort A at Cawthorn was almost as big as the fort itself. At Catterick what is usually described as the annexe lay east of the fort. It not only housed the baths, but also, not far away from it, just the other side of a ditch, was a large midden measuring *c*.71m × 40m and up to 1.5m deep – imagine the smell the bathers might sometimes have had to put up with! The midden accumulated from about the year 80, when the fort was founded, until the early Hadrianic period.[91] Amongst the finds was a large quantity of leather items including discarded footwear.

A Roman fort occupied for any length of time was hardly ever isolated in its surrounding landscape. In most cases small settlements – *vici* – grew up fairly quickly outside them, usually extending along one or more of the main approach roads. They were initially, at any rate, under military supervision, but unlike an annexe they had buildings suitable as residences for soldiers' families and other camp followers, as well as commercial and manufacturing facilities. Testimony to the heterodox nature of Roman religion, there would also have been a number of shrines to those gods favoured by the soldiers for their private devotions in addition to those worshipped at official ceremonies in the fort itself.

In the case of the fortress at York a settlement, located primarily on the south-east and south-west sides of the fortress is sometimes referred to as the *canabae*, which means 'booths' or 'stalls'. The term was used at fortresses elsewhere in the empire, although we do not know if the Romans ever used it at York. However, as described by RCHME in *Eburacum*, using a delightful turn of phrase, it no doubt 'housed the motley crowd of tradesmen and purveyors wont to gather about any large military force'.[92]

The better known fort *vici* of the late first to early second century in Yorkshire include Slack which covered an area of *c*.3.6ha.[93] Now partly under the M62, it stood north-west of the fort and was traversed by the main Roman York–Manchester road alongside which a number of buildings have been identified. Unusually for a *vicus*, it was defended by a bank and ditches. At Catterick, in addition to the annexe, there was civilian settlement along Dere Street for over 2km south of the Swale.[94] Excavations at Bainesse (Illus. 5.6, 10a–b) revealed three timber buildings of the pre-Hadrianic period which were of a type common in Roman Britain in having a long and narrow rectangular plan, hence the term 'strip building'. They were set out, as was usual, end-on to the road so as to maximise the number which could be accommodated on the frontage. As there was usually a shop at the front of the building this made sound commercial sense.

Some 36km south of Catterick lay the fort at Roecliffe, to the east of which was the *vicus*.[95] Timber buildings faced an east–west road leading to the north gate of the fort. Geophysical survey showed that settlement also extended along a road heading north to a crossing over the River Ure and picked up again on the north bank. In a relatively short time it seems that quite a large area had been taken over by what would have been a substantial body of camp followers. There was evidence for metalworking and the finds included pieces of leather tent panels, probably discarded during the repair process.

Further south again at Newton Kyme the enclosures and side streets of a large *vicus* extending for *c*.550m south of the fort have been identified from aerial photography. At Castleford the sites excavated in the *vicus* lay south of the fort on the Doncaster–York road (Illus. 5.5). On Sites 1 and 10 the earliest occupation was dated *c*.71–86 (*Vicus* 1).[96] On Site 1 the road itself was found with a timber-lined drain down its west side. As at Catterick, there were timber strip buildings end-on to the road and also metalworking hearths. In about the years 86–90 these buildings were swept away for a reconstruction of the *vicus* (*Vicus* 2). Five timber strip buildings were recorded, each consisting of a living space and an enclosed open yard behind; a greater air of permanence was confirmed by two properly surfaced alleyways which ran between the buildings. On Site 10 *Vicus* 1 was also represented by timber structures and again there was reconstruction for *Vicus* 2 to create three strip buildings, two with hearths and ovens. An east–west gravelled road completed the redevelopment.

At Doncaster late first- and early second-century occupation material has been found along the line of the Roman approach road from the south-east, including traces of a building close to the road at 8–10 High Street, *c*.50m south-east of the fort (Illus. 5.4).[97] Finally, at Malton, traces of timber structures of a late first- or early second-century *vicus* (or annexe) have been located south-east of the fort in Orchard Field.[98] This was probably defended by a turf rampart and ditch of which a short stretch running roughly north-east/south-west was located in excavations in 1970 (Illus. 7.9).

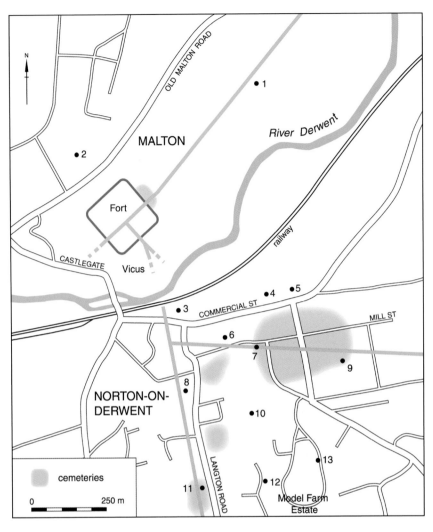

Illus. 5.18 Malton and Norton-on-Derwent: plan showing Roman sites referred to in the text. Key: 1, Rugby Club; 2, Aurelius Macrinus tombstone; 3, Goldsmith's inscription; 4, Kiln (?), Commercial St; 5, Mars Rigas inscription; 6, Wood St, roadside ditch (2007); 7, Roman road at Bright Steels (1994); 8, St Nicholas St / St Peter's St (1951); 9, Eastfield (1946–47); 10, Kiln at Community Primary School; 11, cemetery at 98 Langton Road; 12, Vicarage Garden (1950) / Grove Bungalow; 13, Howe Road pottery kilns.

Roman roads in the Yorkshire region

Of all the engineering achievements of the Romans in Britain, roads are possibly the best known if only because their lines have often survived to become part of the modern world. They can be recognised on a map because they are straight and because their names, acquired in post-Roman times, often end in 'street', e.g. 'Dere Street' and 'Ryknield Street' (south of Templeborough).

The Roman surveyor's eye for landscape was excellent and has rarely been improved upon. Because they did not have to worry about native property rights they could always choose the best and straightest route from A to B. It can be shown, for example, that the main Lincoln–Doncaster road took no account of earlier enclosures at Rossington (Illus. 4.9). This is also the case west of South Elmsall where a link road from Templebrough to Castleford has been recognised heading for Thorp Audlin at the River Went crossing.[99]

However, as well as attempting to minimise journey times for soldiers who had to travel on foot, the Roman surveyors were careful to choose routes which ran on relatively elevated ground in order to ensure good drainage. One can still see this, for example, on much of the road which follows the Roman line between Doncaster and Tadcaster, known appropriately today as Roman Ridge. It sticks largely to the elevated Magnesian Limestone belt avoiding the low-lying ground of the Humberhead Levels and Vale of York.

Although we assume that the principal Roman roads in Yorkshire belong to a period immediately following the Conquest, this is difficult to prove. Excavation of Roman roads usually produces little datable material. Roadside ditches sometimes contain artefacts, but these only date their infilling not the initial digging out. At Catterick, Dere Street was found both at Catterick Triangle, c.1.4km south of the Swale and on two sites north of the Swale (Illus. 5.6, 3–5); at all three a late first- or early second-century date is suggested for the first metalled surface.[100] This corresponds to the date for Dere Street and the first bridge over the Tees further north at Piercebridge.[101] At York the main road from the south-west was excavated at Wellington Row, on the south-west bank of the Ouse, close to the river crossing.[102] Pottery from associated deposits suggests the first metalled surface, again, belonged to the late first or early second century, but this does not necessarily mean the whole of the road along the line from Tadcaster was constructed at this time. On the Brough on Humber to York road at Shiptonthorpe, where a section was dug across its line, pottery from related features suggested metalling was not laid down permanently until the first half of the second century.[103] What the evidence, such as it is, suggests is that it may have been some time before the Romans were happy to turn routes of conquest into proper roads.

Road construction was a considerable enterprise and so it is not surprising that the network took time to complete. In the fifty years or so after the conquest about 650km of main roads, often 10m or more wide, were constructed in Yorkshire demanding vast quantities of materials and a large labour force. Whilst skilled construction work was undertaken by legionaries, fetching and carrying would have been the job of prisoners or local people commandeered for the purpose. An estimate of the material required for a 22km stretch of road, 4–5m wide, between Brough on Noe and Melandra Roman forts in Derbyshire arrived at a total of c.40,000m^3 of stone, gravel etc.[104] It was also estimated that the work took 500 men about eight–nine weeks after an initial seven weeks work clearing a passage through scrub and forest.

The archaeological evidence for Yorkshire's Roman roads shows that construction was undertaken in much the same way as it was elsewhere in Britain. Preparation usually involved careful excavation work to ensure the ground was as level as possible. Other preliminaries might include laying out the line with, for example, two low stone banks 3m apart, as was seen in a 10m stretch on Roman Ridge 2km south of Aberford, or 7m apart with a central line as well, as at Hazel Wood 1km north of Aberford.[105] On occasions, where the ground was unstable elaborate precautions would be needed to prevent subsidence. The consolidation of the ground near the fort at Adel (Leeds) has already been noted and at Scaftworth on the Nottinghamshire side of the River Idle at Bawtry, a wooden corduroy structure of turf and alder wood – well-suited to wet environments – was laid down on marshy ground preparatory to building a stretch of the Lincoln–Doncaster road.[106]

Standing water was the great enemy of good road surfaces, soon causing pot holes, especially if allowed to freeze and thaw regularly. Drainage was therefore crucial and so to ensure the surface was cambered on each side, the lowest layer of road make-up was constructed as a low mound. Locally available materials were used for road construction so that, for example, the mound was composed of clay on Dere Street at Catterick Triangle, of large cobbles at Wellington Row in York, and crushed limestone at the Roman Ridge sites referred to above. In the west of the county, on the road across the Pennines from Slack to Castleshaw the base was composed of large slabs of sandstone.[107] Wherever the roads survive in reasonable condition it can be seen that above the base layer there were hard-packed layers of fine gravel, limestone or other suitable materials giving a smooth surface from which water could run off into a ditch or gutter on each side.

Whilst small becks could be forded, Roman roads had, at intervals, to cross major rivers and here bridges were required. Good examples in our area, which have been studied in detail, are the two which crossed the Tees at Piercebridge.[108] The first bridge with a span of c.70m was probably constructed entirely in timber, surviving as piles driven into the river bed. Timber piles from a rather smaller bridge, probably more typical of the region, have been found on the road from Bawtry to Doncaster in the River Torne near Rossington Bridge.[109]

Although the main Roman roads were initially built for the army, they soon assumed an economic role in opening up the countryside, thereby linking farmland with consumers in the forts and associated settlements. Roads also encouraged travel in a more general sense and allowed the spread of Roman culture represented in the archaeological record by, for example, pottery of Roman type and burials in Roman style. The great highways were supplemented by a network of minor roads and tracks many of which had their origins in pre-Roman times. They often existed as little more than a rough cobbled surface laid to keep the feet of humans and animals reasonably dry.

6 | The Yorkshire Region in the Early Roman Period

Settlement and landscape

A time-traveller returning to Yorkshire in the Roman period would soon notice that the population was very small compared to what we are used to in the twenty-first century. Estimates of the population of Roman Britain as a whole vary, but between three and four million seems most widely accepted.[1] In 1974 the historic county of Yorkshire alone had about five million people, but in Roman times it is unlikely to have had more than about 250,000 at any one time: rather less than present-day Bradford. Furthermore, the Roman population was not evenly spread through the region, being densest in areas best suited to mixed arable and pastoral agriculture. As we have seen in the previous chapter, it is in those areas that enclosed landscapes had begun to develop in the Iron Age. The principal problem of pinning down their development in the early Roman period, the first fifty years or so after the conquest, is a lack of reliable dating material. Enclosure ditches and related features do not usually produce much in the way of finds and any pottery is usually little different from what was made in the pre-conquest period. Roman types such as samian, mortaria and amphorae are usually very scarce in rural areas until the middle of the second century.

An exception to what we may assume was a continuing and unbroken process of landscape development after the conquest may perhaps be identified around Stanwick. The great enclosure was abandoned at about the time of the Roman conquest and the two settlements nearby at Melsonby and Scotch Corner, which also produced unusual artefact assemblages, were no longer occupied either. This was also the case at the site of another enclosure and roundhouse of Late Iron Age date at Rock Castle, c.5km south of Stanwick.[2] Whilst the emergence and demise of settlements all over the region may have been quite a common event as a result of exhaustion of land and other factors, it is none the less possible that the Roman army carried out some form of

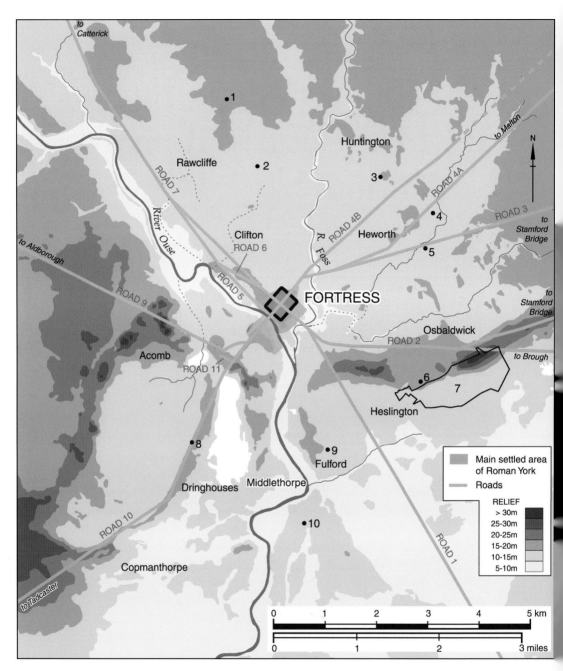

Illus. 6.1   Map showing immediate location of Roman York with relief, principal Roman roads and sites referred to in text. Key: 1, Rawcliffe Moor; 2, Bootham Stray, Roman camps; 3, Huntington South Moor, Roman camps; 4, Ryethorpe Grange Farm; 5, Apple Tree Farm, Heworth; 6, Field Lane, Heslington; 7, Heslington East; 8, Dringhouses Roman settlement; 9, Fulford (coin moulds site); 10, Naburn.

forcible removal of the Brigantian elite and their retinue not only at Stanwick itself but in their estates in the immediate area.

In the environs of York one might also expect to see some immediate impact of the Roman conquest on landscape and settlement. However, one can point to little decisive evidence on the ground. In due course, a pre-Roman settlement may be found in York's historic core, but at present all one can say is that the Roman army did not enter a completely deserted landscape on the banks of the River Ouse. Well-preserved organic material, including plant remains and snail shells, from some of the earliest deposits excavated at York suggests a mixture of woodland scrub and cleared agricultural land.[3] Deposits from sites close to the south-west bank of the Ouse have, as one would expect, produced the remains of organisms which are usually found on river banks, and in marshes and ponds. However, many of the wetland plant species recorded are rather low-growing which may indicate that the land was used for grazing by native farmers.

In a zone c.3–5km from the city centre settled areas had mixed fortunes in the early Roman period, probably due to local environmental factors rather than the impact of the Roman army. For example, at Rawcliffe Moor, north of the city, the settlement noted in Chapter 4 does not seem to have survived the conquest, perhaps because the clay made farming too difficult. At Heslington the late Iron Age field system fell out of use shortly after the conquest, perhaps due to soil exhaustion and, in the low-lying areas at the foot of the York moraine, due to flooding. At Naburn, south of the city, the Iron Age field system survived the conquest, but not the settlement represented by roundhouses.[4]

In assessing the impact of the army on the area around York and the other forts we should consider how the supply of food and raw materials was managed. Local sources would have been preferred, if only for simple cost reasons, and archaeological evidence comes from the grain from York and the animal bone from Castleford already mentioned. Local sources were also preferred for commodities which were expensive relative to their value and/or difficult to transport. These would have included minerals, such as metal ores, and building materials, including stone and timber. One approach the army might take to ensure adequate supplies was to take over an area of land and manage it directly. This is a practice suggested by inscriptions from Dalmatia and Spain which refer to a *prata legionis*, 'the legion's meadow', perhaps used primarily for grazing horses and cattle.[5] By the mid-second century land under legionary control seems to have been referred to as a *territorium*, perhaps because it now included a civilian population and had wider functions than hitherto. The extent of land under direct legionary control is hard to estimate but evidence from Spain suggests it could have been as much as 500km^2. On Bramham Moor, west of Tadcaster, at a distance of c.15km from York, two branches of the York–Ilkley Roman road have been identified and between them three secondary Roman roads or tracks.[6] All these roads run east–west, perpendicular to a major north–south road (now known as The Rudgate). They appear to be later than cropmarks representing field systems thought to be of Iron Age date and more or less contemporary with the Rudgate, thought to be of the conquest period. It has been suggested that there might be evidence here for a Roman re-organisation of the landscape on good agricultural land on the Magnesian Limestone, associated with the requirements of the army for grain. However, whilst this is an intriguing possibility, the location and size of any *prata / territorium* managed by the legion at York remains unknown.

Elsewhere in the region developments in landscape and settlement securely datable to the early Roman period are rare. A common factor linking those sites where developments can be recognised is proximity to forts or Roman roads, presumably because those living in the immediate area could get access to pottery of Roman type more easily than those living in remoter places. For example, at Ferrybridge on the Magnesian Limestone, only 4km east of the main Doncaster–Castleford road, it is possible to say that the principal Iron Age boundaries south and west of the henge were redefined in the early Roman period with the amalgamation of land units (Illus. 4.7, Phase 4).[7] Some of the Iron Age roundhouses are thought to have survived until *c.*100, but another within a discrete enclosure is thought to have been early Roman in origin; it contained a post-built structure with a rectangular plan – an early example for the region.

In east Yorkshire also there are sites at which early post-conquest developments can be identified, including construction in Roman style. This

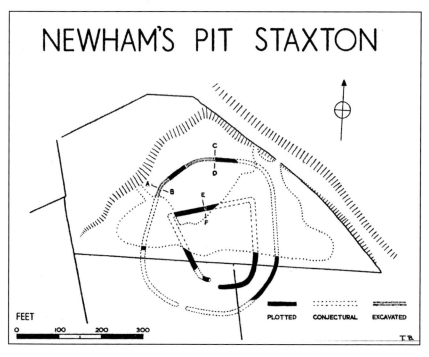

Illus. 6.2 Plan of early Roman site at Newham's Pit, Staxton. (from Brewster 1957, © Yorkshire Archaeological Society).

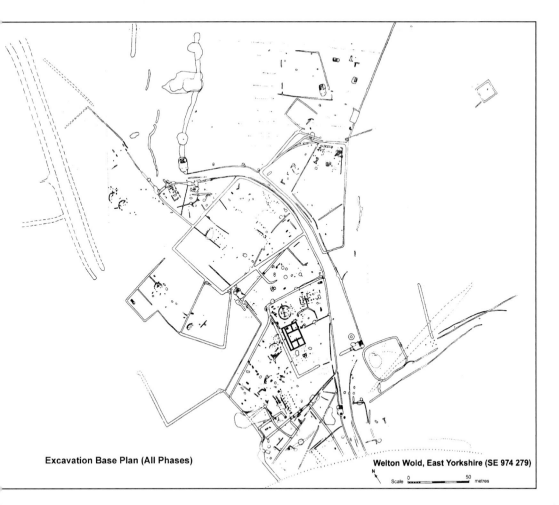

Excavation Base Plan (All Phases)

Welton Wold, East Yorkshire (SE 974 279)

N

Scale 0   50   metres

Illus. 6.3   Welton
Roman villa: plan
of the site based on
excavation and aerial
photography. The main
house is just below
centre and a roundhouse
lies immediately to the
north of it. (© Rodney
Mackey)

can be explained by their being close to Roman roads, in the cases of Langton
and Seamer, and in the case of Staxton to a former Roman fort. The Roman
site at Langton lies on sandstone on the southern slope of Langton Wold, *c.*1km
east of Langton village (Illus. 7.16).[8] Excavations in 1926 and 1930 covered a
large area measuring *c.*192m east–west by 90m north–south (*c.*1.7ha), although
by no means all of this was examined in detail. The principal discovery was
a late Roman villa (see Chapters 9 and 10), but the earliest evidence for
settlement was a small (0.12ha) rectangular, ditched enclosure, divided into
two halves, probably of the early second century. A similar (unexcavated)
enclosure appears on aerial photographs of Whin Fields 0.75km to the east.[9]

North-east of Langton, flanked by watercourses and on sandy deposits just
below the northern scarp of the Wolds, lies Staxton, 8km from the coast.[10] A
double-ditched enclosure of an unusual polygonal shape, measuring *c.*110m ×
94m overall, seems likely to have been a successor to the fort recently identified
here. The site had been partly damaged by quarrying, but within the enclosure
there were traces of three roundhouses occupied in the late first to mid-second

centuries. Pottery included sherds of samian, mortaria and amphorae which may indicate a continuing exchange of commodities with the military after the fort itself had been abandoned. A little to the north-east of Staxton, on the north side of the Vale of Pickering, lies Crossgates, Seamer, an area where archaeological discoveries covering the whole of the Roman period have been found, many of them during gravel quarrying between the late 1940s and mid-1960s.[11] West of the quarried area, at Crab Lane a ditched enclosure of the Iron Age was located in 2000 and within it were the remains of a building of rectangular plan with stone foundations (19m × 9m), dated to the late first century. Whether the building was of stone throughout is unknown, but the use of stone even for foundations is unusually early for the region and suggests a precocious knowledge of Roman building techniques.[12]

On the southern tip of the Wolds at Welton near Brough on Humber extensive excavations in the 1970s revealed a most important sequence which began with a Late Iron Age enclosure of familiar type containing a roundhouse.[13] In the late first or early second century, within a new rectangular ditched enclosure, the farmstead acquired a house of which the stone footings survived. Whether the owner was a native or an incomer, a proximity to the Roman centre at Brough may in some way explain why this house was the earliest example in the region of a 'corridor house'. It had five ground floor rooms and a corridor which, as is common in many Roman houses, ran along one side. A corridor allowed one to move from one part of a house to another without going from room to room thereby allowing a measure of privacy for the residents. A roundhouse was sited immediately to the north of the house, perhaps the residence of the household slaves. These two buildings lay at the centre of a complex of other enclosures and buildings which included a large aisled barn. There was a well almost 30m deep, similar to others on the Wolds chalk where water was often scarce.

At the nearby Melton site already referred to, the landscape with small ditched enclosures attached to the earlier trackways clearly developed without a break from the Late Iron Age through to the mid-second century.[14] The Iron Age roundhouses disappeared, but in an enclosure defined by a 2m deep ditch south-east of the trackway junction there was a post-built structure, rectangular in plan (10m × 8m), another example of early Roman impact on the local architecture. The southern limit of the enclosed landscape and settlement zone at Melton appears to have been reached on alluvial deposits above Melton Ings, c.1.25km south of the road site.[15] Excavation in advance of a waste water treatment works revealed a north–south trackway heading for the Humber nearby and a number of other ditched enclosures, in one of which was a roundhouse gully. The palaeoenvironmental material, indicating a semi-natural environment of saltmarsh, suggested the area was not used for arable. It was probably marginal land used for a short period, probably for pasture, largely in the late first and early second centuries before flooding rendered the land unsuitable for either occupation or agriculture.

An underdeveloped economy

Even after fifty years or so of being Roman, the economy of northern Britain in the early second century was still, in our terms, highly underdeveloped. The vast majority of the population was made up of subsistence farmers who generated few surplus resources above their immediate needs. Production of other commodities such as metalwork, pottery or salt was probably carried out, for the most part, by those same farmers on a part-time basis. However, the Roman conquest of the region led to the introduction of specialists in both manufacturing and craft activities, and in the conduct of trade. They were initially associated with the army, but in due course civilians became involved and began to cluster together in towns and larger settlements. We should probably see the emergence of these specialists as linked, on the one hand, to a higher level of demand than hitherto for manufactured and traded goods, initially as a result of the military presence, and, on the other, to the introduction of new and improved technologies in, for example, metalworking and pottery making. However, after a surge of innovation in the early Roman period further technological change in Roman Britain was a very slow process.

Severe limits to the productive capacity of the Romano-British economy, whether in agriculture or other sectors, were imposed by the availability of power. Animals – principally cattle, horses, donkeys and mules – could be harnessed for pulling carts and wagons, for ploughing and for grinding grain. Water-powered mills were used on occasions for grinding grain, but although sailing ships took advantage of wind power, there were, as far as we know, no windmills. In the end, however, there is no escaping the fact that the principal source of power in the Roman world was manual labour – the arms, backs and legs of its people – from which very few were exempt.

Additional limits on the economy's productive capacity resulted from obstacles to trade whether in raw materials or finished goods. There were, first of all, the shortcomings of the transport network. Although the Romans are famous for their roads, arterial routes of any quality, especially in regions like Yorkshire, were few and archaeological evidence suggests maintenance was not always conducted regularly or to a good standard. Furthermore, roads were not lit and so unless there was moonlight, they were extremely hazardous at night. Poor weather could make even a Roman road near impassable. Water transport was vital, especially for transporting heavy goods such as building stone, but in the near absence of canals it was dependent on the rivers but the navigability of even the best of them could not be guaranteed at all times of the year.

The emperor assumed no responsibility for the economic well-being of his people and did not have an economic policy in the sense that we understand it. He was, however, concerned about raising revenue through taxation in order to pay the army and his officials. It is not known exactly what taxes people in Britain paid; taxation was not uniform throughout the empire. However, there was probably a property tax and a form of poll tax paid by citizens and non-citizens alike. It is also likely that there were customs duties on external and internal trade. Tax collection in the Roman world was usually devolved to local elites (backed up by the army) who were given a total sum to raise for the imperial treasury. They then had to decide on who paid what while no doubt creaming off a certain percentage for themselves. In theory regular censuses kept the tax rolls up to date.

The emperor's interest in the currency was in good part driven by a need to create a mechanism for converting landed wealth into tax revenues. This currency involved a much more complex and sophisticated system than that which had existed under those British kings who minted coins. At the time of the conquest the Roman system fell into two parts, one of which was based on coins made from precious metals (gold or silver) which were supposed to be worth their own weight. They were used for paying the army and were a medium for tax collection. The second part of the system consisted of low value bronze and brass coins which could be exchanged for precious metal coinage (e.g. to pay taxes) at a rate which varied from time to time. This 'small change' which the Romans introduced to Britain for the first time was, in theory at least, beneficial to the economy in allowing greater flexibility in transactions and the use of credit.

Archaeology suggests Roman coinage was used in and around the military sites from the late first century onwards and subsequently in towns and to a lesser extent in rural areas. However, the level of coin supply to Britain varied considerably over time and even in good years it seems that there was never enough for anything like a fully monetised economy.[16] Supply of coin to distant regions of the empire was always awkward because of the distance from the mints. There were only briefly mints in Britain – in the late Roman period – but otherwise Britain relied largely on mints in Gaul and in Rome itself. One has visions of a world in which wagon trains and ships loaded with chests full of coin traversed great distances on a regular basis.

Although money lending was a profitable enterprise for some in the Roman world, there were no banks of the sort we are familiar with today which took deposits from some customers and offered investment opportunities to others through financial products. In these circumstances there were limited options for making use of any surplus, or 'profit', generated by economic activity, surplus which in Britain at any rate was usually in the form of agricultural products, primarily grain, meat carcasses or livestock, and so had a limited life and could not be kept indefinitely. One option for the landowner was sale for money. Another option was to exchange surplus grain etc directly for other commodities and labour services. Whichever option was chosen, a wealthy man might well use his resources to acquire more land and establish facilities on it, such as pottery kilns, quarries, hunting grounds etc, which would yield an income for himself and his heirs. He might also engage in the construction of residential accommodation, whether in town or country, with its accompanying embellishments such as mosaics, wall paintings or sculpture. Such conspicuous consumption was considered an acceptable way of demonstrating wealth and status in the Roman world as was funding the construction of public buildings by which a man would enhance his reputation as a benefactor to his community.

However, whilst construction might boost economic development in a region like Yorkshire from time to time, the sort of underdeveloped economic system I am sketching out was subject to considerable fluctuations in the availability of resources as the dominant productive sector was agriculture, dependent in its turn on the weather and other environmental factors. One effect of these fluctuations was to enhance the difference in life chances between the wealthy few, able to survive the bad times, and the majority of the population who probably found them very hard going.

Agriculture: feeding the army and feeding the people

There is no evidence for any substantial change in the region's agricultural regime in the immediate aftermath of the Roman conquest, although, to feed the army, more land may have been brought into cultivation in certain areas. However, some of the military sites, notably Castleford and York, have produced substantial evidence for cereal and other crops, and for animal husbandry. The evidence for cereals comes, once again, largely from charred material. One of the largest and best-preserved samples for the whole of the Roman period in Yorkshire resulted from the late first-century warehouse fire at Coney Street in York.[17] Spelt wheat was the principal cereal (c.61%), followed by barley (c.25%) and rye. All these cereals may have been brought in from outside the York area to supplement what was available to the army locally. The Roman period saw an increase in the variety of weed flora in grain which probably indicates its movement over longer distances than hitherto; in the Coney Street deposit seeds of larkspur, yellow vetchling and hairy tare, not thought to have grown locally, may indicate import either from southern England or even the Continent.

An improvement in the technology of cereal-based food production in the Yorkshire region, the spread of which can probably be credited to the Roman army, was a new type of quern. The standard military 'rotary' or 'disc' quern usually has an overall diameter greater than the beehive quern — up to 500–600mm — and an upper stone which is much flatter. The lower stone has a flat base and is usually completely penetrated by the socket. These features suggest that the quern was set waist high on a wooden framework so the operator could stand rather than sit or kneel. The upper stone was, in some cases, rotated by a handle set into a socket, but in others rotated by means of a handle set in an iron band fitted around the stone as can be seen on a surviving example from Chesters fort on Hadrian's Wall. Military disc querns were often made of volcanic lava which had an advantage over local ones in sandstone of being lighter and therefore easier to transport; moreover they did not leave so much grit in the flour. The source of the lava was usually the Eiffel mountains in Germany. Imitations of military querns in local stone were made soon after the conquest, but were not readily adopted by the native population and are usually found on military or urban sites. The Romans also introduced the water mill to Britain which enabled production of meal on a considerable scale. No mill structures are known in the Yorkshire region, but millstones have been found at a number of places including forts such as Ilkley and Elslack, and rural sites near York at Heslington and Stamford Bridge.[18]

For other food plants of the early Roman period we may turn once more to Castleford where in the Fort I midden local fruits included sloe, plum and bullace which, along with the hazel nuts also found, were probably gathered in the wild rather than specifically cultivated.[19] Although we may overlook them today, and leave them to the grey squirrels, hazel nuts were probably highly prized in Roman times as a very good staple food, high in protein and fats. As Richard Mabey has noted: 'weight for weight … they contain fifty percent more protein, seven times more fat and five times more carbohydrate than hens' eggs'.[20] Wild celery and black mustard seeds may also come from food remains. Although little trace survived in the ground, vegetables such as beans, leeks and peas probably featured prominently in the diet.

It has been suggested that another agricultural improvement of Roman times, which relates primarily to the feeding of beasts, was the more efficient production of hay taken from managed meadows and grasslands. This would probably have come about in the first instance as a result of the substantial amounts of hay required as winter feed by auxiliary cavalry regiments with several hundred horses to cater for. The principal archaeological evidence for Roman haymaking takes the form of large iron scythe blades.[21]

If we look now at animal husbandry, we find that Castleford has produced the largest assemblage of late first- to early second-century animal bones from the region, and one of the largest from Britain.[22] A count of the bones of the principal meat-giving animals from Forts I and II and also from the early fort at Hayton[23] showed cattle to be far more dominant (over 60%) than in the late Iron Age bone assemblage from Dalton Parlours (see above and Table 1), although the latter may not be typical of the pre-Roman period. In *Vicus* 2 at Castleford (*Vicus* 1 produced very little bone) the percentage of cattle is slightly lower than in the fort, but beef still dominated the diet.

The cattle from Castleford were the native 'shorthorn' type, little different from those of the Iron Age with short tightly curved horns, elliptical in basal cross-section. It is estimated that adults from Fort I deposits had an average height to the withers of *c*.1.07m. This compares closely with the dwarf Dexter breed (Illus. 4.17) farmed today of which the adults weigh on average *c*.300kg, although in the Roman period 200kg–250kg is thought more likely. The Castleford sheep were small, gracile animals, again similar in size to Iron Age beasts. Their average shoulder height was *c*.0.55m–0.56m comparable to modern hill breeds

Table 1 Nos of animal bone fragments of principal meat animals in late first- to early second-century contexts (including Iron Age group from Dalton Parlours for comparative purposes) in descending order of percentage cattle.

Place	Date	Cattle	Sheep/goat	pig	Total	% cattle
Castleford Fort II	85–100	2,353	830	292	3,475	67.71
Hayton Fort	Late C1st	632	318	24	974	64.89
Castleford Fort I	71–85	6,731	2,847	1,158	10,736	62.70
Castleford Vicus 2	85–140	468	394	148	1,010	46.34
Dalton Parlours	Late Iron Age	166	495	34	695	23.88

Table 2 Height to withers of cattle from selected groups, earliest–latest
n = number in sample; n/a = data not available in publication

Site	Date	Min. (m)	Max. (m)	Mean (m)	n
Dalton Parlours	Iron Age	1.06	1.11	1.08	n/a
Castleford, Fort I	Late C1	1.01	1.17	1.07	22
Castleford, Fort II	Late C1	1.04	1.11	1.08	3
Catterick	Late C2–C3	1.02	1.17	1.10	9
York, Tanner Row	Late C2–C3	n/a	n/a	1.11	12
Castleford, Fort IV	c.250–400	1.05	1.25	1.12	9
Dalton Parlours, villa	C3–C4	1.07	1.19	1.14	n/a
Dalton Parlours, well	Late C3–C4	1.10	1.20	1.15	8
Shiptonthorpe	Largely late C3–C4	1.05	1.16	1.12	3
Catterick	Late C3-C4	1.03	1.31	1.13	25

Table 3 Height to shoulder of sheep from selected groups, earliest–latest
n = number in sample; n/a = data not available in publication

Site	Date	Min. (m)	Max. (m)	Mean (m)	n
Dalton Parlours	Iron Age	n/a	n/a	0.58	n/a
Castleford, Fort I	Late C1	0.52	0.64	0.56	33
Castleford, Fort II	Late C1	0.50	0.67	0.57	5
Castleford, Vicus 2	Late C1–mid C2	0.54	0.59	0.57	4
Castleford, Vicus III	c.140–180	0.58	0.59	0.58	2
Castleford, Fort III	c.100–250	0.55	0.57	0.56	2
York, Tanner Row	Late C2–C3	0.53	0.65	0.59	24
Castleford, Vicus 4	c.180–400	0.52	0.59	0.56	2
Castleford, Fort IV	c.250–400	0.53	0.58	0.55	4
Dalton Parlours, villa	C3–C4	n/a	n/a	0.58	n/a
Dalton Parlours, well	Late C3–C4	0.54	0.60	0.57	17
Shiptonthorpe	Late C3–C4	n/a	n/a	0.58	n/a

and the Soay and North Ronaldsay sheep which the Castleford animals would have resembled, for example in having large horns. Over the course of the Roman period in the region the average size of cattle seems to have increased very slightly, but that of sheep remained pretty much the same (Tables 2–3).

At Castleford almost all the cattle were killed when over eighteen months of age and over two-thirds were classified as adult or elderly (c.25%). This confirms that, as in the Iron Age, the beasts were multipurpose and not usually eaten until they had outlived their usefulness in other respects. Butchery practices, as well as aspects of husbandry, can be deduced from bones and Castleford appears to have been typical of Roman military sites. Animals were slaughtered and dressed on site by specialists with types of heavy choppers and cleavers not available in the pre-Roman period. Cattle long bones had their extremities removed and were split for extraction of the marrow used for soup, grease or glue. Shoulder blades pierced for suspension came from joints hung on a hook for curing which would preserve the meat whilst in storage. There is quite a wide spread of age at death for sheep at Castleford, but they were culled most frequently at their prime age for meat in the second or third year of life, although over one third were adult or old (over three years) suggesting they were frequently kept for milk or wool before slaughter. As pigs have no other significant economic use than food, the Castleford evidence is that they were slaughtered for the most part in their second year.

Table 4   Cattle age at death from Roman bone groups in Yorkshire, earliest–latest
m = months

Site	Date	0–18m	18–30m	30–36m	young adult	adult	old/senile	Total no.
Castleford, Fort I	Late C1	3	11	24	25	63	78	204
Castleford, Fort II	Late C1–c.100	0	0	3	6	19	24	52
Castleford, Fort III	c.100–250	1	0	2	2	8	8	21
York, Tanner Row	Mid C2–early C3	0	0	0	0	16	20	36
Ferrybridge, chariot burial	Late C2–early C4	22	125	62	19	2	1	231
Castleford, Fort IV	c.250–400	1	0	2	3	13	17	36

Evidence for human consumption of other mammals is slight throughout the Roman period. Although we think of hunting as a popular leisure activity amongst soldiers, Castleford produced evidence for red deer and roe deer largely in the form of antlers which had probably been gathered as raw material for manufacture of small artefacts. Otherwise hunted animals are only represented by a few hare bones.

Manufacturing and the impact of the Romans: a world of wonders

Production of manufactured goods on native sites would have continued at the same low level as before the conquest. Approaches to crafts such as pottery and metalworking probably changed very little. By contrast Roman military bases produce copious evidence for manufacturing in a wide variety of materials using technologies which were either completely new to the region or much improved when compared with what was previously available. From the sheer quantity of artefacts found at sites like Castleford and Catterick one gets the impression that these bases were hives of manufacturing activity. Each army unit, whether legionary or auxiliary, would have carried specialists in the principal crafts, but is also likely to have recruited unskilled labour from the local population to assist them. We can look at these crafts in turn beginning with those of greatest technological complexity requiring the control of heat.

Ceramics: pottery and tiles

Roman pottery kilns were of the so-called 'updraught type' in which a flue brought hot gas from a stokehole to the furnace chamber where it rose through a raised platform, supported and perforated in various ways, to the stacks of pots above. This was much more sophisticated than the clamp kilns usually used by the native potter. In the early post-conquest period the Roman army's pottery requirements, in terms of the variety of vessel types and their quality of finish, could not be met locally and so it made its own. The earliest Roman kilns in the Yorkshire region were probably at York where there is evidence that pottery and tile manufacture was undertaken in the Peasholme Green area, just outside the east corner of the legionary fortress, from more or less the time the soldiers arrived.[24] Local clays were used to produce *Eboracum* – or 'Ebor' – ware, a wheel-thrown red earthenware similar in overall style to legionary products at Chester, Gloucester and elsewhere. The colour of the vessels and the technology used to create it, which involved an oxidising atmosphere in the kiln, represented a tradition quite alien to the locals. A wide variety of vessels was produced in the legionary kilns for kitchen and table use including bowls, flagons and jars. Tiles – often bearing the Ninth Legion stamp – were made for roofing, flooring and other structural purposes, and were not only used in York, but also in the forts of the region. The Castleford fort bathhouse, for example, produced many Ninth Legion tiles and it may have been built by legionary specialists, although a couple of tiles have a Fourth Cohort of Gauls stamp suggesting supplies from a local kiln also.

Other early military kilns making pottery and tiles existed at Grimescar, *c.*3km north-east of the fort at Slack.[25] The unit stamp was COH IIII BRE – short for *Breucorum* – the Fourth Cohort of *Breuci*. Grimescar tiles were used at Slack itself and at the nearby forts of Castleshaw and Templeborough. It is thought that pottery was also made at Catterick[26] and Aldborough[27] in the

Illus. 6.4 Ebor ware vessels from York. (Photo: York Archaeological Trust)

late first or early second centuries, initially at least under military supervision. At Aldborough kilns were probably located in an area known as 'Red Hills' outside the south-east corner of what would become the Roman walled town.

Metalworking

York and the region's forts have produced numerous metal objects, many, if not all of which, were probably made locally by military specialists or by local craftsmen working for them. The blacksmith's repertoire included armour and weaponry (see above), but equally important were tools and fittings, such as chains, hinges, hooks, staples and the nails which are found in such large numbers. Non-ferrous items included military dress fittings and a range of brooches worn by soldiers and civilians alike. Analysis shows that whereas before the conquest bronze (using tin) was the most common copper alloy, the Romans introduced both brass – copper and zinc – and gun metal – copper, zinc and tin – which were harder and more serviceable.[28] The Romans probably introduced the working of lead on any scale to a region which, as already noted, has sources of the ore. Because of its waterproof qualities, lead was, for example, used as the lining for water tanks and was also formed into pipes for water supply alongside wooden and ceramic pipes.

A particularly interesting discovery at Castleford was a pit in Fort II which produced a large quantity of clay moulds for copper alloy working using the lost wax process.[29] The principal product was a type of cylindrical vessel, finished with enamelled decoration, probably used as a flask for military use. These moulds are a very unusual survival because the clay is so fragile. There are no similar groups of clay vessel moulds from anywhere else in the Roman Empire. In addition, both the fort and the *vicus* produced ceramic crucibles for use in copper alloy and silver working on the sort of hearths found adjacent to the *vicus* buildings. Elsewhere in our region, at Templeborough, in what

Illus. 6.5 Reconstruction drawing of a Castleford flask made from moulds found in the fort (diameter: 132mm; from Bayley and Budd 1998, © ASWYAS).

may have been an annexe outside the fort, there was a walled enclosure with a furnace, and what were identified as a blacksmith's anvil block and quenching tank; a small group of crucibles indicates non-ferrous metalworking also.[30] At Bainesse, in the earliest phase of the Catterick *vicus*, there were hearths adjacent to the strip buildings which were probably used for metalworking. In the Roecliffe *vicus* iron smithing debris was found along with crucibles for copper alloy working.

Leatherworking

It is with the Romans that leather enters the archaeological record in northern Britain. Leather is a highly versatile material, being durable, flexible, waterproof and easily worked. The Roman army had a considerable appetite for leather which was used for, amongst other things, shoes, armour, harness, kit bags, saddles and tents. Yorkshire is fortunate in having two important collections of leather artefacts from late first- or early second-century military sites, one from the midden in Fort I at Castleford (dated 71–85)[31] and the second from the midden near the baths at Catterick (dated 80–120).[32] There is no evidence for the processing of hides themselves at either site (there are no tanning pits, for example), but many of the animal bones they have produced may derive

Illus. 6.6   Left shoe with nailed sole from excavations at Shiptonthorpe (reproduced courtesy of Martin Millett, © Shiptonthorpe project).

from butchery during which the hides were removed. In one of the Vindolanda letters Catterick is referred to as a source of hides.[33] Both Castleford and Catterick provide evidence for the manufacture of new leather items and the repair of old ones.

Without any apparent tradition of leatherworking in pre-Roman Britain, it is not surprising that the material from both Castleford and Catterick conforms to the character of Roman leather goods elsewhere in the western empire. As far as shoes are concerned, Castleford produced examples in cattle hide of the *caliga*, usually thought of as the classic type of military footwear and still in vogue today in pastiche form as the so-called 'gladiator sandals' worn, for the most part, by women. The *caliga* was composed of a separately cut inner and outer sole with the top piece of shoe, i.e. the 'upper', and the middle layer of what would have been three sole layers forming a single piece. The sole layers were nailed together using small dome-headed 'hobnails' which are common archaeological finds. The upper was cut in an open-work manner and straps were wound around the lower leg to secure the shoe on the foot. The *caliga* was going out of fashion in the late first century which may explain why there is only one fragment from the slightly later material from Catterick. Both sites, however, produced examples of another common Roman shoe type, also nailed together, in which there was an insole and outer sole with the upper stitched by its lasting margin (edges) in between the two (Illus. 6.6). Evidence, perhaps, that civilians as well as military personnel were catered for by Castleford's shoemakers, consists of three examples of *carbatinae*, shoes made from a single piece of leather, folded and stitched to fit snugly around the foot. Catterick also produced open-toed sandals, some with their sole layers nailed together.

Roman army tents were made of panels of leather carefully stitched together. Pieces of tent from both Castleford and Catterick show that they were repaired and maintained by patching, re-stitching etc. Whilst cattle hides were usually used for shoes, the sheet leather used for tents at Castleford, as at other northern sites, was largely goatskin, although from Catterick it was cattle hide. Goatskin was lighter and might have been preferred by an army unit on the move. The reason for the difference between the two sites may have been to do either with the availability of the materials or with differences between army units in their preferred approach to procurement and manufacturing.

Wood

Just as versatile as leather as a material was wood. We have already looked at timber buildings, but the production of wooden objects would have been an important aspect of the Roman carpenter's craft. The Castleford forts have produced a collection of typical products ranging from a wooden seat or table top of ash to a boxwood comb for personal grooming.[34] There was also part of a ladder made of oak which had been abandoned in a well. Waste material suggests the production of small cups and bowls on a lathe. A six metre

length of a wattle fence made from hazel rods is good evidence for woodland management by coppicing. This involved cutting back not only hazel bushes, but also alder and willow trees, in such a way as to allow the growth of many thin trunks suitable as rods.

Textiles

The production of woollen textile was obviously important as it provided most of the clothing for the people of Roman Yorkshire. The army may have had specialist weavers, but it was largely a home-based craft and the artefactual evidence for it is widely scattered. Preparation of wool involved removing grease and dirt from the fleece and, on some occasions at least, the fibres were then aligned before spinning using an iron wool comb. An example of the Roman type, 200mm long, flat with long teeth, has been found at Kirby Knowle, on the edge of the Hambleton Hills, c.6km north-east of Thirsk, although as it is the only one from the region, combing may not have been standard practice.[35] Spinning by hand is represented by 'whorls', made of fired clay, bone and other materials, which were used to weight the spindle. Weaving took place on a vertical loom on which the warp (vertical) threads were kept in tension by loom weights of clay or stone. The weft (horizontal) threads were kept tight against each other by either using a pointed object known as a 'pin beater' or using a weaving comb; both types of object were usually made of bone or antler.[36] The commonest weaving pattern in Roman Britain was a plain diamond twill, but checks and other patterns are known; a herringbone twill was found on a fragment of woollen cloth from the late Roman signal station at Huntcliff. Decorative bands and braids were produced by a technique known as tablet weaving.

Little woollen clothing of the Roman period has been found in the Yorkshire region, compared, for example, to Vindolanda where it is abundant. However on a body found preserved in a bog on Grewelthorpe Moor, near Ripon, in 1850,[37] the contemporary account suggests he had worn a green cloak, scarlet tunic and yellow stockings; a fragment survives of the latter, along with a woollen insole from a shoe. The colours confirm evidence from elsewhere in Roman Britain that woollen textiles were routinely dyed in a variety of colours. The Grewelthorpe tunic was probably a garment which fell to the calves on men and ankles on women; it had short, wide sleeves and was sometimes belted at the waist. This so-called 'Gallic coat' was the standard daily wear and can be seen worn by figures such as Aurelius Mercurialis on the tombstone of Julia Velva from York (Illus. 8.6). Worn out of doors over the tunic were a variety of hooded capes and cloaks, usually fastened on the right shoulder with a brooch.

Illus. 6.8 Woman spinning: drawing based on an original Roman depiction of one of the three fates (Parcae) spinning the thread of life (drawn by Sarah Hall Baqai).

Exchange and trade: a chance to network

As in the late Iron Age, exchange or trade in the early Roman period within and between native communities and between those communities and the army would have been largely local involving everyday items. In addition, however, the region was opened up to new trade networks on becoming part of the Roman Empire. These networks extended not only to the rest of Britain, but also to the Continent of Europe and beyond, in some cases involving journeys over hundreds of kilometres, facilitated by an infrastructure of roads and ports. We know little of the exports from our region across these networks, although throughout the Roman period they are likely to have consisted of at least some of those items mentioned by Strabo, including agricultural products and minerals. A lead pig from Faxfleet, probably a small landing place at the mouth of the River Foulness on the Humber, was stamped SOCIOR LUT BR EX ARG or 'product of the Lutudarensian partners: British lead from the lead-silver works' – *Lutudarum* is probably Carsington in Derbyshire.[38] Ten other pigs, mostly unstamped, have been found at Brough on Humber or in the immediate area, suggesting that lead mined in both Yorkshire and Derbyshire was exported via the Humber estuary.

For imports into the Yorkshire region the best evidence comes from pottery on which we are also reliant for suggesting trade patterns in other goods, such as textiles and other commodities in organic materials which have not survived so well in the archaeological record. For the first fifty years or so after the conquest the evidence from Castleford and York (Table 5) suggests that the former was largely supplied from local sources (i.e. from within the Yorkshire region), but that York, conveniently sited on the River Ouse and the base of a legion, with all that implies in terms of the superior social status of its men, used an appreciably higher proportion of imported wares, largely samian from Gaul which supplemented what was made in the legionary kilns.[39] In addition to samian, there were a few other pottery imports to the region, largely mortaria which were made in Kent, but also in northern and central Gaul and the Rhineland. Glass vessels were also imported from the Continent, many of them from the Rhineland, for the most part to supplement pottery as tableware. The range of glass drinking vessels of late first- and early second-century date from Castleford is unrivalled in Roman Britain.[40]

Table 5   No. of pottery sherds in late first- and early second-century groups in descending order of percentage of local wares

Site	Date	Total	Local	British	Samian	Other Continental
Castleford, Fort I	Late C1	8,635	7,822 (91%)	167	529	117
Castleford, Fort II	Late C1–c.100	6,600	5,951 (90%)	120	424	105
Castleford, *Vicus* 2	Late C1–mid-C2	4,553	3,943 (87%)	185	358	67
Castleford, *Vicus* 1	Late C1	848	655 (77%)	24	138	31
York Fortress (Blake Street)	Late C1	2,368	1,662 (70%)	21	615	71
York Roman town, (Wellington Row)	Late C1–early C2	209	147 (70%)	11	43	8

There was a little evidence for imports of food and drink from the Continent, including olives, walnuts, grapes and figs, in both the fort and *vicus* deposits at Castleford, showing that the soldiers of the Fourth Cohort of Gauls were not prepared to abandon their traditional diet. Furthermore, fragments of amphorae from early military sites, including York and Castleford, are common. They are usually of the so-called 'Dressel 20' type, large and bulbous, which brought olive oil from the south of Spain, but there are also examples of types which brought wine from Gaul and the Campania region in Italy, or *liquamen*, a fish sauce considered a great delicacy in the Roman world and produced in the Cadiz region of Spain.[41]

For most of the Yorkshire region York would have been the principal port from which locally produced commodities were despatched and imports landed before they were redistributed along the region's roads and waterways. However, in the early Roman period it is striking that rural settlements received very few goods of what one might call 'Roman type' – pottery, jewellery etc – whether made in the region itself or imported from elsewhere. With the exception of a few sites near roads, samian, for example, is very scarce, usually represented by no more than a few sherds; even scarcer are sherds of the amphorae, flagons or mortaria which would be indicative of a distinctive Roman way of life. The characteristic local Iron Age pottery was still produced and there was, perhaps, little desire or requirement in rural areas for any additional vessel types to cater to local tastes or dining customs. A similar picture of scarcity is found when one looks at metalwork, including coinage, and the conclusion we must draw is that there was only a low level of economic integration, in the sense of regular trade on anything like an equal footing, between native settlements and the military bases, a situation which did not really change until the mid-second century.

The means by which the native population was persuaded to part with goods or assist in their procurement for the Roman army is not entirely clear, although we may assume that some form of requisitioning played a part, perhaps the principal one. This presumably had to be kept in check, however, to prevent the sort of unrest which led to the Boudiccan revolt, and the reciprocal arrangements which sustained relationships with client rulers may have survived the conquest to be taken up again with local notables in the interest of maintaining peace. This may explain such sherds of samian and other types of Roman pottery vessels which do occur on native sites.

Any substantial exports out of the region and imports into it in the early Roman period would have taken place largely in a state-sponsored context and may be seen as a form of administered trade as defined in Chapter 4; in this case commodities were moved around the empire to fulfil military and political objectives. This trade was probably funded largely by taxes in core areas of the empire.[42] The net outflow of resources to Britain and other new provinces on the periphery of empire, in the form of supplies and pay for the army as well as, perhaps, bullion and other commodities distributed to local elites, slowly began to benefit the economies of these provinces and contributed to the rising prosperity of regions like Yorkshire in the second century which will be described in the next chapter.

Although the use of coinage in trade was probably quite limited in the early Roman period, it was an important innovation in the region none the less. Another was the use, on occasions at least, of the sophisticated Roman system of weights and measures. Castleford fort and *vicus*, for example, have produced lead weights; the largest of 15¼ *libra* (pounds) was probably used to weigh sacks of grain and the like.[43] A pre-Hadrianic context at Catterick produced fragments of a steelyard, a type of weighing machine based on moving weights along a balance arm commonly used in the Roman period and still used today.[44]

The visual arts: becoming Roman or staying British?

In the previous chapter we noted that there are important differences between traditions forming the basis of native, or 'Celtic', art and those of Roman art in respect, for example, of representations of the human figure – hardly known in the former and fundamental to the latter. In the immediate post-conquest period we see the continuing slow assimilation in Britain of art styles from elsewhere in the Roman Empire in media such as metalwork. In addition to the influence of new styles, another important development after the conquest concerns the context of artistic expression. Whereas in the native world it was largely to be found on portable items carried around with the owner and used for personal display, the arrival of the Roman army in the region led to the introduction of public art, represented in architecture and in monuments such as altars and tombstones, which employed styles owing little to local traditions. Initially the army probably brought artists and craftsmen with them from other parts of the empire who were, for example, capable of making tombstones like that of the Ninth Legion standard bearer from York, Lucius Duccius Rufinus (Illus. 3.5). A specifically Rhenish influence has been detected in a roughly contemporary tombstone fragment from Templeborough which shows a dining scene of a type well known on tombstones at, for example, Bonn and Cologne (Illus. 6.10).[45]

Sculpture in stone by craftsmen working in a native idiom may have its origins in the late Iron Age (e.g. the chalk figurines) before this was developed further in the Roman period and ultimately became part of the classical mainstream. The Yorkshire region, principally the Millstone Grit area of the old West Riding, has produced a number of carved stone heads, although none comes from a dated archaeological context.[46] Some 400 were recorded by Sidney Jackson amongst which there are medieval or later examples, but others must be of the Roman period, although the simple style of the faces is decidedly non-classical and suggests the work of native craftsmen. For example, they have often have large oval eyes and mouths which are either just a slit or ovals with exaggerated lips. As in the case of the chalk figurines, these heads may depict deities, originally venerated as cult objects.

We should also note the large numbers of small artefacts, usually found in and around military bases, which in their decorative treatment illustrate aspects of Roman artistic styles, some essentially classical, others a mixture of Roman and native. Representing the former are numerous gem stones, known as 'intaglios', which were usually set in a seal ring. They were made from semi-precious stones, notably carnelian (orange to red-brown) and jasper (red), and frequently have images of Roman deities carved into them. Particularly common locally are those associated with good luck, such as Bonus Eventus and Fortuna, or of a martial character such Mars, Minerva and Victory.[47]

Representing the mixture of Roman and native styles are various types of brooch. They include a type of fibula (like a safety pin) known as a trumpet

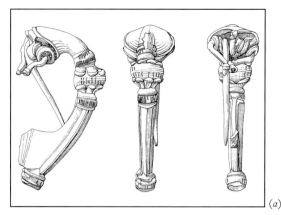

(a)

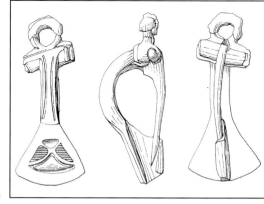

Illus. 6.9   Roman brooches from Castleford:

(a) trumpet,
(b) fantail and
(c) dragonesque

(lengths: 55, 43 and 46mm; from Cool and Philo 1998, © ASWYAS).

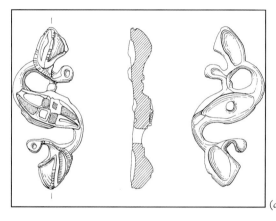

(c)

brooch because of the way the head expands to resemble a trumpet's mouth. Mid-way along the bow there is often a moulding resembling a double acanthus leaf and another moulding usually exists at the base. Amongst the many types of plate brooch, characteristic of the early period is the fan tail, a regional type which is principally known from sites in south Yorkshire, including Castleford,[48] and the north Midlands. However, the most distinctive brooch type of the late first and early second centuries, is probably the dragonesque which is thought to have been particularly popular in the north of Britain.[49] Usually in copper alloy, it is S-shaped with a stylised dragon's head at one end and tail at the other. All these three types of brooch often bore enamelled panels evoking the native tradition of craftsmanship and design.

Another distinctive and prestigious metal item of personal adornment in the native tradition in both Britain and Gaul was the torc, a rigid penannular necklet. Both the woman with plaits from Ilkley in Illus 3.1 and the standard-bearer (from Gaul) Rufinus from York in Illus. 3.5 wear them. A notably fine Yorkshire example was found at Dinnington north-west of Worksop (Notts).[50] Made of hollow tubes, towards the terminals there were a series of spherical expansions or 'beads'. The metallurgy shows the object was made of the sort of brass and gunmetal which was not generally available until after the conquest.

Religion: 'so many gods, so many creeds'

We are little better informed about the religion of the native population immediately after the conquest than we are about it in the late Iron Age. However, those special locations, such as water sources and oak glades, considered particularly sacred presumably continued to witness traditional ceremonies unaffected by political events. The Roman authorities were usually reluctant to offend local religious sensitivities at times of military conquest. A feature of the Roman Empire, frequently commented upon, is its tolerance of almost any religious beliefs – apart from those like Judaism and Christianity which assumed an anti-regime political character. The Romans might even seek to absorb and repackage native cults by associating them with cults of their own.

Although confined initially to the military bases, the great diversity of Roman religious ideas would, in due course, have begun to make itself known to the native population who would have found that the beliefs and cult practices of the conquerors bore many similarities to their own. Both Romans and natives were polytheistic and saw the divine as invested to a greater or lesser extent in all creation. Certain places in the landscape were seen as particularly sacred: a respect for the *genius loci* (spirit of place) may be seen as the inspiration behind the altar dedications from Yorkshire (and other parts of the north) to Bregans (male) or Brigantia (female)[51]– a divinity of a type very common in the Roman world which embodied the spirit of a region. The same idea informed other dedications in the region. One example is an altar at Ilkley dedicated by a prefect of the Second Cohort of Lingones (from what is now Langres on the Marne) to Verbeia, probably the native name for the River Wharfe and its presiding spirit.[52] Another example is a dedication at York to Silvanus by L. Celerinus Vitalis of the Ninth Legion which, no doubt, indicates the concern of a keen huntsman to appease the god of wild places.[53] A sacred quality was also invested in heavenly bodies in both native and Roman religion. In seeking to understand humanity's place in the cosmos people turned as a matter of course to phenomena which had an unchanging or predictable quality such as the alternation of day and night, the changing seasons, the configuration of the stars and the motions of the planets around the earth, then assumed to be the fixed centre of the universe. In the Roman pantheon seven of the more influential gods and goddesses were identified with the planets: Jupiter, Saturn, Venus, Sol (the sun), Mercury, Mars and Luna (the moon). Their approximate distance from the earth and nature of their orbits had been established by astronomical observation over many centuries.

In terms of cult practice both natives and Romans employed sacrifice as a means of communicating with the gods. On the side of the altar from York dedicated to Jupiter by the prefect of an auxiliary unit there is a figure in relief under a wreath holding a large animal, probably a bull.[54] This is probably an abbreviated depiction of a sacrifice of traditional Roman type.

An uninscribed altar from Dunnington Common, near York, has an axe and knife carved on it, representing the standard Roman sacrificial implements.[55] Inscriptions on many Roman altars suggest that the sacrifice by individuals formed the preliminary to establishing a sort of contract whereby the god was asked for a particular favour and, in the event of a good outcome, the altar was set up giving thanks. Communal sacrifice lay at the centre of religious festivals which, in a world dependent more or less entirely on the fortunes of agriculture, occurred at critical times in the cycle of the seasons. Many of the gods were patrons of some aspect of fertility, some quite overtly like the *matres* or 'mother goddesses'.

Whilst the similarities between native and Roman religious ideas are striking, the Romans also brought a range of new ones to Britain and the province's absorption into the Roman world would mean that they would continue to arrive. In respect, for example, of the question of human origins, the Romans subscribed to a number of creation myths, derived mostly from the Greeks. In one of them Euronyme, a goddess of all things, rose naked from Chaos, divided the sea and sky, and created the seven planetary deities with a titan and titaness ruling over each. There is a reference from York to this myth in the form of two small bronze plaques found in 1839–40 on the site of the Old Station, south-west of the Ouse.[56] They carry dedications in Greek by a man named Scribonius Demetrius to, in one case, 'the gods of the military commander's residence' and in the other to 'Ocean and Tethys', the titan and titaness who ruled the goddess Venus.

Certain traditional aspects of Roman religion were officially sponsored. For example, the shrine (*sacellum*) of a military base would have contained statues representing the three principal protective deities of the Roman state, Jupiter, Juno and Minerva, who are often known as the Capitoline Triad because of their temples on the Capitoline Hill in Rome. Dedications to them are well known on altars in Britain, especially in military areas, although there are only two, of uncertain date, both to Jupiter, from Yorkshire. One of them is the York altar, just referred to; on the other, from Aldborough, Jupiter is addressed in the common abbreviated form IOM (Jupiter Optimus Maximus – 'best and greatest') and coupled with the mother goddesses.[57]

In addition to representations of the Capitoline Triad, a *sacellum* probably housed an image of the reigning emperor and members of his family. As the empire's chief priest – *pontifex maximus* as Trajan is described on the King's Square tablet from York – the emperor sought to dominate its sacred as well as its secular life. Strictly speaking, emperors were not considered to be gods while living, although they might be deified after their deaths. The living emperor's spirit (*numen*) was, however, considered to have sacred power and dedications were made to it by soldiers and civilians alike. The cult of the emperor may be seen as traditional Roman ancestor worship on a grand scale, the emperor being regarded as father of his people (*pater patriae* as he is referred to in inscriptions). If one were to be cynical, one might interpret the energetic promotion of the cult as an attempt to provide a unifying spiritual and emotional focus for the disparate people of the empire and secure their loyalty to the ruling emperor, however dubious his right to occupy the throne might be.

Attendance at the official ceremonies honouring the Capitoline Triad and deified emperors would have been compulsory for the soldiers. The commander would have presided as the emperor's representative and carried out important sacrifices. In their own time the men were free to indulge in whatever religious practices they chose. It is, therefore, usual to find that Roman military bases were surrounded by diverse temples and altars. Gods favoured by soldiers would have included those of the classical pantheon who presided over war and combat, such as Mars, as seen, for example, on altars from York[58] and on one linking the god to the health of the emperors found on Staincross Common, near Doncaster.[59] Favoured goddesses included Victoria, patroness of victory, and Fortuna, promoter of fortune or luck, the latter invoked on altars from Bowes[60] and the fort baths at Slack.[61] Dedications to Fortuna were particularly popular in Roman bath houses where games of chance were played and also because men apparently felt vulnerable to evil spirits when naked. In addition to the Classical deities, the men would have worshipped those of their homelands, of countries in which they had seen service and of the locality in which they presently found themselves.

A cult of a more exotic character than most is represented by the depiction of Atys on the early second-century tombstone fragment from Templeborough which also shows a banqueting scene.[62] Atys was part of the cult of Cybele, a great mother goddess who was a patron of fertility. She originated in Asia Minor, but as early as 191 BC had reached Rome where her festivals were celebrated with extravagant and noisy ceremonies.[63] An important part of the mythology associated with Cybele is the story of the shepherd boy Atys who was Cybele's consort. He castrated himself in remorse for infidelity to her with a nymph and, in one version of the myth, was turned into a pine tree, hence achieving eternal life which may explain the use of pine cones on some funerary monuments (such as that of Julia Velva from York – Illus. 8.6). Atys himself is often shown, as at Templeborough, as a mourner. Priests of his cult, known as *galli*, ritually castrated themselves to show their devotion to the goddess.

Treatment of the dead: continuity and change

Just as Roman religious ideas and practice only spread out gradually into the region as a whole in the early Roman period, so did ideas about death and the afterlife, and about how the dead should be treated. Amongst the natives burial of the dead may have remained, as it was in the late Iron Age, the way in which only a minority was treated except, perhaps in the east Yorkshire Arras culture zone. When burial did take place it usually involved inhumation of the body in a shallow grave, often, as in the Iron Age, in a crouched or flexed position. For example, in a small, early Roman cemetery at Blealands Nook near Fimber on the Wolds all fourteen burials were in this native tradition.[64] Alongside the humans were the burials of a pig and a goat which probably had some cult significance rooted in local practice. Of similar date was a group of nine crouched burials found on western edge of the Wolds at Millington, 3km north-east of Pocklington.[65] Another cemetery of crouched inhumations was found nearby at South Newbald.[66] Elsewhere in Yorkshire, identifiably early Roman inhumations are scarce. Examples may include a few of the inhumations in pits near the henge at Ferrybridge and few isolated examples of crouched inhumations found in the York area including Dringhouses, c.3km south-west of the city.[67]

At the time of the conquest of the north of Britain cremation of the dead, except for babies and infants, was usually preferred to inhumation in much of the Roman Empire. Usual practice appears to have required a special site to be set aside for the funeral pyres on which the bodies of the deceased were burnt and there is an example of such a site from York. After a corpse's consumption by the flames, the cremated remains were placed in a suitable container, most commonly a pottery urn. Although one might expect to find early Roman cremation burials associated with military sites in the Yorkshire region, they are quite scarce.

Illus. 6.10
Templeborough: fragment of a tombstone showing the deceased dining (top), his servant next to the table and (bottom) Atys in his role as mourner. (Photo: P. Ottaway, © Rotherham Museum)

This may be partly, at least, because zones outside the defences where the cemeteries would usually lie, have rarely been explored. At York only a few examples have been recorded. A small group comes from a cemetery zone at Fishergate c.1km south-east of the fortress[68] and isolated examples come from the site of the Art Gallery only c.75m from the fortress north-west gate[69] and from Blossom Street, south-west of the Ouse, close to the main road from Tadcaster.[70] Doncaster has also produced a late first- or early second-century cemetery zone, excavated in 2011 on Waterdale where a possible Roman burial mound had been recorded in the early twentieth century (Illus. 5.4, 10). Burnt material from some twenty-six cremation burials showed that, on some occasions at least, glass bottles containing sweet-smelling unguents were cast

Illus. 6.11
Blealands Nook early
Roman cemetery (from
Mortimer 1905).

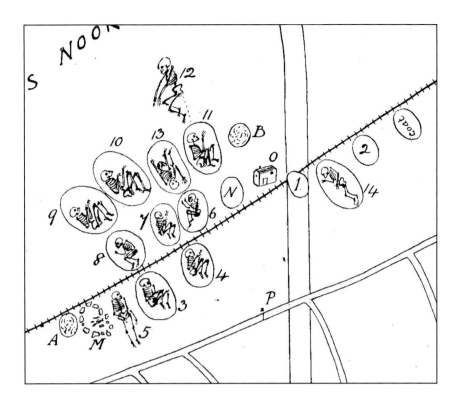

onto the funeral pyres, along with food offerings including figs, grapes and walnuts, delicacies which we have already seen were part of the military diet. Elsewhere in the region some of the cremations found near Slack fort in the nineteenth and early twentieth centuries may have been early Roman.[71] More recently, an urned example was found at Roecliffe.[72]

Early Roman funerary monuments are rare in the region, although there are two Ninth Legion tombstones from York which would originally have marked burial sites. They were both found south-west of the Ouse, close to the main Roman road from Tadcaster. One is that of Lucius Duccius Rufinus (Illus. 3.5), the other is of a man whose name does not survive, from Novaria (now Novara) in Italy; it was found on The Mount where many other later burials would be made.[73] In addition, there are two early tombstones and fragments of two others from Templeborough. Three of them are of men of the Fourth Cohort of Gauls, Cintusmus and Crotus; the name of the third (showing the banquet scene) does not survive. The fourth belongs to a lady named Vercundia Rufilia.[74]

The impact of the conquest

What impact did the Roman conquest have on our region and its people in the first fifty years or so after the Roman army arrived north of the Humber? First of all, we should not ignore quite a substantial increase, perhaps up to as much as 7–8%, in the population although it would have been even greater in certain localities. At its most numerous the garrison probably consisted of at least 15,000 soldiers based at York and the region's forts. In addition, a Roman fort was usually surrounded by a community of non-combatants, many of whom had probably travelled with the army, although others came from the local population. An auxiliary fort housing a unit of 500 men with perhaps another 200 people in the *vicus* would have made a settlement considerably larger than any known to the natives in the region. The incomers were, moreover, from all over the Roman world and brought a richly diverse culture with them.

As a result of this new population, one assumes that the army bases made for quite a substantial increase, at least in the short term, in the demand for food and other resources from the immediate area around them. As we have seen, there is plenty of archaeological evidence for the movement of animals, crops, timber etc into the bases, although it is difficult to pin down clear archaeological evidence for changes in the character of the landscape to indicate either that new land was being taken into cultivation or that there were changes in the agricultural regime. None the less, the pressure on some local landowners to work new land and mobilise additional labour must have been considerable.

Whilst the mechanism by which the army supplied itself is not easy to determine, there seems to have been little in the way of the outflow of manufactured goods to the rural areas in the late first and early second centuries, suggesting a low level of economic integration between Roman and native. Native sites produce very little early Roman pottery and other goods of Roman type. However, this may not only be due to there being no mechanism for their easy acquisition, but also to an innate conservatism in the native way of life. One may envisage a lack of demand for the range of pottery vessels used by the Roman army because native modes of food preparation and consumption remained more or less unchanged. Conservatism can also be seen in the visual arts, religion, and treatment of the dead inasmuch as there is any evidence for what was current in the native milieu.

It has been suggested on the basis of the presence of local hand-made pottery and beehive querns that there was a native element in the population of the *vici* of forts like Castleford and Roecliffe, although the simple equation of artefacts and people is made at one's peril. However, in due course some local people, at least, must have been attracted by the Roman way of life and found opportunities for enrichment and advancement under the new regime, perhaps by supplying or transporting commodities, by working as craftspeople or even by joining the army. As far as local women were concerned, there were presumably opportunities for liaisons arising out of a marked imbalance of the sexes in the military bases. What we do not know, however, is how easy it was for someone to leave the land they worked on and carve out a new career in a fort *vicus*. Any migration of the able-bodied or marriageable may have been strongly resisted by the native elite. Let us also remember that for some locals the coming of Rome offered decidedly negative future prospects as enslavement beckoned, as a result of either capture in battle or sale by their British overlords.

After some fifty years of Roman rule the picture of a somewhat detached relationship between the new elite and the local people began to change. Some native people residing at York or in the *vici* may, under the influence of the army, have already come to embrace new ways of life such as dining in Roman style, adopting Roman styles of dress and toilet, and even burying their dead according to Roman custom. However, the army had largely moved out of Yorkshire by the early 120s and the real force for change was probably the movement through the province of *Britannia* of people, commodities and ideas in many different circumstances only a few of which had a direct military connection.

Some recent commentators have sought to emphasise the idea of a Roman imperialist exploitation of the Britons along the lines of a particular, largely negative, view of the European imperial enterprise of the nineteenth and twentieth centuries. A recent study of Roman Britain by David Mattingly introduces itself by saying, 'My fundamental theme is the fate of Britain as an imperial possession during nearly four centuries of foreign domination'.[75] This use of the word 'domination' seems to me a little misleading; for a start, a Roman emperor did not really have the resources or the communications facilities to control the people of Britain in the way that totalitarian states of recent times, such as the former Soviet Union, controlled their subject peoples. Unfortunately words like 'domination' and 'exploitation' have begun to acquire a somewhat emotive quality in the work of some archaeologists and historians who like to proclaim a loyalty to one side or another in historical conflicts, usually that of the perceived underdog, especially if they were 'natives' rather than 'foreigners'.

Whilst one would not want to endorse the Roman conquest of Britain uncritically, Mattingly's conclusion to his opening chapter: 'And for every winner under Roman rule, there were a hundred losers ...' simply cannot be sustained by the evidence and seems to overlook the inherent ability of human beings to make the best of changed circumstances. I believe that verdicts on historical events like the Roman conquest based on value judgements derived from the ethical priorities of our own time are not really amenable to serious argument. It is the historian's job to record how and why events in the past took place, and not to take sides. In summary, I would suggest that Britain was conquered because she was in Rome's sights at a time when there was a presumption amongst her elite that the empire would continue to expand. Military conquest fed the intense competition between leading families for the power and wealth which was largely gained from acquisition of land and its resources. Furthermore, in going out to conquer new land Roman armies were also sustained by a sense of a divinely sanctioned right to rule and the inherent superiority of their culture. As the god Jupiter proclaims in Book I of *The Aeneid*: 'I set upon the Romans bounds neither of space nor time. I have bestowed upon them empire without limit'. As far as Britain was concerned, Rome knew she could look forward to dealing with an enemy which was not as advanced either technologically or militarily as she was.

The Roman Empire seems to me to have operated on the basis of a bargain to which provincials adapted readily enough after the initial shock of conquest. They had to disarm, pay their taxes and send men to the army whilst Rome, for its part, would keep the peace, internal and external. If the provincials accepted this they could expect to be pretty much left alone to govern themselves. Until this bargain began to fail, in the late fourth century as far as Britain was concerned, one suspects that its people, including the Brigantes and the Parisi, inasmuch as they adopted a new identity, probably came to regard themselves as Romans.

7 | From Hadrian to the Severi

Peace and prosperity

Introduction

As a rule, trying to shoehorn the history of Roman Britain into a structure determined by a few well-documented political or military events can be misleading from the point of view of economic and social history. This relies largely on archaeological evidence which does not lend itself to the precise dating we can establish for an event recorded in a literary source. None the less, the beginning of the Emperor Hadrian's reign (in year 117) appears to make an obvious place for a break in the story of the Yorkshire region because of the impact of the creation of a permanent northern frontier for Roman Britain, instigated by Hadrian when he visited the province in the year 122. From an archaeological point of view there is also a logic to making a break at about this time as it is only shortly after the shift in the principal source of samian pottery, which is so important for dating, from southern Gaul to central Gaul.

Sources of literary evidence for the second century in Britain as a whole are sparse. There is little which bears directly on Yorkshire except, perhaps, for brief references by Cassius Dio and Herodian to military campaigns at the end of the century which must have involved troops based at York and the region's forts. For the early third century Dio and Herodian both give us brief accounts of Septimius Severus's campaigns in Britain and of events surrounding his death in York. However, literary sources may be supplemented by epigraphy in a way that was not possible for the pre-Hadrianic period. The vast majority of the inscriptions on stone from Yorkshire, whether commemorative, religious or funerary, may probably be dated between the reigns of Hadrian and the Severi (Septimius Severus and his immediate descendants). Archaeological sources are also very rich and one could argue that we know more about the century or so discussed in this chapter than about any century in Britain before or after until perhaps that leading up to the Norman conquest almost 800 years later.

In *c.*142, under Antoninus Pius (138–61), the northern frontier was moved north to the line of the Antonine Wall in Scotland, but it was moved back south again to Hadrian's Wall by the end of his reign. However, within the province of Britain these frontier movements did not impinge on a long period of peace which was probably an important factor in what appears to have been one of economic growth and prosperity. In this respect, as far as the Yorkshire region is concerned, the last three to four decades of the second century seem to have been something of a golden age. Nowhere is this more the case than in York.

Had one been in York in the year 120, shortly before Hadrian's visit to Britain, one would probably have seen a legionary fortress which was largely empty of troops. The Ninth Legion had been withdrawn a few years previously and, it is thought, sent to the Rhineland, although its history after leaving York still remains uncertain; the last dated reference to the legion is the inscription on the King's Square tablet (107–08). The civilian settlements on the banks of the Ouse and Foss remained populated places, but one could hardly, perhaps, have expected the extent of growth and development which was to come in the next 100 years and make York by 213 the obvious, indeed the only, candidate to become the capital of Lower Britain (*Britannia Inferior*) when Britain was divided into two provinces in the reign of the Emperor Caracalla. Seen against the backdrop of its region, York would by this time have become a very special place in terms of the composition and size of its population, character of its buildings, extent of its trading contacts, and the diversity of its religious cults and burial practices.

Whether Hadrian stopped in York on the way to the northern frontier we do not know; he may well have sailed directly to the mouth of the Tyne and made landfall at South Shields. The emperor was accompanied to Britain by the Sixth Legion *Victrix* ('victorious') from Xanten in the Rhineland (between the Ruhr and the Dutch border) which was to take over as the garrisoning force at York. In the first instance, the main body of the legion was probably sent straight to the frontier zone where there is evidence for warfare in the early years of Hadrian's reign. However, some troops presumably moved into York and army movements of the time were, perhaps, responsible for a number of camps near York. In the early eighteenth century 'seven or eight' were noted in Francis Drake's *Eburacum*. Two of those surviving into recent times lie on Bootham Stray[1] north of the city and another two, discovered in 2002, are on Huntington South Moor to the north-east (Illus. 6.1).[2] Excavation of one of the latter showed it was Hadrianic, although whether the others are or not remains uncertain.

The subject of Hadrian's Wall lies beyond the scope of this book but construction and then garrisoning of the frontier required a large military force with the result that the number of troops elsewhere in the north of Britain was reduced. In the Yorkshire region only the fort at Bowes (and possibly Templeborough) remained in commission during the reigns of Hadrian and

Antoninus Pius with the others in some way 'mothballed' against possible future use. A stone wall was added to the defences of Bowes and the headquarters and CO's house were rebuilt, the work probably commemorated by a dedicatory inscription (now lost) of 131–33.[3] Slack was unusual in being garrisoned throughout Hadrian's reign, but it was largely abandoned in the 140s. In the 160s there were, once again, changes to the garrison of the north which affected the Yorkshire region. This involved the return in strength of the Sixth Legion to York and the recommissioning of a number of the forts, perhaps to provide a strategic reserve for the frontier or to guard against any continuing threat from episodes of local unrest. It was once thought that there had been a Brigantian revolt in the 150s, but this is now discounted. However, the region may have been affected by events in c.180 when, according to Cassius Dio: 'The tribes in the island crossed the wall [i.e. Hadrian's Wall] that separated them from the Roman army and did a great amount of damage, even cutting down a general together with his troops'.[4] The Emperor Commodus (177–92) then ordered his governor in Britain, Ulpius Marcellus, to lead a punitive expedition; he no doubt used York as his headquarters.

York: the fortress

On its return from the frontier zone in c.160 the Sixth Legion set in train a new episode of construction activity in the fortress at York. A number of buildings previously of timber were rebuilt in stone. Excavations have shown that they included all the barracks hitherto investigated and an accommodation block in the centre of the fortress at 9 Blake Street.[5] Work also resumed on the defences with completion of the stone wall and stone towers to add to the work undertaken in pre-Hadrianic times.[6] The new stretches of wall between the north-east gate and the east corner, in places south-west of the east corner, and immediately north-east of the south corner, were rather different in character from the earlier wall in having a plinth at the base composed of two courses of large blocks, the uppermost being chamfered on the outer face. This plinth is still just about visible at the east corner of the fortress where one can also see that at the top of the fortress wall there was a cornice of flat stones below the parapet (which does not survive). This work on the walls was accompanied by the reconstruction and widening of the rampart in all parts of the circuit of defences, a rampart presumably still thought to be needed in the event of an enemy using a battering ram.

The forts

The recommissioning of forts in the Yorkshire region has been dated to the 160s by an inscription dedicated to Antoninus Pius by the Governor Julius Verus at Brough on Noe in Derbyshire[7] and another from Ilkley, dedicated to the joint Emperors Marcus Aurelius and Lucius Verus (161–69) – 'beloved by Jupiter' – by a prefect, Caecilius Lucanus.[8] It is at Ilkley that a brief review of what is known of reconstruction may begin by noting that the excavations

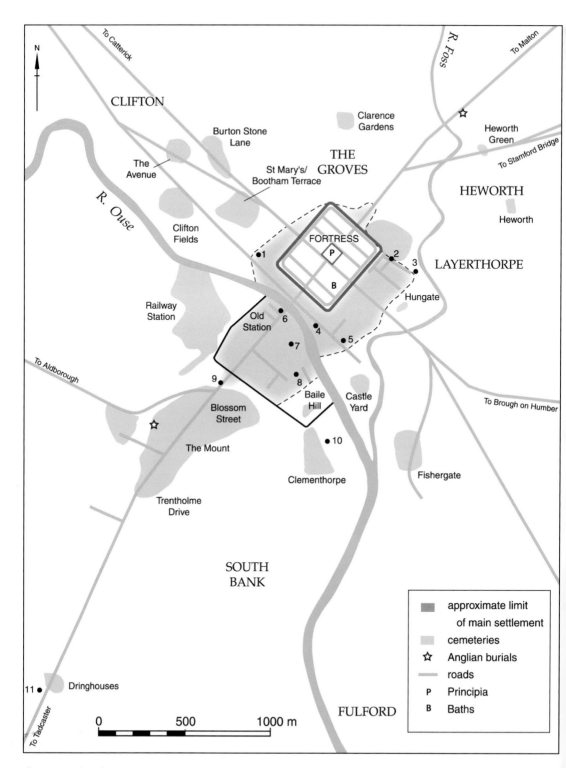

Illus. 7.1 Plan of Roman York. Key to sites: 1, St Mary's Abbey; 2, 21–33 Aldwark; 3, Peasholme Green, pottery and tile production area; 4, Coney Street; 5, Nessgate / Spurriergate; 6, Wellington Row; 7, 1–9 Micklegate (Queen's Hotel); 8, Bishophill; 9, Blossom Street, Roman building; 10, Clementhorpe; 11, Dringhouses Roman buildings.

Illus. 7.2 Copper
alloy baldric pendant
(top–length: 60mm) and
terminal plate (58mm ×
53mm) of the numerum
omnium type from
Aldborough.
(© English Heritage and
M.C. Bishop)

Illus. 7.3 Auxiliary
soldier of the early third
century with baldric,
oval shield, lance and
long sword ('spatha')
as he might have been
shown on a tombstone
(after F. Hilscher-Ehlert
in Horn 1987).

in the north-western quadrant of the fort (the remainder is unexplored) have shown that there was new work on the defences with a redug ditch and reconstructed clay and turf rampart.[9] In addition, there were new barracks for the *cohors equitata* commanded by Lucanus, and a new granary, all built in timber. At Elslack, the next fort to the west, it is possible that enlargement of the original fort to one of 2.2 ha with stone defences took place at this time also, although a late third-century date is more likely based on the form of the south gate.[10] However, at Bainbridge it seems that the stone defences and rebuilt headquarters building, granaries and barracks are late second century.[11]

Little is known in any detail about the new fort at Catterick, although the ditch on its eastern defences has been excavated.[12] However, an indication of Catterick's importance on the main route to the north is provided by two altars, which are probably late second or early third century, set up by *beneficiarii*, legionaries who had some special official status on the governor's staff.[13] In the south of the county a new fort was built at Doncaster, but was somewhat smaller (2.3ha) than that of the conquest period.[14] At

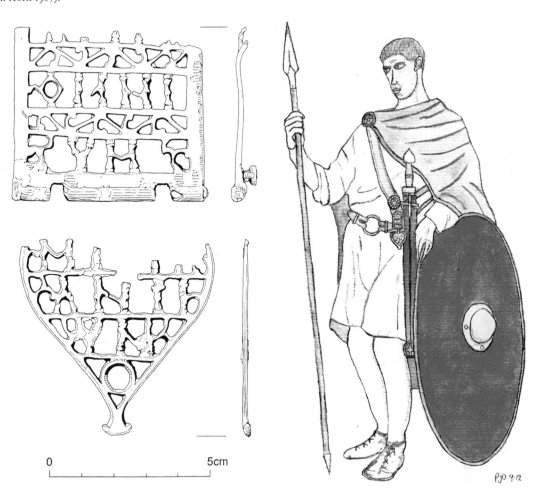

0   5cm

Templeborough Thomas May's excavations suggested the fort was rebuilt with stone defences in the late second century, dating apparently confirmed by excavations in 2008 at the south corner.[15] A new bath house, much larger than that of the first fort, was constructed at the same time (Illus. 5.14). Given its strategic position between York and the coast, it is no surprise that Malton was recommissioned and retained a garrison until the end of the Roman period. It seems more likely that a stone wall was added to the earlier rampart in the late second century than earlier, although the wall was unusually substantial, being 3.5m wide on foundations 4.25m wide. One wonders whether this was, in fact, of later Roman date, when thick walls were more typical, and had perhaps replaced an earlier one of which little trace survived. The accompanying stone-built gate which replaced the double portal timber gate had a single portal of a form which is also typical of the later Roman period.[16] At the north corner of the fort, next to the *intervallum* road, Corder encountered part of a late second-century stone barrack. The garrison of Malton at this time may have been the *Ala Picentiana*, a cavalry unit named on an inscription from the *vicus*.[17]

The road system remained intimately related to the fort network and the region's main roads appear to have been kept in good repair in the century after Hadrian. This extended to the bridges and at Piercebridge a new one over the Tees was built *c.*185m downstream from the first at a point on the flood plain where the banks were less steep; Dere Street was diverted accordingly.[18] The Tees has moved northwards since Roman times leaving remains of the southern bridge abutment high and dry on the bank where they can be seen today. The bridge was constructed on a pavement of large stone slabs above which rose perhaps twelve piers spanning *c.*200m. The piers and abutments were constructed of large blocks of Millstone Grit very carefully cut to leave minimal joints between them and held together with iron clamps, but not mortared; the sheer weight of the blocks kept the structure stable. The superstructure may have been either timber or stone, but the evidence does not survive.

Army dress and equipment

The late second and early third centuries brought changes in military dress and equipment. For example, the sword, usually longer than the old *gladius*, was now worn on the left hip, rather than the right, and the scabbard was suspended from a cross-belt, or baldric, of which the broader end hung down alongside the sword.[19] On occasions the baldric had an openwork terminal composed of two parts hinged together. There are three examples from Aldborough, of which the most complete has IM on one piece, meaning Jupiter Optimus Maximus, with an eagle, and on the other the legend NVMERVM OMNIVM MILITANTIVM meaning 'the number of all those serving' i.e. those men who were being commended to Jupiter.[20] At the waist both soldiers and other government servants wore distinctive wide belts, joined by adjustable rings, with ornamented terminals. As far as armour is concerned, this was now chain mail or made from small scales on a leather base; the *lorica segmentata* of the legionaries having gone out of use.

The creation of the *civitates*

In the previous section I have drawn attention to a number of Roman stone structures on military sites in the Yorkshire region. Until about the second quarter of the second century stone was rarely used in a civilian context, but then stone buildings began to spring up on civilian sites both in the public and private spheres. This indicates, on the one hand, the wealth of certain individuals able to sponsor buildings of stone and, on the other, a wider acceptance and understanding than hitherto of the new ideas in architecture introduced by the Romans. Stone buildings of Roman type are, however, just one outward sign of changes in the region which appear to follow the creation of a permanent northern frontier under Hadrian. Following the creation of the frontier, and the associated reassignment of troops to the frontier zone, Rome appeared to recognise that the army legate in York aided by the fort commanders need not, and could not, continue to administer north-eastern Britain indefinitely.

What Rome preferred to do, and in the south of Britain had done successfully for as much as seventy years or so before Hadrian's time, was to hand over administration, as far as possible, to local elites. As long as taxes were collected, justice was done and public order maintained, autonomy was what worked best in a world of limited imperial resources and poor communications. The vehicle for doing this in Britain was the *civitas* (plural *civitates*), a political entity defined on the basis of pre-existing tribal boundaries. In the early second century, probably under Hadrian, a large part, if not all, of northern Britain, east of the Pennines, was turned over to civilian control, as two *civitates*, one for the Brigantes and the other for the Parisi. Each *civitas* would have been administered by a body, known as an *ordo*, or *curia*, nominally at least, of 100 men (known as 'decurions') who qualified for office on the basis of property ownership.

Whilst the members of the *ordo* might have been drawn from the whole *civitas*, in the Roman world administration was usually exercised from towns. Indeed the Roman Empire has often been characterised as a collection of city states, each of which had considerable autonomy. They were bound together, however, by the common interests and common culture of their ruling elites whose wealth and power were based largely on the ownership of land and the resources – human, agricultural and mineral – which it yielded. These common interests found expression not only in institutions, but in the physical character of towns; their grid-based plans and suites of public buildings were replicated, to a greater or lesser extent, empire-wide from the Euphrates to the Solway Firth.

In Britain, as in much of northern Gaul and Germany, towns of Roman type were introduced into to what had been non-urban communities. One way of doing this was to create *coloniae* (colonies) of Roman citizens, usually veteran soldiers; examples founded in Britain in the first century existed at Colchester, Gloucester and Lincoln. Sometimes the title of *colonia* was given to places alongside important military bases which had developed an urban character as in the case of York which probably became *Colonia Eburacensis* in the reign of Caracalla (211–17). York was not, however, a centre of local administration; its destiny was linked to the army and the provincial government. Local administration of the region, that is for the *civitates* of the Brigantes and the Parisi, was based on towns in which there were at first few Roman citizens. There has been some debate about where the initiative for foundation of these towns came from, but the role of local elites is now considered to be crucial. It is thought that it was their members who furnished, largely at their own expense, the capital of each *civitas* in Britain with its principal facilities and infrastructure. It was here that they, or some of them at least, settled and began to create a version of the urban life that had existed in Mediterranean regions for many centuries. For the Brigantes it was Aldborough, where Dere Street crossed the Ure, which was chosen and for the Parisi the capital was to be Brough on Humber.

York: the town

Expansion and development of the civilian areas of Roman York, on both sides of the River Ouse, began to take off in the third quarter of the second century. This was probably connected, at least in part, with a stimulus to the local economy provided by the return of the Sixth Legion from the northern frontier. North-east of the Ouse the evidence comes largely from small scale excavations and observations which, none the less, suggests the emergence of buildings and streets clustered around all but the north-east side of the legionary fortress.[21] For example, in the mid-second century an important new street was laid out along the Ouse river front, overlying the remains of the Coney Street granary (described above). Another new street ran perpendicular to this riverside street along the south-east side of the fortress. The more substantial buildings in the immediate area included a couple of temples which are known from inscriptions on stone tablets. One was dedicated to Hercules and another to a goddess, probably local, whose name begins IOV, combined with the *numen* of more than one emperor, probably Septimius Severus and his sons Caracalla and Geta.[22] North-west of the fortress a substantial stone wall, presumably from a major building, a street and traces of other buildings have been found in the grounds of St Mary's Abbey.[23] One would like to know more about this area which, some have suggested, was the site of York's Roman amphitheatre.

South-west of the Ouse excavations tell us that development was initially focused on a zone around the main approach road from the south-west.[24] In

c.160, at Wellington Row, the level of the road as it approached the Ouse, was raised by 1m or more, perhaps to create a causeway for a bridge over the river, a companion to the new bridge over the Tees at Piercebridge. Contemporary with the raising of the road level at Wellington Row was a stone building (15.5m × 10.5m) set end-on to the road, originally with a room partitioned off at the front, perhaps for a shop. In living quarters behind there was an oven against the south-west wall. This was probably the source of a spark which caused a major fire, but in spite of considerable destruction – collapsed roof timbers were found on the floor – the building was reconstructed, given a new floor supported on stone blocks and extended north-westwards; it remained standing until the end of the fourth century.

Also found close to the main road from the south-west a little to the south-west of Wellington Row on Tanner Row, was a pair of timber strip buildings which had been constructed of post and plank walls (Illus. 3.4). Large quantities of artefacts had accumulated in surface deposits and timber-lined drains around these buildings, including debris from metalworking and leatherworking.[25] A great range of organic materials, not only wood, was well preserved in the waterlogged ground, including food remains surviving as bones, cereal grains and a great variety of fruit pips, seeds and stones.[26] A somewhat squalid environment was suggested by abundant horse manure, the bones of

Illus. 7.5 York: 1–9
Micklegate (Queen's
Hotel) site looking
south-east showing
walls of the bath house
hypocaust – arches
blocked in the late
Roman period. (© York
Archaeological Trust)

rats and mice, and even the carcases of house flies, lice and fleas. At the end
of the second century there seems to have been a bit of a clean-up when the
timber buildings were replaced by a masonry structure with very substantial
foundations. Insufficient was recovered to allow its function to be determined, but
it may have been part of a suite of public buildings which included the forum. This
is a Latin term which originally referred to a large open space used for markets
and public meetings, but has come to refer to a group of structures ranged
around a central courtyard used for these and other administrative and judicial
purposes. The York forum has not been located, although an altar dedicated
to the *numen* of the emperor linked to the *genius* of *Eboracum*, found near the
Ouse bridgehead (in George Hudson Street) would have been appropriate for
the obligatory forum shrine (*aedes*). This area has also produced a number of
bases for substantial columns, probably as much as 10m high, which must have
stood in a grand public building.[27]

By the early third century the town had spread south-eastwards from the
main road. At 1–9 Micklegate, for example, some very substantial walls, up to
2.5m thick, were found along with flooring of *opus signinum*, a type of Roman
concrete made waterproof – and so suitable for baths – by mixing fragments of
tile into it.[28] The building must have been a large public bath house comparable,
for example, to the *Kaiserthermen* and *Barbarathermen*, of which substantial

remains survive in the former imperial capital at Trier in Germany. Further to the south-east, in the Bishophill area of the city, expansion involved the construction of at least one massive terrace on the steep valley side above the Ouse. Excavations and observations have revealed the remains of a number of town houses on and adjacent to this terrace which would have enjoyed pleasant river views.[29] In what may be classed as a suburban area, at Clementhorpe, on another artificial terrace, there was another large house which faced the Ouse.[30] Although not fully exposed in excavation, it had a large room originally measuring 7.2m × 6m internally, entered from a portico at its east end. This was probably a reception hall providing a suitably impressive venue in which the owner would meet associates in business or officialdom as well as his clients and staff.

In the western corner of the town south-west of the Ouse there was a very grand building c.9m wide and at least 13m long with, at its south-west end, a semicircular apse, an example of an increasingly popular addition to the region's Roman buildings from the late second century onwards.[31] The presence of a hypocaust has prompted the interpretation of this building as the *caldarium* – it would be the largest in Britain – of another bath house. Alternatively, it may have served as the reception hall in a building with some other public function. Further to the south-west, the line of the main Roman approach road was built up for c.250m beyond what is now Micklegate Bar on Blossom Street where there was at least one substantial stone building of the late second century.[32]

At a date which has not been determined, but perhaps most likely in the late second or early third centuries, the Clementhorpe and Blossom Street areas were probably cut off from the rest of the Roman town by the construction of defences. The surviving medieval city walls are thought to follow the line of a Roman circuit of defences, rather as the city walls follow the north-east and north-west fortress defences, north-east of the Ouse. However, a potential Roman town wall has only been found in three places adjacent to the medieval wall, all in the north-western part of the circuit, and it still remains to be conclusively demonstrated that there is indeed a Roman wall beneath the whole circuit of medieval walls.[33] In fact, as there is a Roman cemetery in the south-east corner of the medieval walled town, which ought, according to Roman law, to have been extramural, any Roman defences may have enclosed a rather smaller area.

The population of Roman York is hard to estimate, but it may have reached over 10,000 people at its height if the entire fortress garrison is included, not a large number by modern standards but considerably greater than would have been found anywhere else in the north of Britain. One impact of the growth of Roman York on its immediate hinterland from about the mid-second century onwards was the parcelling up of the land. Previously, enclosed landscapes of the type common in many parts of the region were absent from the immediate York area except on light sandy or gravelly soils as at Heslington. However, beyond the settled areas and cemeteries, archaeology has revealed mid-late second-century ditches on many different sites within a radius of c.3km from the centre of York.[34] The surviving width of these ditches was typically in the range 0.50m–2m and depth 0.25m–1m. They presumably defined fields or stock pens, and may be witness to an intensification of local agricultural production in an attempt to provide more food for a rapidly growing settlement. In a predominantly low-lying area, prone to flood in places, these ditches must also have served to improve drainage. They often appear to be carefully aligned on the nearest Roman road which suggests a major episode of co-ordinated land management. However, although the enclosures themselves may have survived to be defined by hedges, most of the ditches do not appear to have been maintained over a long period and had probably silted up by the early third century if not before.

Also in the York environs a new settlement emerged at Dringhouses, c.3.25km south-west of the city centre, on the main road from the south-west (Illus. 6.1, 8). In the nineteenth century a relief was found here showing Vulcan, the smith god, probably from a shrine dedicated by local metalworkers.[35] More recently, traces of two strip buildings, typical of roadside settlements in the region and beyond, were found.[36] Constructed in the middle of the second century they had substantial clay and cobble footings which probably supported stone walls. Associated pottery included numerous sherds of amphorae and table wares which may indicate that one of the buildings was an inn where travellers to and from York might refresh themselves.

Aldborough and Brough on Humber

According to the Antonine Itinerary Aldborough was known to the Romans as *Isubrigantum* which is a shortening of *Isurium Brigantum*. The second element, based on the name of the tribe (the Brigantes), confirms that Aldborough was its *civitas* capital. The first element is thought to incorporate the British name for the River Ure, *Uria*, the name meaning, perhaps, the 'clean one'.[37] Aldborough was probably chosen as the *civitas* capital for the Brigantes because it was reasonably central to their territory on the eastern side of the Pennines. It was also on Dere Street giving it good communication links to north and south, and it was within easy reach of York (c.25km) from where the Brigantian *curia* could be easily supervised. Where Aldborough differs from many other *civitas* capitals in Britain, such as Cirencester or Canterbury for example, is that it was not near to any important native settlement thereby allowing an easy transfer of authority to the new site (Stanwick is c.50km distant). However, Aldborough was founded in a different historical context from the towns of the first century and should be seen as more comparable to the *civitas* capitals at Carmarthen and Wroxeter, also thought to be Hadrianic, in that its origins probably lie in a Roman fort and associated *vicus*.

Aldborough had clearly begun to develop along the lines of the other *civitas* capitals of Roman Britain by the mid-second century. Having said

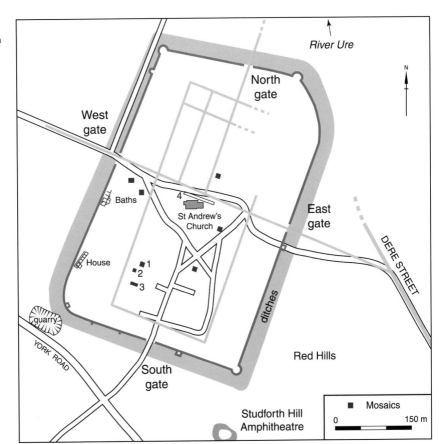

Illus. 7.6   Aldborough: plan showing the location of principal discoveries of the Roman period. Key: 1, Lion mosaic; 2, Flower mosaic; 3, Helicon mosaic; 4, Forum (remains found 1770).

River Ure

North gate

West gate

Baths

4
St Andrew's Church

House

1
2
3

East gate

DERE STREET

ditches

quarry

YORK ROAD

South gate

Red Hills

Studforth Hill Amphitheatre

N

Mosaics

0   150 m

Illus. 7.7   Aldborough: the defences as they survive today near the south gate. (Photo: P. Ottaway)

this, the town is not well known archaeologically. Although recording of Roman antiquities goes back to the eighteenth century and a considerable number of discoveries were published by Ecroyd Smith in 1852, there has been little excavation in recent years except on the line of the defences.[38] There has, however, been a programme of fieldwalking which, for example, identified a zone of early Roman settlement on Dere Street as it approached the Ure, north-east of what would become the defended area.[39] Within the defences aerial photography and chance finds, and in 2010–11 a geophysical survey, indicate the existence of a street grid of the usual Roman type. Its establishment appears to follow the artificial build up of ground level in much of the northern part of the town which was probably intended to prevent flooding from the Ure.[40]

Knowledge of Aldborough's civic buildings within the defences is more or less confined to the forum. As long ago as 1770 widening of the road north of St Andrew's church exposed a range of massively built rooms extending c.52m east–west. This is usually interpreted as the rear range of rooms behind the main hall of the forum; the church itself must stand in the former courtyard. Other buildings discovered in the nineteenth century include baths and part of a house near the western defences and another large house near the south gate with two mosaics dated to the later second century, one depicting a lion – more of the animal was once visible – and the other with a geometrical pattern with a central flower motif (Illus. 7.33). Today they are the only Roman mosaics which can be seen in situ north of the Humber.[41] A room with an apse and a fourth-century mosaic may have been part of the same house. Small scale excavations in the 1950s and 1960s in other parts of Aldborough have revealed sequences in which timber structures of the early second century were replaced by stone buildings.

Visible today in the English Heritage Guardianship site, west of Aldborough's south gate, are the remains of the town wall, including three interval towers, reduced to the lowest courses of stonework. With an enclosed area of c.25ha Aldborough is one of Britain's smaller Roman walled towns. Construction of the defences probably took place in the years 160–80, although a later date is possible.[42] It involved, first of all, a ditch c.6m wide and c.1.83m deep, the material dug out being used to form an earthen rampart. It is now thought that part of the same construction episode was the addition of a stone wall in front of the rampart, along with the erection of the interval towers and gates. No structural remains of the gates survive, but a sequence of roads thought to have passed through the north gate is known from excavation.[43] The wall had a core of sandstone rubble set in white mortar with an interior and exterior facing of red sandstone blocks.

There are examples of towns in Roman Britain which received defences in the late first century, but in the late second and early third so did most others. However, Aldborough is unusual amongst the towns of Roman Britain in having a rampart and a wall built at the same time – it is more common to find a wall added later to the rampart. The reason for the construction of town defences in Britain has been much debated. Protection against a military threat is thought unlikely, but the defences may have served to define an area within which residents enjoyed legal privileges denied to those outside it and / or one which had a particular sacred character under the protection of the Roman gods. We get some intimation that urban spaces might be considered sacred from the Roman author Plutarch, who describing the ritual act of founding Rome itself, tells us in his *Life of Romulus*:

> The founder fitted a brazen ploughshare to the plough, and, yoking together a bull and a cow, drove himself a deep line or furrow round the bounds... With this line they described the wall and called it *pomoerium*... and they consider the whole wall as holy, except where the gates are.'

On a strictly practical level, defences would have allowed the collection of tolls at the gates and exclusion of undesirables. There may also have been an element of competitive civic pride which demanded an architectural show of force to impress townsfolk from elsewhere. Another investment in civic infrastructure at Aldborough took place immediately outside the defences on Studforth Hill, to the south-east, where a most exciting discovery has been made in the recent geophysical survey. It had long been suspected that this was the site of an amphitheatre and the survey seems to show that this is indeed the case with evidence for seating and the outer wall still surviving below the turf.[44] Aldborough now has the only Roman amphitheatre north of the Humber and joins quite a small group of British towns which enjoyed a purpose-built facility for gladiatorial contests and the other robust entertainments of Roman times.

Brough on Humber is usually thought to have been the *civitas* capital of the Parisi, although there is not a great deal of archaeological or epigraphic evidence for urban status. As we have already seen, there was a fort of the conquest period evacuated in the mid-80s, but a base of some sort to the south-west of it (in Wacher's view a 'stores depot') remained in existence until early in the Hadrianic period. The fort was then briefly reoccupied before the defences were slighted for good. By the late second or early third century a defended enclosure had been created, defined by a bank and ditch, but encompassing only *c.*5.25ha (significantly smaller than Aldborough).[45]

Of some importance in determining Brough's status, is an inscribed tablet found in 1937 adjacent to a building (Corder's Building I) within the defences near the east gate, but it was not, unfortunately, in the place for which it was originally intended.[46] The tablet records the gift to his community of a theatre *proscaenium* (stage) by Marcus Ulpius Ianuarius, an *aedile* (junior magistrate) of the *vicus* of *Petuaria*. The form of the imperial dedication to Antoninus Pius dates it to 140–44. The *vicus* is usually assumed to be Brough, although this would not normally be the appropriate status for a *civitas* capital. Furthermore, *Petuaria* has no tribal suffix like Aldborough (*Isurium Brigantum* – 'of the

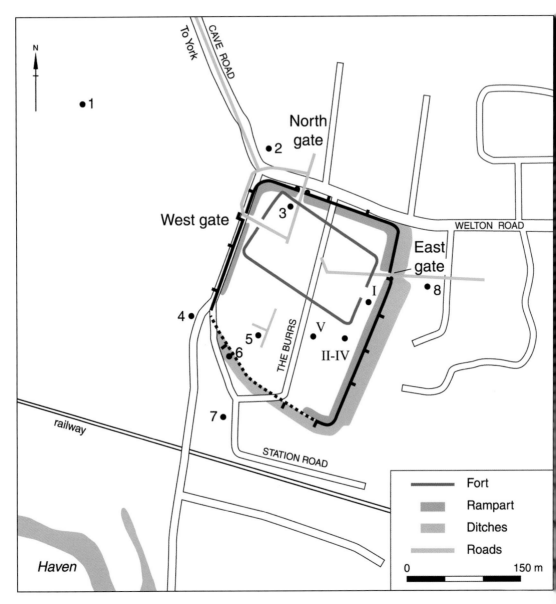

Illus. 7.8 Brough on Humber: plan showing the sites mentioned in the text. Key: I – V sites dug by Corder; 1, Cave Road (1977–78); 2, 12 Cave Road; 3, Brough House; 4, Magistrates' Court; 5, Manor House; 6, 49 Station Road; 7, 66 Station Road; 8, 40–52 Welton Road.

Brigantes') which most other *civitas* capitals have. However, the presence of an aedile suggests a place of some significance, even if such a person would not normally be associated with a *vicus*. The left side of the tablet bears a C, probably standing for *civitas*. The right side is unfortunately missing but had it had a P – for *Parisiorum* ('of the Parisi') – the matter of Brough's status would have been nearer to confirmation.

Little is known of the interior of the defended area at Brough, although a recent geophysical survey of the open land known as Bozzes Field has revealed elements of a regular street pattern.[47] Such excavations as have taken place suggest that from the mid-second century onwards the town was flourishing and began to expand some way outside the defended area. Within the defences a number of stone buildings, largely of simple rectangular plan, were found in Corder's excavations in the 1930s (I–V) and in Wacher's excavations of the 1960s, although it is difficult to place them in a wider townscape context in the absence of excavation on a sufficiently large scale.[48] Wacher's Building A1 at Brough House was thought to pre-date the town defences whilst Corder's Building I, being exactly aligned on the eastern defences, may be a little later. Both Buildings A1 and I yielded evidence for metalworking, the latter having a 'bronze worker's hearth' against the east wall. Another of Wacher's buildings, at Manor House, was of the characteristic strip form (c.14m × 7m) and was set end-on to a major north–south street. Outside the east gate (at 40–52 Welton Road) an extramural settlement south of a road built in the late second century (contemporary with the gate) produced properties defined by ditches in which there were traces of buildings. Kiln wasters were evidence for the manufacture of pottery in the immediate area.[49]

The fortunes of Brough were probably bound up largely with the haven (an inlet from the Humber) where a harbour was presumably located. This is thought to have been west of the defences, although today there is no trace of it and what remains of the haven is well to the south. Excavations immediately west of the town, for example at the Magistrates' Court, suggest the original eastern bank of the haven lay under Station Road, but had moved westwards by the late second century.[50] Further west, west of Cave Road, perhaps near to the original northern limit of the haven there is a record (excavated in 1977–78 and unpublished) of a rectangular stone-walled 'enclosure', of unknown significance, and an adjacent street.[51]

Vici and roadside settlements

The development of York, Aldborough and Brough, relatively large settlements with a number of political, economic and social functions either in the province as a whole, in the case of York, or in their own regions in the cases of the other two, is but one indication of the emergence of a settlement hierarchy quite different and much more complex than had existed in Yorkshire during the Iron Age. In addition to the three principal towns, there were a number of smaller, nucleated settlements not dignified by any particular legal status, their residents possessing no special privileges, but none the less performing roles distinguishing them from mere hamlets or farmsteads. The origin of these settlements varied but they shared a location on important routes across the region and an economic role in marketing, food processing and manufacturing. They lack complex or regular plans and manifest no great architectural ambition. The dominant building type was the strip building for which a shift from timber to stone construction took place fairly generally across the region in the mid-second century.

Settlements outside the forts usually had their origins as *vici* in pre-Hadrianic times and continued to develop through the second century and into the early third. By this time they had probably acquired a life of their own which was not entirely dependent on the military as a source of wealth. In the Pennine region little is known of *vici* at either Elslack or Bainbridge, although at the latter aerial photographs suggest enclosures and structures may lie on relatively gently sloping ground on the east side of the fort. Small scale excavations at Bowes, east of the fort, show a *vicus* settlement extending *c.*150m from the fort along the main approach road.[52] At Greta Bridge, where the fort is thought to have been regarrisoned in *c.*160, remains of a *vicus* were found when the A66 was diverted to avoid today's hamlet and put back on to the line of the Roman road to the north-east of it.[53] Excavations showed that settlement extended *c.*600m along the line of the road which was itself located in the excavations with a stone-lined drain along the side. The earliest excavated building dated to the mid- to late second century. It was large (16m × 12.60m) and probably timber framed with walls infilled with wattle and daub. Its plan is unique for our region with ten or more rooms set around a kitchen facing a courtyard. In the kitchen there was a bread oven with the iron bread shovel found *in situ*. The size and form of this building suggests it was a *mansio*, an inn or guest house of the sort used throughout the empire by the official postal service (*cursus publicus*), although open to other travellers as well.

At Ilkley there has been little excavation outside the fort, but there are enough chance finds to suggest there was an extensive *vicus* taking advantage of a location at the junction of roads through lower Wharfedale and the upper Aire valley.[54] A large Roman millstone in the Manor House Museum suggests the existence of a watermill on the River Wharfe. At Adel numerous chance finds have been made in what would have been the *vicus*, especially to the west of the fort. Geophysical survey has suggested a built-up area either side of the road to Ilkley. Excavations in the 1930s and again in 1956, west of Eccup Lane, produced some remains of buildings including one with stone walls dated to the late second century.[55]

In Yorkshire's lowland zone one of the most successful settlements in the region was at Catterick (Illus. 5.6). It enjoyed continued importance as a crossing point of the River Swale and was a convenient stopping point for travellers to or from the northern frontier. As we have seen, the fort lay on the south side of the Swale and had an annexe to the east. The fort was one of those abandoned *c.*122, but the annexe baths remained standing. In *c.*160 the fort was rebuilt and regarrisoned, and at about the same time a ditched enclosure was established on the north bank of the Swale which has been referred to as a 'stores depot'.[56] North of this enclosure, facing on to Dere Street, there were strip buildings which probably had timber superstructures set over stone footings. They probably belonged to a roadside settlement, comparable to that south of the Swale, which took advantage of a passing trade picking up after the garrison had returned.[57]

In the annexe the baths were enlarged and incorporated into one of the most complex and ambitious Roman buildings known in the region, usually described as the *mansio* (see inset of Illus. 9.5). The building occupied a plot *c*.75m × 50m and its plan can be divided into two main suites of rooms, plus a bath wing and service rooms, probably including stables. Amongst the *mansio*'s appointments was a stone fountain on the head of which a hippocamp – a mythical creature which was half fish, half horse – and a dolphin were depicted in relief.[58] It is suggested that outside the south-west corner of the baths there was a freestanding column for which an extravagant Corinthian capital was found. This may have been a 'Jupiter column', a type of monument rare in Britain, but well known elsewhere in the empire which would have had an image of the god brandishing his thunderbolts on the top.

At Bainesse development of a prosperous suburb really took off in the Hadrianic period with new timber strip buildings facing Dere Street (east side). Subsequently, in the years *c*.138–50 a minor street at 90° to Dere Street appeared. In *c*.150–80 the timber structures were replaced in stone but on the west side of Dere Street there was a timber building which had a blacksmith's hearth. Finally, in *c*.170–220 hearths for non-ferrous metalworking were set out on the east side of Dere Street and a large stone building with an apsed room and heating system was constructed. This latter was altogether more ambitious than the strip buildings and was presumably the residence for a person of greater wealth or status than the norm.

At Castleford, where the fort had been abandoned in *c*.100, the *vicus* outside the fort on the road to York and the north remained occupied (*Vicus* 3; Illus. 5.5). There were timber strip buildings on Site 1, including what had been a pottery shop in which forty or so mortaria, dated 140–50, were stacked up for sale at the time of a very destructive fire.[59] All the vessels, probably made locally, were homogeneous in their fabric, type of pouring spout and the grit fired on to the inner surface to assist the mixing process. They had been broken along the top of the flange separating the rim from the interior as if the roof had fallen directly on top of them. On Site 10 there were two substantial stone structures with internal courtyards, one of which is thought to have been Castleford's version of a *mansio*. Excavation further south in 1987–88 (Sites 44, 45 and 51) suggests the *vicus* expanded in earnest beyond its original limits after *c*.120 with a sequence of timber and then stone buildings facing the road.[60] There was also further evidence for metalworking. In spite of its position at an important river crossing, present evidence suggests the *vicus* at Castleford did not survive beyond the beginning of the third century. Quite why it was abandoned then before re-occupation in the fourth century, is uncertain, although areas not yet excavated may hide a settlement of the missing years.

At the crossing of the River Don at Doncaster, small scale excavations and casual finds suggest a *vicus* lay primarily to the east and south of the fort along the main Roman approach road from the south-east (Illus. 5.4).[61] There is evidence from a site on St Sepulchre Gate that on its south-west side the *vicus* was enclosed by bank and ditch defences in the mid-second century, before the fort was reoccupied. However, the full extent of any defended area is unknown. One of the economic functions of the *vicus* at Doncaster would have been to act as a distribution centre for the important local pottery industry based *c*.5km to the south-east (see below).

Finally the *vicus* which, apart from Catterick, is the best known archaeologically in Yorkshire is at Malton. We have already seen that, on the slope down to the River Derwent (Orchard Field), there was a defended settlement south-east of the fort in the late first century. In the mid-second century, at about the same time as the regarrisoning of the fort, what is usually described as the *vicus* began to expand and timber buildings obliterated the earlier defences (1970 site).[62] The overall picture from the principal excavated sites (Orchard Field, Orchard Cottage and the 1970 site) is that by the early third century buildings, largely of the strip type, faced two roads (1–2) which

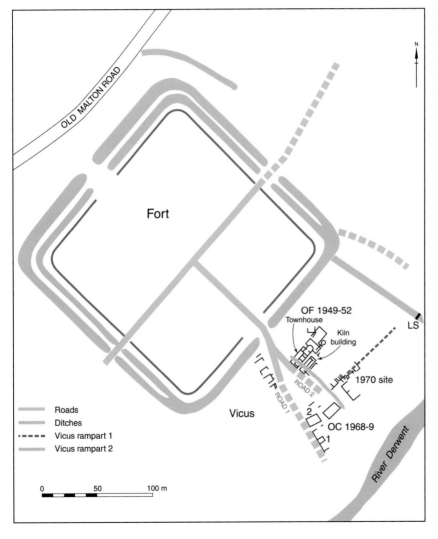

Illus. 7.9   Malton: plan of the Roman settlement south-east of the fort. Key: LS, Lady Spring; OC, Orchard Cottage; OF, Orchard Field.

diverged just outside the fort's south-east gate, Road 2 being an addition of that time. Geophysical survey to the east of the excavated sites shows the presence of a number of other buildings including a house with a courtyard.[63] Timber had been replaced by stone, readily available at Malton (close to sources of Jurassic Limestone) as the principal structural material in the years c.130–60, as at Catterick and elsewhere. On the north-east side of the *vicus* there was an early third-century bank and ditch which ran south-eastwards from the south-east corner of the fort and was picked up at the Lady Spring site where it was shown that the bank was faced with a stone wall.[64] Whether there were defences on the south-west edge of the settlement is unknown, although there do not appear to have been any along the river. In addition to the Orchard Field zone, there was also Roman settlement around the other sides of the fort, probably in the form of ribbon development along the main approach roads as is common elsewhere. The evidence is largely from chance finds, but at the Rugby Club, c.450m north-east of the fort, excavations in 1993 located the approach road from the north-east, a large stone building (18.5 × 7m) and five cremation burials (Illus. 5.18).[65]

Illus. 7.10 Small uninscribed altar from High Catton (near Stamford Bridge, East Riding), probably from a roadside shrine (© Humber Field Archaeology).

On the opposite bank of the Derwent to Malton extensive Roman settlement has been recorded in Norton-on-Derwent.[66] It probably began to develop in the mid-second century around the junction of Roman roads approaching the river. A road from the south, located just west of Langton Road, probably originated in York – it joined Humber Street (from Brough) c.3km south of Norton. Another road approached from the east, perhaps originating in Bridlington on the coast and has been located at sites in Norton itself (Illus. 5.18, 6–7, 9). By the end of the second century Roman Norton appears to have been a manufacturing centre for pottery and metalwork.

Other settlements existed in the Yorkshire region where either a fort had only a brief life or there had been no military presence at all in the vicinity. On the northern boundary of the Yorkshire region at Piercebridge, where Dere Street crossed the Tees, what is referred to as a *vicus* developed both north and south of the river.[67] To the north, on the Durham side, the settlement's origins probably lay in the early second century – hence the assumption of an early (as yet undiscovered) fort nearby. One of the earliest features of the *vicus* was a pottery kiln, but there were soon strip buildings of the usual type facing the road on either side. Settlement development south of the Tees began in c.180 following reconstruction of the bridge. A number of strip buildings have been recorded either side of the rerouted Dere Street. The road itself measured 7.5m wide and was constructed in typical Roman fashion on a base of large cobbles with successive layers of smaller cobbles and a pebble and clay surface.[68]

Further south at Healam Bridge, also on Dere Street, where there was an early fort or camp, recent archaeological work has revealed an extensive roadside settlement either side of the Healam Beck. Full details have yet to be published but it was clearly characterised by ditched enclosures facing the main road in which there were strip buildings surviving as dual rows of post-holes or as stone footings.[69]

Stamford Bridge lies 12.5km east of York; the fort had probably been abandoned by 120, but about c.1km to the south a settlement began to emerge principally around the main Roman road from York to the coast between where it crossed the River Derwent and a junction with a secondary road heading south-east towards Barmby Moor, near Pocklington.[70] Aerial photography, supplemented by small scale excavation, has identified a settled area of c.13ha in which there were small ditched enclosures. Excavation west of the Derwent in 1992 identified part of a building with cobble and clay foundations and a stone-lined well, good indications of a settlement of a status above the purely rustic. East of the Derwent, south of the road to the coast, excavations along the narrow 10m wide corridor of a pipeline revealed enclosures laid out c.120–60. They produced further stone-lined wells and evidence for metalworking as well as burials; buildings were thought to exist in unexcavated areas north of the corridor on the road side.[71] More evidence for ditched enclosures, probably north of the road, was found at High Catton Road where an unusual discovery was a small uninscribed altar, perhaps from a roadside shrine.[72] Another recent discovery is a building with a hypocaust, probably a bath house, located near the north-east edge of the settlement.[73] Near High Catton village, c.1.5km from Stamford Bridge, on the road to the south-east, another small settlement emerged in the mid-second century.[74]

East of the Derwent, at Hayton and Shiptonthorpe, only c.3.75km apart, on the main Roman road from Brough to York, lay two more roadside settlements. Both at beck crossings, on light, well-drained soils, they lie in an area favourable for agriculture, based on a diversity of landscape types within easy reach; to the north and north-east lies the chalk of the Wolds and to the south and south-west are the carrs (meadowland) of the Foulness valley. Fieldwork, as part of the Foulness Valley project, has shown that in the Iron Age settlement in the area had been focused primarily on the river and its tributaries. However, by the early second century, some time after Hayton fort had been abandoned, the Roman road appears to have become an important factor in the reorganisation of settlement. Some of the local population, at least, relocated to the road line, presumably in order to benefit from the exchange of local agricultural products for commodities from further afield.

At Hayton extensive fieldwalking has defined an occupation zone extending over at least 5.6ha in a band c.80m wide on each side of the Roman road.[75] Watching briefs in the area suggest there were stone buildings; aerial photographs and geophysical survey suggest they stood in the sort of small ditched enclosures found in other roadside settlements. On an excavation in Town Street, close to the north-east side of the main road, there were remains of timber buildings and ovens.[76] On Burnby Lane, 450m further east, excavations revealed two Late Iron Age enclosures, each containing a roundhouse. The layout was modified in the early Roman period with one enclosure divided in two, one of which accommodated an aisled timber building 9m wide and at least 11m long, the exterior walls based on stone footings.[77]

By the late second century the Roman road at Shiptonthorpe ran through a corridor 18m wide with drainage ditches on either side.[78] Aerial photographs suggest a settlement zone c.60m wide on each side of the road, extending for c.800m giving an overall area of c.9.6ha. Excavation of c.1050m^2 in 1986–87 and 1990–91 on the south-west side of the Roman road was intended to examine a complete example of one of the plots of land recorded from the air. In the first phase, of the mid-second century, there was, behind a roadside ditch, what was interpreted as the remains of a small roundhouse c.7.4m in diameter – yet another example of the native building tradition still current in the Roman period. In the second phase, dated to the late second or early third centuries, a ditched enclosure was set out. Within this were traces of a second timber structure together with a well and a midden.

Rural settlement and landscape: an emerging Roman countryside

Although some redistribution of the population took place in the Yorkshire region during the second century, the vast majority probably remained where their forefathers had lived and worked. There is good evidence for the rural landscape and settlement of the period covered by this chapter from most parts of the region. The enclosed landscapes defined by ditches, often of Iron Age origin (described in Chapters 4–5) survived and were in some cases modified and expanded. In many cases, however, the ditches seem to have been silting up by the early to mid-third century, never to be used again.

The roundhouse continued to be the characteristic rural building, but, in addition, we find that many farmsteads now acquired one or more stone – or partly stone – buildings of Roman type. The larger complexes are usually referred to as villas and are taken to be estate centres. Unfortunately we have no way of knowing how large these estates were nor do we know whether they were worked primarily by slaves or by freeborn tenants. However, Yorkshire's villas all lay, as one would expect, on good agricultural land which was clearly capable of production above the level required for simple subsistence. The importance of trade in its various forms for stimulating surplus production is indicated by the location of villas; they are close to Roman roads or navigable waterways and within a fairly short distance of the larger settlements, notably

Aldborough, Brough and Malton where markets for produce would be found. Surprisingly, however, there are few villas near York, perhaps because the poorly drained claylands in its hinterland were largely unsuitable for profitable agriculture. Villas usually had a predecessor settlement of native type which is taken to indicate that the estates were owned by local British landowners rather than, for example, retired Roman soldiers or public servants, although some of these people may have acquired a country seat in our region.

In terms of their plans, the region's villas were organised around a main dwelling house, although there are no examples in the region of the integrated building complexes with one or more courtyards seen in some of the larger and more opulent Roman villas in the south of England. In Yorkshire the main house usually faced south or south-east to ensure maximum sunlight for the main rooms. Like the grander town houses, it possessed a number of rooms, often set out such as to offer a measure of privacy to the owner and his family. There may have been upper floors, but no clear evidence survives. As we have already seen at Welton, a corridor or portico might run along one side of the house. The rooms often had the benefit of heating systems and interior decoration which included mosaics and painted wall plaster. There was usually

Illus. 7.11 Gargrave villa in the late third century: plan of the principal buildings (drawn by Brian Hartley, © Elizabeth Hartley).

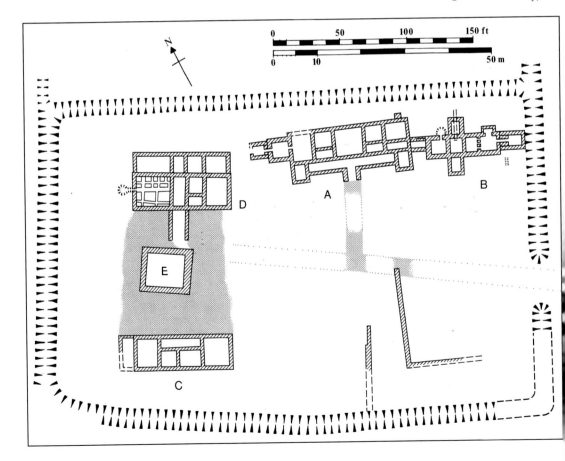

an open yard in front of the house to allow views from within and to show off the façade to best advantage to visitors. Bath houses were an amenity in most cases sited at a distance from the main house rather than incorporated within it, perhaps to reduce the risk of fire. Other buildings, usually dedicated to agricultural use, were loosely grouped around the courtyard or, as the site developed, around secondary courtyards, often behind walls to keep them from impinging on the sensibilities of the owner and his family.

A survey of rural settlement will, as in Chapter 5, move from the west of the county to the east looking, primarily, at examples of sites which have been studied by excavation and survey – many of them have already been referred to in Chapter 4. We may begin in Andrew Fleming's Swaledale study area where Roman period settlements and fields appear to have been fitted into the earlier systems.[79] One of a number of house platforms was excavated at Healaugh, near Reeth. A structure of circular plan was replaced by one of oval plan with a substantial paved floor which produced second-century pottery.

The landscape and settlements of Iron Age origin in Craven continued to develop in the Roman period but dating evidence from these sites is usually very scarce. However, at Attermire Camp East, near Settle, on a south-facing scarp slope at about 400m above sea level, excavation of a number of roundhouses produced second- to third-century pottery, including a little samian, as well as a small hoard of ten coins, hints, perhaps, of more extended links with the wider world than hitherto.[80] Untypical of settlement in the region was a farmstead found at Gargrave which was to attain the status of a villa.[81] This was very much an outlier from the other Yorkshire villas, but in a localised area of well-drained loamy clay over gravel there were ground conditions suitable for productive agriculture. In the early Roman period roundhouses had stood on the site, surrounded by an extensive field system. By the late second century the farmstead had two stone buildings. One of these was a house with a corridor running across the front between two short projecting wings at each end – a 'winged corridor house' (Illus. 7.11, A). Fragments of mosaic floor survived in the main room. The house had a small bath suite, but the other stone building was a detached bath house, perhaps for the use of the estate workers (B). Three second-century timber buildings were presumably used for the farm, along with one of the roundhouses which had survived from earlier times. In the early third century a ditched enclosure surrounded the house and bath house, but excluded the farm buildings, thereby creating a distinction between polite residential space and that dedicated to the agricultural work with its smells and noise.

On the Coal Measures of the southern Pennines, north-west of Sheffield, numerous enclosure sites were recorded in an extensive survey by Leslie Butcher.[82] They were clearly occupied from the second century onwards (although possibly of early or pre-Roman origin). In the Wharncliffe area, east of the River Don and south-east of Stocksbridge, groups of enclosures and probable house sites are, for the most part, defined by stony banks or orthostat walls. At Whitley a rectangular enclosure (c.18m × 9m), located at c.260m above sea level has been excavated.[83] Within the orthostat walls were some cobbled areas and post-holes, which, although making no clear pattern, may have been the remains of structures. Whitley and other settlements in the area had the sandstone to hand to manufacture their own quernstones and a number of 'working floors' associated with roughouts have been found.

North-east of Sheffield, near Rotherham, one of the enclosures defined by banks of earth and stones in Canklow Woods has been excavated. It measured 41m² internally; no clear trace of structures was found, but occupation in the second century was suggested by a few pot sherds.[84] The Wombwell enclosure complex (described in Chapter 4), defined in this case by ditches, produced a little pottery suggesting it too was in use in the second century, but not necessarily later. Nearby at Shafton pottery from the High Street and Bypass sites suggests the enclosures were in use until perhaps the late second or early third century.[85] Wheat chaff and weed seeds from High Street suggested this was a grain producing site, perhaps supplying markets in Doncaster and Castleford. On the eastern edge of the Coal Measures modern arable agriculture means early landscapes are revealed as cropmarks, primarily indicating ditches; any banks or walls are long gone. On the line of the A1–M1 link the Iron Age trackway continued to serve as the spine for the enclosed landscape investigated at Swillington Common (Illus. 4.6).[86] The field system here and at nearby Stile Hill, Colton may have had an earlier origin, but for the most part the ditches contained late second- and third-century pottery, indicating that this was when they were silting up. Notable at the Colton site were traces of four small post-built structures of rectangular plan, most likely used for the accommodation of livestock. Another extensive cropmark landscape lies on gravel terraces either side of the River Calder at Low Common, Whitwood (south-west of Castleford). North of the river a trackway of probable Iron Age origin ran east–west for at least 4km and provided the spine for a co-axial system of enclosed fields. South of the river two enclosures have been excavated and the ditches were, again, found to contain pottery of a date no later than the second or third centuries.[87]

On the drift deposits over the Magnesian Limestone near Ripon (North Yorks.) there is a Roman villa at North Stainley and house at Snape which may also be part of a villa.[88] However, the dating of both sites is uncertain as the buildings which are known at the first were recorded in a nineteenth-century excavation and the house at the second is recorded only on aerial photography. However, also in the same area, at Well, 7km south of Bedale, excavations have revealed an unusual building complex whose origin can be dated to the late second century.[89] The site lies in a little valley running east–west and on its north side there were stone buildings, including a dwelling of simple plan with three rooms linked by a corridor. In the central room there was a mosaic, a part of which can still be seen in the local parish church (Illus. 3.10). To the east was a substantial baths block and south of it the most unusual feature on the site, a large pool, c.12m × 4.5m and 1.8m deep, built of stone blocks and originally lined with lead sheets. Between the house and baths was another structure with a hypocaust which has not been fully explored. Although it is most likely that this complex was a villa, it has been suggested that the size of the baths and pool indicate that it was also a centre for some water-related cult and/or for water-based therapeutic remedies.

On the Magnesian Limestone, about 38km south of Well at Dalton Parlours, near Collingham, lay a villa site where building in stone probably began in c.200 after a break in occupation since the late Iron Age.[90] Thought to be amongst the earliest buildings was the principal dwelling house (Building J). Generously proportioned, with a corridor at the front, it was composed of a large central hall with square rooms at each end and wings projecting from them to the north. On the western side two rooms, one with an apse, may be seen as a reception suite of the sort which became popular in large houses in our region in the later Roman period. The apsed room (sometimes referred to as a *triclinium*), with its half-domed roof, was probably used for the sort of formal dining in Roman style which employed a semicircular couch (*stibadium*) on which one reclined whilst the servants brought the food and drink. On the east side of the house there was a pair of square heated rooms for more intimate dining and sociability. South-west of the main house was another stone building (B), thought to have been a detached bath house, as at Gargrave, with two or more heated rooms. An early third-century date is implied by the style of wall painting on fragments of plaster found in demolition deposits (Illus. 7.34). Immediately south-east of the main house there were two timber structures, X and Y; in the former the bases of four beehive querns were found, clearly indicating its role in grain processing. These buildings were replaced by a large aisled building (M) with exterior walls in part, at least, of stone which was altered on a number of occasions; it may have provided accommodation for slaves and/or estate workers. Other buildings for agricultural use contemporary with the later life of the house are described in Chapter 9. The extensive enclosed landscapes on the Magnesian Limestone, revealed as crop marks on aerial photographs, have been studied by excavation in a number of places including Wattle Syke, just north of Dalton Parlours (Illus. 3.2).[91] As at the villa, numerous querns from this site suggest intensive grain production on what would have been well-drained and fertile land. Other enclosed landscapes on the limestone have been studied on the line of the A1–M1 link at Parlington Hollins (north of Garforth, east of Leeds),[92] at a number of sites excavated in advance of the Darrington–Dishforth A1 upgrade[93] and at the Ferrybridge M1–M62 interchange.[94] A fairly consistent picture emerges of trackways, fields and enclosures for buildings, all defined by ditches. As on the adjacent Coal Measures, these ditches appear for the most part to have been filling up in the late second or early third centuries after which they were not renewed.

South of the Don, enclosure sites on the Magnesian Limestone are often defined, like some of those on the Coal Measures, by walls or banks without

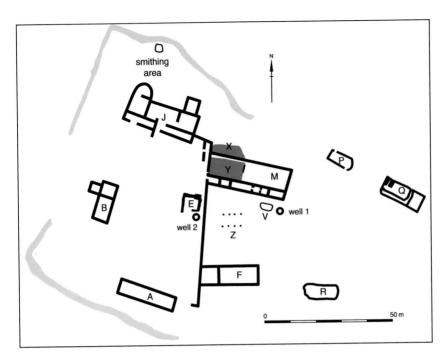

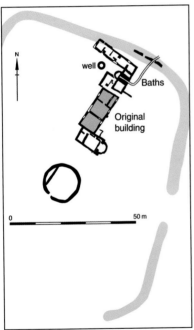

Illus. 7.12 (*top*)   Plan of Dalton Parlours villa- buildings lettered as per text (after Wrathmell and Nicholson 1990).

Illus. 7.13 (*bottom*)   Plan of Holme House villa showing the principal buildings (after Harding 1984).

ditches. At Edlington Wood, 6km south-west of Doncaster, a series of enclosures has been identified within which there were small buildings on a rectangular plan.[95] The apparent absence of any Iron Age settlement in this area suggests that it was in the Roman period that movement on to what may have been an area of marginal land with a poor water supply had taken place, perhaps in response to increasing demand for agricultural products from the fort and

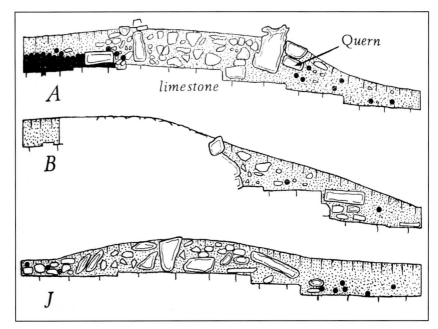

Illus. 7.14 Smarson Hill, South Anston (near Sheffield): cross-sections (lengths: c.11.5m) through an orthostat wall (see p. 55) surrounding a small enclosure (from Radley and Plant 1969, © Hunter Archaeological Society).

vicus just up the road. Between Sheffield and Worksop (Notts.) at Smarson Hill Wood, South Anston enclosures defined by banks covering orthostat walls and lynchets on sloping ground have been revealed, once forming part of a larger Roman landscape which has been largely ploughed away. One of the enclosures, roughly 24m square, has been excavated; there was no obvious building, but an abundance of Roman coarse pottery and some iron slag.[96] The Dinnington torc was found nearby in an area of similar enclosures.

From the Magnesian Limestone belt of West and South Yorkshire we may return to the northern part of the lowland zone in the centre of the county. In the valley of the Tees, near Middlesbrough, there have been excavations at, for example, Bonny Grove Farm,[97] Dixon's Bank,[98] Coulby Newham and Ingleby Barwick.[99] Probably of Iron Age or early Roman origin, these sites appear to have been typical of the area, all taking the form of ditched enclosures on elevated sites close to water, the first three overlooking the Tees Plain to the north whilst Ingleby Barwick lies on a gravel terrace on the plain itself. Separated from the fields by a large ditch was a modest villa complex consisting of a winged corridor house facing east, and, a little to the east, a small detached bath house. Other buildings, loosely grouped around a courtyard, included a large aisled barn, whose outer walls had stone footings. A measure of prosperity in the area is indicated by this site and also appears to have been the case further west where the Tees is crossed by Dere Street where we have already noted the extensive cropmark landscapes around Manfield and the emergence of a road-side settlement at Piercebridge. This was clearly a locality where agriculture flourished assisted by good communications, a combination which may explain the unusually early emergence of a villa at Holme House, *c.*800m east of the river crossing.[100] Within the earlier Iron Age enclosure, but to the north-east

Illus. 7.15
A reconstruction of
Holme House villa in
the mid-second century,
looking north-west.

of the roundhouse, a Roman sequence began with a building of rectangular plan and modest size (*c*.18m × 7.5m). All that survived were footings of clay and cobbles and it is thought that the superstructure may have been timber framed. In the mid-second century the building was enlarged demonstrating a considerable investment by the owner. Added onto the north-east side of the original building was a bath suite of the linear type, similar to military bath houses as, for example, at Catterick. On the south-west side two heated rooms were added, with an apse at the south end, which may be seen as another early example of the type of reception suite also seen at Dalton Parlours.

South-west of the villa, on the site of the earlier roundhouse, and retaining its central position in the enclosure, was an unusual building with a round plan. It was 14.8m (exactly 50 Roman feet) in diameter and the base of the wall, *c*.1m thick, was largely of unmortared cobbles. In the centre were post-holes arranged in a square which had probably supported large timbers integral to the structure; the entrance lay on the south-west side. This building appears different in character and size to the traditional roundhouse and may have had more in common with other Roman round buildings such as one of similar size and ground plan at Winterton villa (Lincs.) or a temple found on Hayling Island (Hants.). Given the thickness of the wall, dry stone construction to a reasonable height seems quite possible – in Illus. 7.15 it has been reconstructed as *c*.7m high, half the diameter. Unfortunately no artefacts give a clue to the function of the round building, but its dominant position and structural sophistication may mean that it is why the villa is here rather than vice versa. A shrine must be a possibility, especially given other evidence for religious activity on the banks of Tees in this area.

Once again there is little settlement to report from the clay lands of the central Vale of York, but the attraction of the morainic ridges is shown by a site on the western edge of the Vale at Flaxby near Knaresborough.[101] It was occupied in the Iron Age and then shifted to higher ground in the mid-second century. Traces of timber structures of subrectangular plan, a cobbled track, and pits and ditches were recorded in trenching.

Investigations in the Humberhead Levels, for example, south of the Aire at Sykehouse, once again suggest that enclosed landscapes did not usually survive into the late Roman period in this low lying area and may have actually been abandoned due to a rising water table.[102] This may also have been the case at Balby Carr, south of Doncaster, where the field system described in Chapter 4 produced no pottery later than the middle of the second century. Also south of the River Don, excavations within a large area (c.27ha) at Gunhills, Armthorpe revealed an organisation of the landscape which was, unusually perhaps, not of Iron Age origin, but began in the mid-second century.[103] The site also shows how enclosures of different types, perhaps for different functions, might co-exist in close proximity. In the later second century, in the western half of the study area, a number of trackways defined by ditches were laid out, around which there were relatively small, irregularly shaped enclosures, but in the eastern half, perpendicular to an east–west aligned trackway, there was a series of very regular, elongated enclosures of the brickwork type common in this area. At Gunhills, and other sites in nearby Edenthorpe, the ditches appear from the pottery, yet again, to be silting up in the early third century.[104]

On the higher ground to the east of the Vale of York, on the south-western edge of the Howardian Hills, a concentration of Roman finds has come from Crayke near Easingwold. There is a spring here, Sike Spa, which one would expect to have attracted settlement and on a gas pipeline traces of five roundhouses were found. They were succeeded in the mid-late second century by a stone building at least 13m long × 8m wide which remained in use until the fourth century.[105] A sandstone block shaped as a plinth or cornice suggests a building of some pretension. In the uplands of the North York Moors evidence specifically for new settlement in the period under discussion is sparse, although those of earlier origin remained in occupation and have produced material culture of the second century. At Crag Bank, Kildale (near Guisborough) a roundhouse was associated with second-century pottery as were houses of rectangular plan at a site in Lonsdale nearby.[106] To the south, on the northern fringes of the Vale of Pickering, at Beadlam, relatively little is known of the site of the well-known fourth-century villa in the second and early third centuries, but there does appear to have been a stone building which belongs to this period.[107]

On the southern edge of the Vale at Brough Hill, Settrington, within a ditched enclosure, aerial photography has recorded three roundhouses, perhaps of Iron Age date, but also a stone building of the simplest linear plan (28m × 6m) with four rooms.[108] This suggests that the generation of surplus on good land had allowed a modest investment in construction with a result probably more typical of the area's farmsteads than the villas which have attracted greater archaeological attention. One of these is Langton, 2.5km to the south-west of Settrington, where the story which began in the late first century continued with the first stone buildings in the late second and early third centuries (Phase 1 on Illus. 7.16).[109] They included 'House 1', although this was not certainly a dwelling. It was a simple elongated structure located in the north-east corner of a walled enclosure where other contemporary buildings may have stood, but were not excavated. To the east, to take advantage of the prevailing wind which would have minimised the annoyance of unpleasant odours from livestock circulating in the house, a complex of other buildings was probably contemporary with it including M and to the east of it Buildings J, U and R. The whole site was now enclosed on three sides by ditches. Aerial photography shows that the 'south ditch' continued to east and west extending, in all, over at least 3km. To the east there are ditched enclosures attached to the north side of this ditch and roughly parallel to it for much of its length were two other ditches, 50–100m apart, to the south. Another farmstead on the line of the ditches, possibly of villa status also, is known at Middle Farm c.400m to the west of Langton villa. The evidence has been taken to suggest the existence of a single estate, but with more than one centre, extending over 3–4km east to west and including an area of pasture on the higher ground of Langton Wold to the north, the whole perhaps occupying 1000ha.[110]

Illus. 7.16 Langton villa: plan of principal buildings (original lettering for Buildings J, L, M, P, Q, R, U, and additional lettering for Buildings A–C; after Corder and Kirk 1930).

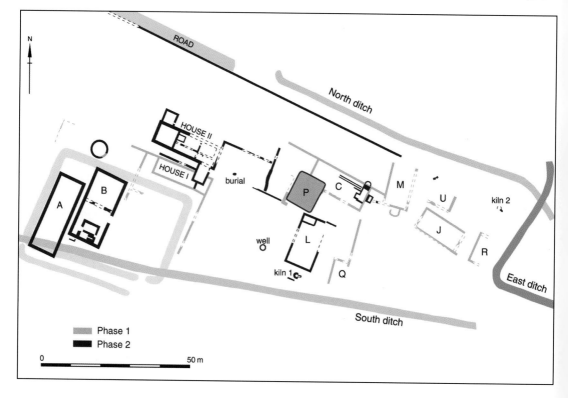

On the Yorkshire Wolds the landscape in the mid-second to early third centuries is similar to that in other areas of Yorkshire in being one of zones of both enclosure and open land with dispersed farmsteads, a few with buildings in stone. At Garton-Wetwang Slack the enclosures of Iron Age origin survived into the second century, but did not, it seems, last much beyond the end of it. However, as in other areas of good agricultural land, the wealth arising from farming combined with the spread of Roman culture led to the construction of a small stone building with a hypocaust, albeit a small one measuring only 4.2m × 2.4m, which was probably a mini-bath house.[111] About 15km to the north-east of Garton at Rudston, another site where a villa would be built in the late third or fourth century, there was evidence that ditched enclosures of late Iron Age origin remained in use until the end of the second century. They formed part of an extensive complex identified by aerial photography to the south of the villa site.[112] The first stone building on the site was constructed in the early third century.[113]

On the southern tip of the Wolds at Welton villa the house remained in occupation, but some change in the character of the site may be suggested by the infilling of the well.[114] This was apparently done as a one-off operation

Illus. 7.17   Plan of Kingston upon Hull showing sites referred to in text. Key: 1, Greylees Avenue; 2, Gibraltar Farm, Kingswood; 3, Saltshouse Road; 4, Malmo Road, Sutton Fields Industrial Estate.

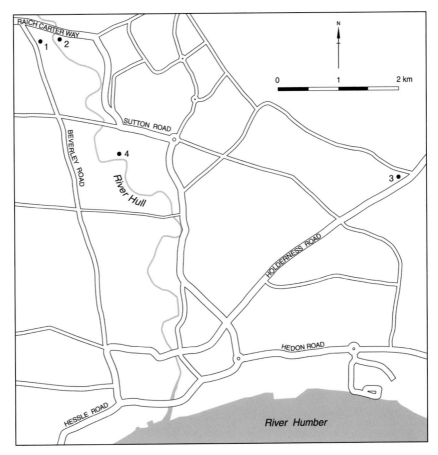

with a vast quantity of animal remains, largely cattle, surviving as a great collection of bones. They may represent a form of ritual closure of the well in a form replicated elsewhere. At nearby Melton, on the road improvement site, the enclosure ditches were, as elsewhere in the region, filling up in the late second or early third century. However, the land was clearly not abandoned as dug into one of the filled-up ditches was a grain-drying kiln.

At the junction of the chalk of the Wolds with the clay of Holderness we may return to the sites at High Wold and Sewerby Cottage Farm on the north side of Bridlington introduced in Chapter 4. At High Wold the late Iron Age rectangular enclosure continued in use, the ditch around it was redug, and the space within was divided into two halves (Illus. 4.11, Phase 3).[115] In the southern half there was a post-built structure on a rectangular plan, probably a farm building. To the east the enclosure was now approached by a trackway defined by ditches, and subsequently the enclosure complex expanded to the south-east (Phase 4) and within it was a grain-drying kiln suggesting the site was a centre for production of cereals. At Sewerby Cottage the large late Iron Age ditched enclosures also continued in use, with the inclusion of at least one small post-built structure.[116] Within the principal enclosure examined there was a group of small enclosures, thought to be Roman, possibly for stock, but in one of them three more grain-drying kilns were found supporting the High Wold evidence for the area's economic base. The latest pottery in the enclosure ditches and other features at both sites was late second or early third century. A similar picture of ditches silting up at this time was apparent at sites with late Iron Age origins at Wansford, just south of the Wolds near Driffield,[117] and also at Aldbrough on the coast of Holderness.[118]

In the lower valley of the River Hull, settlement becomes more visible to archaeology from the second century onwards than hitherto. In what is now the metropolitan area of Kingston upon Hull artefacts dated to the earlier part of the Roman period appear to cluster on land close to the river channel, although many parts of the urban area have been developed without any archaeological investigation.[119] The distribution of these artefacts suggests that, if settled on the river bank, the local population was able to take advantage of the meadows and saltmarshes on lower lying land and slightly higher ground suitable for arable, whether on alluvial silt or clay. On the west bank of the Hull at Greylees Avenue, on the northern edge of the conurbation, an excavation revealed ditches, probably part of a field system, which seem to have silted up in the early third century, although pottery of the later Roman period indicates continuing activity in the area.[120] Roman sequences have also been revealed at two sites excavated on the east bank of the Hull.[121] At Sutton Fields Industrial Estate, Malmo Road, a series of linked enclosures has been identified focused on a cobbled trackway running for at least 60m. At Gibraltar Farm, Kingswood, 2km to the north, a system of ditched enclosures extending over an area c.60m × 25m was identified. At the centre was a timber building of rectangular plan with its origins in the second half of the second century

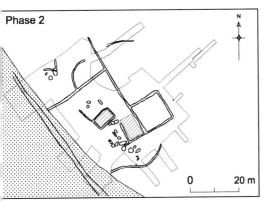

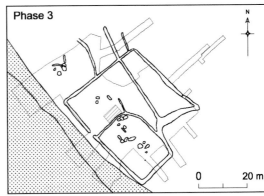

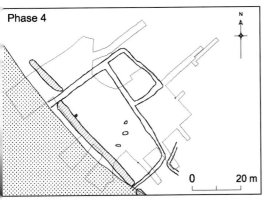

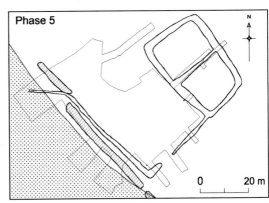

Illus. 7.18
Kingston upon Hull:
Gibraltar Farm,
Kingswood, sequence
of site development
(River Hull, lower
left) (© Humber Field
Archaeology).

(Illus. 7.18, Phase 2). In the early third century the enclosures were redefined and the area enclosed was enlarged (Phase 3).

To sum up, large parts of the Yorkshire region in the period under discussion in this chapter were still characterised by enclosed landscapes which usually survive today as ditches; banks and walls may have been much more common than we imagine, but do not survive except in areas which have escaped post-Roman ploughing. Within these enclosed landscapes there were settlements with a more varied range of building types than hitherto including not only roundhouses of traditional type but others with rectangular plans employing earth-fast timber posts. There were also farmsteads with buildings partly or entirely of stone, sometimes in complexes we regard as villas as at Gargrave, Holme House and Well. By the early third century enclosure ditches appear to have been silting up all over the region, although there are a few sites where ditches were still employed perhaps, as at Gibraltar Farm on the bank of the Hull, where drainage was an issue (Illus. 7.18, Phase 4). It is quite possible that in many cases field systems were now defined primarily by hedges which leave little archaeological trace. Alternatively, we may be seeing a change in the farming regime which required more open landscapes.

Agriculture: some new developments

There may be no means of accurately calculating economic output in Roman times, but there was probably a further increase in agricultural production in our region in the post-Hadrianic period. This answered the demands not only of the military, but of an increasing population in York and the other principal settlements in which a larger proportion than hitherto was engaged in occupations other than agriculture. How production was increased is not entirely clear, but there was probably more land taken into cultivation, in some areas at least, following the clearance of woodland and improvement of drainage.

Evidence for cereal production in the period under discussion, as in others, largely takes the form of charred grain. The largest deposit from the region came from a late second-century context at Rougier Street, south-west of the Ouse at York.[122] This is thought to have been the debris from a granary fire just like the earlier deposit from Coney Street. The Rougier Street deposit was composed of 88% spelt wheat and 11% barley. This may be compared

Illus. 7.19 Bridlington: Sewerby Cottage Farm, sunken-floored building with grain-drying kiln (© On Site Archaeology).

Beam Slot

Sunken feature
Building

Daub

with material from a grain-drying kiln at Ferrybridge which contained a large sample of charred cereals, again largely spelt wheat, but also including some oats and barley.[123] Rather different proportions were found in contemporary deposits at Catterick where barley was dominant for reasons which may be to do with climatic conditions in the immediate area or, perhaps, in the Pennines from where grain was brought for both consumption and, probably, further distribution.[124] The source of the Rougier Street grain is not evident, but unlike Coney Street, it was probably local as it contained seeds of weeds which would have been found in the fields around York, including wild radish, black bindweed and the poisonous corncockle.[125]

It has been suggested that a new type of plough which had a coulter was introduced to Roman Britain in the second or third centuries, although surviving examples of the parts are usually fourth-century, if datable.[126] The coulter is a vertical blade-like component which cut into the soil, aerating it and killing off perennial weeds more effectively than the ard whose share simply made a groove in the surface of the soil. An iron ploughshare and coulter, thought to be Roman, but not closely dated, were found together close to the fortress wall at York.[127] A well-known model of a man using a plough with a coulter comes from Piercebridge on the Co. Durham side of the Tees.[128] How widely the new plough was used is hard to tell, but the ard probably remained in general use.

Whilst there is little evidence for improvement in the crops themselves since the late Iron Age, a development in how crops were processed, which appears to be an introduction to the region of the first half of the second century, is a special type of structure often referred to as a 'grain-drying kiln', 'corn-drying kiln' or 'corn-drier'. As found in the ground, a common type consists of a stoking pit leading to a T-shaped flue made up of a long arm, up to c.5m long, with a short cross arm at the end. A well-preserved late Roman example at Crambe, near Malton, had a limestone flue-lining and some surviving slabs which had covered the flue.[129] However, it is clear from an example at Welton (Illus. 9.14) that on occasions, at least, there was a double slab floor with a narrow space between the two so that any smoke in the main flue would not soot the grain spread out over the upper floor. In addition, vents in the upper flue would have allowed some regulation of the temperature such as to prevent scorching of the grain. Whilst the T-shaped kiln is common, there were others. For example, the Ferrybridge kiln had a short flue leading to a rectangular chamber. Mortice holes in its side are thought to have supported a timber floor.[130] A similar example was found at Sewerby Cottage Farm within a structure with earth-fast posts which would have given the kiln shelter from the weather.[131] Another kiln at the site lay in a sunken-floored timber building. Although they rarely survive in the ground, these buildings must have existed in more or less every case to allow the kilns to function properly. This was shown by Peter Reynolds (Director of Butser Iron Age Farm) in the experimental reconstruction of a grain-drying kiln which also showed that it was preferable to have a hipped or gabled roof which was thatched thereby allowing excess hot gasses to escape into the open air.[132]

There has been debate not only about how corn-drying kilns should be reconstructed, but also about their purpose. Peter Reynolds pointed out that grain can be dried perfectly adequately in sheaves left in the field, if the weather is favourable, or in a barn if not. It seems clear, however, that these kilns, which become very common in the late Roman period, were used to dry damp grain after the harvest. This was probably done, firstly, to prepare it for threshing and, secondly, to prevent it germinating, thereby lessening the risk of rotting during storage.[133] However, prevention of germination was also part of the malting process and Reynolds believed these kilns were used primarily for malting. During germination enzymes in grain break down the starch in it to form sugars used by a plant as it grows. In order to make use of these sugars – i.e. the malt – in brewing or distilling the germination must be stopped.

In the production of meat, cattle remained dominant in relation to sheep and pigs (Table 6). Large groups of animal bones of the mid-second to early third centuries from Yorkshire come from Tanner Row, York,[134] *Vicus* 3 at Castleford[135] and from sites in Catterick.[136] Except for a late second-century group from Thornborough Farm, Catterick, cattle bones make up over 60% of those of the three main meat-giving animals. In addition, and most remarkable of all, was a group of almost 13,000 cattle bones, representing 162 beasts, found in a ditch surrounding an Iron Age chariot burial at Ferry Fryston (near Castleford).[137] The cutting of the ditch itself was probably contemporary with the burial (late third to early second century BC), but the bones were found in the uppermost infilling. Radiocarbon dates suggest that a considerable proportion of the bone was deposited in the period under discussion in this chapter, although deposition continued into the fourth century. The bones had been very carefully selected consisting largely of skulls and right side forelimbs. The inference drawn from this is that the cattle were sacrificed at a site of traditional sacred significance, perhaps the Ferrybridge Henge, and then ritually appropriate parts were consumed before putting the bones in the ditch. Table 6 also shows a markedly lower percentage of cattle from Holme House than elsewhere which may perhaps represent slightly different dietary preferences in rural areas; the percentage of pig bones was correspondingly higher here than elsewhere at *c.*25%.[138]

Aspects of meat preparation and butchery recorded at Tanner Row and Catterick are similar to those thought to have been introduced to Britain by the Roman army, and recorded at Castleford in the late first century, in respect of the specialist tools used, the extraction of marrow and piercing of cattle shoulder blades to allow them to be hung up for smoking.[139]

The Tanner Row cattle had an average shoulder height of 1.11m, and the figure for Catterick was similar, both rather greater than the Iron Age and late first-century groups (Table 2). Although the samples are small, there

Table 6 Nos of animal bone fragments from principal meat sources from second- or early third-century contexts in descending order of percentage of cattle

Place	Date	Cattle	Sheep/ goat	pig	Total	% cattle
Castleford Fort III	*c*.100–250	1,985	380	198	2,563	77.45
Catterick Bridge	Early C3	639	185	83	907	70.45
York Tanner Row	Mid-C2	384	79	96	559	68.69
York Tanner Row	Mid C2–early C3	4,912	1,408	1,064	7,384	66.54
Castleford *Vicus* 3	*c*.140–180	1,693	611	334	2,638	64.18
Catterick, Thornborough	Late C2	567	302	135	1,004	56.47
Holme House Villa	Largely C2	363	273	211	847	33.00

may have been a slight increase in size of the region's cattle. The reason for any increase is not entirely clear, but it has been suggested that during the Roman period new breeding stock was introduced to Britain in an attempt to create a larger animal.

Age at death patterns for cattle at Tanner Row and Catterick were much the same as at Castleford in the late first century with no evidence for cattle slaughtered below three years of age (Table 4). These data are quite typical of Roman Britain as a whole reflecting the multi-purpose character of the animals. It is very striking, therefore, that a quite different age at death pattern comes from the cattle bones at Ferry Fryston where the vast majority were killed between the ages of eighteen months and three years. Whoever organised the feasts at which these beasts were eaten was sufficiently wealthy to forego any use of them past their prime age for eating.

The age data for sheep at Tanner Row and Catterick are much the same as they are for late first-century Castleford with slaughter in the second or third year of life, although there is evidence from Tanner Row for the early slaughter of lambs at two–four months which is thought to be the result of a reducing surplus in a flock kept, at least in part, for milk production. Pigs were usually slaughtered at Tanner Row and Catterick, as elsewhere, when immature at about two years of age, but there is some evidence from Tanner Row for very young pigs, perhaps reflecting a taste in York for the sucking pig referred to in some Roman recipes. An unusual animal recorded in the bones from Tanner Row, which is also mentioned in Roman recipes, was dormouse, although it was a species (*eliomys quercinus*) native to Gaul rather than the classic edible type (*glis glis*) enjoyed in Mediterranean regions. As in the pre-Hadrianic period, hunted wild mammals – boar, deer and hare – appear to have made little contribution to the region's diet.

Fowl remained a component of diet as far as birds are concerned. However, the Roman hen would have looked rather like our little bantams and hardly recognisable to anyone used to their plump successors of today which are the result of selective breeding over hundreds of years. A remarkable range of other birds was represented at Tanner Row, if usually by no more than one or two bones, but some species, at least, must have been eaten on occasions. They were, for the most part, ducks, such as gadwall, mallard, shoveller, teal, tufted duck and wigeon. Geese were probably the native greylag, very common in the city today, but they cannot be easily distinguished from other species by their bones. In addition, there were bones from black grouse, rook and wood pigeon, all birds which no doubt made good eating as well.

Fish bones have not usually been recovered in any numbers from Roman sites in Yorkshire, but at Tanner Row there were bones of estuarine fish such as smelt (related to salmon), although those of freshwater species such as barbell, burbot, grayling and salmon predominated, suggesting the River Ouse was cleaner and better oxygenated in Roman times.[140] A roof antefix from York has an image in relief of a fisherman with a trap and net, forerunner of the many anglers who can be seen on the banks of the Ouse today.[141] Sea fish did not feature in Roman diet but a marine peculiarity from the roadside settlement at Dringhouses was a large whale vertebra, probably from a beached specimen, not one caught at sea.[142] It seems unlikely that whale meat was regularly eaten in Roman Britain, but the sheer size of the creatures seen off our shores seems to have aroused an interest which apparently got as far as Rome itself. In *Satire IX* the poet Juvenal refers to the fortunes acquired by certain unscrupulous individuals which '… dwarf any normal inheritance until they look like some puny dolphin beside a British whale.'

Animals were not only bred for food and other economic reasons and this section may be concluded by reference to dogs. A feature of the Roman period as a whole is a greater diversity in the size of dogs than has been recorded in pre-Roman material. Seven fairly large specimens, known from their partial skeletons found at Bainesse, Catterick, measured 306–374mm to the shoulder which suggests they worked as guard dogs or hunting dogs.[143] However, bones from Castleford suggested a range of sizes with those at the smaller end comparable to modern dachshunds.[144] The British enjoyment of the keeping of a dog purely as a pet may, therefore, have had its origins in Roman times.

Manufacturing: from strength to strength

The range and quantity of manufactured goods, and extent of their distribution appears to have increased considerably in our region from the second quarter of the second century onwards to judge by what has been recovered from archaeological sites, not just in the principal settlements, but also in the rural areas. The evidence for specialist manufacturing sites is, as in other periods, dominated by those of the pottery industry, although it also extends

Illus. 7.21 (*opposite*) Typical products of the Doncaster pottery kilns including: Rusticated ware (rear row, left), Black-burnished ware jar with lattice decoration (rear row, second from left), Parisian ware (rear row, right), mortaria (front row, first and second on right) (© Doncaster Museum Service, Doncaster Metropolitan Borough Council).

to metalworking and glassworking. Specialists in these relatively high tech. industries worked primarily in or near the larger places in the region where they could find a regular market. Other materials, such as bone and textile, were worked largely in households, whether in town or country.

Pottery

It is clear that until the mid-second century people in many parts of the Yorkshire region used mainly hand-made pottery, largely cooking jars, in the native tradition. This only gradually died out to be replaced by mass-produced

wheel-made vessels of Roman type, hitherto largely confined to York and a few other major settlements. At York the direct involvement of the military in making pottery had apparently ceased by the Hadrianic period. It is thought that red earthenware of Ebor Ware type was now produced by civilian entrepreneurs, for example at Apple Tree Farm, Heworth, *c.*3 km north-east of the fortress.[145] This development may have been prompted by the departure of the Ninth Legion and one can envisage legionary veterans taking up the production of ceramics as a second career. However, on its arrival to form the new garrison in York after 122, the Sixth Legion felt the need to make its own pots. A Hadrianic phase of manufacture has been identified in the material from the kiln zone east of the fortress. Vivien Swan has shown that the vessel forms and their decorative motifs mark a radical change in the legionary approach to potting at York.[146] For example, there are vessels coated in white clay slip with simple stamped motifs and other decoration. Swan suggests that the origins of the new Hadrianic styles are to be found in the province of *Germania Superior* (Upper Germany) notably the Wetterau region, east of Mainz. It is for this reason that she suggests the presence in York of a potter familiar with the styles of the Twenty-second Legion *Primigenia* based at Mainz itself. This is not surprising, perhaps, as many of the Sixth Legion's recruits would have come from the neighbouring province of *Germania Inferior* (Lower Germany) as the legion had previously been based at Xanten before coming to Britain. That the new types of vessel from York were not distributed widely in the region, only occasionally being found elsewhere and usually on military sites, may, perhaps, indicate that the army in the Hadrianic period still remained something of a community living apart from the population as a whole. However, by *c.*140 the legionary kilns had once more ceased to operate, although production continued at Heworth. New products from the Heworth workshop included mortaria stamped with potters' names including that of a man named Agrippa. In the early third century there was a final episode of production in the legionary kilns at York, probably associated with the presence of the Emperor Septimius Severus (see below).

The other important regional production centre in the second century lay south-east of Doncaster in what are now the parishes of Auckley, Bessacarr, Branton, Cantley and Rossington.[147] Production probably began in the late first century, but the earliest known kilns date to *c.*135. There was an enormous increase in output in the 140s and 150s. Workshops included one at Rossington, established by an enterprising individual named Sarrius, known from his mortaria stamps, whose career had begun at the Mancetter and Hartshill potteries in Warwickshire. Other potters, possibly his assistants, are named on stamps as Secunda and Setibocius. Sarrius, the enterprising fellow, also had a workshop at Bearsden on the Antonine Wall. It is thought that one can detect the influence of pottery traditions from north-west Lincolnshire in the Doncaster kilns, suggesting craftsmen, taking their cue from Sarrius, who had moved north following the expanding military market.

The products of the Doncaster kilns were usually grey wares with cooking jars of various sorts the dominant functional type answering to the demands of local consumers. In addition, black or near black vessels with a slightly shiny finish of a type known as 'Black-burnished ware' were produced at Rossington, probably for military clients. A more specialised product was a distinctive table ware known as 'Parisian ware' (first identified at Brough on Humber hence the name) distinguished by patterns of stamped decoration.[148] Doncaster products were distributed widely in the late second century reaching York and the northern frontier. Transportation of bulk consignments was, perhaps, effected largely by water via the Don, Humber Estuary and east coast. By the early third century, however, production levels appear to have declined such that distribution was largely local.

Elsewhere in Yorkshire there was production of pottery at Castleford and Catterick until the mid-second century, and at Aldborough, probably until the end of the second century, although less is known about industries in these places in the absence of kiln sites. By the late second or early third century new centres had emerged in east Yorkshire, notably in the Holme-on-Spalding Moor area[149] and at Norton-on-Derwent.[150] Both places produced good quality grey wares in a range of vessel types for kitchen and table. Distribution was largely local, but presumably production was answering an increasing demand, even in remote areas, for Romanised types of pottery.

Metalworking

The best evidence for metalworking in the period under discussion comes from York, south-west of the Ouse, and other larger settlements. At Tanner Row, York, deposits around the timber buildings described above produced smithing slag, hearth linings, several metalworking tools, including drifts and punches, and probable scrap items, including part of a sword, all suggesting there was a smithy nearby.[151] Also south-west of the Ouse, on the site of the former church of St Mary Bishophill Senior, a hearth was found associated with a small pit in which there were two wooden boxes containing copper alloy filings, probably part of a smith's store of material for recycling. As already noted, two buildings at Brough produced evidence for metalworking, and a smithing hearth was found at Bainesse, Catterick.[152] Amongst the pottery kilns at Cantley, Doncaster an iron smelting furnace was found and it may not have been unusual to find the two principal heat-using technologies practiced in the same places if not by the same people.[153] Other settlements must have had metalworkers supplying local needs and small quantities of smithing slag are found on many sites in the region.

Gold artefacts are very rare in the region's archaeological record being confined to a few coins and pieces of jewellery. However, unusual evidence for goldworking comes from an inscribed tablet found in Norton-on-Derwent which combines a dedication to the *genius loci* of a goldsmith's workshop with an injunction to a young slave to make use of, or perhaps work hard in

Illus. 7.22 Pottery kiln (late second- to early third-century) found at Norton Community Primary School, Norton-on-Derwent (© MAP).

Illus. 7.23 Norton-on-Derwent: inscribed tablet from a goldsmith's shop (0.33m × 0.2m; photo: P. Ottaway).

it.[154] Although he is not named, any reference to a slave in an inscription is almost unknown in Britain so this individual may have been a craftsman of unusual skill.

Glass

Evidence for a glassworks, the only one known in Roman Britain, was located at Coppergate, York, immediately south-east of the Roman fortress, and dated to about the year 200.[155] Excavations on what has become famous as the 'Viking Dig' produced some small blocks of a material which suggested that the glass was actually being made here from the raw ingredients – silica and an alkali – and not just worked. In addition, the manufacture of glass artefacts is indicated by some 3kg of pottery sherds derived from receptacles used to melt both colourless and green soda glass. This suggests an episode of glass melting on a relatively large scale; one product is thought to have been window panes. In addition there were a few glass fragments derived from the use of a blowing iron to form glass vessels. In view of its location, the glassworks may have been under military control; however, window panes were probably destined for both military and civilian building at a time of increasingly sophisticated architecture in the region.

Building materials

Other aspects of an increasing diversity of products for building construction in the region in the second century include new types of ceramic material such as chimney pots and the box flues used to take the hot air from under-floor hypocausts up the walls of a room. Rather more rare are the ceramic water pipes found in the fortress at York.[156] For floors there were *tesserae*, cubes either of tile used to make 'tessellated pavements' or of a variety of other materials used to make mosaics; the late second century saw the laying of the first mosaics in the region with examples known at Aldborough, and the villas at Gargrave, Holme House and Well.[157]

Other crafts

Although there are no collections of second- to early third-century leatherwork from the region comparable to those of the late first and early second centuries from Castleford and Catterick, there is a certain amount from Tanner Row, York, probably debris from a local cobbler.[158] There are about eighty nailed shoe soles from the site of which about a quarter showed evidence for repairs, including renailing. In addition, there were sandals decorated with impressed lines on the uppers and decorative nailing patterns on the soles. Fragments of leather sheet and a near complete panel suggest that army tents were also repaired in the vicinity.

Bone and antler remained important materials for making simple tools such as needles, weaving combs and spindle whorls as well as items for recreation such as counters and dice. In addition, the period under discussion is one in which pins were widely used by women to secure their hair and bone examples are particularly common finds. A more distinctive bone object, often known as a 'perforated spoon', has a hole of various shapes in its flat 'bowl'. The type seems to be something of a Yorkshire speciality hardly known elsewhere. Examples come primarily from the caves in Craven, although a few others have been found in York, the Castleford *vicus*[159] and one or two other places. The function of these spoons is uncertain, but they may have been used for some craft purpose, perhaps for drawing and twisting yarn, or, given their occurrence in the caves, in some ritual context. One possibility is that in divination a viscous material, possibly blood, was passed through the hole and observations were made of how it dripped on to a surface marked out in some special way.

In addition to being made from metal or bone, jewellery and small dress items were made in jet (and similar materials) which became fashionable at the end of the second century.[160] The electrostatic properties of jet – it gives off visible sparks when rubbed in the dark – may have lent it a certain magical quality. Pliny believed that when burnt, the fumes would drive off snakes and also relieve suffering of the uterus.[161] Jet was, for the most part, collected on the Yorkshire coast near Whitby and was then brought to workshops in York to be made up into such things as beads, bracelets, hair pins and rings. Most production was for local consumption, but some pieces may have been exported to other parts of Britain and even as far as Gaul or Germany.[162]

Exchange and trade: wider and still wider

Most trade in the Yorkshire region remained local and would have involved commodities of relatively low value. However, from the mid-second century onwards trade connections within the region began to expand such that, for example, pottery, including samian, and metalwork of Roman types begin to appear, if only in small quantities, in even quite remote upland areas. Furthermore it is in the period up to the early third century that trade beyond the purely local flourished to its greatest extent in the Roman era. Although a good deal of the interregional and interprovincial movement of goods would have been administered by the state, largely to supply the army, at a smaller scale wealthy individuals probably commissioned merchants to bring them consignments of wine, silk or glassware etc for their personal consumption. As in previous periods, these people would, in turn, have redistributed these commodities to their local clients.

Goods exported from our region to other parts of Britain and to other provinces would, as in pre-Hadrianic times, presumably have been primarily agricultural products and minerals such as lead and silver. However imports have a rather more varied tale to tell. An impression of the balance between the local, interregional and interprovincial import trade and how its extent varied from place to place is gained primarily from data for pottery which, by default, is usually taken to represent other commodities which have not survived (Table 7). Locally produced wares provided most of the pottery for the region, although certain British sources of specialist pottery outside it

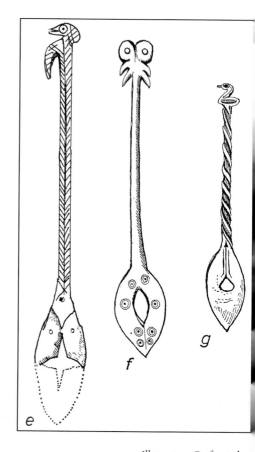

Illus. 7.24 Perforated spoons from Dowkerbottom Cave (left and centre) and Attermire Cave (spoon in centre L. 104mm). Reproduced courtesy of Alan King (from King 1974).

Table 7 No. of pot sherds of local, British and Continental origin from
mid-second- to early third-century groups in descending order of percentage local.

Site	Date	Total	Local		British	Samian	Other Continental
Castleford, Vicus 3	c.140–180	20,820	18788	(90%)	342	1380	307
York, Blake Street	Early –mid-C2	3,771	3095	(82%)	55	444	177
York, Wellington Row	Late C2-early C3	2,950	2327	(79%)	85	433	105
York, Blake Street	Late C2-C3	2,620	2017	(77%)	222	268	113
York, Wellington Row	Mid-C2	2,138	1430	(67%)	103	463	142
York, Wellington Row	Early C3	7,429	2880	(39%)	1,469	2117	958

became significant in the second century. They include Mancetter and Hartshill
in Warwickshire from where both the army and civilians acquired large
quantities of mortaria. Imports of pottery from outside Britain are primarily
represented by samian from Gaul, although there were some other types,
usually from the near Continent, notably colour-coated wares from Trier and
Cologne in Roman Germany.[163] Colour-coated vessels were given a surface
clay 'slip' of a different colour from that of the main fabric – purple was very
popular for much of the Roman period.

The pottery from York exhibits its greatest variety in groups of the late
second and mid-third centuries and the percentage which was imported from
outside Britain was at its highest, reaching as much as 40% by sherd count
on occasions. As it had been since the early conquest years, York enjoyed a
pre-eminent position in the region as a road hub and river port which was
closely associated with its role in supplying the legionary fortress and other
military sites in the region, and also its status as the home of some of the
wealthier members of regional society. By the end of the second century, a
small merchant class had apparently emerged in York. They included, amongst
others known from inscriptions, Lucius Viducius Placidus, who described
himself as a *negotiator* (merchant) from the Rouen area in northern Gaul on the
tablet commemorating the construction of part of a temple in the year 221.[164]
Those involved in interprovincial trade had to be prepared for considerable
risk when sending ships across the North Sea and many voyages must have
come to grief. However with a modicum of luck the rewards were considerable.

In other settlements, and especially those in rural areas, non-local pottery
was much less common than in York, although taking Gunhills, Armthorpe
(near Doncaster) as an example of a rural site with quite a large quantity
of pottery (7475 sherds), the late second- and early third-century phase
of occupation produced a more varied collection than was usual in South
Yorkshire hitherto. There were mortaria from Mancetter and Hartshill, colour-
coated wares from the Nene Valley (the Peterborough area), as well as
samian.[165] The quantity and variety of pottery on rural sites may, to an extent,

be related to their distance from market centres and ease of access. The size and make-up of the Armthorpe pottery group may be due to its proximity to Doncaster; even allowing for comparatively less extensive excavations, much smaller and less varied groups of pottery come from more remote sites in South Yorkshire such as, for example, Shafton and Wombwell.

Other commodities with a non-local origin found in the region suggest a similar, if less detailed, picture of expanding trade networks than that revealed by pottery, especially in material from York. For example, high status burials in its cemeteries have produced examples of the best Rhineland glass of the period.[166] Food, of which a good sample of remains has been found in York, especially at Tanner Row, appears to have been largely locally sourced. However, if not available locally, comestibles did, it seems, also come from further afield. For example, crab and herring came from the coast.[167] As in the first-century fort at Castleford, but now in a civilian context, there were olives, figs and grapes from the Continent. Amphorae brought olive oil and fish sauce from Spain and wine, largely from the Rhône valley, but also from Campania.[168] Whilst the more exotic commodities may have been imported to satisfy the appetites of the army and upper echelons of civilian society, from the mid-second century onwards amphorae, in small quantities, were beginning to reach rural sites, although in some cases, perhaps, probably re-used as convenient containers for other commodities such as grain or water. Also, lava querns, previously almost unknown outside military sites, appear in small quantities at sites like Shiptonthorpe[169] and Dalton Parlours villa,[170] although they remain rare in most rural areas.

A rather more unusual import was cinnabar (mercuric sulphide), a red pigment used in wall paintings. It was probably imported from Spain where, according to Pliny, it was found in the silver mines.[171] Other perishable imports such as clothes made of silk, or comestibles such as cinnamon and pepper, may have come to our region in the same ships as the amphorae of olive oil and wine. Such things are hard to recognise in the archaeological record, although the fortress sewer at York did produce a fragment of silk which must have originated in China.[172] On rare occasions, unusual materials travelled long distances before being worked or reworked into artefacts here in Yorkshire. For example, buckets made of silver fir, which is not native to Britain, have been found in wells in York and elsewhere in the region. The wood may have started life in wine barrels imported from Gaul. Not so much unusual as exotic was a piece of elephant ivory which seems to have been made locally into a woodworker's plane. Surprisingly perhaps, it was found in an otherwise ordinary rural settlement at Goodmanham on the edge of the Wolds, although not far from the port at Brough on Humber.[173] One can imagine the ivory having quite a journey, perhaps originating as a traded commodity somewhere in Africa and then being passed from hand to hand, before eventually arriving in Yorkshire after a journey across the Roman world. Why it was preferred to local wood for a fairly humble tool must, however, remain a mystery.

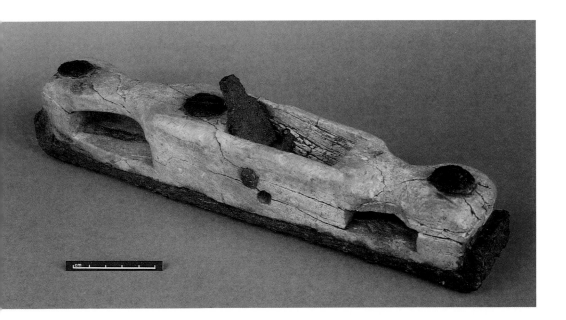

The money supply

For state administered trade or private deals by the wealthy the medium of exchange would usually have been gold and silver coin or bullion. However, the extent to which one could use coinage day to day in the markets of our region to buy such things as a chicken for tea or a pair of shoes at a price expressed in money terms is uncertain. Between the reigns of Trajan and Commodus there appears to have been a remarkable consistency in the level of supply of new coin to Britain, but trade using money would, as in the pre-Hadrianic period, have been limited by the restricted quantity available and what there was probably stuck to relatively few hands.[174] Furthermore, many of the coins available were still not particularly suitable for low value transactions. Archaeological finds imply that trade based on money did take place at military sites, in towns and in other large settlements in the region, but until the late third century coinage seems only rarely to have reached rural areas, especially those at all remote from the road network.

Until the middle of the second century the value of the imperial currency retained a fair degree of stability, which would have benefited trade using money, but then the mints began to steadily reduce the silver content of the principal silver coin, the denarius, until it reached c.50% by the end of the reign of Septimius Severus. This probably occurred because rising imperial expenditure, especially on the army, outstripped the supply of silver and it was not possible to bridge the gap by increasing the tax yield. There may also have been inflation in some important commodity prices including, perhaps, that of the grain and other supplies which were bought in bulk for the army. Reduction in silver content tended to lead to a vicious circle as once people realised that silver coins were not worth their weight in the metal, prices of goods reckoned in money terms went up to compensate. In due course it is likely that the uncertainty that a combination of debasement of the coinage and inflation caused for those engaged in commerce was a contributory factor in the sort of decline in trade, other than the purely local, for which we find evidence in mid-third-century Roman Britain including the Yorkshire region.

The visual arts: an embarrassment of riches

What did a valuable item like a gold brooch or a mosaic pavement cost a Roman consumer in our region? How was it paid for? Such questions may be hard to answer, but we can say something about the art styles and the role of the visual arts in local Roman society. From the mid-second century onwards there appears to have been a much greater availability of art objects, as of material culture generally, in the Yorkshire region. In all sorts of media, objects rendered in various versions of Roman style were now no longer seen largely in the military bases, but had become available in the wider civilian world, although the evidence still comes principally from the major settlements. Smaller personal items of jewellery and/or of religious significance are very common, although in the absence of a large body of elite patrons, except perhaps in York, the amount of public art displayed as architectural features or sculpture, including tombstones, was restricted even compared to other parts of Roman Britain.

In York in particular, and in the region as a whole, artists' works imported from outside Britain would have circulated in small quantities. There is, for example, a charming little sculpture in white marble of a naked youth, perhaps an athlete, from York, probably imported for a wealthy connoisseur.[175] However, the majority of art objects were locally made – or at least made in Britain. They exhibit the eclecticism of provincial artists whose influences ranged from the almost purely native to the classical traditions of Greece and Rome and its adaptations in other parts of the Roman world.

Representation of the human figure is an important aspect of what set Roman art apart from that of the native Britons. At their best, local examples show good skill in execution and sympathy with the subject, but more usually expression is very stylised, indeed to our modern eyes rather crude. The subject matter may be divided into two groups: deities and members of the local elite, the latter usually on their tombstones. As far as deities are concerned, York has produced some good figure sculpture in provincial classical style, notably a Mars carved life-size in Millstone Grit.[176] He is shown as a young man with a crested helmet of Greek type over his curly hair and he bears military equipment and armour. Other figure sculpture of note, if simpler in style, includes an unidentified goddess from Well, originally c.0.80m high, probably from the villa,[177] two reliefs of Mercury from Aldborough[178] and a lively relief of the goddess Victoria (victory) from Bolton, East Riding.[179] In a style rather further from the classical ideal is a none the less striking low relief depiction of a native god from York.[180] He is shown with large lentoid eyes in a face with a drooping moustache framed in a wild mass of stylised flowing locks. It is an image similar to the much better known face of the god Sulis from the Bath temple pediment and suggests a local craftsman struggling to come to terms with the classical tradition of portraiture. This can also be seen on tombstones where heads are too large for their bodies, and eyes and ears are oversized. However, as far as the patrons of those tombstones were concerned, a strictly accurate likeness of the deceased was probably of secondary importance to the very fact of having a sculpted monument in Roman style. It would have been more important to emphasise certain marks of status such as good clothes and well-groomed hair, preferably in fashions espoused by the emperor and his coterie. A rather dramatic example is to be found in the image on a tombstone from Ilkley which shows a seated woman with a centre parting and elongated plaits which extend as far as her waist – their maintenance would surely have required maidservants and this was no doubt one of the messages the viewer was expected to take away (Illus. 3.1).[181]

Whilst good clothes, elegantly worn, were considered a means of demonstrating social status, another aspect of Roman figural art is the nude. A naked male may either be a defeated native warrior, a savage deprived of what makes him human, or a hero whose nudity evokes a primal and manly vigour. The latter is evoked both by the marble statuette of the athlete from York, with his curly hair wreathed by a victor's laurels, and in much cruder form by a small relief of what may be a native version of either Mercury or Hercules, with a winged or horned hat and possibly holding a club, now in the church at Kirby Underdale near Stamford Bridge.[182] Female nudes are usually representations of the goddess Venus, the most famous from Yorkshire being on a fourth-century mosaic at Rudston (Illus. 9.20). Showing the goddess nude was an artistic convention and, as such, not considered problematic from the point of view of decency. In any event, representations of Venus often show her bathing which provided a legitimate excuse for her nudity, but also referred to the sensuality of female grooming and to sexual fertility, emphasised by the association with water. Similar references occur on a crudely executed dedication slab to the nymphs – water spirits – from the Castleford *vicus* showing two female heads depicted alongside combs for grooming their hair and trees symbolising the life force in nature.[183]

Depictions of figures in media other than stone also illustrate versions of the provincial classical style. For example, there is a most attractive copper alloy oilflask from Aldborough in the form of a young slave dozing off while awaiting his master.[184] A slight lack of crispness in its execution suggests that this was made by a local craftsman who had made a mould from an imported original. In addition, we can enjoy a striking group of jet medallions from York depicting figures in relief.[185] There is one of the gorgon Medusa with her winged head dress and snake hair in stylised form. In imitation of the goddess Minerva, who bore Medusa on her breastplate, this medallion was

Illus. 7.26 (*left*) York: statue of the god Mars (height: 1.59m; © York Museums Trust).

Illus. 7.27 (*below*) Relief of Mercury from Aldborough, now in the church of St Andrew (height 1.07mm; Photo: Blackthorn Press).

probably worn to avert the evil eye. Portrait medallions include one with a man and woman facing each other, probably a betrothed couple, whilst another depicts a group of three people recalling images of Septimius Severus and his family. Figurines suitable for domestic and other shrines are quite common finds. Examples in pipeclay were usually imported from Gaul; representations of Dea Nutrix, shown suckling a child, and Venus were particularly popular.

Illus. 7.28 Relief of the goddess Victory from Bolton, East Riding (height: 0.3m; © Peter Halkon).

Illus. 7.29 Relief of native version of a Roman god, possibly Mercury or Hercules, from Kirby Underdale, East Riding (height: 0.35m; photo: P. Ottaway).

Illus. 7.30 Castleford: inscribed stone (0.27m × 0.18m) with a dedication to the nymphs (from Tomlin 1998, © ASWYAS).

Illus. 7.31 Aldborough: copper alloy flask in the shape of a sleeping slave boy with a lantern between his legs (© British Museum).

Amongst those in copper alloy, there is a delightful figurine of the smith god
Vulcan from Catterick. He wears the *exomis*, originally a Greek tunic, but
adopted by Roman craftsmen, which left one side of the torso bare, and on
his head is a conical cap (*pileus*).[186] The man's hands probably grasped tools
which have not survived. Whilst the prototype may be found in the Hellenistic
world, the extravagant curly hair and beard on the Yorkshire version recall
the abstract patterns of local 'Celtic' art.

As well as representations of the human figure, Roman art is also rich
in depictions of natural phenomena, including animals, birds, plants and
heavenly bodies. Examples from the Yorkshire region may be sought in media
from stone sculpture to figurines and gemstones. There is insufficient space
here for an exhaustive discussion, but as far as animals are concerned, there
was a preference for those which had strong symbolic value in representing
particular qualities. As in the Iron Age, the bull and the stag, for example,
were probably seen as combining strength, ferocity and male sexual power.[187]
It is not surprising, therefore to find that the bull was the emblem of the Sixth
Legion at York. A bull's skull, or 'bucranium', a common motif in Roman art,
can be seen at the head of a centurion's tombstone from the city.[188] The stag
was a spirit of the forest and its annual growing and shedding of antlers would
have been an obvious symbol of the cycle of fertility. We have already seen
the horned head on a chariot fitting (probably late Iron Age) from Aldborough
(Illus. 4.19) thought, perhaps, to have invoked Cerunnos, a stag god of native
origin, and the stag was probably the inspiration of other horned gods in
Roman Britain, a local example being the Kirby Underdale 'Mercury'. The

stag also featured in the iconography of hunting, a popular past-time for the Roman elite, along with the hare and the hounds the animals were hunted with. Hares are represented by two small brooches from Catterick[189] whilst an incomplete stone relief from York depicts a hound and a horse in what was probably a hunting scene.[190]

Another animal of great symbolic significance in Roman art was the lion, king of beasts, admired for his ferocity. The Emperor Commodus took the lion as a badge as part of his identification with the god Hercules who had slain the Nemean lion and wore its skin as protection. Representations of lions from Roman Britain are numerous but of widely varying quality as local craftsmen are unlikely to have seen one in the flesh. However, two splendid stone lions each holding down a bull's head, probably from a tomb monument, were found in Catterick – here they represent the all devouring power of death.[191] Also from Catterick is a fairly respectable, if stylised, lion on a bronze brooch.[192]

Pride of place amongst birds represented in Roman art is the eagle which was considered a suitable companion for the gods, especially Jupiter, and had a particular significance as the sacred emblem of the Roman legions. One of two stone reliefs from York showing an eagle has the bird in a typical pose with a wreath around its neck while the other shows it with wings outstretched.[193] Smaller objects from York incorporating an eagle include a pin from the Minster excavations[194] and a seal box lid from Blake Street.[195] Also popular was the cockerel, companion of Mercury and messenger of the gods who appears, for example, on a small stone relief from York.[196] More exotic is an Indian parrot carved on a gemstone of red jasper from the Castleford *vicus*.[197]

As far as the embellishment of buildings is concerned, new and typically Roman modes of artistic expression represented in mosaic and painted wall plaster began to appear in the region during the second century. Mosaics will be further considered in Chapter 9, but as for painted plaster, there were clearly some elaborate designs employing a variety of mineral-based pigments, including red ochre (red and brown), yellow ochre, glauconite (green), calcium-copper tetrasilicate, more commonly known as 'Egyptian Blue', and imported cinnabar (red). They were usually applied using the fresco technique when the plaster was still damp so as to prevent fading. For example, a wall of one of the rooms in the *mansio* at Catterick had the tripartite division into dado (at the base), central zone and frieze, very common in Roman buildings of the better sort.[198] The dado exhibited a fake marbling effect and there had been plant motifs in the central zone. What must have been some of the most attractive designs from the region come from the bath house at Dalton Parlours villa.[199] Fragments of plaster have been reconstructed to reveal not only wall decoration, but also part of a ceiling decoration with a pattern of continuous octagons containing roundels. On a white ground these motifs are defined in various colours and painted in such a way as to suggest relief. At the centre of the roundels are stylised rosettes and palmettes in red, not painted but, very unusually, made with a stamp.

Illus. 7.33   Second-century mosaic at Aldborough with a geometric pattern and central star motif. (Photo P. Ottaway)

Religion: staying with the old but welcoming the new

For the first fifty years or so after the conquest there is little evidence for the adoption of Romanised religious ideas in Yorkshire except at York and the forts. By the mid-second century the situation had begun to change, although once again the evidence from York is more abundant than from anywhere else in the region.

Understanding the beliefs and practices of the native population remains difficult. Native cults derived from pre-Roman forebears required neither man-made locations for observance nor representation of the gods in human form; inscriptions would have been largely meaningless to the illiterate. One imagines that British people continued to interact with the divine at such places as rivers and streams, and the tops of mountains. If certain native cults continued to flourish more or less unaffected by the conquest, alongside them we find those which had been given a Romanised veneer. One way of doing this was the use of artefacts of Roman type. For example, for a considerable period before the conquest a particular sacred quality may have been invested in the caves of the Craven area. Their dark, silent and confined interiors, to which access was often

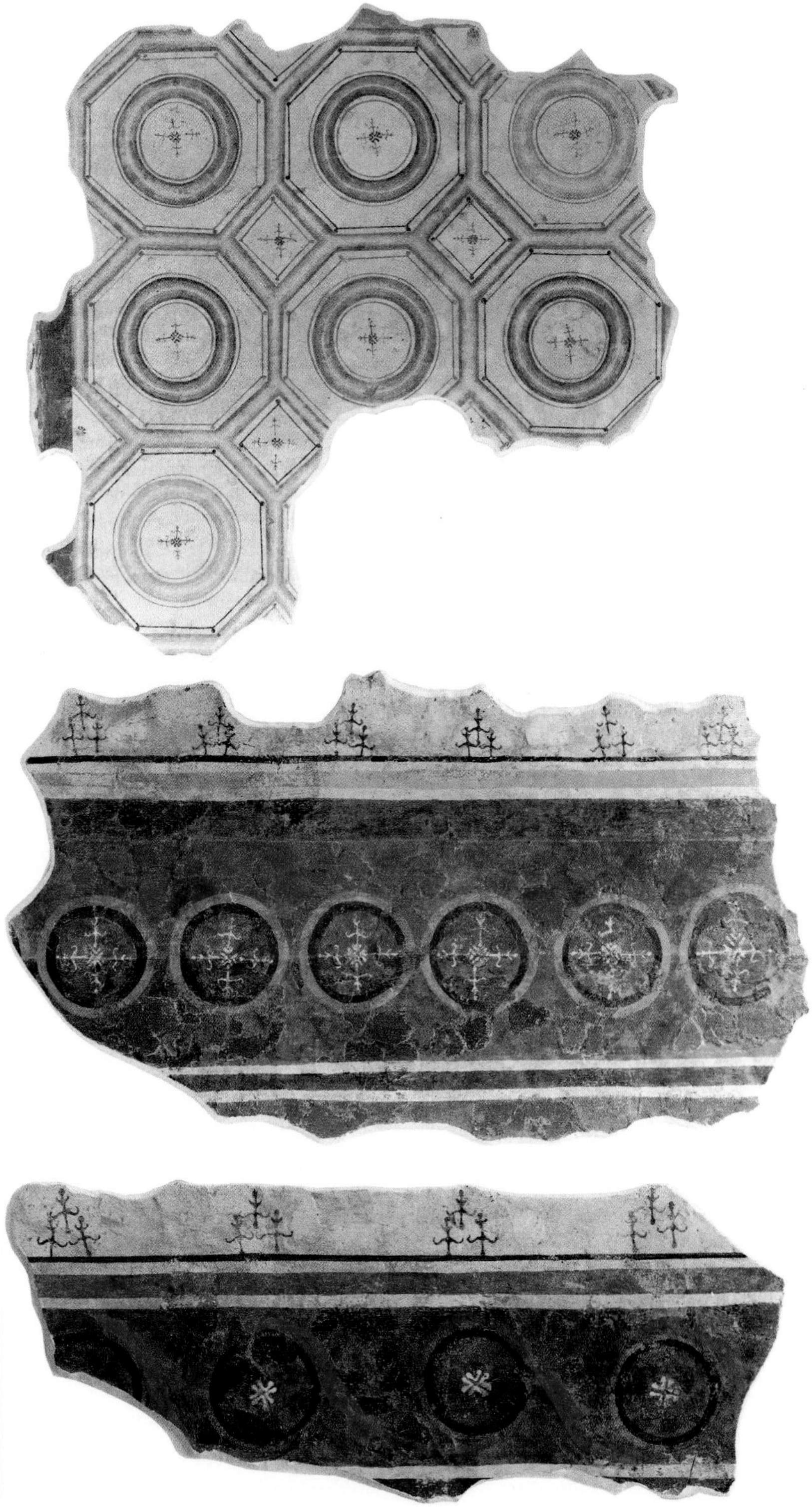

Illus. 7.34
Reconstructed areas of painted ceiling (top) and wall plaster from Dalton Parlours villa (© English Heritage).

difficult, may have been deemed appropriate for the sort of sensory deprivation conducive to trances associated with certain cults. However, it seems that it was only from the early second century that these cults, or activities incidental to them, began to leave substantial traces visible to archaeology with the deposition of pottery, coins, brooches, other personal ornaments and a diverse range of fittings and tools, including the pierced bone spoons.[200]

At Piercebridge the sort of water cult common in the native milieu was represented by the casting of coins and other items into the River Tees.[201] By 2008 local divers had recovered a rich collection, including 415 identifiable coins, largely of the mid-second and early third centuries. A peak in the Severan period could relate to the arrival of soldiers who wished to appease the local *genius* on their arrival to garrison a new fort nearby. There were a number of fakes amongst the official coin issues, but this was not apparently sufficient to detract from their suitability as offerings; a number of the fakes had been deliberately defaced perhaps as part of some sort of ritual. Other items include brooches, rings (one of gold with a garnet setting), other jewellery, and some fittings from military uniforms and armour. There are also two bronze figurines depicting winged cupids, and a pipeclay figurine thought to be Mercury.

The Romans might absorb deities into their pantheon by rebranding them with a Latin version of their original names. There is, for example, Arciacus, a god, probably of native origin, local to York, who is linked to the imperial *numen* in a dedication on an altar found in Walmgate on the south-east side of the city.[202] In addition to Romanised native gods, there are examples of those with a dual character created by giving a Roman god a title incorporating a Latinised version of a native word. An altar from Malton is dedicated to Mars Rigas; the second word is thought to be derived from a British word for king.[203] There is also Mars Emnenogenus for whom an altar was dedicated at Greta Bridge.[204] Another Roman strategy was to represent native deities as human beings, often in a classical style. A popular cult in Roman Britain, as well as Gaul, whose origins probably lay in fertility cults of the native world was that of the *matres* (Latin for mothers).[205] A York relief shows the *matres* (without an inscription), as is usual, seated and in triplicate to emphasise their power, a device well known for deities in Romano-Celtic art.[206] In addition, the *matres* are named in inscriptions on three altars from York, one of which was dedicated to the mother goddesses of Gaul, Africa and Italy by Marcus Minucius Audens a river pilot, perhaps mindful of the origins and destinations of the ships he was dealing with.[207] Dedications to the *matres* also appear on altars from Adel,[208] Aldborough,[209] Catterick[210] and Doncaster.[211]

Once a native god had acquired a Roman personality, the cult might be transferred from the wild outdoors to the man-made environment of a temple or shrine. Examples known from their structural remains appear to have existed at Elmswell[212] and Millington,[213] both in the East Riding. The Elmswell site is close to a spring, a common location for native cult sites in Britain. Trenching in 1950–52 located the remains of stone buildings and fragments of carved stones. Three of the latter belonged to a relief with human figures and two others were parts of altars, one of which bore the small part of an inscription. The only lettering which can be seen is DIIO = DEO – 'to the god'. The site has also produced two uninscribed altars. At Millington (near Pocklington) the temple site lies 1km north-east of the village on a spur of land overlooking the Millington Beck from where any buildings would have been visible from the main Brough to Malton Roman road to the east. The existence of Roman buildings has been known since the first half of the eighteenth century and they were relocated in recent fieldwork. Usually thought to be part of a complex associated with a water cult, they include what may have been a substantial temple of circular plan, 13.7m in diameter, with some surviving stonework and foundations 1.5m thick. In addition, to the south, are two buildings of rectangular plan, apparently with hypocausts, and another with a mosaic of which a few fragments survive.

Whilst knowledge of traditional classical deities may have spread gradually through the region as a whole, York retained a distinctive role as a centre for cults of Roman origin. They included the officially sponsored imperial cult described in Chapter 6. In addition to dedications to the imperial *numen* from Nessgate, George Hudson Street and Walmgate, we know of two men from York who had belonged to a college of priests responsible for maintaining the imperial cult, the *seviri augustales*. These men were usually wealthy freedmen (i.e. ex-slaves) who nominally owed their freedom to their ultimate master, the emperor. Verecundius Diogenes is known from the inscription on his coffin.[214] Marcus Aurelius Lunaris, who was a *sevir augustalis* of the *coloniae* at both York and Lincoln, set up an altar made of Yorkshire Millstone Grit in Bordeaux in 237.[215] This was dedicated to the Tutela Boudiga, a presiding local deity, and probably part of Lunaris's preparations to sail back across the Bay of Biscay and up the Channel to his home in Britain.

Also known almost exclusively from York in our region is the evidence for religious cults of eastern origin which, probably as a result of the movement of soldiers and merchants, swept through the western empire in the second and third centuries. These cults were rather different in character from those associated with traditional Roman religion. They claimed to offer adherents a more intimate relationship with a deity and access to revelations of secret knowledge ('mysteries') guaranteeing spiritual renewal and eternal life. Admission to these 'mystery cults' was governed by rites of initiation and they were practiced in dedicated buildings or enclosed spaces unlike traditional Roman ceremonies which were held in public and were open to all comers.

York's mystery cults included that of Mithras, originally from Persia, which offered its adherents a spiritual journey from the darkness of death to the light of everlasting life.[216] The central myth involved the sacrifice of a great bull which had been created at the beginning of time. From the blood of the bull came all life and so an apparent act of destruction was transformed into

Illus. 7.35 Gallery at the rear of Victoria Cave. (Photo: P. Ottaway)

one of creation. This sacrifice, known as 'the tauroctony', can be seen on the Mithraic relief found on Micklegate which suggests the presence of a temple in the heart of the town south-west of the Ouse (Illus. 3.8).[217] Mithras was opposed by the evil god Arimanius who is represented by a statue which shows him as a winged figure, naked except for a fringed loin cloth tied with a knotted snake, symbolising the tortuous course of both the sun through the sky and of the initiate to revelation.[218] He carries the keys of heaven and a sceptre to symbolise his power. Mithras was particularly revered by the upper echelons of the Roman army and merchant class, but the cult did not accept women or the lower orders and it appears to have declined in popularity in the fourth century.

The mysteries of the cult of the goddess Isis and her consort Serapis, which originated in Egypt, were also known at York.[219] A temple stood in the town south-west of the Ouse for which there is a fine inscribed tablet commemorating its construction at the behest of a legionary commander named Claudius Hieronymianus who may, himself, have been an Egyptian (Illus. 3.8). The central myth, like that of Mithraism, also contains the idea of eternal life beyond death. In one version Serapis was killed by his brother, the evil god Seth, but, on achieving manhood, Harpokrates, son of Isis and Serapis, defeated Seth and avenged the death of his father whom Isis then restored to life. There is no date for the York tablet, but the early third century would be appropriate as Septimius Severus and his family were keen adherents of the cult; Caracalla even had a Serapeum constructed on the Quirinal Hill in the centre of Rome.

Treatment of the dead: why York was special

Whereas emperors might consort with the gods after death, ordinary mortals had no such lofty destiny. None the less, there was considerable interest in the Roman world in the transition from the present life to another state of being, or non-being, after death. Views on the subject were diverse and need not be discussed in detail here, but there is some evidence from both burials and funerary monuments for the introduction of traditional Roman ideas to the Yorkshire region as a whole and to York in particular.

One version of the next world, ultimately of Greek origin, can be found in Aeneas's visit to the Underworld described in Virgil's *Aeneid*. Our hero follows the journey of the dead to a shadow land beyond the River Acheron, or Styx, in the care of Charon, the ferryman. On the other side, having passed the ferocious multiheaded dog Cerberus, he finds himself where Hades (Pluto to the Romans), brother of Zeus (Roman Jupiter), presided. Here, fortunate souls might in due course make their way to Elysium where they drank of Lethe, the fountain or river of forgetfulness, before being reborn. Others less fortunate were persecuted in Tartarus, a version of hell, by the furies, frightful winged maidens with serpents twined in their hair and blood dripping from their eyes. That these ideas found some currency in York is to be found in the epitaph on thirteen-year old Corellia Optata's tombstone with its reference to 'Pluto's Acherusian realms'.[220] In addition, there are a number of examples from York and Catterick of coins buried around the head or hands of the dead which may have been intended as payment for the ferryman.

The scarcity of Roman burials in Yorkshire for the first fifty years or so after the conquest may, as we have seen, be due to the persistence of a native custom which did not commit the dead to the ground, at least in any formal sense. In the period with which this chapter is concerned, burials remain scarce in the region except at York, although small numbers have been recorded elsewhere, largely at settlements of military origin. Both cremation and inhumation were practiced side by side.

It is, perhaps, the extent of its cemeteries, and the variety and, in some cases, the richness of its burials which, as much as almost anything else, make Roman York stand out as a special place in its region.[221] Conforming to practice elsewhere in the Roman world, the cemeteries lay outside areas inhabited by the living, usually on or adjacent to the main approach roads.

Only babies and young infants could be buried in or around buildings within the settled areas. The roadside location allowed passers-by to pay due respect to the dead and keep their memory green. The York evidence shows that the development of Roman cemeteries was a complex business, probably depending on the availability of suitable land and on whom the land's owner was prepared to accept for burial. There would probably have been distinct plots owned by families and other social groups and, as in other cities of the empire, those of dedicated burial clubs whose members paid a subscription for a funeral following their demise. The rich and powerful usually strove to secure plots in prominent locations close to the roads where their monuments would remind visitors and locals alike of who the most important people in the community were. It is no surprise, therefore, that at York a popular location for tombstones and other funerary monuments lay close to the main road from the south-west on the high ground at the top of The Mount.

The earliest cemetery zones at York are those with cremation burials, cremation being, at least until the mid-late second century, the preferred, although not exclusive rite for the treatment of the dead. These zones lay at some distance from the fortress or other settled areas, perhaps in anticipation of the expansion of those areas in due course. Cemeteries at Burton Stone Lane and Clifton Fields, for example, are about 0.7km north-west of the fortress

Illus. 7.36 York: reconstructed view of the Roman cemetery on The Mount looking north-east towards the town.

while two cemeteries at Heworth are 0.85km north-east of the fortress, and the cemetery at Fishergate is about 1km south-east of it. The largest Roman cemetery zone excavated archaeologically in York, at Trentholme Drive, which produced fifty-three cremations, was over 1km south-west of the River Ouse.[222]

From the mid-second century onwards some very large cemeteries were to develop in York. Trentholme Drive, which also produced some 342 inhumations dating from the mid-second century to the early fourth, was at the limit of a cemetery which extended along both sides of the main Roman road from the south-west. Elsewhere, south-west of the Ouse, another major cemetery developed on the site of what is now the Railway Station, around a minor Roman road which approached York from the north-west. Other cemeteries, as well as small groups of burials and isolated individuals, have been found in many different parts of York.

Elsewhere in the region, no cemeteries are yet known at Aldborough, the Brigantian *civitas* capital, although a few burials have been found outside its walls and there is a tombstone of Felicula, the 'dearest wife' of a man named Gaius.[223] Also, probably of the period under discussion, was a female inhumation found in Marton-cum-Grafton, c.4km south of Aldborough. She had been interred in a lead coffin within a stone structure which was set on a prominent rise close to the approach road from York.[224] The deceased was, perhaps, a member of the curial class of the *civitas* who belonged to a family owning land adjacent to its principal town.

Few burials have been recorded at Brough on Humber, but they include one with very remarkable contents (described below). However, at Catterick, Doncaster and Malton rather better evidence for the dead has been found. At Catterick four graves were found near one another, west of Dere Street, near the Bainesse settlement (Illus. 5.6).[225] The early Roman cremation burials at Waterdale, Doncaster were described in Chapter 6, but five others probably from the period covered by this chapter were were found in a small cemetery at 53–54 Hall Gate in which there were also nine inhumations (Illus. 5.4).[226] Two inhumations of the second or third century were found at Waterdale and nearer the fort, two more were found at 8–10 High Street, c.30m north of the main Roman approach road from the south-east.[227] Also in a roadside location were a group of four found about 6km up the main road to the north at Adwick-le-Street.[228]

At Malton (Illus. 5.18) a cemetery lay outside the north-east gate of the fort and other Roman burials were found in various locations in the nineteenth century; many of them are difficult to date accurately.[229] More recently (in 1993), five cremations, one in a mid-third-century beaker, were found at the Rugby Club on Old Malton Road on the line of the Roman road approaching the fort from the north-east.[230] However, the most remarkable person known to have been buried at Malton was Aurelius Macrinus whose tombstone (now lost) was found in 1753, c.200m north of the fort. He had served with the highly prestigious *equites singulares Augusti* (Imperial Household Cavalry), a mounted bodyguard for the emperor selected from the best men in the auxiliary regiments.[231] Quite what this man was doing in a remote outpost like Malton is hard to understand – unless, perhaps, he had returned to his birthplace on retirement. In Norton-on-Derwent extensive cemetery zones are known, largely from chance finds, adjacent to the roads from the south and the east.

In addition to the lady found near Aldborough, other burials of the landowning class near their country seats include those of Titia Pinta and Valerius Adjutor whose inscribed sarcophagus was found at East Ness near Helmsley,[232] and Aurelius Serenus and Cosciana Mammiola named on a sarcophagus from nearby Hood Grange at Sutton under Whitestonecliffe.[233] As far as the humbler members of society are concerned, second- and early third-century burials in the smaller settlements and rural areas in Yorkshire are very scarce. However, providing another instance of how Roman culture spread out along the region's roads, a cremation, possibly as early as the reign of Hadrian, placed in an urn and buried with a flagon, a jar and a bowl, was found *c*.3km from York, clearly a centre for new ideas on funerary customs, on the road to Malton (at Ryethorpe Grange Farm, Illus. 6.1, 4).[234] Slightly later in date, an isolated urned cremation came from Heslington East at a similar distance from the city. Also close to a road from York, in this case to Brough on Humber, was a group of three cremations, all in urns, found in the roadside settlement at Hayton (Burnby Lane).[235] From a rural settlement at Fairburn, near Castleford we may note an urned cremation burial and a female inhumation accompanied by a copper alloy necklet and a late second-/early third-century pottery jar.[236] More remote from centres of Roman culture, at Sewerby Cottage Farm, Bridlington, were two cremation burials, one accompanied by glass beads and a bone pin.[237]

Within a cemetery individual graves were presumably marked, if at all, by simple mounds of earth and / or wooden posts, but these were, of course, not permanent and have not been recorded in excavation. At Trentholme Drive and in other York cemetery zones a lack of permanent grave markers may have contributed to an apparent disorder with graves lying on a variety of different alignments and frequently cutting into one another. More permanent markers, such as tombstones, would have been needed to keep a grave intact over a longer period. However, they are rare in the Yorkshire region, the majority coming from York. Even less common is evidence for the funerary structures well known in other parts of the Roman world. However, the presence of inscriptions on sarcophagi, of which there are a few examples from Yorkshire, suggests that they had probably been displayed above ground in funerary structures of some sort, although rather more modest in style than some of those still visible today outside Rome and other Mediterranean cities. More typical of the region, perhaps, was a small mausoleum of early third-century date whose demolished remains were found at a site south-east of Blossom Street site in York, close to the main road from the south-west.[238] It had

Illus. 7.37 A decapitated male skeleton found on Driffield Terrace, The Mount, York (© York Archaeological Trust).

been built of stone with a ground plan measuring 6m square. The walls were plastered and the floor was of *opus signinum*. A woman of about 40–50 years and a juvenile had been buried within. The structure was probably covered by a tunnel vault similar to that which still survives nearby covering a stone coffin in a small mausoleum in the cellar of 104 The Mount, right on the edge of the Roman road from the south-west.[239] An example of another type of tomb was found near the fort at Slack. Within a small stone structure there was a sort of tent made of roof tiles, three along one side, two at one end and one at the other which covered cremated human remains.[240] Some fifteen examples of similar tile tents have been found at York, some of which, at least, were used for inhumations. A rather grander tomb structure at Catterick is hinted at by the stone lions found there which had probably stood guard on the remains of someone of special status.

Funerary practices

Although there are some distinctive and unusual burials from York and the region, in general terms burial practice seems to conform to what is found elsewhere in Roman Britain. At Trentholme Drive there was an *ustrina*, a public space where the bodies of the deceased were burnt. A stone structure, probably used for the pyres, was surrounded by a dense layer of charcoal but it seems that coal as well as wood was used as fuel.[241] As at Doncaster, the evidence, described in Chapter 6, suggests, while the bodies were burning, offerings, for example of unguents in glass jars, were made, no doubt accompanied by appropriate mourning rituals. After cremation it was usual at York, as elsewhere, for the charred remains to be interred in a pottery urn, although glass urns and lead canisters are also known. Unusually for a smaller settlement, a glass cremation urn was found in an isolated burial at Stamford Bridge (near York).[242] Cremation had probably fallen out of favour in Yorkshire and much of the Roman world by the early third century, although there are late Roman cremations from the region, and it remained current in elite social circles as in the case of the emperor Septimius Severus himself who was cremated after his death in York in 211.

In inhumation graves bodies were usually laid out fully extended and supine with their arms by their sides or crossed over the waist, although there are a few cases at York of the Iron Age custom in which the body was laid on one side in a flexed or crouched position. However, the most remarkable skeletons from York of the period under discussion were found on a site in Driffield Terrace on The Mount.[243] They are remarkable, first of all, because, apart from seven non-adults, all the fifty-three adult skeletons were of males – most Roman cemeteries have a roughly equal mix of men and women – and, secondly, because at least thirty had been decapitated, the skulls being placed in the grave by the feet, lower legs or pelvis. Throughout Roman Britain decapitated bodies have been found in small numbers, but the heads were usually removed post-mortem, probably for some ritual purpose. Specialist analysis of the Driffield Terrace bodies suggests, however, that they were execution victims, men whose heads were removed with a sword or axe, in some cases clearly whilst under physical restraint. The most remarkable of all the burials was that of two individuals interred one above the other in the same grave, both decapitated, one of whom had heavy iron rings around his ankles. These had been applied during life and had presumably been a form of punishment for a criminal offence. In addition, the skulls had been switched so that the man at the base of the grave was given the skull of the man buried above him and vice versa.

None of the Driffield Terrace burials had been in coffins, but iron nails surviving in many graves at York and elsewhere in the region show that wooden coffins were frequently used. However, lead and stone coffins (sarcophagi) were very expensive items and their use would normally have been restricted to the richer families. The fact that some ninety stone and twenty-five lead coffins have been recorded from York, a greater number than from any other Roman centre in Britain, says something about not only the wealth, but also the cultural affiliations, of at least some members of city's population who had adopted what was considered a mark of status in much of the Roman world. There also appears to be something of a concentration of stone coffins, although not usually closely datable, in the immediate York hinterland, presumably used for the burial of prosperous local landowners. Within 3km of the city centre examples have been found at Acomb, Askham Richard, Dringhouses, Middlethorpe, Naburn and Stockton on the Forest.[244] Further afield they have been found, for example, at the two sites near Helmsley noted above, and at Adel (six),[245] and Sherburn in Elmet.

Often associated with burial in a stone or lead coffin was the use of gypsum (hydrated calcium sulphate) which, on occasions, completely encased the deceased, but in most cases was simply a thin layer spread over the body.[246] When gypsum is mixed with water to make a paste – usually known as Plaster of Paris – it invokes an exothermic reaction causing the solution to heat up to $c.150°$C as it sets. Once the mixture hardens it cools down. This process may well have been seen as mysterious by the Romans and in some way symbolic of the consumption and purification of the dead before passage to the next world. There are at least forty burials with some gypsum in them from York and others come from its hinterland. Gypsum burials are usually thought to be late Roman, but early third-century examples have been found at Trentholme Drive and Mill Mount in York[247] and the custom probably began at about this time.

Gypsum casts show that on occasions, at least, the deceased were buried clothed, although all that usually survives of dress are jewellery items, such as rings and bracelets, and the iron hobnails from boots and shoes. Unfortunately records of many of the York burials cannot tell us whether the jewellery was worn by the deceased or simply put in the grave as furnishing. Whichever is the case, however, York has produced a number of female burials richly endowed with jewellery for which there is nothing comparable elsewhere in

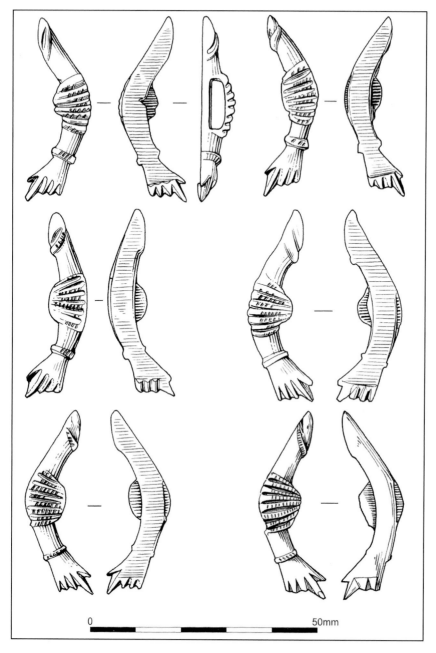

Illus. 7.38 A group of amulets for the inducement of good fortune from an infant burial at Catterick (© English Heritage).

the region. One of the richest, dated to the early third century by a coin of Septimius Severus, comes from Walmgate. The body, covered in gypsum and interred in a lead coffin, was accompanied by two necklaces made in one case of 237 and in the other of ninety-three jet beads, one of which carried a medallion depicting Medusa. Items in the grave also included a glass bracelet, a necklet of glass beads and freshwater pearls, eight glass beads, sixteen jet hairpins and one of bone, and as well as two glass bottles.[248]

There are other richly furnished burials from York, some of which are probably late Roman (see below), but in general grave goods are rare both in York and the region. For example, fewer than 10% of the inhumations from Trentholme Drive in York were furnished, the commonest item by far being a pottery vessel. A few burials were accompanied by a fowl (surviving as the skeleton), probably a symbol of Mercury and intended as an offering to the god in his role as escort of the dead to the next world. In the region as a whole pottery vessels, usually one, but occasionally two or three, were, as in York, the most common type of grave good. They may originally have contained food, either to provide nourishment for the deceased's journey to the spirit world or to symbolise participation with the living in a funeral meal of the sort depicted on the tombstone of Julia Velva from York (Illus. 8.6).

More unusual grave goods from York include a fan, of which the ivory handles were found with a burial in a stone coffin in the Railway Station cemetery,[249] and a figurine of Hercules with his club from a burial north-east of the Ouse near Peasholme Green.[250] At Catterick an unusual infant burial, found near the *mansio* in the foundations of what may have been a sacred enclosure (*temenos* – see inset of Illus. 9.5), was accompanied by five copper alloy amulets. Each had at one end a female hand with a pointing finger – to ward off evil spirits – and at the other a phallus, symbol of fertility and good fortune.[251] From the cemetery outside the north-east gate of the fort at Malton, another infant burial, unusual for being furnished, was accompanied by a tiny jet bear, as well as a jet bead, a copper alloy bracelet and a coin of 215–18.[252] Finally, perhaps the most remarkable grave goods of the period under discussion were found with a burial made close to Humber Street, just north of Brough.[253] Apparently lying below limestone slabs were two skeletons, one of which was accompanied by a small wooden bucket represented by iron hoops and a copper alloy escutcheon in the form of a stylised human bust. In addition, there were two iron sceptres, both of which were topped with busts in copper alloy wearing what are taken to be Roman cavalry helmets.

Cemeteries and population

The first cemetery in the region to be studied systematically to determine the physical characteristics of the Roman population was Trentholme Drive in York.[254] Apparently there were four times as many men as women buried there, although it is also possible that some of the identifications of males were incorrect as the study was done in the 1960s when methodology was not as well developed as it is today. However, assuming there was an imbalance between the sexes, this may have had something to do with soldiers being amongst the deceased. Another possibility is that men from the region around York were brought to its principal town for burial because it offered a more prestigious starting point for a journey to the next world than their farmsteads. In this case women, being generally seen as of lower status, would have been interred close to home.

Age distribution of the Trentholme Drive people reveals a population with high mortality in the 20s and 30s but few over 50s. As far as those whose ages are recorded on tombstones from Yorkshire are concerned, the oldest is Aurelius Romulus from Greta Bridge who died aged 60 years,[255] a little older than Antonius Gargilianus, a camp prefect from York, who died aged 56.[256] These two people probably benefitted from the relatively good diet and living conditions available to the wealthier members of society. However, no-one was exempt from the ravages of the infectious diseases for which there were no cures in Roman times. In Roman Britain as a whole mortality in the 20s and 30s was greater for women than men because of the hazards of pregnancy and child birth. There were hardly any infants at Trentholme Drive, probably because they were buried less formally elsewhere, although we suspect that infant mortality was high in Roman Britain. Very few infants and children were commemorated on funerary monuments and they belonged to the social elite including, for example, Simplicia Florentina, described on her sarcophagus from York as 'a most innocent soul' who died aged ten months.[257] From Greta Bridge there is the tombstone of Salvia Donata who died aged eight years.[258]

In respect of stature, the men buried at Trentholme Drive were on average 1.7m (5 ft 7 in.) tall and women 1.55m (5 ft 1 in.). Contrary to popular belief about people in the past being much smaller than they are today, these averages remained more or less unchanged in the British population until World War II; since then there has been a slight rise due to better nutrition. There is as yet no more recent study of human skeletons in the Yorkshire region on a similar scale to that for Trentholme Drive; the broad conclusions about age and stature are, however, borne out by recent work on other Roman cemeteries in Britain.

It is rare to find clear evidence from a Roman burial for a person's ethnic affiliation or place of origin. We assume, however, that the vast majority of the people living in Roman Britain were of native stock, although immigrants from elsewhere in the empire came to serve in the Roman army and government. Many would have settled here only temporarily, but those who did make our region their home can be glimpsed on a few inscriptions such as those found on the sarcophagi from York of Verecundius Diogenes who came from Bourges in Gaul and his wife Julia Fortunata from Sardinia.[259] Native people also moved from region to region during the Roman period as we can see on two Yorkshire tombstones. One is from Ilkley which tells us that the lady with the plaits was from the *Cornovii*, people who lived in what are now Cheshire and Shropshire.[260] The other, from Templeborough, is Vercundia Rufilia of the *Dobunni* whose territory lay in what is now Gloucestershire.[261]

8 | Septimius Severus in Yorkshire

The Severan campaign

Had you been standing at the main gate of the Roman fortress at York in the year 208 you might well have seen a magnificent procession led by the Emperor Septimius Severus and his entourage, although, according to Herodian, Severus, now an old man in Roman terms, being 62 or 63, suffered from gout so that he was carried in a litter rather than riding on horseback.[1] Severus was accompanied by his Empress, Julia Domna, a priest's daughter from Emesa (Homs) in Syria, and their sons Antoninus and Geta. Antoninus, who was usually known as Caracalla on account of the type of cloak he wore, had been declared co-emperor with his father in 198; his younger brother Geta was only promoted to the same rank in 209 when he was in Britain. This led to considerable rivalry between the brothers which intensified as Severus's health deteriorated. Also in the imperial party was Aemelius Papinianus (Papinian), the Praetorian Prefect who had responsibility for the imperial guard as well as being experienced in legal matters. Government of the empire was directed from wherever the emperor happened to be and so, albeit briefly, York found itself a place of considerable political importance at the centre of the Roman world.

To understand why Severus visited our region we should go back to the murder of the Emperor Commodus on 31 December 192. He was succeeded by P. Helvius Pertinax whose career was one of the more remarkable examples of social mobility known from the Roman world. Born in 126, he was the son of a freedman, in other words the son of a former slave, who had been a timber merchant. Pertinax himself became a school master before joining the army and was appointed a tribune of the Sixth Legion at York in the 160s. The year 175 found him serving as Consul and Prefect of Rome. In 185–87 he returned to Britain as governor, following Ulpius Marcellus who may have had to deal with unrest in the north. Apparently Pertinax was a strict disciplinarian and this led to a mutiny by British troops. Although this was quelled, he had to resign his command. This was not the end of Pertinax's career, however, and following the murder of Commodus, he reluctantly accepted

ROMAN YORKSHIRE

Ilus. 8.1
Reconstruction
Illustration of Roman
York as it might have
looked at the time of
Septimius Severus,
looking north-east. The
River Ouse runs left to
right across the centre,
the legionary fortress
is at the top and the
principal urban area is
in the lower half of the
picture.

the imperial throne from the emperor's assassins. However, only eighty-six days later Pertinax was, himself, murdered by mutinous Praetorian Guards.

After the death of Pertinax, the Roman governor of Britain, Clodius Albinus, was proclaimed emperor by the three British legions. At the same time as Albinus staked his claim, Septimius Severus was hailed as emperor by his legions in Pannonia (now parts of Austria, Hungary and Slovenia) and moved west to secure Rome. Initially Albinus was offered a role as junior emperor, but once Severus had defeated another claimant, Pescennius Niger, a civil war with Albinus became unavoidable. This was settled in Severus's favour in 197 by a battle at Lyon, in Gaul, in which Albinus was killed.

Lucius Septimius Severus was born in Leptis Magna, now in Libya, in 146. A successful soldier, Severus, to an even greater extent than emperors before him, made the basis of his rule the support of the army. His attitude is epitomised in his reported dying words to his sons: 'enrich the troops and never mind the rest'.[2] Severus did as much as he could to secure the army's loyalty, for a start by giving them only their second pay rise since Augustus's time. In addition, Severus allowed soldiers to regularise their private lives and cohabit with women outside the camp; this was not quite the same as allowing soldiers to marry, although this is sometimes how the change is presented. It was by now normal imperial policy to assign army units to permanent bases and not move them around from province to province as had often been done at the time of the conquest of Britain some 150 years earlier. Recruitment became largely local, although units might keep the names they had acquired when raised in particular regions like Gaul or Germany.

It is thought that Albinus took much of the army of Britain with him to Gaul and in so doing set a precedent, to be repeated later in the Roman period, of stripping Britain's defences to pursue a power struggle elsewhere in the empire. A question which has taxed scholars is whether Albinus's actions were seen as an opportunity by the barbarians north of Hadrian's Wall to attack the Roman province. Cassius Dio seems to suggest that in about the year 197 there was a threat to Britain from the Caledonians, living in what is now Scotland. They gave assistance to a people referred to as the Maetae, living near the Wall, from whom peace had to be purchased 'for a large sum'.[3] Archaeological evidence for reconstruction in the Hadrian's Wall zone, for example at Corbridge, and in the Pennine forts in Yorkshire, was once claimed as evidence for the Roman response to an attack on northern Britain in the early part of Severus's reign. However, reconstruction is now seen more as the routine maintenance and modification of buildings and fortifications.

Work known to have taken place in the Yorkshire forts in the early third century includes the heightening of the rampart behind the fort wall at Bowes and rebuilding of a building range north of the headquarters and of at least part of the baths in the CO's house.[4] Of greater interest in light of the debate on enemy action, is the fort bath house immediately outside the defences. An inscription records that it was reconstructed after a fire in the governorship of Virius Lupus (197–200/2), the work being undertaken by a cavalry unit of Vettones (originally from central Spain) and by the First Cohort of Thracians who formed the principal garrison at the time.[5] There need be no question of an attack, however, as accidental fires were a constant hazard in Roman times, especially in bath houses.

At Ilkley an inscription (now lost) took the form of a dedication to Septimius Severus and Caracalla by Virius Lupus in 197–98 which may have commemorated a stone wall added to the defences here at this time – a short stretch of this can be seen near the Manor House museum.[6] The new, stone-built, north gate, revealed in excavation, had, in the style of the time, a single, rather than double, arch.[7] New stone buildings known within the fort included the CO's house and a barrack block.

Lucius Alfenus Senecio – an African from Cuicul (Djemila) – became governor of Britain in about 205 and Cassius Dio tells us that he had a military success in 206, presumably in the north. According to Herodian, Senecio made an appeal for reinforcements which may have led to Severus visiting Britain in person.[8] Dio claims that Severus welcomed the opportunity to campaign in Britain, one reason being that he saw it as good training for Caracalla and Geta who had grown soft in the flesh pots of Rome. Before Senecio moved on in 208 he was probably charged with making York ready for the emperor, although a *domus palatina* (palace) referred to in the *Augustan History* is likely to have been the commanding officer's house in the fortress rather than a completely new building.

The impact of the imperial presence in York must have been considerable if only because of the numbers of additional troops in Severus's army to be accommodated. For some civilians there were probably opportunties for making a bit of a killing out all those new customers. Some of the troops brought to York are thought to have come from Africa; Severus would, perhaps, have been more confident of the loyalty of men from the part of the empire from which he himself came than of local men who may have backed Albinus. Amongst the Africans there may have been a man named Gaius Cosurtius Saturninus of the Sixth Legion from Hippo Regius whose tombstone was found at Birdoswald fort on Hadrian's Wall.[9]

Severus's campaigns took him as far north as the banks of the River Tay where a fortress was established at Carpow. It was probably at this time, rather than later in the century, as has also been suggested, that a large (4.58ha) new fort was built at Piercebridge (Co. Durham) just north of the Tees.[10] Archaeology has also revealed striking evidence for Severus's campaigns in the Hadrian's Wall zone. At South Shields, for example, the fort was extended in the early third century and much of the interior was devoted to granaries, presumably to make a dedicated supply base. A similar supply role was probably played by Corbridge, at the crossing of Dere Street over the Tyne, and this may explain the so-called 'military works depot' occupied by soldiers of the Sixth Legion from York and those of the Second Legion from Caerleon. An altar, now in the Corbridge site museum, was set up by an officer in charge of the granaries which refers to 'the most successful expedition to Britain'.[11]

Dedications to Severus and his sons in some of the Pennine forts in Yorkshire, which name Senecio as governor, may relate to construction specifically for the expedition. A tablet from Bowes cannot be related to a particular building,[12] but another from Greta Bridge was found near the north gate of the fort and may have commemorated work on the gate itself and the defences.[13] At Bainbridge an inscription bearing the name of Gaius Valerius Pudens, governor immediately before Senecio, records the building of barracks in 205 by the Sixth Cohort of Nervians, originally from western Gaul.[14] Work of the period was identified in barracks excavated in the south-east part of the fort. Another inscribed tablet from Bainbridge, in this case of Senecio, may commemorate other construction work of the Severan period, also recorded in excavation, including that of a new headquarters, with a fine cellar below the shrine for the storage of valuables, and a new granary next door.[15] During Senecio's governorship a walled extension was added to the east of the fort, the *Bracchium Caementicum* (outwork of stone) referred to in an inscription (now lost).[16] The extension may have been intended to house prisoners from Severus's campaigns and/or to accommodate extra troops. The lead seal of the Second Cohort of Asturians (originally recruited in northern Spain) found at Bainbridge perhaps shows that they served here briefly alongside the Nervians.[17]

Pots and cults

Whilst there may be little in the way of buildings which can be ascribed with certainty to the Severan period in York, a distinctive artefact often associated with it is the so-called 'head pot', a jar made in the shape of a human head.[18] The heads are usually female and, in some cases at least, are thought to represent the Empress Julia Domna; male heads may represent Caracalla. Head pots were sometimes used for the burial of cremated remains and in view of the semi-divine status of the imperial family it may have been believed that there was merit in consigning one's friend or relative to the hereafter in the care, symbolically at least, of one of its members.

It is thought by pottery specialists Jason Monaghan and Vivien Swan that these head pots were made in a style with its origins in North Africa. Further evidence for the introduction of North African ceramic styles to York at about the time of Septimius Severus has been identified by Swan in cooking vessels, especially a type of flat casserole dish with a lid.[19] The way in which the junction of side wall and base is formed would have served to hold the vessel steady on the sort of fired-clay brazier used for cooking in the North African provinces. This contrasts with the usual British and north-west European mode of cooking using a jar set in hot ashes. Who the potters making these

Illus. 8.2 Bainbridge Roman fort: aerial view looking north. The walled extension of the early third century lies largely to the right of the small barn by the south-east corner of the fort (© Anthony Crawshaw).

distinctive vessels in African style were is not clear, but it is quite possible that they belonged to new detachments sent to join the Sixth Legion at York. Swan has also identified vessels, including mortaria, cooking jars and serving bowls, made by potters from the Rhineland which seems to suggest that the Severan army also drew reinforcements from this region for the campaign in the north.[20]

The imperial cult was assiduously promoted in Severus's reign, in part at least, as cover for his attempt to give himself a false legitimacy as the son of Marcus Aurelius and a bogus ancestry going back to Vespasian and the Flavian emperors. His oldest son (Caracalla), originally called Bassianus, was renamed Marcus Aurelius Antoninus to bolster his claim. In addition to dedications at York referring to the imperial *numen*, there is another coupled with the goddess Victoria Brigantia – appropriate for the times – on the altar found at Greetland near Halifax.[21]

Two shrines which probably have their origin in the Severan period, stood on Scargill Moor, 3km south of the fort at Bowes.[22] There seems to be a good example here of the way a native god was absorbed into the Roman pantheon with a Roman name and a Roman home. The deity's Latin name is Vinotonus, mentioned on three inscriptions from the site. The first shrine was

Illus. 8.3 York: pot in the form of a female head, thought to be the Empress Julia Domna (© York Museums Trust).

a small structure of rectangular plan (5.2m × 2.6m) and, remarkably, the altar was found still standing where it was originally set up. It bore an inscription dedicated by Julius Secundus, a centurion of the First Cohort of Thracians, known from other inscriptions at Bowes to have been posted here in the early third century. The dedication is to Vinotonus coupled with Silvanus, Roman god of wild places and also of the boundaries where wild places and cultivated lands meet. This is appropriate as the site, at the confluence of two becks, is on the edge of the wild even today; to the north there is pasture, but to the south is uncultivated high moorland. The Thracian cohort no doubt entertained themselves with hunting in the area for the success of which they required the god's blessing. A second shrine a little to the north of the first was circular in plan with a diameter of 5.2m. It also had an altar surviving, although pushed over and damaged, which was dedicated by Lucius Caesius Frontinus, prefect (commander) from Parma (Italy) also of the First Cohort of Thracians. Fragments of six other altars were found, one of which bore a V for Vinotonus, and the shrine was probably in use until the fourth century to judge by pottery recovered.

The death of an emperor

In the event Severus did not enjoy a particularly 'successful expedition' and the campaign in the north was brought to an abrupt end with the death of the emperor in York on 2 February 211. According to the colourful, if somewhat unreliable, account in the *Augustan History* Severus's imminent demise was foretold by a number of omens of the sort by which the Romans set great store. For example, he is said to have dreamed that 'he was dragged up into the sky by four eagles' – eminently appropriate for an imperial personage on a voyage to join the immortals. The death of an emperor was regarded in the Roman world as an event of great cosmic significance given his place half-way between men and gods, and the funeral, leading to his apotheosis (journey to heaven), would have been correspondingly splendid. According to Cassius Dio:

> ... his body arrayed in military garb was placed upon a pyre, and as a mark of honour the soldiers and his sons ran about it; and as for the soldiers'

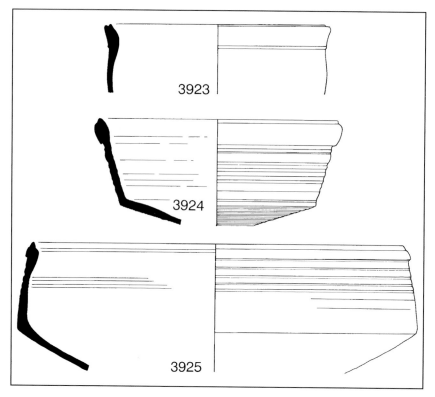

Illus. 8.4 York: cross-section drawing of early third-century 'casserole' dishes (from Monaghan 1997; © York Archaeological Trust).

gifts, those who had things at hand to offer threw them upon it and his sons applied the fire.[23]

Severus was probably cremated somewhere immediately outside the fortress at York, but he was not buried in one of its cemeteries and we are told that the emperor's ashes were taken to Rome in an urn described by Cassius Dio as made of porphyry (a valuable purple stone) and in the *Augustan History* as made of gold. Empress Julia Domna and her sons, Caracalla and Geta, left Britain, apparently with precipitate haste to secure the crown against possible rivals with all thoughts of further conquest in the north forgotten. Caracalla soon murdered his younger brother and ruled alone. He gets a very bad press from both Cassius Dio and the *Augustan History* on account of murdering as many possible rivals and enemies as he could lay hands on – some of his victims may even lie in the execution cemetery at York.

The tombstone of Julia Velva

A desire to appease the gods was never far from people's thoughts, especially at times of death and burial. This could be done by appropriate iconography such as the pair of charming *amorini* delicately carved in relief on the sarcophagus of Julia Victorina. A more sophisticated attempt to secure divine favour can be found in the tombstone of Julia Velva from York.[24] We do

not see the tombstone brightly painted as it
would have been in its full glory, but it is
still an example of the way that emphasis was
placed on those features which had a symbolic
significance for demonstrating the status of the
deceased and of members of his or her family
who were still alive. The upper part of the
tombstone depicts, in relief, a group of four
people within an arch framing a scene which
was intended to represent an apsed dining
room. This is the sort of room which would
be found in a high-status house where a patron
not only received his friends, but also his
clients to whom favours were dispensed. Julia
Velva herself reclines on a couch to dine,
as one did in polite circles. We see that her
hair is parted in the centre, hiding her ears
in a manner recalling images of Julia Domna
and other early third-century empresses. This
little portrait serves to show that the women of the family sponsoring the
monument have maintained the standards of grooming and apparel expected of
members of the Roman elite which, it was thought, set them apart from their
inferiors – the 'great unwashed'. The man standing to Julia Velva's left must
be the Aurelius Mercurialis named in the inscription, possibly her husband,
or, alternatively, the son-in-law who is now her heir. He holds a scroll which
is probably intended to indicate his status as literate and perhaps as a member
of the local curia. A child sits in a wicker-backed chair holding a bird, a
symbol of youth seen on other Roman tombstones from York and elsewhere.
A small male figure is probably a servant – in a convention of Roman art
social inferiors are shown smaller than their betters.

The inscription reads:

D(IS) M(ANIBUS)
IVLI(A)E VELV(A)E PIENTISSI
M(A)E VIXIT AN(NOS) L AVREL(IVS)
MERCVRIALIS HER(ES) FACI
VNDVM CVRAVIT VIVVS
SIBI ET SVIS FECIT

The inscription begins with the standard abbreviated dedication to the Manes,
spirits of the departed in the form DM (*dis manibus*), seen on many Roman
tombstones. The rest translates as 'To Julia Velva. She lived fifty years, most
dutifully. Aurelius Mercurialis, her heir, had this made. He made it while alive
for himself and his family.' The phrase 'most dutifully' is a common epithet
for women, also found describing Cosciana Mammiola on the Hood Grange

sarcophagus. Duty to the household and to the gods was considered an estimable female virtue.

On occasions, Roman funerary inscriptions have levels of meaning other than the immediately obvious. In this case we should look closely at the numerical structure of the inscription. When we count the number of letters (ignoring the DM), the three ligatured letters counting as one, we find there are eighty-one (9^2). In addition, the number of words is sixteen and the number of Is is also sixteen (4^2). These numbers, eighty-one and sixteen, which have square roots as whole numbers relate the inscription to the number of people depicted (four) and the initial letters of Julia Velva in Latin: IV ($4 = 2^2$). All this is surely deliberate and is probably an attempt to use numbers, considered somewhat magical in a world of poor numeracy, and especially the concept of the square root, to create a dedication and memorial with an added harmonious quality in an imitation of the divine. Although intellectual passers-by might have found the number patterns interesting, they were primarily intended to appeal to the gods.

Illus. 8.6   York: the tombstone of Julia Velva (height: 1.63m; © York Museums Trust).

Emperor Caracalla

There is a loyal dedication to the *Domus Divina* (divine house) of Caracalla on a stone block re-used in the church at Kirby Hill, perhaps originally from nearby Aldborough, although he was one of the bloodthirstiest of Rome's rulers and it can be no surprise that he himself was murdered in 217.[25] However, two important events took place in Caracalla's brief reign. The first was the division of Britain into two provinces: Upper Britain (*Britannia Superior*) and Lower Britain (*Britannia Inferior*). The former had its capital at London and the latter at York which was probably given the status of *colonia* at the same time (the only dated reference is on the Lunaris altar of 237); its distinct role as the main centre of imperial power in the north was thus confirmed. The division would have curbed the power of a British governor with three legions and numerous auxiliaries at his command which had been revealed at the time of Clodius Albinus in 196. Caracalla saw that it was now time to separate the control of the legion in the south (at Caerleon) from the two in the more distant north (at Chester and York).

The second event was the proclamation of the so-called *Constitutio Antoniniana* in the year 212 which awarded citizenship to all free born people

in the empire, i.e. all who were not slaves. This was not quite as revolutionary as it might seem as there were, by the early third century, considerably more citizens in the empire than in the first. The award may have had more to do with tax requirements as, paradoxically perhaps, citizens were taxed more heavily than non-citizens. The coffin of a Sixth Legion centurion, Aurelius Super, from York is probably that of a local man who had become a citizen in 212 and was thereby eligible for legionary service.[26] His name reminds us that the creation of new citizens led to the sudden popularity of the family name Aurelius (or Aurelia) —assumed fraudulently by Caracalla — which, in traditional manner, many took in gratitude for their new status. Another example of how a name might change with the acquisition of citizenship is that of Lucius Viducius Placidus the Gallic merchant from York.[27] It is thought that the same man, known simply as Placidus, son of Viducus, is named on an inscription dredged from the Rhine estuary in the Netherlands. In typical native fashion he Romanised his father's name to form the family name, Viducius, and kept Placidus (Latin for 'quiet' or 'gentle') as his familiar name — one wonders whether this really did describe his temperament!

Although many non-citizens may have been delighted with their new status, as the numbers of citizens increased, social distinctions continued to separate the privileged upper echelons, the *honestiores*, from the rest, the *humiliores*. As far as Britain was concerned, members of the former remained few in number, being largely legionary veterans and the political elite who, as far as our region is concerned, probably lived largely in York.

The inscription on the sarcophagus of one of the city's great Roman ladies, Aelia Severa, tells us proudly that she was a member of the *honestiores*.[28] In addition, it gives us a little story of social mobility, quite possibly from Severan times. We learn that a freed slave, Caecilius Musicus, had set the sarcophagus in place. He was probably a musician in the household of his master Caecilius Rufus from whom he had received his freedom, perhaps purchasing it after saving up sufficient funds. On becoming free Musicus, as was often the case, took his master's family name, Caecilius, as his own. When his former mistress Severa died he inherited the family fortune and was able to afford a splendid inscribed coffin for her. The coffin was found on top of The Mount close to the main road from the south-west and had probably been set up in a family mausoleum occupying a prominent site befitting the family's status where it would have been admired by all who passed by. Another former slave, like Musicus, named on an inscription from York was one Nikomedes, a name which suggests he was a Greek, who made a dedication on a statue base to the goddess *Britannia*, probably during the reign of Septimius Severus.[29] He describes himself as a 'freedman of the emperors' meaning that he had been a very superior sort of slave, probably with a role in the government and administration of the empire.

Another stage in the history of the Yorkshire region in Roman times can now be brought to a close, but before doing so we may note that the first governor of the new province of *Britannia Inferior* that we know of, was a Marcus Antonius Gordianus from Cappadocia (now Turkey), already fairly elderly at the age of fifty-nine, who may well have regarded his posting to York in 216 as the crowning achievement of his career. A surviving trace of his sojourn in the city may be an inscription, now built into the foundations of York Minster. It appears to refer to a college or club of *beneficiarii* who had dedicated themselves to their governor and commander.[30] Fate was to have another card to play in Gordian's career because no less than 22 years after coming to York, in 238, when aged 81, very venerable indeed in the Roman world, he became emperor for a year and even then he would die by suicide rather than natural causes.

From the Severi to the House of Constantine

Introduction

According to the great historian of the later Roman world, Peter Brown: 'After 240 the sprawling empire had to face barbarian invasion and political instability on a scale for which it was totally unprepared'.[1] However, although many turbulent events in the empire as a whole in the middle years of the third century may be documented in contemporary accounts, our understanding of the period in Britain is not aided by much in the way of written sources. After the death of Cassius Dio historians of the empire have little to tell us of direct relevance until the time of the usurper Carausius at the end of the third century and that of the Emperor Constantine in the early fourth. There are, moreover, few inscriptions on stone from Britain which can be securely dated after the time of the Severi; as in other parts of the empire people were giving up the habit of public commemoration in written form. Inscriptions on other media are also scarcer than hitherto.

Understanding the mid-third century on the basis of archaeological evidence is challenging because of a reduced occurrence of two important tools for dating: samian pottery and coinage. The supply of samian to Britain had more or less come to an end by 230 and it was not replaced by any other imported fine ware. In addition, difficulties in managing the imperial economy led to a reduction in the supply of coin to Britain to a trickle until the 260s. The history of the later third and early fourth centuries in our region is easier to describe, first of all because of the emergence of a new local pottery industry at Crambeck near Malton, the distinctive products of which were widely distributed.[2] Secondly, as far as coinage is concerned, attempts to restore the stability of the imperial currency led on several occasions, beginning in the reign of Gallienus (253–68), to a deluge of coins of very low intrinsic value engulfing the empire. However, although they may have been of relatively little worth at the time, they are invaluable to today's archaeologists.

The death at Mainz in 235 of the last of the Severi, Severus Alexander, was followed by the accession of Maximinus the Thracian, the first of some fifty soldier-emperors who would rule until the accession of the Emperor Diocletian in 284. These were men able to seize power simply by virtue of commanding a substantial part of the Roman army, but they were usually unable to do a great deal with that power before being replaced by a rival. As well as being fractured by claims of rival army commanders, the empire was also under pressure from the Sassanid Persian Empire in the east and from the Franks on the Rhine frontier. In the year 253 the Emperor Valerian was defeated by the Sassanids, and in 256–57 and again in 259 the Franks crossed the imperial frontier along the Rhine. Worse was to follow in Mesopotamia with the capture of Valerian by the Sassanids in 260, an event which must have sent shock waves even as far as Yorkshire. In the same year the whole of the western empire broke away from the rule of a Rome which had failed to defend it to form the so-called 'Gallic Empire'. The secession collapsed in 273 in the reign of Emperor Aurelian, but the unity of the empire in the west was threatened again in 286 when the usurper Carausius set up his own breakaway regime encompassing Britain and northern Gaul. Said by the contemporary historian

Illus. 9.1   The Tetrarchs in porphyry, looted from Constantinople and now built into St Mark's Cathedral in Venice. (Photo: P.Ottaway)

Eutropius to be 'a man of very low birth' from what is now Belgium, Carausius had been a naval commander based in Boulogne charged with policing the Channel but, although effective in seizing booty from pirates, he was caught keeping it for himself, giving him no option but to become a rebel.

In the meantime the Emperor Diocletian (284–305) reformed the government and administration of the empire. He created the so-called 'Tetrarchy' (rule of four) recognising the empire was too large to be governed by one man. It would now have two senior emperors, each of whom took the title 'Augustus', one in the west and one in the east. There was also a junior emperor in the two halves of the empire, known as a 'Caesar', who would in due course succeed to the top job. Diocletian added new layers of administration and bureaucracy with the further subdivision of the empire's provinces. Britain was divided into four with York the capital of a province probably named *Flavia Caesariensis* and usually thought to have been the former *Britannia Inferior* minus some territory south of the Humber–Mersey line. The four provinces formed the diocese of Britain under a *vicarius* (vicar) who was himself answerable to the Prefect of the Gauls at Trier rather than, as the old governors had been, directly to the emperor in Rome. Unlike the old governors also, the *vicarius* was a wholly civilian administrator who no longer controlled the army. The effects of this reorganisation have been much debated, but it has been suggested that one consequence was to add to the tax burden on the population because the new bureaucracy was more efficient at collecting taxes than the old and also because the state apparatus, including the army, was now larger than hitherto and more expensive to run. An increased tax burden may have had some negative effects on the economy of the empire, for example reducing the ability of the curial class to sponsor construction of public buildings and infrastructure. However, the early fourth century appears to have been a time of renewed prosperity in much of Britain including the Yorkshire region.

The career of Carausius came to an end in 293 when he was murdered by his aide, Allectus who succeeded him. Allectus was, in turn, defeated by the Caesar in the west, Constantius in 297 – in honour of whom the province *Flavia Caesariensis* was named. While on campaign in Britain in the years 305–06, Constantius I, by now Augustus, became the second emperor to die in York.[3] The tetrarchy system prescribed a successor, but not Constantius's son, Constantine who, however, at the head of his father's army, immediately claimed the crown. The soldiers, it is said by the fifth- sixth-century writer Zosimus,[4] supported Constantine because they were hopeful of a large donation on his accession – and probably got it! According to *Epitome de Caesaribus* by an anonymous late fourth- fifth-century author, Constantine inherited an entourage which included one Crocus, a king of the Alemanni, a Germanic people, quite likely to have been accompanied by a number of his retainers. In this case it would be further evidence, additional to that from other sources, for the extensive incorporation of troops of non-Roman origin into the late Roman army to make up a shortfall in recruits from the empire itself.[5]

In Yorkshire we would like to think that Constantine was actually acclaimed emperor in York, perhaps in a colourful, dramatic and vivid ceremony, accompanied by the appropriate sacrifices to the gods of Rome, in the courtyard of the great fortress headquarters. A larger than life marble head of a late Roman emperor found near the Minster is thought to represent Constantine and may have come from a grand commemorative statue.[6] In any event, Constantine would not have lingered in York, but set off to fight for his inheritance against other claimants, only becoming supreme ruler of the empire in 318. Perhaps the most famous event in his struggle came before a battle against his rival Maxentius at the Milvian Bridge outside Rome in 312. On the night before, Constantine allegedly had a vision of the chi-rho – the first two letters of Christ's name in Greek – which he was told by God to put on his soldiers' banners with the injunction 'By this sign conquer'.

After the death of Severus the Roman army in Britain was, as far as we know, a garrisoning rather than a campaigning force until the end of the third century when it was caught up in the rebellion of Carausius and subsequent defeat of Allectus. It has been suggested that in the long period of peace troop numbers declined, perhaps because detachments were removed to fight in trouble spots elsewhere. As far as Yorkshire is concerned, this suggestion is not easy to assess on the basis of the archaeological evidence. Also difficult to determine locally is the effect of changes in the way the army had been organised since the time of Severus which created a rather different sort of force from that which he commanded in the north in the years 208–11, and one even more different from the army of Vespasian in 71. By the early fourth century command of a province's army came under the authority of senior officers with regional briefs and we know of several in Britain from the *Notitia Dignitatum*, an early fifth-century list of governmental and military personnel (see Chapter 10). It includes the *Dux Britanniarum* (Duke of the Britains – meaning the provinces of Britain) who may have been based in York as his subordinates all commanded units based in the north. There were still garrisons on the frontiers, the heirs of the auxiliaries, who were recruited locally. However, the principal defence of the empire was entrusted to a mobile field army – the emperor's *comitatus* (companions). It moved about to where it was needed rather than being stationed permanently in fortresses, like York, on the periphery of the empire. Furthermore, instead of preferring to fight its adversaries in the field, as in earlier times, the late Roman army was prepared to defend itself against either an outside enemy or internal rebellion in heavily fortified strong points, including towns. This may, up to a point at least, explain the walling of Brough on Humber and Catterick, and the addition of bastions to the town wall at Aldborough, in all three cases work for which either Carausius or Constantius I could have been responsible, the one to defend his illegal regime and the other to prevent a recurrence of rebellion. It is characteristic of late Roman walls, whether of towns or forts, that they are much thicker (up to 3m and more) than those of earlier times (up to c.1.5m) and higher (up to 9m) in order to deter attacks by battering, undermining or scaling during sieges. The walls and any towers projecting from them could also be used as solid platforms for *ballistae*, Roman artillery engines which could fire arrow-like projectiles or stone balls. The defensive ditches outside the walls were often much wider than hitherto in order to create an effective killing ground which could be bombarded by artillery.

At York there was no new construction on the fortress defences but there was a strengthening of the rampart behind the wall on the south-west side where it was extended from a width of *c*.9–10m to *c*.12.8m.[7] Presumably this was to create a more solid obstruction to a frontal assault, although the work may also have been intended simply to keep soldiers busy! More usually in the forts, and towns, we find that new defensive walls were built freestanding in the late Roman fashion, and in some cases pre-existing ramparts appear to have been deliberately removed. Within the fortress at York there is evidence for early fourth-century reconstruction in some of the barracks, but there was a more interesting development in the headquarters basilica.[8] Built out into the portico space at the north-west end was an additional room decorated with a very fine scheme of painted wall plaster (what survives is on display in the Minster). As in the Catterick *mansio*, there were three zones of decoration: a dado, with, as is common in the Roman world, a fake marbled effect, a middle zone with architectural features and figures, and a frieze which featured paired masks of comedy and tragedy (only the latter surviving), a common motif. The function of this room is unknown, but it may have provided private accommodation for a senior officer, perhaps the *Dux Britanniarum* himself.

In the Pennines the defences of the fort at Bowes received a rebuilt stone wall. As recorded on the south side, this was 2.33m thick and and largely freestanding, the rampart having been cut back for a new *intervallum* street.[9] There was also some rebuilding in *principia* at the same time. At Greta Bridge a geophysical survey by University of Durham students has produced intriguing evidence for a reorganisation of the plan in the late Roman period, although how late cannot be determined without excavation. The significance of a late fourth-century buckle-plate, found at the site by chance, therefore remains uncertain.[10] In the centre of the fort, where one would expect the headquarters, it looks as though there was a bath house, formerly, one assumes, it was outside the defences. Where one would expect the typical long low barracks, there appear to be small detached buildings for accommodation of the garrison, similar to those found late in the structural sequence in forts on Hadrian's Wall, for example, at Housesteads or Wallsend.

At Bainbridge fort a new east gate was constructed and the east wall of the fort was restored as a freestanding structure; the earlier wall had been removed when the annexe was built.[11] At Ilkley evidence from the excavations in the north-western corner of the fort suggested that the rampart had been partly removed to accommodate an *intervallum* street leaving the wall on the defences freestanding.[12] In addition, the flanking towers of the north gate had been removed so that it now resembled the new Bainbridge east gate as the sort of simple arched opening which was common in forts of the later Roman period. In the centre of the fort at Ilkley a new commanding officer's house was constructed on a truly grand scale with baths and heated rooms showing that the status of the man in charge of an army unit, however remote its base, remained as prestigious as it always had been.[13] To the south of the CO's house excavations located a contemporary granary of the traditional type with thick exterior walls, buttressed at intervals. Further up Wharfedale, at Elslack, the enlarged fort is, as already suggested, more likely to be late third or early fourth century than earlier. The defences were provided with a wall of Millstone Grit blocks, with foundations 2.9m thick, in front of which was a new ditch 4m wide. Characteristically late Roman in plan was the south gate with the towers flanking the entrance set behind the wall line, instead of directly on it as in earlier times, thereby creating a narrow court between the inner and outer arches in which visitors could be confined before being admitted.[14] A building c.20m square with heated rooms found inside the fort at Elslack may also be late Roman.

In the lowlands of Yorkshire at Newton Kyme, where the Rudgate crosses the River Wharfe, there had been camps and a fort of the conquest period, but in the late Roman period a new and larger fort (4.35ha within the defences) was built of which little is known in detail, although it had a c.3m thick wall and a 15m wide defensive ditch typical of the period.[15] At Castleford, at the Aire crossing, a new fort was built on more or less the same site as Fort II of the late first century (Illus. 5.5).[16] Although its full extent has not yet been fully determined, the north side being as yet unlocated, the late fort was probably larger than its predecessor. It had a freestanding wall with foundations c.2.5m thick, as well as two wide, encircling ditches. Little is known of the interior of this new fort because of later disturbance, although a pit produced the most remarkable discovery of over 800 clay moulds for casting spoons of late Roman type (see below). At Doncaster, it was probably in the late third or early fourth century that the fort was given a stone wall, 2m thick, recorded most recently on the north-east side on sites off Church Way (Illus. 5.4, 1–3), accompanied by a wide (6.6m) and deep ditch (2.4m). Pottery from the ditch suggests a garrison in occupation until the mid-fourth century. Templeborough was apparently rebuilt for the second time on a slightly smaller scale than previously, but with a free-standing wall.[17]

Finally, at Malton, Corder's excavations showed that the north-east gate had been built, or rebuilt, in a manner similar to the south gate at Elslack with guard chambers at the base of towers behind the line of a thick fort wall.[18] Little is known of the late Roman interior, but pressure on space may account for the encroachment of buildings onto the adjoining rampart. They included an apsed structure parallel with the fort wall, with a forge, dated by a coin to later than 330–37, in a courtyard south-east of it. Another building, found near the north corner of the fort, was probably a barrack block and cut into the latest floor were ten new born infant burials, suggesting to the excavator

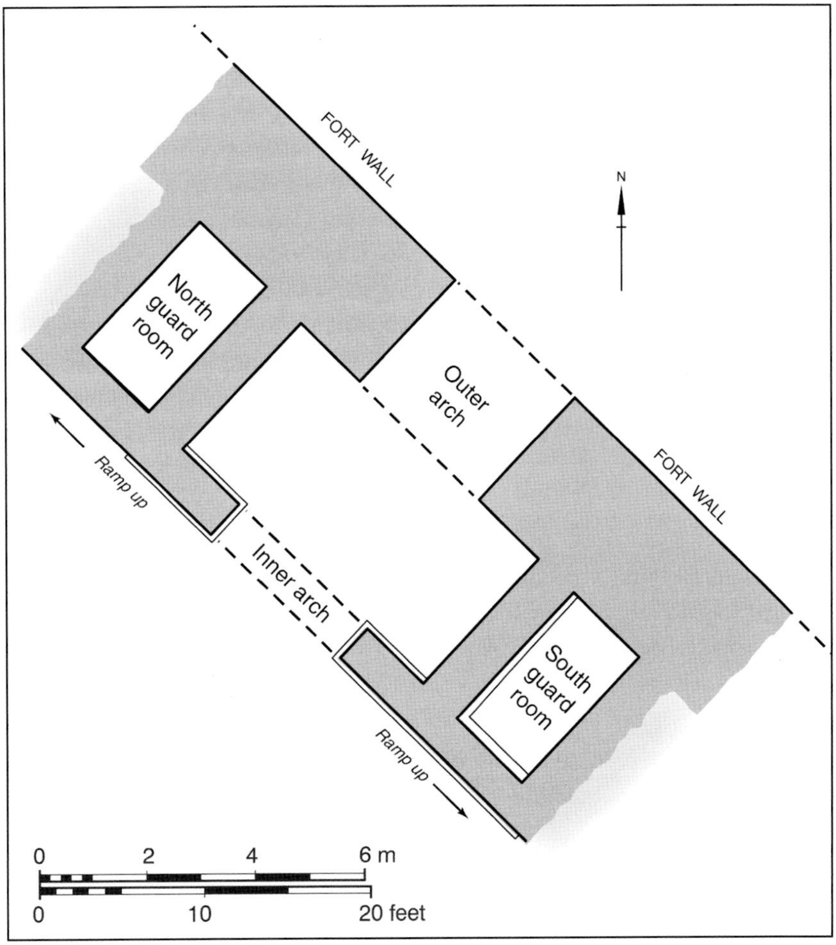

Illus. 9.2 Malton: plan of the north-east gate of the fort as rebuilt in the fourth century (after Corder 1930).

that 'strict military discipline did not hold in the fort in the late third and early fourth century', although the presence of infant burials in forts is by no means unusual.

The towns and principal settlements

The archaeological evidence from the towns and other principal settlements of the Yorkshire region suggests a revival of the local economy at the end of the third century with a particularly prosperous period during the reigns of Constantine the Great and his sons in the first half of the fourth century.

York

York does not seem to have been embellished with new public buildings in a manner comparable to other late Roman imperial capitals, like Arles or Trier, but there is good evidence for new construction, especially of houses, in the late third and early fourth centuries. North-east of the Ouse, at Coppergate, a large house dated to the late third century was built on what had been marginal land sloping down to the River Foss, although little except its plan was revealed as the walls had been almost completely demolished in the later Roman period or Viking Age.[19] A mosaic found in the nineteenth century at the nearby church of St Mary Castlegate probably belonged to a contemporary building.[20] At 21–33 Aldwark (Illus. 7.1), outside the east corner of the fortress, part of another town house was found, the walls of which had also been completely demolished, but it was dated to the early fourth century by a mosaic pavement depicting a female bust in the centre.[21]

South-west of the Ouse several new or extended houses are known from excavations. In the Bishophill area (at St Mary Bishophill Senior) a late second-century stone house was upgraded with additional ranges built around a courtyard.[22] The south range was most extensively examined and consisted of four rooms connected by a corridor of which three had underfloor heating. One of these rooms acquired an apse, that typical flourish of the late Roman period, thereby becoming a good example of the type of elongated reception hall of which examples at Holme House and Dalton Parlours villas have already been referred to. Newly constructed in the late third century, immediately north of the later church of St Mary Bishophill Junior,[23] was a house with several rooms around a courtyard to one of which an apse was added in the fourth century. In the north-western part of the town, on Toft Green, three rooms of another large house (discovered in 1853) had mosaic pavements of the early fourth century.[24] One, now on display in the Yorkshire Museum, has a design incorporating female busts representing the four seasons, one at each corner. Another house, nearby, at Bar Lane is also known from a mosaic recorded in 1814, but subsequently destroyed.[25]

At Clementhorpe, immediately south-east of the presumed town defences, the principal reception room of the house described in Chapter 7 had a polygonal apse, rather than one of the usual semicircular plan, added to it at the west end.[26] This room now became very large indeed; at 71.5m^2 it was the fourth largest room in a house in Yorkshire (Table 8) with the length to width ratio of 2.12:1 appropriate to a reception hall. Whereas a room of sides of more or less equal size is conducive to social gatherings amongst equals, an elongated room, especially one with an apse which focused attention on anyone framed by its arched opening, was suitable for social interaction between unequal parties. Length emphasised social distance, making a client take time to approach a patron and reflect the while on his inferiority. He may even have prostrated himself before his superior as was now common practice at Constantine's court. The Clementhorpe room was also given a new floor; only red *tesserae* had survived making a semicircular pattern around the edge of the room, but they may have framed a mosaic or architectural feature in the apse. In an adjacent room to the north there were remains of a mosaic dated 325–50, of which the border survived as a band of *pelta* (shield) motifs outside a band of guilloche (knot work).[27]

Table 8   Size of the ten largest rooms (excluding bath houses and passages) in Roman houses in Yorkshire in descending order of area

Site	Length (m)	Width (m)	Area (m²)	Proportions L:W
Malton, Town House	15.49	7.11	110.13	2.18:1
Brantingham villa	11.13	7.77	86.48	1.43:1
Aldborough, Helicon mosaic room	11.64	7.83	83.34	1.49:1
York, Clementhorpe house	12.50	5.90	71.50	2.12:1
Dalton Parlours villa, J Room 3	12.70	5.50	69.85	2.31:1
Harpham villa, main room	9.15	6.40	58.56	1.43:1
Dalton Parlours villa, J Room 2	7.60	6.20	47.12	1.23:1
Dalton Parlours villa, J Room 4	6.85	6.85	46.92	1:1
Beadlam villa Room 2	6.40	6.40	40.96	1:1
York, St Mary B'Hill Senior	7.88	5.63	40.41	1.40:1

In the immediate environs of Roman York there are very few examples of enclosures defined by ditches remaining in use in the late Roman period except on the well-drained morainic ridge at Heslington. Here a second-century landscape of ditched enclosures was extended. It surrounded a farmstead with several timber buildings and one partly built in stone, which had an underfloor heating system, the latter setting the place apart from most rural settlements in the region. There was evidence for the processing of crops, including two grain-drying kilns, as well as for the forging of iron on the site. A group of wells, including an impressive example, over 4m deep, with a substantial stone lining, suggested a greater investment in ensuring a ready water supply than is usual in the countryside except in villas. In sum, the evidence suggests a farming family who, with easy access to the York market, found agriculture reasonably profitable. The heated room shows them acquiring one of the luxuries of the traditional Roman way of life. In addition, what has been interpreted as a stone-built tomb monument standing at the western entrance to the farmstead represented another distinctive symbol of Roman culture, one rarely found in a rural setting in Britain.

Aldborough and Brough on Humber

At Aldborough six projecting towers, often referred to as 'bastions', are known to have been added to the second-century town wall (others presumably remain undiscovered), probably in the early fourth century (Illus. 7.6).[28] Two towers have a semicircular plan, one is rectangular and three, at the corners, have a semi-elliptical plan. They were built, at least in part, of Millstone Grit rather than local red sandstone. To accommodate the towers, the original ditch around the town had to be filled in and a new, wider one dug further from the wall.

Illus. 9.3
Heslington near York,
fourth-century well:
a) at the beginning of
excavation; b) stone
lining at the base.
(Photos: P. Ottaway)

(b)

Illus. 9.4
Reconstruction of the
north gate at Brough
on Humber after the
addition of flanking
towers in the mid-fourth
century.

Aldborough's late Roman defences may be well known from excavation, but the evidence for contemporary occupation within them is difficult to assess. There are, however, some seventeen early to mid-fourth-century mosaics, mostly discovered in the nineteenth century.[29] Although we do not usually have a clear idea of the buildings in which they were laid, they are a witness to a population of which some at least were wealthy members of a local elite enjoying life in handsome and luxurious residences. A particularly grand house may have existed in the south-west corner of the town. Its origins lay in the second century when the mosaics noted in Chapter 7 were laid. By the fourth century it was probably this same house which acquired a large reception hall with an eastern apse; at $c.86m^2$ this was the third largest room in a house in the region. It was endowed with a splendid mosaic pavement of which one part depicted Mount Helicon, home of the muses (see below).[30]

At Brough on Humber the earlier town defences composed of a rampart and ditch were strengthened with a limestone wall, 2.5m thick at the base, perhaps as much as 7m high or more, with an extended and heightened rampart (Illus. 7.8).[31] One of John Wacher's principal excavations was at the north gate which was built as a single portal with a short internal passage before recesses on either side making it a rather exaggerated version of the late Roman south gate at Elslack fort and north-east gate at Malton fort. Subsequently added to the outer face of the wall, probably before the mid-fourth century, was a series of substantial towers of rectangular plan (7.75m × 3.1m). Towers of semicircular plan were added flanking the north gate, and on one side of the east gate. The impression created as a result of this very substantial investment in construction on the defences must have been of a place not unlike some of the late Roman forts on the Rhine, such as Andernach (Germany) and Kaiseraugst (Switzerland), both of similar area to Brough, which also had high walls bristling with towers. It is tempting to see Brough now as not so much a town as part of a system of coastal defence for late Roman Britain, the northern end of a system of forts of the so-called 'Saxon Shore' on the east and south coasts. Within the defences Corder's Building I and Wacher's strip building at Manor House remained in use until the middle of the fourth century, although the Brough House building had gone by c.270.[32] In its latest phase the Manor House building had a number of hearths showing it was used for metalworking. Immediately outside the north-west corner of the defences, at 12 Cave Road, part of a stone building was occupied in the early fourth century.[33] However, outside the east gate, at the large site on Welton Road, occupation had probably ceased by this time.

What has sometimes been suggested as a decline in Brough's importance in the later fourth century may have resulted from deposition of silt in the haven which rendered it unsuitable for vessels, whether commercial or belonging to

Illus. 9.5 Catterick: plan of the fort and town in the late Roman period (© English Heritage, published in Current Archaeology 166, 1999). Note the extent of the Bypass site excavated by Wacher in 1959. The inset shows the area of the mansio and baths in the mid-second century.

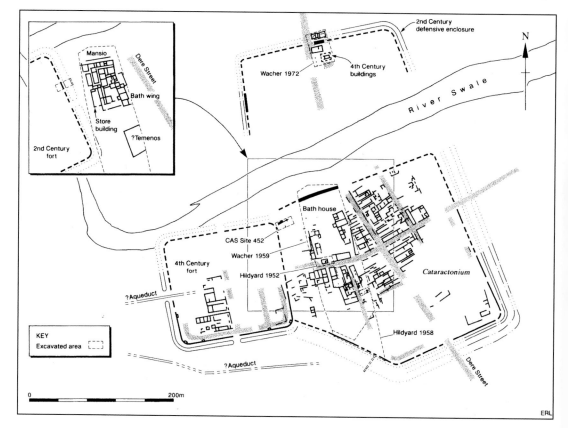

the Roman navy. This silting may have been due to the effects of rising sea level which also affected other low-lying areas in the Humber Basin. Recent excavations west of the walled area at Brough, for example at 66 Station Road, have identified waterlain silt and alluvial deposits in the haven area, although it has not been possible to date them with certainty to the late Roman period.[34]

Other principal settlements

Whilst the evidence for the fortunes of Aldborough and Brough in the late Roman period remains limited and not easy to understand, this is not the case for two of the other principal settlements in the region: Catterick and Malton.

At Catterick what may now be described as a small town was contiguous with the fort and included the former annexe.[35] The town was defended, like many contemporary forts, with a thick wall, $c.2.5$m at the base, which probably stood $c.5$m high, but had no rampart behind it. In front of the wall there were two ditches, the outer, typical of its period in being 10m wide (and $c.2$m deep). Within the walled town we have something like the complete late Roman plan in outline thanks to a combination of excavation, aerial photography and geophysical survey. There appears to have been a grid of streets based, firstly, on Dere Street, which ran north–south through the centre, and, secondly, on the east–west street, recorded on the Bypass Site, which ran towards the fort's east gate.

On the Bypass Site abandonment of the fort for a period in the third century may account for the demolition of the *mansio*, with the exception of a store house and the bath wing. Subsequently, it was rebuilt as a bath house of the usual row type. This was a building whose walls survived to a considerable height, especially on its west side where it was terraced into rising ground below the fort platform. Also on the Bypass Site, perpendicular to the main east–west street and on its south side, a new north–south street was laid out creating two blocks of urban space, often referred to in a Roman town as *insulae* (islands).[36] Facing end-on to the east–west street in these two *insulae* were a number of strip buildings, initially constructed in the mid- to late third century (for a late fourth-century view see Illus. 10.9). Small towns in Roman Britain, like Catterick, often had an important role in the production and marketing of manufactured goods for their regions and in one of the strip buildings there was evidence for metalworking (see below).

There was also a flourishing settlement outside the walls of Catterick. On the north side of the Swale, the earlier defended enclosure was no longer in commission. A strip building stood over its infilled ditch, facing Dere Street, another lay to the south of it and next to that was a possible roadside shrine (Illus. 5.6, 3). North of the former ditch, earlier buildings remained in use until the mid-fourth century. Outside the town wall to the south the process of construction and reconstruction, largely of strip buildings on Dere Street, was recorded in the Bainesse area. A smith's forge on the west side of the road may be set alongside the evidence for metalworking within the walled area.

At Malton the three major campaigns of excavation in the *vicus* south-east of the fort all produced considerable evidence for occupation in the late third /early fourth centuries, giving the impression of space being at a premium (Illus. 7.9). At Orchard Field, following the sequence of stone buildings described in Chapter 7, the so-called 'Town House' was erected in *c*.300, facing end-on to the easternmost road (2) emerging from the south-east gate of the fort.[37] Although firmly in the strip house tradition, it was a substantial structure measuring 28m × 8.5m with an apsed room at the south-east end. An impressive façade of large limestone blocks appears to have had a main door below a lintel bearing a sculptured representation of Victory. The door led to a room which at 110m[2] was the largest in a Roman house in Yorkshire. Beyond this, to the south-east, there was a suite of two rooms of a size and proportions suited to formal reception and entertainment. The first had a hypocaust and on the floor above it was a mosaic pavement, partly destroyed when found, which had probably featured the four seasons as at one corner a bust of winter survived.[38] In the surviving panel next to it was the image of a hunting dog and opposite was a panel with a deer; perhaps other animals from the hunt were depicted on the other two sides. Plaster debris showed the walls were painted, perhaps with the principal deities of Rome (see below). The second room existed as an apsed *triclinium* in which, no doubt, diners reclined on couches in traditional Roman style.

To the south-east of the town house lay the so-called 'Kiln Building' creating a juxtaposition of residence and commercial activity which shows that

Illus. 9.6 Hayton: detail of an inlaid wooden strut from a piece of panelled furniture. (Photo by Jennifer Jones, University of Durham; reproduced courtesy of the Hayton Project)

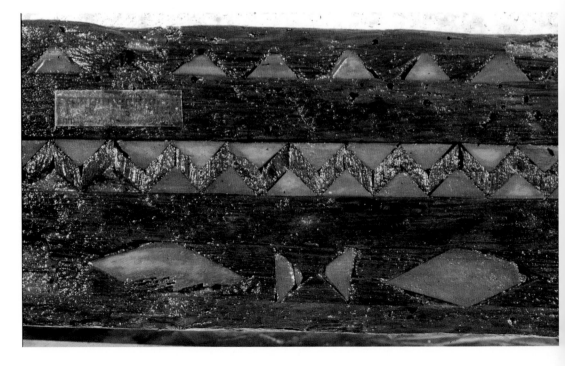

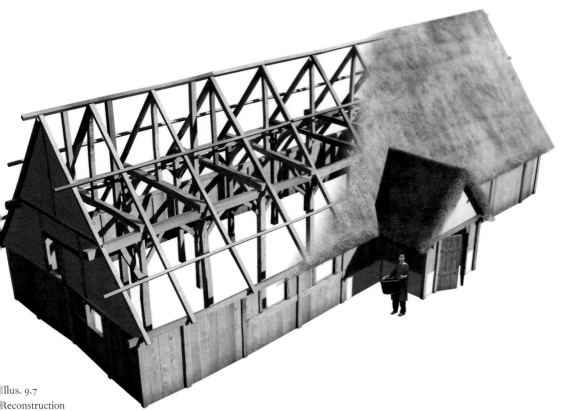

the zoning one might find in a large Roman town was not rigidly adhered to in smaller settlements. The Kiln Building probably looked superficially similar to the Town House on the street frontage with, again, a façade of large blocks, but within there were a number of stone-lined pits, rectangular in plan with a flue at one end, probably used for drying grain or for malting. To the south, at the 1970 site, part of a new strip building facing Road 2 was found. Like the Town House, it had a hypocaust in the rear room. Behind it were two other buildings.[39] They were all subsequently linked together to make one large house and the rooms were linked by a corridor on the south-east side.

Catterick and Malton (with Norton-on-Derwent) evidently flourished in the first half of the fourth century; other significant settlements in the region may also have done so, but the evidence is scarce in most cases. However, in the roadside *vicus* at Greta Bridge the timber building described in Chapter 6 burnt down in the last quarter of the third century after a fire in the kitchen.[40] In *c.*275 a number of stone-built strip buildings were built end-on to the south side of the road. Similar buildings have been identified in the western part of the *vicus*. Whether due to a running down or even abandonment of the fort, the *vicus* seems to have been in decline by the middle of the fourth century and buildings on the sites investigated were probably abandoned.

The extent and character of the roadside settlements in east Yorkshire may have remained much as before, but excavation has revealed interesting new developments at both Hayton and Shiptonthorpe. At Hayton, Burnby Lane site, where three ditched enclosures had been created in the early Roman period, the enclosure with the aisled building was reduced in size and to the north of it a small stone-built bath house, only about 8m × 5m, was constructed, served by a timber-lined well.[41] Amongst the contents of the well was a most remarkable and very well-preserved piece of oak, c.1m long, probably a strut, or stile, from a panelled piece of furniture such as a chest or cupboard.[42] Set into it were three narrow bands of wood and bone inlay in patterns of triangles, lozenges and running zigzag. This is not really what one would expect to find in a humble roadside settlement, but it gives us an unexpected glimpse of what Roman furniture was like on occasions; the complete object from which it came must have been most attractive. To the east of the baths were the foundations for a contemporary building, perhaps a house, built, at least in part, in stone.

At Shiptonthorpe, in the enclosure selected for detailed excavation, there was a major rebuilding episode in the mid- to late third century with the erection of an aisled hall measuring 21m × 8m.[43] It was defined on the ground by a wall trench in which it is thought that vertical boards had been set between vertical posts, but the main weight of the roof was carried on two rows of very substantial aisle posts, and additional posts in the space between them which gave added support to the ridge pole and what was probably a thatched roof. In the centre of the floor was an oven, originally with a domed cover. This hall represents an important timber building tradition in the region of which there were other examples at Hayton, Spaunton (see below), Dalton Parlours villa (Buildings A and M), and Ingleby Barwick villa. The Shiptonthorpe hall remained in use in the early fourth century, but the enclosure ditch is thought to have silted up to be replaced by a fence. North of it there was a large pit, roughly circular in plan, with a ramp down the west side. This was a water hole or pond, rather than a proper well, and had presumably served as a communal facility.

Rural settlement and landscape: a hey day for the Yorkshire villa

In Chapter 7 we saw that many of the ditches defining the region's enclosed landscapes had silted up by the early third century, perhaps replaced by hedges, although there were still places where the use of ditches continued in the late Roman period, especially, perhaps, where drainage was an issue. In those areas where ditched enclosures no longer existed, the presence of late third- and early fourth-century pottery clearly shows that some, if not all, these landscapes remained in use. On at least some of the region's estates prosperous times had returned by the end of the third century to judge by the evidence for new construction at farmsteads and villas.

For a review of rural settlement in the period covered by this chapter Yorkshire's subregions may be reviewed in the same order as in previous chapters with a return to some of the sites considered previously and a look at some new ones. Once again the evidence is more extensive for the lowland areas and the Wolds than it is for the uplands.

In the Pennines the settlements and fields defined by stoney banks (described in Chapter 4) produce few finds and it can be difficult to be certain that they survived into the late Roman period. However, the latest coin in the Attermire Camp hoard was late third century and was associated with two pots of the same period. Another excavation, by Alan King, on the west side of the site, produced pottery of late third- and fourth-century date.[44] At New Ing Barn in Littondale excavations in 1992 produced pottery of the late third and early fourth centuries associated with cobbled and paved areas, probably representing timber buildings within a landscape of enclosures defined by banks.[45]

Also in Craven, the villa at Gargrave acquired two new houses in the later third century, one of them with a heated room and both with at least one mosaic pavement, although fragmentary when found (Illus. 7.11, C–D).[46] An additional square building (E) was linked to the north house by a covered walk. The implications for social organisation of what were now apparently three residences are hard to determine, but there may have been accommodation for an owner, for other family members and, perhaps, for an estate manager. What may have been a walled stockyard was built in the south-east corner of the villa enclosure. Another Dales villa may have existed on the eastern edge of the limestone uplands at Middleham where excavations in 1881, 1940 and 1956 have revealed two undated buildings each with a hypocaust, probably both belonging to a bath house.[47]

The only villa known on the Yorkshire Coal Measures has been found at Conisbrough, c.5km south-west of Doncaster. A bath house and other buildings have been excavated by the landowner, but unfortunately few details of the work have been made public.[48] Some enclosed landscapes in the Coal Measures had disappeared by the early third century (or are no longer visible to archaeology), but others continued to develop. On a half hectare site at Thurnscoe near Barnsley,[49] two small enclosures of the late second or third century (Illus. 9.8, I) were replaced in the late third or early fourth century by two larger enclosures, one D-shaped and the other rectangular, associated with a trackway (II). Subsequently the D-shaped enclosure survived on its own (III). In all three phases there were subordinate enclosures and probable structures which are witness to considerable activity, related presumably to the site's arable farming function represented by quern fragments and a good example of a T-shaped grain-drying kiln. The charred plant remains in the kiln were composed of cereal grains (principally wheat), chaff and weed seeds, suggesting it was primarily used for drying wheat before pounding and winnowing.

On the Magnesian Limestone belt at Well, the fate of the main villa house is uncertain, but the baths continued in use in the fourth century and a small

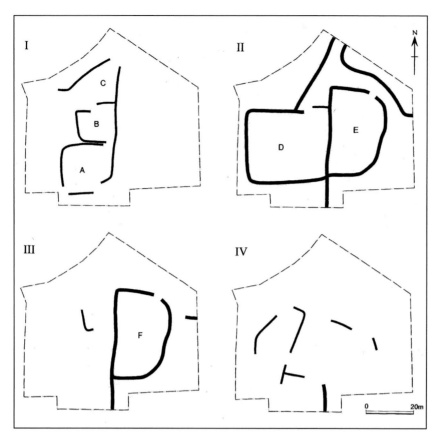

I

C
B
A

II

D
E

N

III

L
F

IV

0   20m

Illus. 9.8   Thurnscoe (near Barnsley): plan of the site sequence. (© Northern Archaeological Associates)

annexe was added mid-century.[50] The open air pool had, however, been backfilled by this time. To the south of Well lay a villa at Castle Dykes, North Stainley.[51] The date of the buildings excavated in 1866 and 1870 is uncertain, but it is likely that they were, at least in part, constructed in the fourth century. The site lies on the north side of the Lightwater Beck, south of the present village. Still prominent today are three sides of an enclosure defined by a double ditch – this is undated but may be prehistoric rather than Roman defining the precinct of an elite family whose descendants would in due course express their high social status through the villa building. Recorded within the enclosure were two wings of a large house of more than one phase, probably with a central courtyard. Revd Lukis's excavations concentrated on the bath house in the east wing which clearly went through a number of alterations in its life. In the south-west corner of the ditched enclosure another building with two heated rooms was found, probably a second bath house.

At Dalton Parlours, the layout of the villa seems to have reached its final form by the early fourth century (Illus. 7.12).[52] Like others in Yorkshire, such as Gargrave, Langton and Rudston, there was a series of self-contained buildings located with reference to the main house (Structure J). The apsed reception suite in the west wing of the house acquired a fine mosaic, featuring

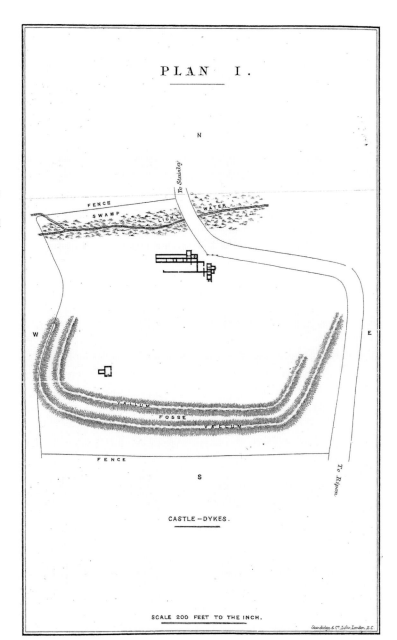

Illus. 9.9 Castle Dykes
villa, North Stainley:
plan of the buildings and
earthwork to the south
(from Lukis 1875).

the head of Medusa. In addition to the bath house in the courtyard (Building
B), another building (E) on the eastern edge of the courtyard is also thought
to have been a bath house given its proximity to a well (2). The courtyard was
partly walled, in this case on the east and possibly south sides to divide the
residential area from the working farm. On the south side of the courtyard was
a large aisled hall (A). The other (M), located east of the courtyard wall, is
thought to have had an exclusively agricultural function when built. However,
it was extended eastwards with new walls on a stone base, to become c.32m
long and it then acquired a row of small rooms on the south side making it

13m wide. Two of the rooms had hypocausts suggesting they were residential, perhaps for estate workers. Contemporary with the extension was a T-shaped grain-drying kiln and an oven at the west end of the hall. In the subsequent, third, phase the south aisle was divided into seven rooms; three in the centre had hypocausts, possibly representing a bath suite.

Immediately south-east of Building M was a well (1). It was 16m deep and had been filled up in the later fourth century, although it was presumably dug at an earlier date. Amongst the pottery were numerous jars of a type often found in wells, with lugs to which a cord might be attached so as to draw water; wooden buckets were represented by surviving iron fittings. Other, smaller, farm buildings included two (P and Q) which, although on stone footings, had superstructures of timber. Structure P must have been used for processing grain; it had an oven base and hearth near the centre and the lower stones of two beehive querns were set into the floor whilst other quern fragments were found on the floor surface. More quern fragments came from Structure Q which in its final phase had a grain-drying kiln at one end. Slag, coal and hammer scale (from welding) were found associated with a small stone-lined pit north of the house which may indicate that iron tools, fittings etc were forged on the villa site.

Not far from Dalton Parlours another villa on the Magnesian Limestone probably existed at Kirkby Wharfe near Tadcaster.[53] It was investigated early in the eighteenth century and a mosaic was reputedly found, and again in 1972, but the report is not widely available. Although the extent to which the extensive enclosed landscapes on the Magnesian Limestone belt were maintained in the fourth century is uncertain, there seems no doubt that agriculture continued to flourish. In addition to the villa complexes, there are signs that other farmsteads acquired stone buildings, or buildings partly in stone. They include an example found during A1 widening near Micklefield between Leeds and York.[54] At Hampole, just north of Doncaster and close to the main Roman road to the north, an L-shaped bath building with at least four rooms was found.[55] This was not apparently part of a villa, but it may have served as a facility for local people and travellers. What was probably another stone-built bath house, again with no adjacent villa yet known, was found at Stancil near the southern limit of Yorkshire, 3km north of Tickhill.[56] In its final form the building measured at least c.14m × 3.5m and contained a room with a hypocaust. Unfortunately excavations in 1938–39 were interrupted by World War II, but traces of two other stone structures were found, one possibly an apsidal room at the east end of the main building which had a floor of 'pink cement', probably the *opus signinum* typical of bath houses.

On the A1-M1 Link at Swillington Common South the north–south trackway, probably of Iron Age origin, was now extended to the south or at least defined for the first time by ditches in its southern part (Illus. 4.6). To the east of this extension the land was divided into three broad strips of similar size. Further east, at Parlington Hollins, there was another example of a landscape still divided up by ditches in the late third or early fourth centuries.[57] A major north–south ditch formed an important land boundary and there were wide strip fields, defined by ditches, to the west of it and at least one ditched enclosure to the east. Another phase of activity, perhaps of the mid-fourth century, saw the ditch restated and a new enclosure set out to the east of it. In contrast to the two sites just described, at Ferrybridge the extensive enclosed landscape of Iron Age origin south of the Ferrybridge Henge seems to have almost completely disappeared by the late Roman period with the possible exception of one small enclosure.[58]

In the Tees valley the villa at Holme House appears to have been abandoned, although there was apparently later Roman settlement nearby. However, there was little evidence of late Roman occupation at two of the other sites (Bonny Grove Farm and Dixon's Bank, Coulby Newham) referred to in Chapter 7. At Ingleby Barwick villa changing fortunes may be indicated by the conversion of the small baths *caldarium* into a grain-drying kiln.[59] Another villa of similar character lay *c.*16km to the west at Dalton-on-Tees.[60] The site, discovered in 1992, lies east of the village on a scarp above the river. The villa, like Ingleby Barwick, lies in an area of earlier ditched enclosures and, in this case, stood within a dedicated enclosure of its own. The full story of the site is unknown as excavations concentrated on its later history. However, also as at Ingleby Barwick, there were three rectangular buildings, but although on stone footings, they may not have been of stone throughout. One of the buildings, of winged corridor plan, would have offered the residents fine views to the south and east. Another, facing south, of several phases of construction may originally have been an aisled structure with the aisles divided into rooms. Three apses were later added on the north side, the largest, opposite the main door to the south, had had painted plaster walls; this central part of the building was presumably a reception and dining area. A substantial well supplying the villa with water was *c.*4.8m deep and lined with sandstone blocks.

In the Vale of York, one might, perhaps, expect to find farmsteads which reached villa status in the late Roman period given the potential income to be made from York's considerable appetite for agricultural products. However, only two potential villa sites have been found. One is at Wilstrop, *c.*12km west of the city, overlooking the River Nidd to the west.[61] Part of a bath house has been revealed in excavation and fieldwalking has produced tesserae, box flue tile and fragments of wall plaster; most of the pottery is late third or early fourth century. About the same distance north-east of York lay another possible villa at West Lilling in the middle of an extensive cropmark landscape on sand and gravel at the foot of the Howardian Hills, 200m south of the River Foss by which trade with York would have been easy enough.[62] Foundations for stone buildings were revealed in advance of pipe laying. Pottery suggests occupation from the second century onwards, but most of it was fourth century. This is yet another site in Yorkshire that one would like to know a good deal more about.

In the flat country east and south-east of York the agricultural economy continued to flourish as far as one can tell from excavations. For example, at a site near Wheldrake, c.10km south of York, the fourth century was the principal period of activity in a landscape of ditched enclosures attached to a trackway.[63] Immediately east of the River Derwent, just east of Stamford Bridge village, on Moor Lane, the landscape was apparently reorganised in the late third or early fourth century with new ditched enclosures around a T-junction between an earlier north–south trackway and another running east–west. There were also traces of settlement in the form of a roundhouse and a few pits, one of which contained a number of pottery kiln wasters suggesting a production site nearby.[64] Also close to the east bank of the Derwent, at Sutton on Derwent, 12km south-east of York, geophysical survey identified an east–west road along an old river course either side of which were rectilinear enclosures thought to represent a settlement in existence c.230–370.[65] In light of the favourable conditions for agriculture between York and the edge of Wolds it is surprising that no villas have been recognised, although Peter Halkon has recently identified a possible example within an enclosed landscape of earlier origin at Ousethorpe, c.2km north-east of Pocklington about midway between Humber Street and the Roman road to York. Aerial photography has revealed a house of winged corridor type and fieldwalking has produced mosaic tesserae and painted wall plaster fragments.[66]

Some parts of the Humberhead Levels may have become marginal land if they were increasingly prone to flood as a result of climate change. However, this does not seem to have been a widespread problem. For example, in what might be thought a vulnerable area immediately south of the River Ouse at Drax, excavations in 1961–64, in advance of the construction of the power station, revealed a substantial late Roman stone building, presumably at an estate centre.[67] This was a house built in the mid- or late third century, initially of five rooms with a verandah, supported by timber posts, facing south-east into a walled courtyard. There may have been other associated buildings but they were not clearly identified by the excavation. Later alterations to the house added a room on the south-east, a new verandah founded on stone walls and a corridor connecting the internal rooms.

South of the River Aire at Womersley, the ditches of an extensive (over 2ha) field system produced pot of the fourth century.[68] A small enclosure, containing a timber building of rectangular plan founded on sill beams, was carved out of the fields in a manner typical of the region since the late Iron Age. Another late Roman site at Womersley, just on the Magnesian Limestone, produced a grain-drying kiln built of limestone rubble.[69] Evidence for ready access to money, by the fourth century even in areas like Womersley a little removed from main Roman roads, came from a hoard of 3300 coins deposited in c.345 (at Cridling Stubbs). Further south at Gunhills, Armthorpe the later Roman period saw continued use of the field system and settlement described in Chapter 7.[70] Dated to the late third or early fourth century were two great dumps of pottery in the enclosure ditches, one of which was composed of as many as 4000 sherds. They do not appear to derive from middens accumulating over a period of time and it is possible that they were the result of a one-off event, perhaps a feast held to mark some special occasion, after which some sort of ritual considerations forbad the reuse of the associated vessels and instead demanded their disposal.

In the completely different upland environment of the North York Moors, late third- and fourth-century settlement is better documented than in earlier periods thanks to its having had a greater access to Roman material culture. For example, at Newbiggin overlooking Eskdale, traces of a small dwelling consisting of an oval pavement of stone (5.5m × 4m) were found; it probably had timber and turf walls.[71] There were few associated finds, but sufficient to show occupation in the period under discussion. On the south side of the Moors similar traces were found at Hutton le Hole with stony surfaces suggesting buildings with circular, oval or rectangular plans.[72] Nearby at Spaunton there was a farmstead with a rather more ambitious timber building on an aisled plan.[73] Overall it measured c.7.3m × 6m; there were two rows of four posts, 2m apart, flanking a central space 3.65m wide in which there was a pit for a hearth. Stonework, of which some traces were found, probably served as infill between the posts. Only slight traces of a later stone building with stone-lined drains survived and are difficult to interpret. South of Spaunton, on the northern edge of the Vale of Pickering, another late Roman farmstead was found at Sinnington, sited on a low promontory overlooking a beck to the north.[74] There were traces of what would have been a small timber building on a roughly oval plan (c.4.9m × 3.35m). It survived as a floor surface of large

Illus. 9.10 Beadlam villa: plan of the principal buildings (after Neal 1996).

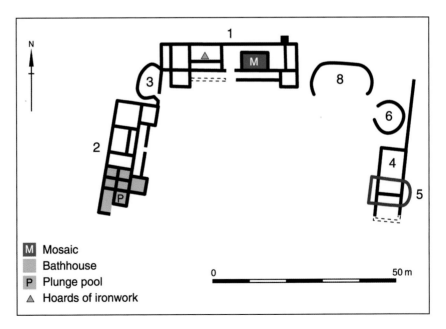

M Mosaic
Bathhouse
P Plunge pool
▲ Hoards of ironwork

0   50 m

Illus. 9.11 Beadlam villa: a reconstruction looking north-west towards Buildings 1 (*right*) and 2 (*left*).

rounded cobbles and limestone slabs set in clay, but it probably had walls of timber or turf. Further east, 4.8km north-east of Pickering, yet another late Roman farmstead has been identified at Stonygate in Newtondale,[75] whilst at the foot of Newtondale excavations at Blansby Park in 2002 located a building with a hypocaust, probably a bath house, suggesting the presence of a villa.[76]

If we stay on the southern edge of the Moors, but move west we may now look at the villa about which most is known in this area at Beadlam, 2.5km east of Helmsley, at the foot of Wykeham Dale.[77] This is a favourable location for settlement as it lies close to three different ecological zones, each offering good opportunities for agriculture. To the north lie the well-drained lower slopes of the Moors on Corallian (Jurassic) sandstone suitable for arable, and also a source of building material, and further north was higher ground more suitable for grazing sheep. To the south lay the Vale of Pickering in which, in Roman times, the heavy clay soil was poorly drained, but would have been suitable for pasture. Settlement at Beadlam probably has a long history going back to pre-Roman times, but in the area excavated in 1966–78 there was little pre-dating the stone buildings, the earliest of which was late second century.

The principal stone buildings at Beadlam, dated to the early fourth century, were ranged around a courtyard. The large building on the north side (1), which measured *c*.37.8m × 12.8m, may originally have been constructed as a barn as it seems to have had a wide door on the south side. However, it was converted into a dwelling which, on the east side of a new, narrower entrance, was given a reception room which possessed a hypocaust below a mosaic pavement.[78] On the west side of the courtyard was another house (2), in this case of winged corridor plan, composed of two suites of rooms with a lobby between them. The southern suite contained a bath house. Between this and Building 1 was added a subsidiary building (3) with straight sides and rounded ends, perhaps serving as a stable or byre. On the east side of the courtyard was a wall which, as in other villas, may have divided it off from a farmyard beyond. In due course Buildings 4, 6 and 8 were built up against this wall. Building 6 had an oval plan and with a maximum width of 9m looks like a version of the traditional roundhouse.

In the Hambleton Hills to the west of the Vale of Pickering is Cold Cam, Cockerdale Wood, where, spared from the plough, a typical upland field system defined by boundary walls rather than ditches, was found in 1953.[79] These walls ran north-eastwards up a hill slope reaching nearly 250m above sea level and defined small enclosures up to 90m × 55m. East of the main group a pottery kiln was found on the edge of three small enclosures, each c.18m square. Pottery recovered from excavation was late third or early fourth century, although, as elsewhere, the enclosures may have had earlier origins. The Hood Grange sarcophagus was found nearby which may indicate that a farmstead of villa status awaits discovery. Another has long been thought to have existed in the same area at East Ness. The 'ness', a Viking Age name for a promontory, refers to a little ridge of the Hambleton Hills projecting into the Vale of Pickering and overlooking the River Rye to the north. The inscribed stone coffin was found by the plough here as long ago as 1619, but it is only recently that a geophysical survey has revealed the remains of a villa composed of three stone buildings.

South-west of the Vale of Pickering, in the Howardian Hills west of Malton, but within easy reach of it by road in Roman times, lie Musley Bank and, adjacent to it, Roughborough, identified as villa sites. This is largely on account of the discovery of buildings with mosaics in the nineteenth century, although not much else is known about either of them.[80] Farther west at Hovingham, remains, presumably representing another villa, were found in 1745 in front of the Worsley family seat at Hovingham Hall. They consisted of a hypocaust forming part of a bath building, c.16m long, with three or four other rooms floored with a mosaic and other tessellated pavements.[81]

Of the villas in Malton's hinterland most is known about Langton to the south-east where a further phase of construction took place in the early fourth century (Phase 2 on Illus. 7.16).[82] This perpetuated the rather loose arrangement of buildings of earlier times, but respected the new dwelling house (2) which, assuming House 1 had been demolished, faced an open space to the south. House 2 had a simple plan with two large rooms, both heated, at each end with a corridor and another room linking them. Subsequently a verandah was constructed across the façade and two more heated rooms were attached, one to the north-west and the other to the south-east. Internal arrangements are hard to determine, but the larger western room produced wall plaster in the demolition debris with dark red and white panels and flower motifs. Both this room and a room added to the north-west probably had mosaic pavements.

South-west of the house were two substantial buildings (A and B), presumably used, in the main, for agricultural purposes. The eastern building was divided into two halves and had a substantial doorway 2.5m wide, suitable for carts. Two road surfaces were recorded leading to the doorway of which the earlier yielded a coin of c.324. At the southern end there was a small bathroom with a hypocaust and the base for a hot tub above the flue for the furnace. One wonders how happy bathers were to share the building with

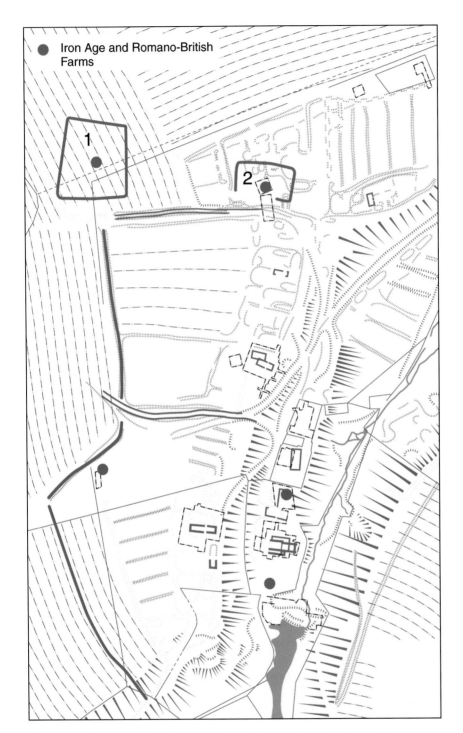

Illus. 9.12   Wharram Percy: plan of the village earthworks showing Iron Age and Romano-British farms / enclosures, trackways and boundaries; 1, north-west enclosure; 2, north manor enclosure. (After Beresford and Hurst 1990; by courtesy of English Heritage)

farm animals or bales of hay? East of the main house other buildings were partly walled off from the main house. Building C had a small bath complex built into the east end which may have served the estate workers rather like that added to the aisled building at Dalton Parlours. The rest of the building may have been demolished by this time as at the west end it had been cut into by a large flat-bottomed shallow pit with a rough stone base. This may have been the sub-floor of a timber building, although it has been identified as a threshing floor or a rick stand because of the proximity of Building L to the south which may have been a barn for storing and processing cereals. In its north-west corner there was a small room in which a quantity of burnt wheat grain was found. South of this building was an oven or grain-drying kiln. West of Building L in the courtyard was the obligatory villa well, c.13.5m deep, thought to have been last used in c.335. A glimpse of an excavation in the pre-health and safety era is captured in the Langton report as follows: 'Bertie Gott who was working in waders in semi-darkness, in eighteen inches of water, lugged water jars from the base'.

Just as Malton had a group of villa estates around it, so did Brough on Humber. One of these lay at Brantingham, 1.5km to the north, between the Walling Fen and the Wolds and a little to east of the road to Brough from York.[83] Although much of the site has been lost in sand quarrying, it has been excavated on three occasions in 1948, 1962 and 1983. Like Langton and other east Yorkshire villas, it probably enjoyed its best days in the early fourth century. The 1983 work showed that since the late Iron Age there had been a field system typical of the area before the estate owner decided to build himself a splendid house, probably with rooms ranged around a courtyard. Other buildings presumably existed on the site, but have not been found. In 1948 two rooms in the southern part of the house were excavated and two mosaics were found, one of which was mysteriously stolen the night before it was due to be taken to Hull Museum. In 1962, 70m to the north, five rooms in a probable north range of the same building were examined. One of these rooms was the second largest in a Roman house in Yorkshire with a floor area of 86.48m^2. However, it is not strictly comparable to the elongated reception halls we have seen in Aldborough or York, for example, being more nearly square (11.13 × 7.77m). The room possessed one of the finest mosaics in the region known as the 'Tyche mosaic' (see below) which was dated to after 330 as a coin of about that date was found beneath it. North of Brantingham there were other villas, also close to the road to York, at South Newbald and South Cave, although little is known about them.[84]

On the Wolds we may look first at the area around Wharram Percy, east of Malton, where research has shown the value of studying a Roman landscape over a large area using excavation, fieldwalking and survey such that the interrelationship between settlement sites can be studied as they developed over time.[85] For example, on the North Manor site at Wharram Percy, within an enclosed landscape of Iron Age origin, an east–west trackway was a focus

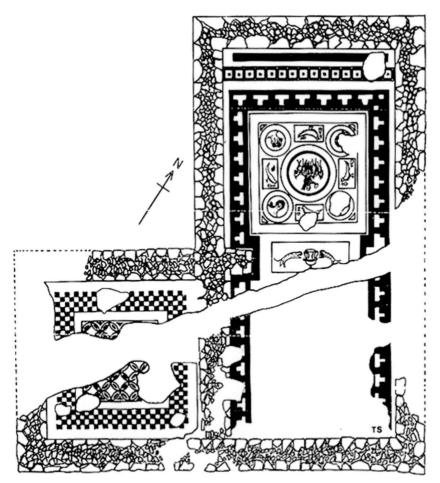

Illus. 9.13 Rudston villa: plan of the main house – length 12.6m (drawn by T. Suthers, from Smith 1976).

for settlement until the end of the Roman period. However, an enclosure to the west (the 'north-west enclosure') produced little evidence for fourth-century activity serving to make the point that accidents of sampling can be misleading in assessing settlement history unless individual sites are seen in a wider landscape context. Two other Roman farmsteads, but in these cases with stone buildings, have been identified in the vicinity, although not extensively excavated, at Wharram Grange and Wharram le Street.[86] They both stood within well-defined, rectangular ditched enclosures surrounded by complex enclosed landscapes, again probably of Iron Age origin, which were clearly occupied into the fourth century.

Further east again on the Wolds is Thwing where a single stone building of winged corridor plan, in its final form, has been found, which does not seem to have been part of a villa complex.[87] However, at Rudston, only 5km to the south-east, is one of Yorkshire's best-known villas.[88] The site has a long history going back to the late Iron Age but became a farmstead with stone buildings by the early third century. In the late third and early fourth centuries Rudston received further stone buildings loosely arranged around a central yard. They included a bath house with a row of rooms through which one progressed in the usual manner. At the north end there was probably the changing room on the floor of which was the famous Venus mosaic (Illus. 9.20 and described below). Having commended oneself to the goddess, one advanced to the two intermediate rooms, one of which had a geometric mosaic. They were, perhaps, used for exercise or simply socialising. In the next room there was a striking mosaic depicting a bust of the god Oceanus and sea creatures, a theme appropriate as an introduction to the actual bathing suite next door. Two rooms with internal apses at their western ends functioned as the *tepidarium* and *caldarium*. Finally there was a warm plunge bath; the excavator comments, thinking of winters on the Wolds, 'classical convention required a cold plunge, but convention was sacrificed for comfort'. Immediately west of the baths was the well, although the baths must have been supplied by spring water also. Of all the Roman wells in Yorkshire this was, at *c*.30m, the joint deepest (with Welton) showing the great effort to which one must sometimes go on the Wolds to find water. It was an audacious piece of engineering to dig and also, latterly, to excavate archaeologically.

A little later than the baths, judging by what is thought to be the date of its mosaics, a house was constructed *c*.50m to the north-west. Unfortunately a complete plan could not be recovered because part of it lies under the Kilham–Rudston road, but what we can see is a large room, internally 9.4m × 4.17m, facing south, flanked on the west at the south end by another room. The former, with length: width ratio of 2.25:1, was clearly intended to be a reception suite. Stub walls projecting from the sides at about the mid-point suggest a partition, or even an arch, across the centre to allow for the maintenance of social distinctions amongst visitors. Those admitted to the northern half would have seen the very fine mosaic featuring a charioteer (discussed below) dated to the second quarter of the fourth century.

Other buildings standing in the late Roman period at Rudston included one on the south side of the courtyard in which there were the remains of a hearth and ovens and, more remarkable, small piles of tesserae against the western wall. They were sorted by size and colour, and may have been surplus from making the bath house mosaics. In another building, on the west side of the courtyard, there was another pile of tesserae. One can envisage the great day when the mosaicists arrived with their sacks of raw materials and set up their workshops on site, no doubt causing considerable disruption to the residents before the project was completed and then annoyance when debris was left behind.

Another villa on the Wolds lies near Harpham, *c*.3km south of Rudston.[89] Inadequately published excavations of 1904 and 1951 and aerial photographs have revealed a large building, at least 50m long, on a reversed E-shaped plan with a large central reception room and wings to the north and south. Mosaics or tesselated pavements of the early fourth century were found in all nine rooms.[90] There were other buildings about which little is known and the photographs suggest the villa stood within an extensive field system, but they also show that the site is very badly damaged by ploughing. On the southern arm of the Wolds the Welton villa site described previously appears to have reached its maximum extent, although the original house was not extended.[91] New construction included two more aisled barns and three sunken-floored structures in which there were grain-drying kilns; no fewer than fourteen existed on the site as a whole in this period. Carbonised grain suggests barley rather than wheat was now the principal crop. Another possible villa on the Wolds lay at Bishop Burton near Beverley where two mosaics, one a '...

Illus. 9.14 Welton villa: sunken-floored building with grain-drying kiln. The stoke-hole is in the foreground (the flue is blocked) and, unusually, part of the double floor survives (© Rodney Mackey).

curious Pavement of red, white and blue stones; each about an Inch Square, placed in a beautiful Order ...', were found in the early eighteenth century.[92]

On the gravel at the junction of the Wolds and Plain of Holderness, we should now return to Elmswell.[93] On the site examined in the 1930s there was a settlement bounded by large ditches on the west and the Elmswell Beck to the south and east. Dating of individual features is a bit sketchy in the report, but occupation of an undefined character had clearly begun in the first century AD. Ascribed to the third century was a building ('hut' in the report) of rectangular plan (c.5m × 3m) represented by traces of a cobbled floor set in mortar. Elsewhere on the site 'many paved areas' may represent other structures. At least one of six pits on the site was apparently third century; it contained tips of ash and layers of burnt clay. It is possible that this was in some way associated with what was thought to be 'a smithy' – a bowl-shaped hearth c.1m in diameter, surrounded by an area of chalk and gravel, which was filled with ash. The excavations produced half a ton of iron smelting slag which testifies to a major production operation, although the date of the material is uncertain. In any event, occupation at Elmswell clearly continued through to the end of the fourth century and beyond.

Finally, we can look again at the lower Hull valley where the river level may have risen with the marine transgression which probably began in the mid-third century.[94] At the Gibraltar Farm site, Kingswood, a reorganisation of the settlement in the late third and early fourth century was represented by a reduction in the area enclosed (Illus. 7.17, Phase 4).[95] Subsequently (Phase 5) a substantial new enclosure was created to the north-east of the former enclosure complex, perhaps in response to a rising river level, before the site was abandoned in the mid-fourth century.

Agriculture

The previous section has indicated that there may have been changes in the organisation of the landscape in many parts of the region with a decline in the extent of enclosed landscapes. Otherwise there is little evidence to suggest an agricultural regime much different from that which had prevailed since the Iron Age, although in cereal processing the use of the grain-drying kiln was now well established.

As far as animal husbandry is concerned, numbers of bones from archaeological sites (Table 9) show that cattle remained the principal source of meat throughout the region, although they seem to be slightly less dominant than hitherto as one moves away from sites with close military associations (Castleford fort[96] and Catterick Bridge[97]). Percentages for cattle bone around and below 50% may indicate a slight shift in husbandry towards sheep, perhaps reflecting a growing consumer preference for mutton on sites such as the Castleford *vicus*, Bainesse at Catterick[98] or the roadside settlement at Shiptonthorpe.[99] The Wharram Percy figures[100] – especially North Manor (although only a small sample) – seem to suggest that in rural areas, as in previous periods, mutton retained a significant place in the diet. (The two latest dated groups, from York and Filey, are discussed further in the next chapter).

Table 9 Nos of animal bones from principal meat sources: late third- to fourth-century contexts in descending order of percentage of cattle

Place	Date	Cattle	Sheep/ goat	Pig	Total	% Cattle
Castleford Fort IV	*c.*250–400	1,945	607	274	2,826	68.83
Catterick Bridge	Late C3–C4	321	97	70	488	66.00
Castleford Vicus 4	*c.*180–400	536	258	166	960	55.83
Catterick, Bainesse	Largely late C3–C4	3,284	2,143	926	6,353	51.69
Dalton Parlours well	Mid- to late C4	1,321	1,047	360	2,728	48.42
Wharram north-west enclosure	Late C3–C4	212	202	41	455	46.59
Shiptonthorpe Trench 3	Mid-C4	369	409	92	870	42.41
Shiptonthorpe Trench 3	Mid-C3 to early C4	277	332	76	685	40.44
Wharram north manor	Late C3–4	107	215	28	350	30.57
York Minster	Late C4	234	311	415	960	24.38
Filey signal station	Late C4	175	436	334	945	18.52

Manufacturing

Manufactured goods found in the region were once again overwhelmingly produced for local consumption, perhaps to an even greater extent than before as supplies of imported commodities from outside the region seem to have largely dried up.

Pottery

One of the new pottery production centres of the early third century was located around Holme-on-Spalding Moor in east Yorkshire. In the Foulness Valley Project area sixteen pottery producing sites have been recorded, usually sited on low ridges of land near the river where thin sand deposits overlie clay.[101] The first kiln excavated in the area (in 1930) was at Throlam farm.[102] Philip Corder found a huge mound – 'pot hill' – *c.*30m in diameter and 2m high within which there were kilns and vast quantities of discarded pottery. The kilns had stoke pits with flues leading to furnace chambers dug up to *c.*0.5m into the ground and lined with clay; within them the vessels were placed on a raised platform for firing. Products included bowls (a variety with a perforated base was used as a cheese press), large jars with two handles at the neck and large storage jars. Similar pottery has been found locally associated with kilns at Hasholme Hall[103] and Bursea House,[104] and others north of the former Tollingham airfield.[105]

At Norton-on-Derwent pottery kilns have been found principally in the Model Farm estate area, but at least one other may have existed on Commercial Street (Illus. 5.18).[106] They were probably in operation during the first half of the third century although one (Grove Cottage) was dated to the late third or early fourth century. These kilns had distinctive small circular or oval furnace chambers with long, relatively wide flues often lined with stone; temporary stands for the vessels were made of prefabricated clay bars set on a central support. Vivien Swann suggests that the kiln type shows that the first Norton potters had moved to the area from north-west Lincolnshire where similar kilns have been found. The incomers may have sought to take advantage of the local military market – the fort had been regarrisoned after c.160 – which may explain the production of vessels in the black-burnished ware traditionally favoured by the army. Most of the Norton pottery is in wheel-thrown grey ware, although some hand-made jars in a local tradition (sometimes known as 'Knapton ware') were probably made in the same kilns.

Another new centre for pottery production lay in an extensive zone around Crambeck which is c.7km south-west of Malton on the York road and was therefore well placed for distribution to local markets.[107] The industry took advantage of a local bed of Jurassic 'Oxford Clay', preferred for potting purposes to the boulder clay of glacial origin which is found in much of the area. The kiln flues were lined with limestone slabs and sloped upwards slightly to the furnace chambers which were circular pits dug into the ground and lined

Illus. 9.15a   Doncaster (Cantley): a late third- / fourth-century Roman pottery kiln (No.33) with three small cylindrical pedestals, and supplementary supports for radiating fire-bars (© Doncaster Museum Service, Doncaster Metropolitan Borough Council).

Illus. 9.15b   Plan and cross-section of Kiln 33 (© Doncaster Museum Service, Doncaster Metropolitan Borough Council).

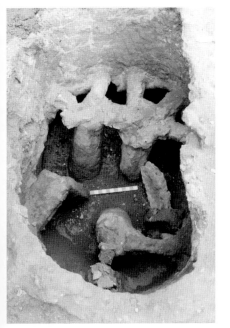

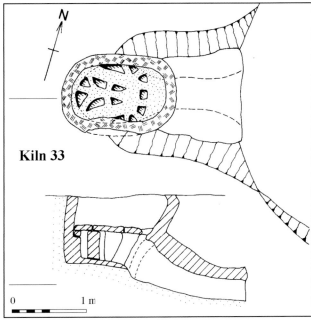

Kiln 33

0   1 m

with clay. Examples excavated in 1928 and 1937 were arranged in pairs with a common stoke-hole. Vivien Swann suggested that the Crambeck industry was founded by potters moving in from the established local centres at Norton and Holme-on-Spalding Moor.[108] The kilns largely produced good quality table wares (dishes and bowls) in a burnished gun-metal grey fabric and to a lesser extent in red earthenware imitating certain samian forms. Elsewhere in the Yorkshire region a small early fourth-century kiln, similar to some of those at Crambeck, was found at Bainesse, Catterick which also produced vessels in black-burnished ware, in part, presumably, for the local military market.[109] Pottery production continued at Doncaster in kilns at Cantley and Branton, apparently on a considerable scale, perhaps primarily to supply a newly beefed up garrison in the fort.[110]

Metalworking

Evidence for late Roman metalworking is found widely in the region and the villas and farmsteads may have been largely self-sufficient at least in production of day to day iron tools and structural fittings. That the army continued to have specialist metalworkers is suggested by the presence of a forge in the fort at Malton. However, perhaps the most important single metalworking-related discovery in a late Roman fort in the region comes from Castleford.[111] In a pit, unfortunately not related to any structure, were buried some eight hundred fragments of two-piece clay moulds for making spoons in leaded gun metal by the lost wax method. The spoons would have been *c*.150mm long with a purse-shaped bowl typical of the period.

Good archaeological evidence for late Roman metalworking, both ferrous and non-ferrous also comes from the town at Catterick, both within the

Illus. 9.16a and 9.16b Castleford: spoon moulds and reconstruction drawing of a spoon (length: 150mm; from Bayley and Budd 1998, © English Heritage).

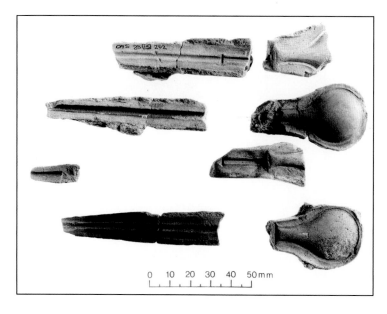

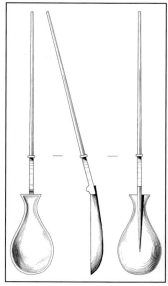

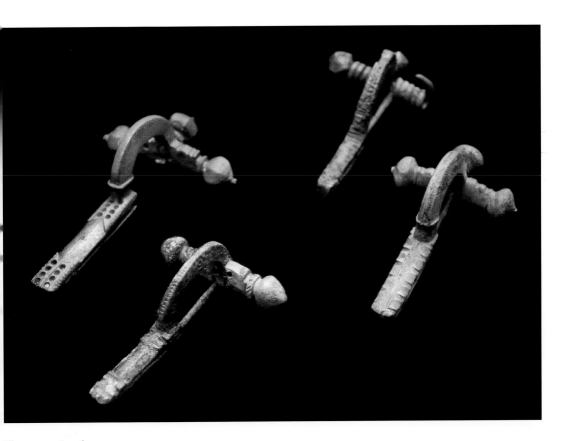

Illus. 9.17 Crossbow brooches from Malton (photo: Gwen Jones ©).

walls and on the roadside settlement at Bainesse.[112] Within the walls, one of the strip buildings on the Bypass site housed a smith working in copper alloy. Set into the floor were a waste bin and two trays – wooden boxes *c.*0.5m square – containing the filings and other debris arising from cleaning castings etc. Although there was no evidence for the actual products made here, we can guess that they included jewellery such as armlets and bracelets that were in fashion for female attire in late Roman Britain. Types made from twisted wire were particularly favoured and a number of examples come from Catterick itself. Also fashionable in the fourth century, although quite rare in the Yorkshire region, was a development of the fibula known as the crossbow brooch.[113] Occurring in silver (sometimes gilded), as well as copper alloy, these brooches are often quite weighty and, when closed, are characterised by a P-shaped profile with a transverse bar at the top of the P. Decoration with knobs at the ends of the bar and with small notches and ring-and-dot motifs is common. These brooches were worn principally, it is thought, on the basis of contemporary illustrations, by men for clasping their cloaks high on the right shoulder, the loop of the P downwards.

A stone mould found on the Catterick Bypass Site was probably used for making plates of pewter (tin–lead alloy) and another was found at Langton villa.[114] As tin is not found in Yorkshire, the pewter was probably brought in as cakes from elsewhere in Britain for working locally. More remarkable evidence for the skill of the metalworkers at Catterick, however, is represented by two iron beams from the bath house of the sort which, as can be still seen *in situ* at Pompeii, were used to support the water boilers.[115] They had to be laboriously, but very skilfully, fabricated from numerous bars of iron; the complete example, 1.72m long and 0.18 square in section, weighs *c*.1275kg.

Other crafts

There is little new to say about the manufacture of basic building materials in this period, except perhaps that clay roof tiles were increasingly replaced by stone roofing slabs in York and elsewhere. However, one product which became much more widely demanded for the embellishment of buildings, albeit belatedly compared to many other parts of Britain, was the mosaic pavement. As we saw in Chapter 7, a few second-century Yorkshire examples are known but all the rest are thought to be of the early to mid-fourth century. In their great corpus of Britain's Roman mosaics Neal and Cosh recorded up to about sixty from Yorkshire.[116] The largest number (about twenty) from a single place come from Aldborough, although the somewhat smaller figure (about twelve) recorded for York is largely due to the lack of excavation in its Roman residential areas. There were probably several mosaic workshops in the region working largely within what Neal has called a 'northern style' (see below).

Exchange and trade: back to basics

Based primarily on the evidence of pottery and metalwork, two general comments may be made about trade in the late third and early fourth centuries. Firstly, there appears to have been a greater availability of manufactured goods than hitherto in areas, especially the uplands of the Pennine Dales and North York Moors, at a distance from the principal market centres and the main roads and waterways.[117] Settlements which may have existed in the Iron Age and early Roman period now become visible because they produce late Roman pottery and other artefacts. This suggests both changing tastes and lifestyles in remoter areas and a more integrated regional economy. Secondly, it appears that imported commodities whether from outside the region or from outside Britain itself were scarce. Whether in groups from York or elsewhere the non-local component of the pottery is much lower than hitherto, partly because samian was no longer imported and there was no replacement for it, but even pottery from elsewhere in Britain was scarce except for wares from the Nene Valley (usually *c*.4% in groups from York). On rural sites pottery remained overwhelmingly locally made and the products of the region's potteries were, in turn, largely locally distributed. For example, vessels from the new industries in the Holme-on-Spalding Moor area are mostly found in east Yorkshire and those made at Crambeck are usually found in a zone defined by Catterick, Malton and York.[118]

Although samian was no longer imported to Britain, import of at least a few Continental goods to the region is indicated by sherds of amphora. Largely found in York, these are from types usually dated to the third and fourth centuries and suggest that olive oil and wine was continuing to arrive from the Mediterranean, if in smaller volume than before. Whereas until the early third century the principal source of oil had been southern Spain, a new source supplying Britain was North Africa. For example, the top half of a vessel made in the Sahel region of central Tunisia (centred on the town of *Byzacena*) was found at York Minster.[119] York has also produced sherds of 'hollow foot' amphorae which probably brought wine from the Aegean.[120]

Imports of glass to the region from Continental Europe, the Rhineland and northern Gaul continued, although in smaller quantities than previously, to meet the requirements of discerning and wealthy customers, principally based in York. A number of complete vessels found their way into burials, although sites in urban areas and the fortress only produce fragments; for example, the York Minster excavations produced two fragments of fourth-century vessels, probably from the Rhineland, on which images had been made by cutting with a wheel or by abrasion of the surface. Two other fragments came from mould-blown cylindrical bottles manufactured in Gaul.[121]

One inference which is usually drawn from the sort of data just referred to is that supply of the army from other parts of the empire was not such an important factor in the economy of Roman Britain as it had been. This may have been due not only to a lower level of demand from a smaller garrison than hitherto, but also to the reorganisation of the supply of food and other commodities such that they now came almost exclusively from the local areas around the bases in which the soldiers themselves were recruited. Individual army officers and other wealthy individuals may have continued to commission merchants to bring luxury goods to them in York and elsewhere, but this was apparently rare.

As far as use of money in the region's trade is concerned, this was, as in other periods, related to fluctuations in the supply of coinage. Under Caracalla a new coin, the *antoninianus*, had been introduced, notionally equal to two silver denarii, but only 1½ times the weight of the denarius and containing virtually no silver. A continuing shortage of silver in state coffers eventually meant the end for the denarius and reduced the supply of coinage to the provinces including Britain. One consequence was that taxes could no longer be paid wholly in money and had to be paid, at least in part, in kind, primarily as agricultural products.[122] However, at a time of a shortage of good quality silver coins, supply was supplemented by local manufacture which probably received official sanction and so was not exactly forging in its traditional sense. These forgeries were made in a mould, rather than struck as was usual for coins. At York, broken moulds have been found both near the fortress and more surprisingly in an otherwise unremarkable rural settlement at Fulford *c*.3km to the south (Illus. 6.1, 9). They were used for making coins of Septimius

Severus and Caracalla, although they probably date to the mid-third century when coins of these earlier emperors retained some prestige in terms of metal content compared to what was then available.[123]

In an attempt to restore the stability of the currency, large quantities of coinage, albeit with a very low silver content (or none), were minted from c.260 onwards both by the emperors in Rome and by the Gallic emperors who ruled the breakaway western empire (including Britain). The emperor is shown on these coins wearing a radiate crown, imitating the sun's rays – hence the coins are known as 'radiates'. After the collapse of the Gallic empire in 273 the Emperor Aurelian reformed the coinage, but a shortage of coin in Britain was remedied by local copies of earlier coins known as 'barbarous radiates'. Coin moulds for making barbarous radiates have been found in our region at Lofthouse near Wakefield.[124] Although not expressly intended by the state, one effect of the circulation of large numbers of low value coins was probably to increase the use of money in trade, even in the rural areas of regions like Yorkshire. In addition, mid-third-century coin hoards from Britain, including a number from Yorkshire, are often very substantial. For example, a hoard from Nunburnholme (East Riding), in which the latest coins were of Aurelian, contained c.6000 coins.

The usurper Carausius (287–93) set himself apart from the legitimate emperors by minting good quality silver coins, probably because he needed to pay his army properly to keep them loyal. He had two mints, one in London and the other at an unknown location. After the reconquest of Britain the provinces were subject once again to the imperial monetary and fiscal regime. In 301 the Emperor Diocletian issued an edict in an attempt to control certain commodity prices in the empire which suggests that inflation remained a problem for the imperial government. However, the contemporary view that it was greedy speculators who drove prices up, rather than shortages of supply or other structural factors, meant that the edict's success was limited and stabilising the currency remained a problem. In 309 a reform of the currency involved the establishment of a new gold coin, the *solidus*, as a viable, empire-wide, standard unit of value.[125] Gold was now increasingly used for paying soldiers and imperial servants, and for tax exactions, although payment of taxes in kind directly to the state continued. However, payment in gold made more sense in an era when the army was no longer permanently based in large numbers in fortresses like York, but moved around to where it was needed. It has been suggested that now that the frontier garrisons were smaller, the net flow of gold in the empire had changed direction, no longer passing from the centre to the frontier provinces, via army pay, but flowing towards Rome and the main imperial capitals as tax revenues. One consequence of this was, perhaps, that neither York nor London became the sort of opulent late Roman capitals that existed in Gaul at Trier or Arles.

Diocletian also reformed the silver and copper alloy coinage, although barbarous radiates continued to circulate as small change. There were further reforms under Constantine and his sons, but they were followed by periods of steady reduction in coin sizes and silver content. Supply to Britain fluctuated somewhat and in the years *c*.335–45 a shortage of official coins led to extensive local copying. As in the late third century, circulation of large numbers of low value coins probably allowed a good deal of trade in our region – as well as tax payment – to be conducted using coinage. The high number in circulation was also a factor in hoards; for example, four of Yorkshire's ten largest coin hoards are dated to the years 335–55, including the two largest which were found in the East Riding at Cowlam (1858), with at least 10,000 coins, and Langwith near York (1891), with over 6000.[126] Apparently the ploughmen who found the Cowlam hoard '… meant for the future to live like gentlemen', but, sadly for them, the coins were confiscated by the landowner and sold to a London dealer.[127]

Illus. 9.18   Rudston villa: panel from the mosaic in the main house showing the charioteer (© Bridgeman Art Library / Hull Museum).

The visual arts: the age of the mosaic

The early fourth century is the golden age of the mosaic in Yorkshire whether in the town houses of York or Aldborough or in the country villas. The majority have geometric patterns only; scenes featuring human figures and/ or animals are relatively rare. In this most northerly cluster of mosaics in the Roman empire, the overall style of execution is similar to what is found in other parts of Roman Britain, but there are elements of a distinctive, even idiosyncratic, local flavour.

Table 10   Fourth-century Roman figured mosaics from Yorkshire

Site	Motifs	Present location
Aldborough[128]	Muses at Mount Helicon	Aldborough
Aldborough[129]	Wolf and twins	Leeds Museum
Brantingham villa[130]	Tyche and nymphs or muses	Hull Museum
Dalton Parlours – main house[131]	Medusa	Yorkshire Museum
Malton 'town house'[132]	Bust of winter, dog and deer	In English Heritage store
Oulston villa[133]	Bust of Bacchus?	Yorkshire Museum
Rudston villa[134]	Venus, merman, animals	Hull Museum
Rudston villa[135]	Sea creatures	Hull Museum
Rudston villa[136]	Charioteer and seasons	Hull Museum
York–Aldwark[137]	Female bust	Yorkshire Museum
York – Toft Green[138]	Bull	Yorkshire Museum
York – Toft Green[139]	Four seasons	Yorkshire Museum
York – Bar Lane[140]	Dancers or seasons	Lost

The most common figures represented, of which there are three, or possibly four, examples, are the female spirits of the four seasons, not surprising perhaps in a world depending so much on agriculture. As is usual in Roman Britain, the spirit of spring is symbolised by a swallow, summer by a bunch of grapes or poppies, autumn by a rake, and winter by a bare bough. The seasons appear in the corners of perhaps the most sophisticated of all Yorkshire's mosaics from the main house at Rudston villa which, made with tesserae in as many as ten different colours, features a charioteer in his *quadriga* – a vehicle drawn by four horses (Illus. 9.13; 9.18). At the opposite end of the mosaic is a panel depicting leopards and urns known as *canthari* (singular *cantharus*). The border resembles the battlements of a town or fort wall. As is usually the case, a superior mosaic of this sort probably carried several different layers of meaning to its intended audience. On one level a charioteer, successful and victorious, may be seen as an icon of good luck whilst the leopards and canthari may refer to the god Bacchus, associated with wining and dining and other pleasures of life. Roger Ling has suggested that, in addition, the mosaic may be interpreted in terms of a series of cosmic allusions beginning with the depiction of the seasons which invite us to think of the circus as a microcosm of the universe.[141] The usual twelve chariots in a race allude to the months, the twenty-four heats of a contest to the hours and the seven circuits to the days of the week and to the planets known to the Romans.

Equally sophisticated, perhaps, was the mosaic of the muses from Aldborough of which only a fragment survives. Originally it was laid in the large room with an apsidal end described above. The main part of the room may have had a mosaic – now lost – but the mosaic in the apse depicted the nine muses, the presiding goddesses of the arts, who lived on Mount Helicon, named in Greek on the surviving fragment. This also bears one of the goddesses who, when a bit more of the mosaic existed, could be seen to have a mask suspended at her right side which identified her as either Melpomene, muse of tragedy, or Thalia, muse of comedy. This is the only mosaic from Britain with an inscription in Greek and must say something about the unusual intellectual abilities and interests of its patron. The use of glass tesserae in the mosaic is also very rare, indicating work of high quality.

The largest Roman mosaic from Yorkshire comes from Brantingham villa. In the central octagon is the bust of a woman wearing a white dalmatic with red vertical stripes. This is a type of tunic introduced in the late Roman period with tight fitting sleeves down to the wrist which were often woven separately allowing the tunic itself to be narrower than the rather baggy ones of earlier times.[142] The woman also appears to wear a crown in the form of a battlemented town wall which has led to her being called a tyche, usually the presiding deity of a city, but here of the Parisian *civitas* perhaps. Around the sides of the octagon are eight reclining females usually thought to be water nymphs, although an alternative is that they and the central figure are, once again, the nine muses, in which case rather than a mural crown the woman in the centre wears the feathers worn by the muses after winning a singing contest with the sirens. At each end of the mosaic are panels in each of which there are four more female busts, again wearing dalmatics, but with blue stripes.

Less competently executed than the three mosaics just described, are the Venus mosaic from Rudston and the Wolf and Twins mosaic from Aldborough, although their eccentricity and vitality are arresting. The former has a circular central panel in which the female figure may be identified, as is traditional, by being naked and holding a mirror (Illus. 9.20). A certain disproportion and her prominent genitalia are made up for by a pleasing earthy vigour. Next to her is a curious figure, usually described as a merman, whose sudden appearance has, perhaps, caused Venus to drop her mirror in surprise. On each side of the mosaic, in a semicircular panel, there is an animal: a lion, a bull, a deer and a leopard. Across one end there is a panel with a bust of Mercury in the centre. The animals take us back to the amphitheatre and may confirm the interests of a patron who also commissioned the charioteer, although in this case he was unable to secure an equally competent craftsman. The impact of the mosaic is made all the greater by its sheer colourfulness, no less than twelve different shades of tesserae being employed. Roger Wilson has suggested that

Illus. 9.19 Brantingham villa: central panel from the 'tyche' mosaic (© Bridgeman Art Library / Hull Museum).

Illus. 9.20 Venus mosaic from Rudston (© Hull and East Riding Museums).

Illus. 9.21 The 'Malton Venus' painted on wall plaster from the Town House. (Photo: Gwen Jones ©)

both the Venus and the aquatic mosaic from Rudston baths show the use of a pattern book with an African design influence.[143] In respect of the former he cites, for example, the way vine scrolls spring from *canthari* in the end panel, and the labelling of two of the amphitheatre animals (*bestiarii*) with their stage names which is unique in Roman Britain – the lion probably FLAMMEFER, meaning 'fiery', and the bull OMACIDA, 'man killing'. That the patron was aware of an African connection seems unlikely, but none the less these mosaics remind us of the continuing pan-imperial character of some aspects of material culture which extended as far as remote regions like the Yorkshire Wolds. The same can be said about the least competently executed figured mosaic from Yorkshire which comes from Aldborough. It shows a she wolf, looking rather like a demented cat, and, as tiny figures, the twins – Romulus and Remus – whom, Roman legend relates, she suckled after they were abandoned by their mother, a vestal virgin seduced by Mars. Clumsy though it may be, however, the pavement shows that even in one of its most distant urban outposts, a fundamental founding myth of Rome was known and proudly displayed by someone who presumably thought of himself as a Roman after over 200 years of his region's incorporation in the empire.

Scholars have sought to identify local mosaicists' workshops in Britain based on the distribution of pavements exhibiting common features; one suggestion has been that there was a Brough on Humber school which executed pavements in villas both north and south of the Humber, although there are no mosaics known from Brough itself. Aldborough and York would seem to be equally likely as workshop locations. However, whether the products of one or more workshops, Neal and Cosh have, on stylistic grounds, identified a 'northern group' of fourth-century mosaics, found in Yorkshire and Lincolnshire, characterised by certain commonly occurring motifs.[144] Taken together, the Yorkshire mosaics tell us that, by the early fourth century, members of the wealthy elite regarded them as an appropriate part of the repertoire of status expression in the context of their cultural and social aspirations. The figured scenes suggest some acquaintance with the enduring mythologies of the Roman and Hellenistic worlds, and an endorsement – at Rudston and Malton respectively – of the part played by the circus and hunting in the local elite's sense of its identity.

In addition to mosaic, painted wall plaster continued to embellish the grander sort of dwellings, sometimes with figured scenes clearly drawn from classical mythology supplementing purely geometric designs. For example, in the Town House at Malton painted plaster from the reception room with the mosaic depicted a female with a nimbus, probably Venus, and a male with a staff of office, possibly Jupiter, both, perhaps, in attendance at an assembly of Olympians.[145] In Brantingham villa plaster fragments from the largest room suggest a ceiling painted to create a trompe l'oeil effect of coffering with a design featuring female faces echoing that of the mosaic on the floor.[146]

At Rudston the baths produced evidence for painted plaster in all the principal rooms.[147] The most complete scheme that can now be reconstructed came from the *caldarium*: a dado with a white ground on which there was a pattern of green leaves around a central red roundel and other foliate motifs. Above this was a band with a design in purple and green with white highlights forming a lower border for panels in dark red. From the reception room in the main house the evidence comes in particular from the north wall where there was a dado painted to imitate marble veneer. Above this was a design including a scheme with white panels framed by green bands outlined in black representing a niche in the wall seen in false perspective. Above this was a cornice of two horizontal red bands with purple motifs separated by another green band. At the top of the wall was a frieze of green vegetation with occasional purple and yellow flowers in front of a fence or trellis. Along with more fragmentary evidence for other walls, these paintings reveal a considerable sophistication of design and taste to set alongside the charioteer mosaic.

Religion: a return to obscurity

What we lack in Yorkshire's mosaics is much evidence for the sort of philosophical and religious debate and inquiry which can be read into some of the mosaics of southern Britain and the Continent. Indeed, for the period under discussion evidence for the religious beliefs of the region's population and how they were expressed in cult practice is very sparse. One must assume that the range of pagan beliefs and practices for which there is better evidence in earlier periods continued to flourish. None the less, artefacts occasionally provide a window into what was thought and done locally in the late Roman period, an example, perhaps, being the so-called 'smith's pots' found principally in Malton and, appropriately, in Norton-on-Derwent and Elmswell as ironworking is known at both places. The cult of a British version of Vulcan is probably implied by the application to pottery vessels of small model hammers and tongs.[148]

Temples such as those at Elmswell and Millington may well have continued in use, but we have little in the way of altars or other artefacts bearing inscriptions. However, a possible temple or shrine which is thought to be late Roman in date has come to light at Bawtry, near the south-eastern edge of Yorkshire, during removal of material on the banks of the River Idle, east of the town.[149] In about ¼ha of land a large collection of late third- and early fourth-century Roman pottery was found, but more significant were three dressed stone column bases, two probably still *in situ*. A scatter of seventy-one coins was largely of the same date as the pottery, although a few pieces were later fourth century. The columns must be from a special structure of some sort whilst the disposition and make-up of the coins has suggested that they were the sort of offerings one might expect to find at a sacred site, rather than simply a dispersed hoard.

Illus. 9.22 Malton: drawing of a fragment of a smith pot (from Wenham and Heywood 1997, © Yorkshire Archaeological Society).

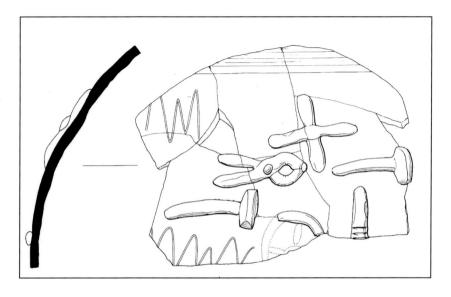

Emerging alongside the traditional native and Roman cults in the early fourth century, one might, perhaps, expect to see some sign of a Christian community, at least in York, in the wake of the installation of a man named Eborius as bishop. In 314 he was summoned by the Emperor Constantine, along with three other bishops from Britain, to discuss doctrinal matters at the Council of Arles. However, for the fourth century as a whole Yorkshire is remarkably devoid of evidence for Christianity when compared to some other regions of Britain. Only two possible examples of the chi-rho symbol have been found, one scratched on a tile from the *principia* basilica at York[150] and the other (now lost) on a sandstone block in the bath house at Catterick.[151] However, more remarkable is a cornelian intaglio from York, for which there is nothing comparable in Roman Britain. On it are carved two fish hanging from the crossbar of an anchor.[152] Both are Christian symbols, the anchor recalling the hope of salvation and the fish Christ's mission to create 'fishers of men' whilst the letters of the Greek word for fish – *icthys* – was a mnemonic (in Greek) for 'Jesus Christ, Son of God Saviour'.

Treatment of the dead: more from York and 'Catterick camp'

Whilst the evidence from our region for religion in the period covered by this chapter is poor, that for burials is as good as it is for any other part of the Roman era. Having said this, it remains the case that, as in earlier times, burials in any numbers have only been found at the principal settlements such as York, Catterick, and Malton and Norton. In other settlements burials remain rare. Inhumation remained the dominant means of treatment of the dead, but cremation was also practiced in York and elsewhere in the region. Bodies in inhumation graves were usually laid out extended and supine, but examples of the crouched or flexed position are also found, suggesting burial customs of native origin persisted in the local community which may have extended to other aspects of behaviour at funerals for which there is no surviving evidence.

At York the earlier Roman cemeteries may have been sited at some remove from settled areas, but from the late third century onwards it looks as though there was an attempt to fill in any empty space close to either the fortress or civilian settlements. For example, a new cemetery zone was found at Castle Yard (north-east of the Ouse), only 200m from a Roman building on Castlegate.[153] A small group of six, apparently high status, inhumations was found including three in stone sarcophagi, two of which were inscribed, one in a lead coffin and two more in wooden coffins. One of the coffins, that dedicated to the centurion of the Sixth Legion, Aurelius Super, had been reused for another, later, burial; reuse of sarcophagi has been recorded elsewhere in York and the region in the late Roman period.

South-west of the Ouse the site on Blossom Street, *c.*150m from the Roman town, was used more intensively for burial than hitherto in the

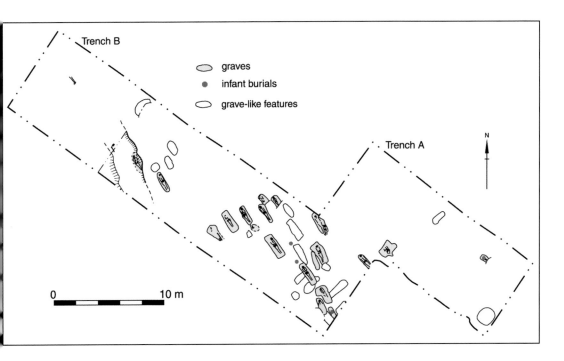

Trench B

graves
infant burials
grave-like features

Trench A

N

0   10 m

early to mid-fourth century.[154] After the demolition of the early third-century mausoleum described in Chapter 7, a cemetery of about twenty-five inhumations was laid out. The graves were aligned north-west/south-east at 90° to the nearby main road from the south-west, and spaced in a fairly regular manner reminiscent of the large so-called 'managed cemeteries' of late Roman Britain. They have common alignments for the burials, usually coffined, in rows or lines with little intercutting.[155] Elsewhere in the Mount cemetery zone, on Driffield Terrace, burial of execution victims continued.[156] A little to the south-west of the site referred to in Chapter 7 another group of decapitated males was found. There were twenty-one, although accommodated in only fifteen graves as there were three multiple interments. One very remarkable burial contained as many as four individuals all buried in a large wooden chest held together with nails. Also in the chest were parts of the skeletons from at least four horses, although why they had been deposited with the men is hard to understand.[157] A few of the bones had come from butchered skeletons and it is possible that what we have here are the remains of a funeral feast in which, unusually for Roman Britain, horse was eaten. This may have taken place in the context of ritual observance as the horse had a status as a totemic animal in both the native and Roman world. The horse was also associated with Epona whose cult is thought to have been brought to Britain from Gaul by Roman cavalry for whom she was a protective deity.[158]

Amongst the Roman burials of York there are a few which can be assigned to the late third or mid-fourth century on the basis of their grave goods. For example, a burial in a stone coffin with a lead lining from the Railway Station cemetery contained a female buried with two jet hair pins, their heads in the shape of *canthari*.[159] Another burial was found at Field Lane, Heslington (3km east of the city, Illus. 6.1, 6) of a woman who may have been a member of the family which owned what was, as we know from excavations, good farm land nearby – hence the gypsum in the stone coffin and the gold earrings, a silver ring, two necklaces, one of glass beads and one of coral beads, and other jewellery.[160] Other burials, including many with stone coffins, may be of the same period as these two, but they lack associated dating evidence. As is usual in Roman Britain generally, grave goods are exceptional in the late Roman period. At Blossom Street, for example, no more than four graves contained artefacts; two had pottery vessels, in one of which there was a chicken skeleton, and one contained shoes betrayed by the surviving hobnails. In addition, an infant burial was accompanied by two glass beads and two shale bracelets.

At Catterick no large, organised late Roman cemeteries have been found, but some twenty-five mid-third to mid-fourth-century burials came from various locations adjacent to settled areas (Illus. 5.6). Three burials from the roadside settlement at Bainesse, east of Dere Street, were, perhaps, made after the nearby buildings had been abandoned in view of the Roman practice of keeping the dead away from the living.[161] Another six burials were found close to Dere Street at Catterick Race Course; two of the deceased individuals, one male and one female, were buried in the crouched position. As at York, only a few of the Catterick burials were accompanied by grave goods, principally pottery vessels, although there was also a burial with a glass vessel and a coin of Septimius Severus, the latter perhaps as much as 100 years old when interred. However, the burial which has aroused the greatest interest of all from Catterick (Bainesse) was that of a 20–25-year-old adult male buried wearing a range of jewellery items including a very elaborate jet necklace, a jet bracelet and a shale armlet on the left arm, and a bronze anklet on the right leg. This is a very unusual collection and has, not surprisingly, given rise to some speculation as to the identity of the deceased, especially as his attire is thought by some to be more appropriate to a female. There is no obvious ethnic or religious group who habitually bury males in this way. However, although there is a fair degree of standardisation in late Roman burials, egregious examples of one sort or another do come to light from time to time and cannot be easily explained. Ideas circulated at the time of publication that the man from Catterick was a transvestite or a *gallus*, one of the emasculated priests of the cult of Cybele, may seem a bit far fetched, but they served the purpose of attracting some extensive press coverage. The apparent cross-dressing aspect led the *Daily Telegraph* to use the witty headline 'Catterick Camp' and the *Daily Mail* to announce 'Meet Crossus Dresseus – our first transvestite'.[162]

Burials from Malton (Illus. 5.18) recovered in the nineteenth century are usually difficult to date closely, but in the cemetery outside the north-eastern defences of the fort the 1920s excavations revealed a female gypsum burial in a wooden coffin which is thought to be early fourth century.[163] Across the Derwent on Langton Road, Norton-on-Derwent a small cemetery, thought to be mid- to late third century contained twenty-six inhumations, a few in the crouched position, and four or five cremation burials.[164] As at York in the same period, the alignment of graves was not standardised, although they were mostly north–south with a minority laid out east–west. Grave goods were, as one would expect, scarce being confined to jewellery – four skeletons were accompanied by bracelets and two by a ring, and a child had nine jet beads, possibly from a necklace. Immediately to the north investigation of another area during building work revealed some thirty more inhumation burials, three of which were accompanied by crossbow brooches.[165] These burials are unusual in the region, but whether the brooches indicate the deceased had some distinct status is uncertain, although it has been suggested they were worn primarily by government officials or soldiers. Other late Roman inhumations have been found in Norton-on-Derwent scattered along the main approach roads. At Malton, as elsewhere in the region, infant burials were still made within settled areas. As well as those already noted in the fort, in the *vicus* eleven were found in the Kiln Building and another eight in the Town House.[166]

As far as lesser settlements in the region are concerned, the only formal cemetery known appears to be that at Hayton, found a little to the north-east of the main Roman road from York to Brough. There were two groups of graves laid out in an orderly fashion, at right angles to the road; in one there were eight side by side whilst twenty-five or so others lay further to the south-west beyond an empty zone. Burial probably continued until the end of the fourth century and at least one of the graves was Anglo-Saxon.

In the region's rural areas late third- and early fourth-century burials are, as in earlier periods, quite rare. They usually occur in ones and twos on the margins of what were probably fields, as in the case, for example, of two crouched inhumations and a cremation found at Parlington Hollins (near Leeds).[167] Burials associated with the villas are also scarce, although four dated to the early fourth century were found in the courtyard at Ingleby Barwick.[168]

Decline and Fall | 10

Introduction

Today you hardly notice the steep-sided little valley of the Cram Beck, with its stone bridge at the bottom, as you drive along the A64 from York to Malton, although heading east just beyond the bridge you might have to downshift quickly if you get stuck behind a horse box on Golden Hill. Coming west you put your foot down as the dual carriageway approaches just after the Welburn turn. However, if you had been here in the fourth century all around you there would have been the smoke from clusters of pottery kilns. Everywhere you looked there would have been people making pots, carrying pots, and loading pots onto wagons pulled by oxen. Crambeck was the site of one of the great pottery centres of late Roman Britain, making use of the local clay deposits on the southern edge of the Howardian Hills, the local woodlands and water from springs and the beck itself.[1]

In the middle of the fourth century someone at Crambeck had the bright idea of introducing types of vessels made in a whitish-buff fabric which were given attractive red-painted designs. These appear largely abstract, although a few vessel fragments from Malton had faces painted on them and on a sherd from York a 'stick man' warrior is depicted.[2] Production of this so-called 'Parchment ware', one of the most attractive ceramics of late Roman Britain, continued for perhaps forty years. Although Parchment ware only made up about 3–4% of Crambeck production, it soon became popular, and together with the other products of the kilns, had a wide distribution in northern England. For archaeologists it is very important for dating, both because it is so distinctive and because production has a fairly clear start date; any deposit containing Parchment Ware must be dated after about 360.

The Crambeck potteries in the late fourth century were a success as an industrial enterprise due to their role in supplying the army and they therefore stand out from the traditional narrative of the period which is usually dominated by the signs of economic failure. This is manifested most obviously in the Yorkshire region by a lack of new building, either public or private, and of substantial refurbishments to old buildings, except in a few military

contexts, as well as a continuing decline in trade, other than the purely local, to more or less nothing as far as we can tell.

An important source for Britain in the late fourth century is the history of Rome written by Ammianus Marcellinus covering the years 354–78, although his attention was focused principally on the eastern empire. Another more or less contemporary writer was the poet Claudian who in praising the Emperor Honorius and his general Stilicho mentions Britain in passing. A few authors of the fifth and sixth centuries, such as the historian Zosimus, who worked in Byzantium, also refer to events in Britain in the late fourth century. In addition to historical literature, a documentary source of considerable value for late Roman military and political matters is the *Notitia Dignitatum* ('the *Notitia*'), a list of officials probably produced in the early fifth century, but incorporating earlier material. The list for Britain begins with the *Vir Spectabilis*, Vicar of Britain, and goes through senior provincial officials and military commanders, including the *Dux Britanniarum*, down to the commanders of individual units such as the Prefect of the Sixth Legion at York.

Although it is difficult to quantify in any meaningful way, one, none the less, has the clear impression that there is a good deal less archaeological evidence for our region in the sixty years after the year 350 than there is for the previous sixty. In places reoccupied in post-Roman times the latest

Roman archaeological deposits are vulnerable to disturbance and truncation, but this on its own cannot explain the deficit in the region as a whole. We cannot explain it either by a lack of material usable for dating the latest Roman deposits, at least in the eastern and central parts of the region. Not only was coinage supplied on a fairly regular basis until *c.*402, but we are fortunate in having two types of distinctive late Roman pottery: Crambeck ware and calcite gritted ware in a variant usually known as Huntcliff ware because it was first identified at Huntcliff near Saltburn, one of the late Roman signal station sites on the east coast. Both types occur widely across the much of the county, although they are relatively scarce in the west.

The unavoidable conclusion that we should probably draw from the archaeology is that the level of activity, including landscape management, building, manufacturing and even rubbish disposal, which generates archaeo-logical remains, was lower in the second half than had been the case in the first half of the fourth century. At York and the other principal settlements in the region one can say that the settled areas diminished in extent and in rural areas settlements often seem to disappear totally. Whether there was a decline in the region's population remains an open question, but it would be one way of interpreting the data.

A summary of the military and political events in Roman Britain which form a backdrop to the history of the Yorkshire region itself in the second half of the fourth century may begin in the last years of the reign of the Emperor Constantius II (337–61), the second of Constantine's sons. In 353 he finally destroyed Magnentius, a usurper in the west who may have enjoyed considerable support in Britain. As a direct result Paul, an official known as a Secretary, was sent to Britain to seek out conspirators. Ammianus Marcellinus tells us that:

> Like a flood he suddenly overwhelmed the fortunes of many, sweeping forward amidst the widespread slaughter and ruin, casting freeborn men into prison and degrading some with fetters, all this by fabricating charges that were far removed from the truth.[3]

He exceeded his terms of reference such that he acquired the sobriquet 'The Chain' after threatening to take the Vicar himself in chains to the emperor's court to answer for his supposed crimes.

Although Britain had been largely immune from major barbarian incursions that had hitherto occurred elsewhere in the fourth century, there was, according to Ammianus Marcellinus, an attack on Britain in 360 at the end of Constantius's reign when:

> invasions by the fierce tribes of the Scots [then in Ireland] and the Picts who had broken the peace they had agreed upon, were causing destruction in those areas near the frontiers, and the provinces, worn out by the numerous disasters in the past, were caught in the grip of fear.[4]

The then Caesar in the West, Julian sent one Lupicinus to 'settle matters either by force or negotiation'. The urgency of the situation demanded that he cross from Boulogne to Richborough in the middle of winter.

Constantius II died in 361 and was succeeded as Augustus by Julian, principally notable as the last pagan emperor. On his death in Persia in 363 he was, in turn, succeeded by Valentinian I (364–75), originally a soldier from Pannonia who was faced with two barbarian attacks on Britain. In 364 '… trumpets sounded for war all through the Roman world … and the Picts, Saxons, Scots and Attacotti harassed the Britons with continual calamities'.[5] An even more serious attack took place in 367 when 'a conspiracy of the barbarians' led to the slaying of Nectaridus, 'Count of the Coastal District' (unfortunately it is not known which one) and the Duke Fullofaudes was surrounded and captured.[6] In an attempt to restore order Valentinian sent a senior general, Count Theodosius, 'a man with a very good reputation in military affairs', to Britain.

The 'barbarian conspiracy' is an event which has exercised a powerful hold over the imagination of archaeologists. Considerable effort has been made to identify, on the one hand, destruction at Roman sites which could be ascribed to the barbarians and, on the other hand, restoration work which could be ascribed to Theodosius, even when the actual dating evidence is equivocal to say the least. In excavation reports one sometimes reads of the 'Theodosian period' and finds what now appear to be rather rash assumptions about what happened in 367. In the 1966 report on Drax villa, for example, it is concluded: 'Probably the damage done to Malton in the raids of 367–69 prompted the inhabitants to leave'.[7] In 1978 Ramm asserted 'The vicus at Malton … was laid waste in 367 …'.[8] It is now recognised, however, that it is simply not possible to either identify 'damage' and 'waste' caused by 'raids' or refine the dating of late Roman structures to a point where a date for (re)construction in the late 360s can be given with any confidence.

Serious though the events of the 360s would have been for Roman Britain, there may well have been other unrecorded incursions in the second half of the fourth century. The most threatening hostile forces as far as Yorkshire was concerned were probably the Picts – 'the painted people' – who lived north of Hadrian's Wall. The inference to be drawn from contemporary Roman sources is that they were typical barbarians in the sense that their principal interest in the Roman Empire was the booty which could be extracted from it, either by hit and run attacks or by treaties which paid them to go away. The great hoard of late Roman silver from Traprain Law on the East Lothian coastal plain in south-east Scotland was probably accumulated by one or both means.[9]

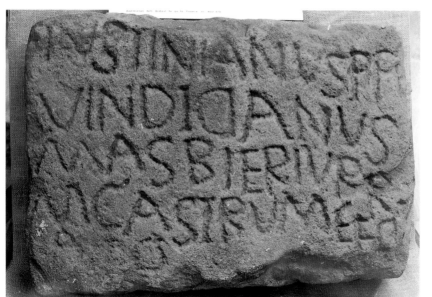

Illus. 10.2 Ravenscar: the latest Roman inscription from Britain; a commemoration of the construction of a camp and tower (© Whitby Museum).

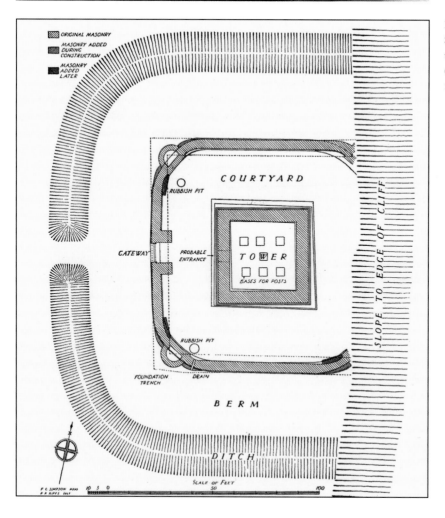

Illus. 10.3 Scarborough: plan of the Roman signal station (from Collingwood 1931).

The late Roman garrison

The Yorkshire signal stations

Although one cannot now point to any work specifically associated with Theodosius, there is a group of small fortifications in Yorkshire which can be considered a Roman military response to the sort of attacks on Britain described by Ammianus Marcellinus, if not to those actual events themselves. These are the so-called 'signal stations' located on the coast of Yorkshire at, from north to south, Huntcliff,[10] Goldsborough,[11] Ravenscar,[12] Scarborough[13] and Filey.[14] There may have been others, for example at Whitby and Flamborough Head, which have yet to be found, although they may have already gone into the sea, as what is left of the Huntcliff and Filey sites will before long.

The story of the discovery of the signal stations begins at Ravenscar in 1776 when a stone tablet came to light bearing an inscription, thought

Illus. 10.4
Scarborough: the Roman signal station site looking south-east with the ditch, line of courtyard wall (*upper left*) and site of the tower (*extreme left*). (Photo: P. Ottaway)

Illus. 10.5   Filey Roman signal station: a) the stone blocks laid out in Crescent Gardens; b) detail of the hare and hounds relief. (Photos: P. Ottaway)

DECLINE AND FALL   295

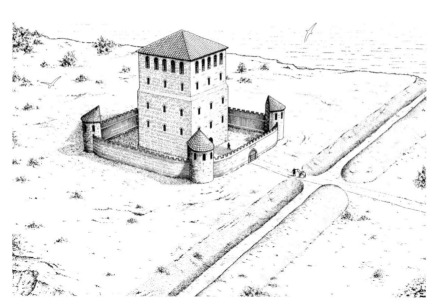

Illus. 10.6   Filey:
reconstruction drawing
of the Roman signal
station (from Ottaway
2000).

to be the latest from Roman Britain.[15] This refers to a 'camp and tower',
apparently constructed at the behest of a commander named Justinianus and
'master' named Vindicianus. No Roman structural remains have been found at
Ravenscar itself, but it is assumed that the tablet comes from a signal station
similar to the other four as the structures described on it appear to correspond
to what has been found elsewhere by excavation.

At all the signal station sites the structures have been substantially
demolished so that their original form can only be conjectured. However,
we do know that at each one what was presumably the tower referred to in
the Ravenscar inscription stood in a small courtyard surrounded by a wall;
at each of the rounded corners there was a small turret of semicircular plan.
Within the courtyards at Goldsborough and Huntcliff a well was found.
Usually a signal station was surrounded by a ditch and measured *c.*50m
between the outer edges of the ditch. At Filey, however, there was only a
ditch on the landward side of the Carr Naze peninsular on which the station
stands (Illus. 2.3). At the base of all the towers there were very substantial
socketed stone blocks into which upright timbers would have been set. They
presumably fulfilled a role in supporting the upper part of the structure. One
of the blocks from Filey has a hare and hounds in relief on one face. The
tower walls could have been either vertical (as in Illus 10.6) or stepped in at
intervals towards the top as in the case of the Roman lighthouse at Dover
and as shown in an artist's impression on display at Scarborough Castle.
Alternatively, the tower may have tapered towards the top as is shown in an
illustration of Scarborough by Alan Sorrell derived from the representation
of an early second-century signalling tower on Trajan's Column in Rome. As
far as the top itself is concerned, there appear to be two principal options.

One is a pitched roof above a room with windows of sufficient size to be used for observation. A balcony around the top of a tower with this type of roof is shown in the Sorrell illustration. The other option is that there was a flat roof, perhaps with crenellations like a medieval keep.

The height of the signal station structures may be estimated if it is assumed that the Romans wished to prevent the ditch being a safe zone in which attackers could take refuge. At Filey, to ensure that projectiles discharged from the courtyard wall reached all parts of the ditch, the height above ground level of the walkway at the top of the wall would probably have been about 3m. The full height of the wall with its parapet might have been 4.50m. Based on the same principles, the height at which a man stood in the tower would have been some 12m above ground to ensure that any projectiles he fired cleared the parapet of the courtyard wall. If the tower was roofed, as shown in the reconstruction in Illus. 10.6, then it is possible that the tower had an overall height of about 18m, a figure which is similar to that estimated for the height of the Dover lighthouse.

Although a date of construction after 367 is very likely, the exact date of the signal stations must remain somewhat conjectural as it relies largely on coins found in deposits accumulating in the courtyards and therefore deposited some time after construction. An alternative to an immediate post-367 date is the time of Magnus Maximus, a general in Britain in the early 380s who is credited with defeating the Picts. It is possible that part of his strategy was the creation of the Yorkshire signal stations, perhaps before he was emboldened to take an army from Britain to Gaul in 383 to claim the imperial crown.[16]

The function of the signal stations has also been the subject of some debate, although their location above beaches suitable for landing small craft suggests they were intended to combat a danger coming from the sea, probably from hostile raiders working their way along the coast rather than from across the North Sea.[17] It has been thought that the signal stations' particular role – hence their modern name – was to give an early warning of attack by serving as watch towers from which signals were sent either inland or up and down the coast. One possibility is that this was done by some form of beacon. There may have been intermediate beacons between the coast and Malton or York from where troops were despatched if danger threatened, although beacons would have been useless in the sea frets which are quite common on the Yorkshire coast. A unit known as the *Numerus Supervenientium Petuarensium* (usually translated as the 'unit of anticipators from Brough'), an appropriate name for a unit involved in coastal patrols, was based at *Derventio* (probably Malton) according to the *Notitia Dignitatum*. More useful than beacons, however, would have been a man on a horse who could convey detailed information about an enemy's whereabouts and capabilities. In any event, it is reasonable to assume that assistance would have been required to repel raiders as the signal stations themselves only had accommodation for a small garrison. However, another

Illus. 10.7 Bowes Moor: signal station reconstruction (© Tees Archaeology).

role which the signal stations were well suited to perform was as places of refuge where local people could go in troubled times.

Whilst the coastal signal stations may have been principally concerned with a sea-borne enemy, there was also a chain of smaller signal stations of late Roman date on the Stainmore road across the Pennines. This was one of the principal arteries of communication in the north, and the signal stations were, perhaps, a response to the danger posed by land-based attacks on imperial assets.[18] Between the forts at Bowes and Brough on Stainmore (Cumbria) there are up to ten sites which may belong to the chain. In Yorkshire they include (from east to west) Bowes Moor, Vale House, Roper Castle, a recommissioned Rey Cross, and, formerly in Yorkshire, Maiden Castle (now Cumbria). Excavations have taken place at Bowes Moor where earthworks survive both of the signal station defences, which enclose an area 10m × 6.5m, and of a larger defended annexe of rectangular plan. Excavation of the signal station revealed a structure in the centre, presumably a tower, which had employed large pad stones rather similar to those in the towers of the coastal signal stations.

York and the forts

Although it is no longer possible to associate it with Count Theodosius, there is evidence for construction and refurbishment work at some of the other military sites of the Yorkshire region in the middle of the fourth century. In York some strengthening of the fortress defences is probably represented by the 'Anglian tower', just north of the west corner, which, inspite of the name given to it by its excavator in 1972, is most likely to be late Roman and was probably a replacement for an earlier interval tower nearby which had collapsed.[19] Two of the principal fortress streets were resurfaced after *c*.350, at least in places. On the south-east side, near the east corner, a new cobbled surface of the *intervallum* street was laid down after an accumulation of silt on the late second-century street. In Low Petergate the *via principalis* was observed in a series of sewer repair trenches; it appeared to have been relaid in a rather rough and ready manner incorporating a certain amount of re-used stonework, also after the silting over of the previous surface. Some of the barracks, including those of the first cohort, were altered in the mid-fourth century indicating continued use, although the character and size of the Sixth Legion at this time is unknown. A hint that it may have been smaller than hitherto comes from Blake Street where the principal building range had been demolished and the space cleared by the mid-fourth century.[20]

Of particular interest is the evidence from the great aisled hall of the headquarters where bases were found for new statues in front of the nave columns.[21] In front of one column a railed enclosure, presumably around some special statue or altar, was put in place. Socketed bases sunk into the floor suggest that it had been possible to screen off the north-western bays of the

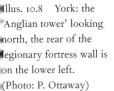

Illus. 10.8   York: the 'Anglian tower' looking north, the rear of the legionary fortress wall is on the lower left.
(Photo: P. Ottaway)

nave and aisles from the rest of the hall, but for what purpose is uncertain. Subsequently there was an episode which suggests a radical change of use for the hall in the last days of a garrison either about to be withdrawn from York or simply left to fend for itself once Britain had ceased to be ruled by Rome. At the south-east end a room in the rear range, behind the north-east aisle, became a workshop with a number of metalworking hearths. At the north-west end of the hall more or less contemporary deposits contained a group of animal bones, largely of pig (especially very young animals) and sheep, perhaps the result of feasting and/or butchery in the vicinity (see below). Radiocarbon dating of the animal bones places them in the late fourth or early fifth century.[22]

A brief review of the evidence from the forts may begin at Bowes where, according to the *Notitia*, a unit of *exploratores* (scouts) commanded by a prefect was based. Some late fourth-century repair on the southern fort wall was recorded in excavation.[23] At Bainbridge excavations produced evidence for its continuing occupation by a late Roman garrison and maintenance of the traditional, regular fort layout. In the final phase of the headquarters, however, there appears, as at York, to have been a change of use in which the main hall became a metalworking workshop. Whether the smiths still considered themselves to be part of the Sixth Cohort of Nervii referred to in the *Notitia* is not known. In the south-east corner of the fort there were newly erected stone buildings, presumably barracks.[24]

At *Olenacum*, thought most likely to be Elslack, the *Notitia* records the prefect of a cavalry unit named as First *Ala Herculea*, but no obvious archaeological evidence for its presence was recovered in the 1909 excavations. At Ilkley, although not mentioned in the *Notitia* (unless it, rather than Elslack, was *Olenacum*), there were, none the less, developments in the late fourth century.[25] On the defences the north gate was blocked; gate blocking in forts was common in the late Roman period, perhaps indicating an increased concern for security or simply that forts were now over provided with gates as their garrisons were smaller than hitherto. In the centre of the fort the commander's house had a new range of heated rooms and baths added to the rear. Even right at the end of the Roman period it seems the CO still demanded the luxurious accommodation his predecessors had enjoyed over the previous three hundred years or so. None the less, part of the house on south side was demolished for a new granary, still in the traditional style with thick buttressed walls.

Little can be said about the lowland forts of Castleford, Doncaster, Newton Kyme and Templeborough in the late fourth century. According to the *Notitia* Doncaster was garrisoned by a cavalry unit from Crispiana in Pannonia, but little trace of their presence has been found in the excavations. However, control of the main Roman road to Doncaster from the south may have been stepped up by the construction of a new fortlet, only 0.4ha in area but strongly fortified with a triple ditch system, on the east bank of the River Idle at Scaftworth, just over the Yorkshire border in Nottinghamshire.[26]

Finally, the archaeological evidence for the fort at Malton, likely to have been the base of the 'anticipators', is difficult to interpret because of the restricted areas of excavation, although undoubtedly there was activity in and around the north-east gate which was partly blocked, reducing it to the status of a postern.[27] A ditch was later dug along the north-east side of the fort, close to the wall, which served to close off the gate completely; this is undated but it may have been related to a post-Roman use of the fort as a local strongpoint.

Magnus Maximus's attempt to usurp the imperial crown came to an end in 388 with his defeat at the hands of the legitimate emperor, Theodosius I (379–95). However, he may have permanently weakened Britain's defences if his army did not return here, but was incorporated in units fighting elsewhere. The last serious attempt to shore up the defences of Roman Britain may have taken place in c.398 when, according to a passage in *On the Consulship of Stilicho* by Claudian, the Picts and Scots were defeated by an army commanded by Flavius Stilicho who, in effect, ruled the western Roman empire on behalf of the young Honorius (393–423), successor to his father Theodosius.

Although Britain had not been as badly affected by the crises of the late fourth century as some other parts of the Roman Empire, political and military events in the west conspired to weaken the capacity of the imperial court, now in Milan rather than Rome, to rule those provinces distant from the centre. Remnants of any effective fighting force were apparently removed from Britain and taken to Gaul in 407 by a would-be usurper based in Britain who styled himself Constantine III. By 409 Constantine had lost control of Britain and Spain and was eventually captured and executed in 411 by the army of Honorius. The intervening year, 410, is sometimes taken to mark the end of Roman Britain because this is when the city of Rome itself fell to an army of Goths. However, it is likely that, as far as Britain is concerned, that long-standing bargain between the Roman state and its people, in which internal peace and protection against their enemies was provided in return for taxes and army recruits, had already broken down. In the early fifth century the Roman provinces on this island ceased to be part of the empire, although it would be difficult to say that this happened in any particular year.

The towns and principal settlements: still going, but not very strong?

York

At York (Illus. 7.1) no site excavated in the Roman urban areas either side of the River Ouse has produced evidence for new construction in the second half of the fourth century, although pottery and coinage imply occupation up to the end of the century and beyond.[28] However, this did not take place in the flourishing environment that had existed previously. In the two most important recent excavations south-west of the Ouse, 1–9 Micklegate and Wellington

Row, it was found that before the end of the fourth century the baths at the former had probably been demolished, and that the building at the latter was deserted and had either begun to collapse or had also been demolished. Maintenance of streets appears to have ceased in many cases and silt and rubble accumulated over their surfaces. However inadequately maintained, some of the main approach roads must, none the less, have continued in use as they are still followed by roads today. Outside the settled areas a few burials may belong to the late Roman period (see below). Otherwise in the immediate environs of Roman York there is very little to report for the late fourth century, even the roadside settlement at Dringhouses appears to have been abandoned.

Aldborough and Brough on Humber

The late Roman history of Aldborough, now heavily defended by the projecting towers added to the walls, has yet to be examined archaeologically in any detail, although the excavations on the defences have produced plenty of late pottery and coinage indicating a community surviving up to the end of the Roman period. However, hinting at some break-up of the traditional urban order, in which the dead were kept away from the living, are two burials cut into the floor of the reception room with the Helicon mosaic.[29] They are undated and may be a good deal later than the Roman period, but if not they should be considered alongside other late or immediately post-Roman burials in Roman buildings in the region (see below). Outside the defences survival of what was part of Dere Street to become the Dunsforth road in post-Roman times may suggest the continuing occupation of Aldborough's eastern suburb.

The fate of Brough on Humber in the late Roman period is often thought to have been related to changes in sea level which affected the viability of the haven. Although more archaeological investigation is clearly needed to give us an understanding of the matter, it is striking that both within the walled town at Brough and in what had been fairly extensive suburbs there seems to be relatively little evidence for activity and occupation at the end of the fourth century.[30] On the defences an excavation at 49 Station Road (near the south-west corner) suggested the town ditch had filled up by the mid-fourth century and one wonders whether the walls and towers had begun falling into disrepair.

Catterick and Malton

At Catterick the evidence suggests a late fourth-century settlement not obviously in decline, at least within the walled area (Illus. 5.6).[31] Of particular interest is the Bypass site where there were sequences of building development both north and south of the east–west street. To the north of the street the bath house was still standing; on the street frontage and parallel to it was a substantial stone building, apparently at least 27.5m long × 10.3m wide. To the west of this building was a smaller one (c.8m × 6m) of three rooms in one of

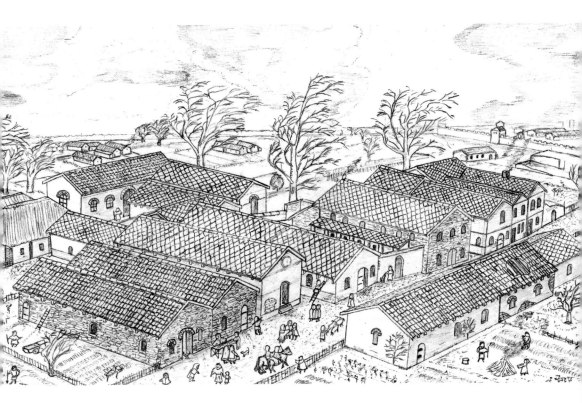

Illus. 10.9 Catterick:
reconstruction of the
bypass site at the end
of the fourth century
looking south-west. The
buildings on the right
are those north of the
main east-west street
(that producing the late
Roman buckles is at the
extreme right). On the
south (left) side of the
main street the first three
buildings on the left
lie east of a subsidiary
north–south street (©
P.Ottaway).

which was found a remarkable group of five belt buckles of types which are
usually dated to *c*.375 or later (see below).[32]

On the south side of the street, east of a subsidiary north–south street,
three strip buildings were identified. At the rear of one of them a room with
a hypocaust was added very late in the fourth century. The westernmost of
the three seems to have been deliberately built on a raised platform above
street level from which it was, perhaps, accessed by steps. This feature has
led to the suggestion that it was a temple or shrine, although there is no
other evidence for this. The building was given a southern extension late in
the fourth century. At the rear of the block (or *insula*) there was a structure,
referred to in the excavation report as the 'best preserved of unquestionably
fifth-century buildings'. Measuring 14m × 6m it had much less substantial
remains than earlier buildings, surviving only as post-holes and slight stone
footings for the timber sill beams which had supported the walls. Part of a
similar structure was found further to the south.

On the west side of a block, west of the north–south side street, another
group of three strip buildings was identified. Added at the rear late in the
sequence was a single depth of additional rooms. Two strip buildings on the
east side of the same block were altered after *c*.350, the easternmost being
provided with a hypocaust whilst that to the west of it had a verandah added
on its east side. Behind these two buildings two others were amalgamated
into a single, large one (25.5m × 18.5m) comprising, perhaps, as many as three

reception halls, one of which had a small room with a hypocaust carved out of it during the late fourth century.

What the evidence summarised here seems to show is that late in the fourth century there was a streetscape in at least part of Catterick which was, in essence, very similar to what had become familiar in towns all over Britain over the previous three hundred years or so. Within it there was construction and reconstruction of buildings in typical Roman style with appointments, notably hypocausts, added to them. It is possible that Catterick is unusual because a military presence gave it a wealth and population not generally found elsewhere in the region. The exact status of the fort in the late fourth century is unclear (Catterick is not in the *Notitia*), but deposits of this period on the Bypass site produced five spearheads and an arrowhead, all thought to be of late Roman types.[33] We cannot tell how long the Catterick streetscape survived; strictly speaking all the recorded structural changes could have taken place before 410, but it is quite possible that some of them belonged to the subsqequent ten years or so and that final abandonment did not occur before the middle of the fifth century. Unfortunately we do not know how typical the Bypass site is of the walled town as a whole, but outside the walls the evidence is for a marked change in the character, if not complete abandonment, of settled areas before the end of the fourth century. On the north bank of the Swale, occupation of the strip buildings facing Dere Street (described above) ceased in *c.*360–70. However, although the areas excavated were partly turned over to burial, there were some traces of later timber structures on the Dere Street frontage.[34] At Bainesse, to the south of the town, there were no buildings surviving in the excavated areas after *c.*350 in what had been a flourishing roadside settlement, the land continuing in use only for the occasional burial.

Malton and Norton-on-Derwent were not on quite so important a route as Catterick, but the *vicus* south-east of the fort was clearly still occupied at the end of the fourth century, if not, perhaps, to the same extent as earlier in the century (Illus. 7.9). On the Orchard Field site the Town House is thought to have become derelict after a roof collapse by *c.*370.[35] At the 1970 site the dismantling of the hypocaust in the building on the street frontage and its infilling with debris, including painted wall plaster, suggests standards of maintenance had declined, but not that it was deserted as a flagstone floor was laid over the disused hypocaust. However, the building is thought to have been finally abandoned before the end of the fourth century. In a room at the rear an adult burial was dug into the floor to the unusually substantial depth of 1.5m, some time after the mid-fourth century.[36] At Orchard Cottage what were probably grain-drying kilns were constructed in Buildings 1 and 2, the latter being a large new building of the mid-fourth century.[37] However, Road 2 may have been disused before the end of the century. Cutting through the 1970 site buildings and the Town House and Kiln Building was a substantial ditch, *c.*3.5m wide and *c.*1.5m deep, on a north-west/south-east line, with a low rampart and palisade on its south-west side. This ditch was, perhaps, intended to defend a surviving settlement zone to the west at the very end of the Roman period, although it is more likely to have been post-Roman, like the ditch immediately outside the fort defences.

On the opposite bank of the Derwent, at Norton, pottery production on any scale probably came to an end soon after the mid-fourth century, but occupation clearly continued.[38] For example, excavations at Eastfield (in 1946–47) suggested 'intense late fourth-century occupation' of buildings surviving as paved floors near the Roman road approaching from the east (Illus. 5.18, 8). A similar picture was revealed in the Vicarage Garden, Langton Road near the road heading south to York and Brough on Humber (Illus. 5.18, 6).

At the small roadside settlements in east Yorkshire the finds suggest continuing occupation through to the end of the fourth century. On the basis of the pottery from fieldwalking at Hayton it has even been suggested that the settlement was at its greatest extent in the late fourth century and this may be a context for the continuing use of the cemetery on Town Street (see above). Nearby, at Shiptonthorpe, the excavated enclosure produced little evidence for activity in the late fourth century, although the latest deposits may have been lost to ploughing.[39] However, fieldwalking has produced many late coins and the settlement may, like Hayton, have continued to fulfil a significant role in the locality. Evidence for appreciable late Roman settlement also comes from Stamford Bridge[40] whilst at nearby High Catton a new series of ditched enclosures on the road heading south-east towards Barmby Moor is thought to be late fourth century.[41]

Rural settlement and landscape: deserted or impoverished?

In rural areas a diminished occurrence of material culture, principally pottery, appears widespread in the Yorkshire region as a whole, although the picture is by no means an even one. A lack of material culture in an area does not necessarily mean there was a lack of people. However, it is the case that many of the sites referred to in previous chapters produce little or no pottery of the late fourth century, especially those west of the Magnesian Limestone belt which appear to have been largely beyond the reach of the Crambeck and Huntcliff distribution networks. By contrast in much of east Yorkshire, within those networks, settlement evidence remains highly visible.

Where the pottery sequence does continue into the late fourth century it is often difficult to identify what it means in terms of either land management or the fortunes of agriculture. In many cases late Roman pottery comes from the upper filling of ditches which were presumably silting up for the last time before going out of use. The ditch systems which had been such a feature of the enclosed landscapes of the first to early third centuries in the region, surviving in some cases into the early fourth century, appear to have largely disappeared by 350. Although ditches may have been replaced by hedges, we may now be seeing evidence for a real decline in the fortunes of agriculture involving desertion of land and a reduction in surplus production above subsistence level, especially in areas which, because of soil quality, climate, drainage and other factors, were less favourable for cultivation. This impression is supported by changes in the character of the villas at the end of the fourth century; their owners were, for example, clearly finding it difficult to maintain bath suites, hypocausts and wells.

In previous chapters a review of rural settlement has proceeded from west to east. In this chapter, largely because of a lack of datable finds, it is very difficult to say much about the Pennine regions, although life must have continued as before in many of the farmsteads and fields. At the Gargrave villa, in Craven, the main houses are thought to have been abandoned before the end of the fourth century. The excavator, Brian Hartley, commented that the final activity for which evidence was found derived from a hearth of tiles in

Illus. 10.10 Wattle Syke near Wetherby: remains of a late fourth-century sunken-floored building with flagged floor (© ASWYAS).

the northern house, '... probably used to cook a meal, or meals, by a shepherd sheltering in the ruins of the building'.[42] One wonders whether this was eaten from a pot or were wooden vessels now routinely used for food preparation?

On the Coal Measures there is also little to report for the late fourth century, although on their eastern edge at Swillington Common South (Illus. 4.6) there was an appreciable quantity of pottery in the ditches suggesting continuing farming activity and settlement here.[43] However, one would expect this in an area of good agricultural land linked to the landscapes on the Magnesian Limestone immediately to the east which must have remained a bread basket for York. Another site within easy reach of York, on the limestone, is that already mentioned at Wattle Syke near Wetherby.[44] A number of timber buildings with slightly sunken floors, some with stone footings, and flagged floors and hearths, remained in use in the final decades of the fourth century. Although we sometimes think of sunken-floored buildings as typically Anglo-Saxon, it seems that they were quite widespread in the late Roman period and not necessarily an introduction of Germanic newcomers. Presumably the villa near Wattle Syke, at Dalton Parlours, was also occupied at the end of the fourth century, although Well 1 was apparently filling up with refuse by the middle of the century.[45]

The northern part of the Magnesian Limestone belt, where the solid geology is largely below drift deposits, is also good agricultural land which probably explains why, for example, the villa at Well was still occupied at the end of the fourth century. As an unusual example of construction in the region in this period, another annexe was added to the baths after c.370.[46] On the boulder clay of the Tees lowlands there is very little evidence for settlement in the late fourth century, although excavations at Ingleby Barwick villa identified new construction in the form of a circular building with stone footings. This may have been another late Roman example of the roundhouse or, it has been suggested, a building where grain was ground by animal power – the so-called 'donkey mill', well known in other parts of the Roman world, if not in Britain.[47] Unfortunately the main villa house was not excavated so its fortunes in the late Roman period are unknown. Evidence for the late fourth century in the rest of the lowland zone as far south as York is also sparse, although just on the eastern edge, at the possible villa site of West Lilling there was pottery dated to the late fourth century and also some of the early Anglo-Saxon period suggesting continuity of settlement into the fifth century and beyond.[48]

On the Humberhead Levels the effects of rising sea level may, by the end of the fourth century, have seriously affected the viability of settlement in areas liable to flood. The landing place at Faxfleet on the Humber is thought to have been buried under flood deposits at some time in the fourth century.[49] On the south bank of the River Ouse at Drax the villa was abandoned in c.370, perhaps due to more frequent flooding of the surrounding land rather than the 'barbarian conspiracy' as proposed by the excavator.[50] In the southern part of the Levels overbank flooding of the Rivers Don, Torne and Idle may have been a particularly serious problem.[51] The potential impact was assessed on a sandy ridge near Sandtoft in the former fen and raised bog known as Hatfield Chase, just over the Yorkshire border in North Lincolnshire.[52] Cropmarks and a finds scatter on the banks of the old River Idle led to an excavation which examined two adjoining rectangular ditched enclosures (182m² and 71m²). They were probably in use during the fourth century, but alluvium overlying ditches on the north side of the site suggested that flooding had led to migration eastwards to a large enclosure (120m across) on slightly higher ground where the ditches produced late fourth-century pottery.

If we now return to the area of good agricultural land at the foot of the North York Moors at Beadlam, we find, again unusually for Yorkshire, some further construction had taken place in the villa in the late fourth century, principally on the east side of the courtyard (Buildings 3, 5, 7–8; Illus. 9.10).[53] This included an unusual apsed building (Building 5) about which further comment is made below. However, the picture is not all positive as during this period there was a change in the status of the dwelling house (Building 1) indicated by the digging of a grain-drying kiln, of the common T-shaped form, through the mosaic in the dining room; what better indicator could there be for the disappearance of the traditional lifestyle of the Roman rural gentry? At much the same time, Building 2 on the west side of the courtyard was probably abandoned except, perhaps, for a part of the baths housing the latest phase of the plunge pool.

East of Beadlam at Crossgates, Seamer discoveries at the gravel pit immediately south of Seamer station began in 1947 with a roughly circular stone floor, c.5.5m in diameter, with a central hearth, presumably representing the remains of a roundhouse.[54] Subsequently, more extensive work revealed the floors of another six roundhouses.[55] A date for these buildings in the late fourth century is given by the associated pottery of which almost half was Huntcliff ware. Nearby at Knapton, on the south side of the Vale of Pickering, the remains of two more late Roman roundhouses have been found.[56]

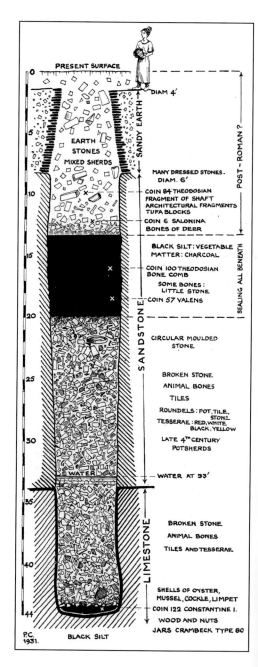

Illus. 10.11 Langton villa: cross-section of the well (from Corder and Kirk 1932).

At Langton villa there appears to have been no new construction in the late fourth-century, although the site clearly remained occupied.[57] The well, thought to have been last used in c.335, apparently remained open, but presumably fenced off, until the end of the fourth century at which time it was still c.7m deep. The infilling up to this point included a lot of animal remains (surviving as bones) and building materials, the latter probably arising from demolition or reconstruction somewhere nearby. There was then an accumulation of organic black silt. However, from a depth of c.4m below ground level the well appears to have been deliberately filled up. The contents included two fragments of ornamental balustrade and a broken pillar which may have resulted from further demolition or the collapse of buildings at the very end of, or even after, the Roman period.

A short distance from Langton, on the Wolds at Wharram Percy there is also good evidence for the late fourth century.[58] At North Manor a considerable quantity of pottery of the period was recovered in deposits associated with the north-west/south-east running trackway (Illus. 9.12). North of it were what were identified as 'outbuildings' with pebbled floors, thought, perhaps, to have been part of a farmstead whose main buildings were in an unexcavated part of the site. In addition, a grain-drying kiln was constructed in the second half of the fourth century. The two villa sites in the Wharram area – Wharram-le-Street and Wharram Grange – both produced late Roman pottery, although no details of what this signifies are apparent in the absence of much excavation.[59]

Further east at Rudston the history of the villa site at the end of the fourth century is difficult to determine because of plough damage to the latest Roman deposits.[60] However, as elsewhere, the fate of the well may be taken as an indicator of the residents' lack of ability to maintain the building complex to former standards. Infilling of the well is thought to have begun after it had fallen out of use in c.330 (a similar date to disuse of the well at Langton). The lowest deposit, largely chalk rubble, contained the remains of iron buckets, presumably once used to draw water. Between a depth of c.28m and 26m below ground level there was an accumulation of peaty material, largely moss, interpreted as a dump of the Roman equivalent of toilet paper (the Langton 'silt' may have had a similar origin).[61] The well was then used for dumping rubbish to a depth of c.24.5m. At this point the sandstone lining began collapsing into the shaft, due to a lack of maintenance. There was then a deposit containing rubble, including tesserae and wall plaster, thought to be from the demolition of the bath house. From a depth of c.3m the well gradually silted up, a process probably not complete until after the end of the Roman period. At the beginning of the silting the body of a human male 35–45 years old was buried in the well in the crouched position; two large chalk blocks formed a deliberate covering.

On the southern limb of the Wolds at Welton villa the area of activity and settlement was much reduced after the mid-fourth century.[62] The ditches of the surrounding field system had silted up and the only new ditch defined the south side of a compound containing the main house, aisled buildings and a small cemetery (see below). A new sunken-floored building contained a crop drier which after its last use was dug into to make a female burial. The skeleton showed signs of burning, probably as a result of a fire which also destroyed the house and one of the aisled barns. There was no sign of reconstruction after the fire.

On the eastern edge of the Wolds at Elmswell occupation continued up to the end of the Roman period and beyond.[63] The so-called 'hut' of the third century was enlarged slightly and the floor was resurfaced with cobbles and chalk in c.370; set into the floor was a Huntcliff ware vessel. Further east at Bridlington surprisingly little evidence for fourth-century activity is reported from the relatively large scale excavations at High Wolds and Sewerby Cottage Farm. However at Bessingby Hill, on the south side of the town 'a crude round hut', c.9m × 8.25m, represented by a chalk floor and post-holes was found, dated by two coins of 364–75.[64]

On the boulder clay of Holderness there seems to be little evidence for late Roman settlement, although this may be an accident of recovery rather than a real phenomenon. However, on the Leven–Brandsburton bypass a complex of ditches and remains of timber buildings dated to the mid- to late fourth century has been recorded.[65] In the lower Hull valley marine transgression may have made settlement untenable in some places formerly occupied, although it did continue up to the end of the century at sites excavated in 1991–97 on Malmo Road in Hull.[66]

The settlement evidence described above and other indicators, especially the distribution and quantity of material culture, suggest that, in general terms, the economy in the Yorkshire region, in line with most of Britain, was in decline after c.350–70 and no longer functioning as it had done in the early fourth century. Were we to have reliable statistics, we would probably see that agricultural and manufacturing output steadily fell, although production of certain commodities, including pottery, may have been less affected if it was required by the army. However, a diminishing level of demand from the military in the region both because of a progressively smaller garrison and a decline in purchasing power was probably a factor in reducing the generation of agricultural surplus, the principal source of wealth, and thereby the impoverishment of the elite and, in turn, the population as a whole. Any drop in population size would have exacerbated the situation.

Agriculture: the decline of the cow?

The archaeological evidence for the Yorkshire region's agriculture in the late fourth century is minimal in the absence of large and well-dated samples of either plant material or animal bones. One of the few late fourth-century sites in the region which has something useful to tell us is Filey Signal Station.[67] Refuse deposits produced a few charred peas and grains of spelt wheat, but more important, if a relatively small group compared to some from Roman military sites, were the animal bones (Table 9). What is immediately striking is an apparently reduced reliance on beef in the diet as cattle bones make up only 18% of those of the three main meat–producing animals. Although not perhaps excavated as systematically as Filey, some bones were evidently collected at Goldsborough signal station and those of pig (not cattle) are said in the report to have been the most common.[68] Late fourth- and early fifth-century deposits in the York fortress basilica tell a somewhat similar story to Filey. Cattle bones only made up 24% of a group of similar size, whilst pig bones formed a much higher proportion than in any Roman group quoted in this book at 43%[69] – only Filey comes close at 35%. Whether these data tell us something about the changing tastes in meat of the late Roman military or about some problem in rearing cattle in the region is hard to tell. We may simply be seeing two untypical groups of bones in which the remains of army hog roasts feature prominently.

Manufacturing

Pottery

Two major pottery industries were located in the Yorkshire region, one at Crambeck (described above) and the other at an unknown location, thought by some to lie at the eastern end of the Vale of Pickering. The latter produced Huntcliff or 'Signal Station' ware which occurs largely as jars, but also as bowls, dishes and the occasional flagon, in a black, coarse fabric with calcite temper.[70] Jar rims characteristically have a seating for a lid, although very few ceramic lids are known and they were probably made of reused tiles or wood. Pottery production may also have continued in the late fourth century at other centres such as Doncaster, but on a small scale and distribution was purely local.

Metalwork

No metalworking sites of this latest Roman period are known in the Yorkshire region. Many, if not most, smiths in rural areas probably remained peripatetic, although villa estates might still be able to retain one on a permanent basis. The presence of a smith at Beadlam villa at the end of the fourth century is suggested by two hoards of ironwork found close together against the south wall of Room 6 in the main dwelling house.[71] Hoard I, containing about thirty objects, included tools such as two axe blades and two scythe blades, three door hinges and miscellaneous strips and bars. Hoard 2, some fifteen objects, included a trowel blade and a spear head. These items may have been set aside towards the end of the building's life for a future recycling episode which never happened. Alternatively, they may represent deliberate 'structured' deposits ritually marking a particular event, perhaps the demolition of all or part of the building. Another hoard of about fifty iron objects, undated, but possibly contemporary, comes from a pit at Ingleby Barwick villa; it included ten woodworking tools and three metalworking files.[72]

As far as non-ferrous metalwork is concerned, jewellery items such as the crossbow brooch and bracelet types of the early fourth century remained fashionable. However, the belt buckles found at Catterick are thought to be particularly characteristic of the later fourth century and to have been made in state-run factories for soldiers and imperial officials. Four of them have animal head terminals and are decorated in the so-called 'chip-carved' technique which involved the use of a punch with a wedge-shaped tip.[73]

Another craft to produce distinctive items in the latest Roman period were the antler and bone workers who made distinctive combs, some single sided and others double, often attractively finished with anthropomorphic motifs, such as the stylised horses seen on a double-sided comb from Beadlam villa.[74]

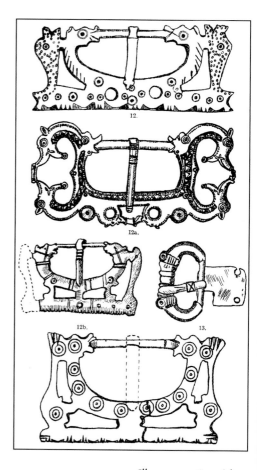

Exchange and trade

Whilst most trade remained very local, there was still a Roman military supply system in the latter part of the fourth century which could move commodities over a long distance between provinces. Ammianus Marcellinus records that when the future Emperor Julian had been Caesar he ordered the transport of grain from Britain to the Rhineland in the year 359.[75] A supply system with more of a regional reach is revealed by the distribution of Crambeck ware.[76] The pattern of find spots is not one would normally expect for a commodity in Roman Britain, with a steady diminution in numbers as distance from the

Illus. 10.12 Catterick: late fourth-century buckles (from Hildyard 1957, © Yorkshire Archaeological Society).

source increased, but rather it is one with a concentration at one of the limits of distribution – on Hadrian's Wall. Very little Crambeck ware is found south of the Humber; this cannot be due to transport costs as expensive, land-based transport would have been needed to take pottery from Crambeck to the frontier, although part of that journey might have been made by water from York to South Shields at the mouth of the Tyne. Another aspect of regional military supply was revealed by the animal bone from Filey Signal Station. This showed that the garrison had not been reduced to a militia which had to fend for itself as part-time farmers. On the contrary, the parts of the cattle and sheep skeletons found were largely the meat-yielding ones and did not include skulls or feet. It seems clear that slaughter took place elsewhere – at York or on a local estate perhaps – and joints were then sent by an army quartermaster to the signal station for consumption.

Crambeck ware apart, distribution of pottery from other local sources suggests that in the late fourth century a return was made to something like the Iron Age pattern. On the one hand, there is very little late pottery from sites west of the Magnesian Limestone belt, but, on the other hand, it occurs widely in the eastern part of the Yorkshire region. Non-local pottery imports from elsewhere in Britain, except from the Nene Valley, almost completely disappeared and wares of Continental origin were more or less unknown.[77] One remarkable exception to the dearth of evidence for interprovincial trade which should be added here is the pieces of a glass vessel with floral patterns in brilliant colours found at Ingleby Barwick villa.[78] There was little else to suggest extravagance of tastes here, but somehow an item of probable Egyptian origin had ended up in Teesside.

Local and regional trade probably continued to use coinage fairly widely until the end of the fourth century, although, as in earlier times, supply to the Yorkshire region reflected the fluctuations experienced by Britain as a whole.[79] For some years after 353 there was a shortage of coin, partly because that of the usurper Magnentius (350–53) was no longer legal tender; this led to the local production of copies of coins of Constantius II (d. 361) bearing the legend FEL TEMP REPARATIO ('happy times are here again'). Following a further reform, official coinage of Valentinian I (364–75) and his co-emperor Valens (364–78) was supplied to Britain in large quantities judging by the number lost. A low level of loss after the death of Valens until the defeat of the usurper Magnus Maximus in 388 suggests supply dipped for a ten year period, but it then revived with the production of large numbers of small bronze coins, usually known as *nummi*. In about 402, however, supply of coinage to Britain more or less ceased for good, presumably meaning the army was no longer being paid. Furthermore no local copies were made of late fourth-century coins to compensate for the failure of supply. This probably indicates that there was now no need for coin to pay taxes, even if there were still sufficient coins available to allow money to be used in some transactions in the early fifth century.

Late Roman hoards

Hoarding of coins continued in the second half of the fourth century, but there are relatively few known from the north compared to the south and south-west of England. A large hoard of 2795 coins from Heslington near York of *c.*360 reflects the plentiful supply of coin to the city at that time,[80] but this is one of only four hoards from Yorkshire of the period *c.*355–75 recorded in Anne Robertson's survey of year 2000. Dated between *c.*375 and the end of the fourth century, eleven hoards were recorded by Robertson, all of which come from the north-east of the county. Three of these late hoards (two from Filey and one from Scarborough) come from the signal stations.[81] Another late hoard, a substantial one (for the time) of 75 coins, was recorded from Filey (unspecified location) in 2008.[82] These hoards may reflect a greater availability of coin in the coastal zone than elsewhere in the region due to continuing supply to the army on the coast.

A feature of British hoards in the late Roman period is that they sometimes included valuables other than coins. One example from Yorkshire was a huge hoard of metal vessels found at Knaresborough of which only a few pieces now survive in the Yorkshire Museum. Another hoard was found in 1810 at Whorlton, on the northern edge of the Cleveland Hills.[83] Unfortunately much of the contents is lost, including a silver 'urn' in which they were buried. A few pieces survive in the British Museum and we must otherwise rely on a near contemporary account which estimated the whole as weighing about 14kg. There may have been several thousand coins but the thirty-eight in the BM suggest a date of deposition of c.410–25. There was also bullion in the form of silver bars and 'ornaments' of which a spoon, two finger-rings and a buckle tongue survive. This was not, however, a hoard of barbarian loot like Traprain Law, as coins were the dominant component; it seems more likely to have been the wealth of a local estate buried at a time of political uncertainty to be recovered in happier times.

The Visual Arts: the age of invisibility

Examples of the late Roman minor decorative arts as applied to pottery, metalwork and bone have already been referred to. However, local traditions of architectural embellishment, sculpture, mosaic and wall painting appear to have more or less come to an end after the mid-fourth century and, with a very few possible exceptions, new examples cannot be found whether at York, the other major settlements or the villas where they might be expected. If we see this as a result of a dearth of economic surplus available for conspicuous consumption by the elite on any sort of scale, then there is perhaps no more obvious indicator of the declining productive capacity of the region at the end of the fourth century.

Religion: even more obscure

Without any sculpture or artefacts with a clear cult function from a late fourth-century context it is difficult to say anything useful about religion in the Yorkshire region at this time. One must presume that pagan practices of the sort described in previous chapters continued unabated. Evidence for the spread of Christianity in the region remains scarce, in contrast to some other regions of Britain, although one might have expected aggressive sponsorship of the faith by the Emperor Theodosius I to have had some impact in making

Christian worship more widespread. A church for the bishops of York may have existed, but otherwise worshippers must have convened in private houses.

The sort of building which might have been used as a private church is Building 5 on the east side of the courtyard at Beadlam villa which replaced an earlier building in the late fourth century (Illus. 9.10).[84] Building 5 was aligned more or less east–west and had an eastern apse as one would expect in a church of this period, although this is a feature which also occurred in many secular buildings. In addition, however, the building was apparently exactly 36 Roman feet (10.66m) long × 25 (7.40m) wide. The choice of two dimensions incorporating whole number square roots suggests a building carefully designed with the harmony appropriate to a sacred milieu. Sixty-six metres due west was the bath suite in Building 2 and the latest phase of the plunge pool has the octagonal form common in late Roman baptisteries, an allusion both to Noah and his family in I Peter III, 20 – 'eight were saved by water' – and to the Resurrection on the eighth day. The excavator concedes that Building 5 could have been a shrine but the pool in its liturgically correct place to the west of it raises the possibility, at least, of this being a Christian church.

At the other end of what we might call the religious spectrum, where it merges into superstition, we may return to the matter of the ritually structured deposits described in Chapter 4. A type, well-known in other parts of Roman Britain, of which there are a number of probable examples in the Yorkshire region, largely of the late Roman period, involved the burial of animals or parts of animals, notably in wells. At Shiptonthorpe during the infilling of the well or water hole referred to in Chapter 9, probably in the mid-fourth century, four pigs, a young bull and a calf were deliberately buried nearby.[85] In the upper filling of the well at Langton villa there were the bones of red deer, still numerous, perhaps, in an area from which they have long since disappeared; the report refers to 'seven or eight individuals', although it is not clear if they were whole skeletons.[86] A distinctive group of bones near the base of the stone-lined well at Heslington included the partial skeletons of a young red deer, a calf and of several puppies. There were antlers from at least six stags in the well at Rudston and at a depth of 8.5m–10.5m below the surface there was a deposit containing three neonatal lambs.[87]

Although the animals whose bones are found in Roman wells, whether as whole or partial skeletons, may have sometimes simply died due to natural causes or accident and were then disposed of in the nearest hole in the ground, it seems unlikely that a last resting place in or near a well was always a matter of chance. As water sources wells were of great importance for daily life, and, like other water sources, they also assumed a sacred significance in the Roman period – as some holy wells still do today. After a well had ceased to function it may have seemed incumbent on the local people to mark this within the context of a water cult; the sacrifice of life to a place which had given life would have been an obvious symbol of closure. Deer, especially the stags, and perhaps just their antlers, would, perhaps, have been seen as particularly appropriate for a closure deposit in light of their long-standing role as symbols of fertility in pre-Roman and Roman Britain; the antlers, shed and regrown every year would have evoked the cycle of death and rebirth in nature as whole.

Whilst it can be easily accepted that animals were dedicated to the gods, it is rather more controversial to suggest that human beings might, on occasions, have been considered suitable offerings. However, at Garton Slack the great well, 29m deep, thought to have been abandoned by the early fourth century, produced at a depth of 14m the skeleton of a boy about fourteen years old with, it is reported, 'a badly smashed skull' (it is not clear how this was caused) lying prone above the skeleton of a dog in pup close to that of a sheep.[88] At first sight this looks like the remains of an accident, testimony to the dangers of an unfilled hole in remote countryside, in which a shepherd boy had fallen down the well with his dog whilst trying to save a sheep. However, it does not seem entirely plausible that a well was simply left open given the obvious danger to both sheep and people and it must be a possibility that something more deliberate, and sinister, had taken place and what we have here is another form of ritual closure of a well. The same phenomenon may be represented by the burial in the well at Rudston, although he may simply have been put in a convenient hollow where the ground was relatively soft.

Treatment of the dead: where is everybody?

Evidence for human burials in late fourth-century Yorkshire is sparse, being divided between formal cemeteries, primarily at York and Catterick, and burials in one and twos made in apparently less formal circumstances, including abandoned town and villa buildings, which suggest the breaking down of established Roman practice. The preferred method of treating the body remained inhumation, but cremation was still practised on occasions. A few people, at least, in Yorkshire may have known that this would acquire renewed imperial sanction when the Emperor Julian, an avowed pagan in a world rapidly turning to Christianity, was cremated in traditional fashion on his death in 363.[89]

At York a few of the burials from the 35–41 Blossom Street cemetery may belong to the period after c.350 but this cannot be determined with certainty. The same may be said of the Castle Yard burials. More confidence for a post-350 date can be given to a small cemetery of six inhumations found at 16–22 Coppergate only 175m south-east of the fortress defences, another example of the trend in the later Roman period of moving cemeteries closer to settled areas, in this case one where the buildings on the site may have only just been abandoned.[90] Other burials from York, recovered in the less than ideal circumstances of the nineteenth and early twentieth centuries, may be of late fourth-century or even later date, but this cannot be proved. However, a burial recently discovered at Hungate has been radiocarbon dated to the very late fourth or early fifth century. In addition an unusual burial found in

Sycamore Terrace, north-west of the legionary fortress, in 1902 has some claim to belong to the second half of the fourth century, primarily on the basis of the date of a blue glass jug it contained.[91] A stone coffin, lying north–south, contained a female inhumation and a rich array of grave goods. In addition to the jug there were two jet bangles, a bracelet of blue glass, glass beads, silver and bronze lockets, two yellow glass earrings and a small round crystal mirror. Most unusual, however, was a small bone plaque bearing a motto thought to be Christian in sentiment: SOROR AVE VIVAS IN DEO ('Hail sister may you live in God'), although the alignment and the provision of grave goods would appear to be contrary to Christian practice.

At Catterick, Bainesse, two late fourth-century inhumation burials were found in an area where occupation of buildings is thought to have ceased by c.350.[92] One had a stone-lined grave, but they were otherwise unremarkable. However, a cemetery of the latest Roman period was found north of the Swale at Catterick Bridge. There were nineteen inhumations; all the bodies were extended and supine except for one female who was buried in the crouched position. Nine burials were accompanied by some sort of grave good. The crouched female had four armlets, two of copper alloy and two of jet. An infant burial had three armlets, two of copper alloy and one of antler. Most unusual was an infant burial which, in addition to an early fourth-century coin, was buried with a miniature (uninscribed) stone altar, possibly after its use in the funerary rites.[93] Small cemeteries at places other than the region's principal settlements include one at Welton villa outside the main house where a number of graves were ordered on a common north–south alignment, some in wooden coffins. Also likely to be very late Roman is a cemetery with at least eleven burials at Wetherby, found south of the church in 1928–30 in an area previously part of a settlement.[94] Three had their legs either flexed or contracted under the chest. Four of the burials were in so-called 'cists', graves which were lined and capped with stone slabs. In some cases these slabs were probably reused roofing material, perhaps from a demolished building such as the nearby Dalton Parlours villa. This in itself might suggest a late fourth-century date, but the cist is a type of burial which is thought to be largely, if not exclusively, late fourth century in the region, on the basis of examples from the Crambeck area. At the Jamie's Crags site there were two cist burials, one of which appeared to post-date a disused kiln and the other was buried with two pots thought to be late Crambeck ware.[95] Other cist burials, which may well be of late fourth-century date, include two more from Crambeck (found in the nineteenth century)[96] and others in the limestone hills north of the Vale of Pickering include examples from Nawton and Appleton-le-Moors.[97] Another was dug into the Helicon mosaic in the town house at Aldborough[98] and yet another was found in the courtyard of Ingleby Barwick villa. An unusually late Roman example of a burial in a stone coffin, dated by the style of an accompanying bone comb, was found at Glass Houghton, near Wakefield.[99]

The Aldborough burial was one of a pair, aligned east–west, which are but two examples of burials made in the region's Roman buildings, presumably after they had been abandoned and had perhaps become derelict, probably in the late fourth or early fifth centuries (although later dates are also possible). In addition to that found cut into a building floor at the Malton 1970 site, there was a burial in Room 7 of Building 1 (the main house) at Beadlam villa,[100] and there were two more in the Castle Dykes villa bath house.[101] The discovery of one of the latter prompted the excavator, the Reverend Lukis, to give free reign to an imagination influenced by the prevailing late nineteenth-century notions of the violent end of Roman Britain and arrival of the Anglo-Saxons:

> But when we uncovered the human remains, their remarkable position, encased in the debris of a wall which had been battered about his ears, told the story of the young man's last moments in the clearest language. It was plain that he had rushed out of one of the adjoining rooms when the place was assaulted, and was seeking concealment and safety when he received his death blow. Perhaps he was feeling the effects of the blinding smoke which was filling the house and was staggering along the wall side. Whatever was the mental misery and horror of his condition at that moment, it is evident that an arrow from the hand of an unseen enemy struck him on the left side of the head, and he dropped upon one knee, with his hands raised to defend his head. In this position he has been found after a lapse of sixteen or seventeen centuries.

One would like to know whether an arrowhead was actually found, and about a bronze armlet which was found 'under the bones' – perhaps, in fact, a perfectly respectable grave good for a burial of the late fourth century.

The end of Roman Yorkshire

There is little which can be said with any certainty about Yorkshire at the beginning of the fifth century. From an archaeological point of view one of the principal problems we face is a lack of diagnostic artefactual material to date structures and other features. Not only is there no newly minted Roman coinage, but there is no distinctive pottery. Industries such as that based at Crambeck probably ceased to function once the army was no longer paid and contracts had ceased. There are hand-made wares from the region which are thought to represent a return to a tradition of low-tech local potting as seen in the late Iron Age/early Roman period but they are difficult to date closely. Furthermore, Yorkshire has produced no fifth-century imported vessels, such as the wine amphorae recorded on sites in western Britain, which can be tied in to dated sequences in Mediterranean countries.

Prevailing opinion is that the sort of apocalyptic vision of the end of Roman Yorkshire conjured up by Revd Lukis cannot be sustained; invaders from Germanic lands across the North Sea did not, it is thought, rush into ill-defended Roman towns and villas to seize booty and slaughter the residents. However, the idea of a gentle transition to the post-Roman era can be overplayed, at least when applied to the Roman empire in the west as a whole, parts of which witnessed plenty of spilt blood — not least Rome itself when sacked by the Goths. Whilst remote from more destructive conflict, Yorkshire may have experienced at least some reverberations of the turmoil elsewhere. For example, there are what the excavators of Goldsborough signal station in 1931 called 'discoveries which can only be described as sensational'.[102] Digging within the south-east corner of the tower revealed a skeleton of a thick-set muscular individual, but only *c*.1.55m tall, with serious head wounds inflicted, it was claimed, by a sword or some other heavy item. He had fallen face down across a hearth, perhaps after being stabbed in the back. Another skeleton, face down, lay above the skeleton of a large dog, its head against the man's throat and its paws on his shoulders. This was thought to represent the faithful friend of the first man defending the tower against an intruder. The ensemble was called 'a grim record of a thrilling drama' and proof of a 'sudden and violent end …'. It is usually assumed that this occurred more or less at the end of the Roman occupation of the site, although it could have taken place much later. There is nothing comparable from the other signal station buildings, although parts of fourteen human skeletons were found in the well at Huntcliff.[103] They are hard to explain, but may simply have resulted from the disturbance of earlier burials in the area, or, alternatively, are they evidence for some rather unsavoury closure ritual?

At Filey signal station the latest deposits in the courtyard conjure up their own distinctive, and peaceful, vision of the end of Roman Yorkshire. They produced the bones of mice, shrews and lizards, and even of a snake, all of which were probably the remains of meals consumed by barn owls resident in the tower.[104] These are birds which tend to shun human company and so it is quite likely that they only moved in after the tower was deserted by its garrison, but, none the less, still stood sentinel above Filey Bay waiting in vain for Rome's legions to return. Meanwhile, in the evening light, the owls swooped silently down over the Carr Naze and the rocks of Filey Brigg beyond in search of their nightly prey.

Yorkshire's Roman Legacy

The new politics

There are parts of Europe where the legacy of the Roman era, in both culture and landscape, is much more obvious than it is in any part of Britain. This country seems to have experienced a complete and fairly rapid collapse of the Roman political, economic and social system, followed in due course by the emergence of systems of a very different character in the ensuing 200 years or so. Contemporary or near contemporary sources which throw light on the transition from Roman Britain in the early fifth century to Anglo-Saxon England a century later are very few indeed and their relevance for Yorkshire is marginal. Furthermore, good archaeological evidence for much of the fifth century is more or less non-existent in the region except for a number of early Anglo-Saxon burials.

Although the year 410 has sometimes been given as the date for the end of Roman Britain, there is no question of Britain suddenly ceasing to be part of the Roman Empire with the legions packing their bags rather like the British army leaving Hong Kong. How many troops the usurper Constantine III actually removed from Britain in 409 and how many remained is debatable. The sixth-century historian Zosimus suggests, for what it is worth, that at about the time of Constantine III a rebellion in Britain led to the expulsion of much of the remaining Roman garrison.[1] As far as new settlers in Britain are concerned, contemporary or near contemporary sources are more or less silent. The *Anglo-Saxon Chronicle*, first written down in the late ninth century, tells us that in 449 a British ruler named, or with the title of, Vortigern invited groups of Angles – from Angeln in southern Denmark – to settle in Britain on condition that they fought for him against the Picts. In this case they would presumably have settled on land north of the Humber. In any event, this is why fifth-century Germanic settlers in the Yorkshire region are often referred to as the Angles (from which 'Anglian') rather than Anglo-Saxons.

A question which immediately arises when considering the early fifth century is how was Britain now governed? Did some sort of Roman structure survive? Did the *civitates* continue to form a basis for administration with a curial class able to continue exercising its authority and raising revenue on the basis of legitimacy inherited from Rome? Alternatively, was the inheritance of Roman power seized by local autocrats simply able to command sufficient numbers of armed warriors, rather in the manner of an Iron Age chieftain, and impose their will on territories of varying and shifting size, and exact tribute from them? Either route could have been the basis for the creation of new political units such as that thought to have existed until the early seventh century in west Yorkshire, known as the Kingdom of Elmet.[2] The principal historical source for Elmet is the Venerable Bede who was writing at Jarrow in the eighth century. In addition, however, there is a certain amount of place-name evidence which scholars have used to define the boundaries of Elmet. There is also a remarkable sixth-century memorial stone of one Aliortus, a man of Elmet, found at Llanaelheaer in north Wales.[3] Elmet is assumed to have been a Christian polity – its people continuing to worship in the late Roman manner, but whether there was still a bishop at York is unknown. Nine place-names in what is thought to have been Elmet derive from the Latin word *ecclesia* meaning a church. Examples, on the western side of Elmet, near Bradford, include Eccleshill and fields named Great and Little Eccles at Allerton. Another post-Roman British polity has been identified in Craven, largely on the basis of its survival as a distinct territorial unit in the late Anglo-Saxon period;[4] others may have existed but are now lost to history.

Settlement and population

If we consider the question of settlement in the fifth century, and how the pattern changed after the end of the Roman period, a fundamental question is whether population size changed greatly. Did any new settlers from Angeln or anywhere else find great swathes of more or less empty landscape? In the absence of reliable archaeological data, any estimate of fifth-century population becomes very difficult. However, as we have seen, one could be forgiven for concluding that the population of the Yorkshire region had been in decline during the second half of the fourth century. Are we now to believe that a near absence of material culture which can be ascribed to the fifth century is to be equated with a further decline in population or, alternatively, with a collapse of all but the most fundamental of subsistence and craft activities which leave few archaeological traces?

In some circumstances a useful indicator of changes in the size of an ancient population, if not its absolute level, might be derived from burials. However, although there may be fifth-century burials in the Roman cemeteries at York and other places, none has yet been identified for certain. It has been suggested that the tradition of cist burial which is known in parts of Yorkshire in the fourth century continued into the fifth and beyond, but there is little conclusive evidence for this and in any event numbers of them are small. Radiocarbon dating has, none the less, begun to identify inhumations of the 'Elmet period' as in the case of a couple found at Ferrybridge (Illus. 4.7, Phase 5),[5] and three more at Parlington Hollins (near Leeds);[6] others may eventually come to light giving us a bit more information on population, but it is unlikely that this will ever allow a satisfactory estimate of numbers to be arrived at.

Although descendants of late Roman Britain may be hard to find, it is through their cemeteries, with burials often accompanied by distinctive items of material culture, that the Germanic settlers in Yorkshire announce themselves. In their pagan world burial provided an opportunity for statements about identity and status in which, fortunately for archaeologists, pottery, jewellery and other items had a part to play. It seems clear that the Humber estuary exerted a powerful attraction on these settlers who used it to gain access to the land drained by its tributaries. On the Yorkshire (north) side of the Humber the largest – extending over *c.*10ha – and most important early Anglo-Saxon cemeteries, probably serving a large part of east Yorkshire, lay at Sancton.[7] This is on Humber Street, the Brough on Humber–Malton Roman road, just to the north of the junction with the road to York and just below the western edge of the Wolds. Based on comparison of the ceramics in the cemetery with those in the Anglian homelands, the earliest burials at Sancton are thought to be of the early fifth century. Numbers of burials steadily increased, especially after the middle of the century. Other east Yorkshire cemeteries, in which the earliest burials are thought to be of fifth- or sixth century date are known on the northern edge of the Wolds at West Heslerton[8] and on the coast at Hornsea.[9]

Illus. 11.1 Bainbridge: the line of the Roman road across the Pennines to Ribchester looking west.
(Photo: P. Ottaway)

The fifth and sixth centuries: continuity and change

Whilst the Sancton cemetery testifies to the continuing importance of the Roman road network in Yorkshire, there is, as yet, little good evidence for Anglian settlement anywhere in Yorkshire before the late fifth and sixth centuries. However, there are places where settlement continuity from the late Roman to the Anglian period can be inferred. A brief survey may begin at York itself where the earliest post-Roman archaeological evidence takes the form of two small, late fifth- /early sixth-century cremation cemeteries. There was one on The Mount (south-west of the Ouse) and another at Heworth (north-east of the Ouse); they were both in areas previously used for Roman burial and, like Sancton, close to Roman roads which may explain their location rather than any continuity of funerary associations, somehow maintained over at least 100 years.[10] Where had the dead been living? Were the former fortress and urban areas deserted? These are impossible questions to answer. One would imagine the Roman defences and other infrastructure at York exerted some attraction for any local lord wishing to cast himself as Rome's heir. However, excavations have so far failed to help us test this idea. For example, at the Minster, in the heart of the former legionary fortress, archaeology is silent from the early fifth until, perhaps, the late seventh or eighth centuries, although we know from Bede that in the year 627 King Edwin of Northumbria was baptised in York

and built himself a wooden church. At Wellington Row, by the Roman river crossing immediately south-west of the Ouse, the archaeology has yet to be fully analysed and published. However, unlike many other sites in York there was no major ground clearance or pit digging in medieval times within the shell of the stone building, originally of the mid-second century. There was a complex sequence of deposits representing refuse disposal and cultivation, as well as natural accumulation, after the latest identifiably Roman level. This sequence may belong, in part at least, to the fifth–seventh centuries before the adaptation of the surviving Roman walls for a timber structure.[11]

At the two *civitas* capitals in Yorkshire, at Aldborough and Brough on Humber, the archaeological evidence is more or less non-existent for the early Anglian period, although, for the benefit of any local lord, the walls of both places presumably remained standing, if in a derelict condition, for a considerable period of time. Aldborough is thought by some scholars to have been the '*municipium*' described by Bede as held in 633–35 by Caswallon of Gwynedd where he was besieged by Osric of Northumberland whom he later killed.[12] At Catterick there may have been continuity of settlement from the Roman period, although the earliest post-Roman archaeological evidence appears to belong to the sixth rather than the fifth century. Anglian pottery and a brooch were found in the fill of the town ditch which may derive from settlement within the walls.[13] Outside the walls a structure was found at Catterick Triangle and there were Anglian burials at Bainesse and Catterick Bridge.[14] Catterick's continuing importance is also suggested on the basis of written sources, although the earliest is *The Gododdin*, thought to have been written in the seventh century by the poet Aneirin. This refers to a battle, probably of c.600 at *Catraeth*, fought unsuccessfully against the Angles by a British expedition originating near Edinburgh. Bede refers to Catterick as a royal vill of Northumbria which suggests a place of long-established importance.

Outside the principal Roman settlements, it is in rural areas of east Yorkshire that one may most readily see continuity of settlement from the late Roman to the Anglian period on archaeological grounds, primarily because of the relative abundance of pottery compared to other parts of the region. An important site for the study of continuity is Crossgates, Seamer (near Scarborough) where, as we have already seen, there was an extensive late Roman settlement, but immediately to the west of it there were a number of Anglian houses and additional hearths. They may have been within buildings of which no other remains survive.[15] The earliest of an appreciable quantity of pottery is thought be fifth century and speaks of a slight shift of settlement in about 400–50. At the foot of the Wolds at West Heslerton a settlement contemporary with the early Anglian cemetery was excavated and appears to have directly succeeded one of the Late Roman period.[16] A similar picture of the typical Anglo-Saxon structures with sunken floors (*Grubenhäuser*) on or closely adjacent to late Roman settlement has emerged on the Wolds at Caythorpe[17] and on an east facing slope 1km south of Kilham village.[18] On the North

Manor site at Wharram Percy the trackway which had been a feature of the landscape throughout the Roman period probably continued to function until two structures dated to the sixth century were dug into it.[19]

Quite how the local British people and incoming Anglians interacted is difficult to determine. Philip Corder commenting on the Anglian pottery and other artefacts from Elmswell, another site where continuity of settlement after the end of the Roman period is likely, suggested:

> It is on just such a native site as this where one might expect to find the enslavement of a sub-Roman population. They had never been deeply Romanized and would exchange one master for another without serious dislocation of their way of life.[20]

Whether enslavement was the context for relations or not is unknown, but it is quite possible that a small warrior elite was able to assume control of a population descended from native stock who simply adopted the material culture and customs, with regard to burial for example, of their new overlords.

To conclude, the history of Yorkshire in the 100 years or so after what we usually think of as the end of Britain's inclusion in the Roman Empire remains obscure, although new archaeological evidence is gradually shedding light where previously there was precious little. For much of the region it was apparently a period when a small and fugitive population sought to come to terms with the final stages of the collapse of a political and economic system which had ensured peace and a measure of prosperity, even in remote areas, for over three hundred years. In the Pennines and central lowlands there may have been a brief interlude when independent British political units assumed the mantle of Rome, but in the east of the county – the nucleus of the Anglian kingdom of Deira – the natives soon had to come to terms with a dynamic new and alien elite intent on settlement, reorganisation of landholding and introduction of new social customs.

However different in character Yorkshire may have seemed in 600 from what it had been in 400, the impact of Rome would not disappear completely in our region. In due course important Roman settlements usually became important settlements once again. We can see evidence for this in the names of places which betray their Roman past, such as, for example, Aldborough ('the old fortification'), and Doncaster and Tadcaster which incorporate 'caster' derived from Latin *castra*, a camp. Many Roman roads also survived as routeways, even if they were not well maintained, because they provided a well-drained ridge of fairly solid material which could be traversed in most weather conditions. In 1789 Gough's edition of Camden's *Britannia* could describe the Roman road from Castleford to Tadcaster at Hazel Wood, about 1km north of Aberford, as 'in many places exceeding perfect' and it can still be seen as a mound *c.*11m wide and 1m high. There are also place-names which include 'le street', such as Adwick le Street, near Doncaster, or Appleton le Street, near Malton, which refer to Roman roads remaining in use many years after the end of the fourth

century. Another vehicle for continuity was the Christian church. In spite of there being a brief period in which there were probably few if any Christians in the Yorkshire region, when the faith returned in strength sites which were inhabited and defendable were chosen for churches. This can be seen, for example, at Doncaster and Ilkley where the parish churches stand within the former forts, and in particular at York where the Minster stands in the centre of the legionary fortress.

York was still referred to as *Eboracum* on maps well over 1000 years after it had lost its status as provincial capital, although the name was refashioned by both the Anglians – as *Eoforwic* – and the Vikings – as *Jorvik* – to create the modern version. The original Latin also survives today in various contexts often abbreviated to 'Ebor'. They include the signature of the Archbishop who uses his Christian name followed by Ebor, in recognition of Eborius, the first of his line. However, more important even than Eborius was a decision taken for strategic purposes by a Roman general in about the year 71, nearly two thousand years ago. This would create a central place in the economic, political and social geography of a region which was, in due course, to take its name and become Yorkshire.

References

Abbreviations

Eburacum   Royal Commission on Historical Monuments for England, 1962.
An Inventory of the Historical Monuments in the City of York: 1,
Eburacum, Roman York

RIB I   Collingwood, R. G. and Wright, R. P. 1965. *The Roman Inscriptions
of Britain* I

RIB II, 1   Frere, S. S., Roxan, M. and Tomlin, R. S. O. (eds) 1990. *The Roman
Inscriptions of Britain* II, *Instrumentum Domesticum*, fascicule 1

RIB III   Tomlin, R. S. O., Wright, R. P. and Hassall, M. W. C. 2009. *The
Roman Inscriptions of Britain*, III

Tab. Vindol. II (*Tabulae Vindolandenses II*).
Bowman, A. and Thomas, J.D. 1994. *The Vindolanda Writing
Tablets*

Notes and references

Chapter 1
1. *Annals* XII, 32; Wilson 2009.
2. *Annals* XII, 40.
3. *Histories* III, 45.

Chapter 2
1. Raistrick 1935; Frere and St Joseph 1983, 215–16.
2. Rivet and Smith 1979, 493.
3. Halkon and Millett 1999, 75–81; Halkon 2012; www.ironmasters.hull.ac.uk.
4. Buckland and Gaunt 2003.
5. King 1974, 199–200; Dearne and Lord 1998.
6. Buckland 1976a, 33–5; 1988; Phillips 1995, 41.
7. Buckland 1988, 249–53.
8. ibid., 255–60.
9. Monaghan 1997, 869; Swan and McBride 2002, 190–1.
10. Hall and Kenward 1990, 413–14.
11. Buckland 1976a, 36–7; 1988, 262–5.
12. *Strabo* IV, 5, 2.
13. Bridgland et al. 2011, 266.
14. Lamb 1981, 56.
15. Kenward et al. 1986, 265.

16. van de Noort 2004, 107–12.
17. Williams 1979, 57–60; Bastow 1999, 176; Huntley 2002, 439.
18. Fleming 1998, 138.
19. Yarwood 1981, 50–3; Berg 2001.
20. Simmons et al. 1982, 44.
21. Close et al. 1975, 67.
22. Roberts 2010, 61.
23. Hall and Kenward 1990; Bastow 1999.
24. Bastow and Murray 1990, 266.

25. Hall and Kenward 1990.
26. Stallibrass 2002, 400.
27. O'Connor 1988; Berg 1990, 256.
28. Stallibrass 2002, 400.
29. O'Connor 1988, 100-02.
30. Dobney et al. 2000, 157–8.
31. Stallibrass 2002, 401.
32. O'Connor 1988, 115–16.
33. Hall and Kenward 1990, 419.
34. Sudell 1990.

Chapter 3

1. *Strabo* IV, 5, 2.
2. *Annals* XII, 32.
3. *Annals* XII, 40.
4. *Histories* III, 45.
5. Jones and Mattingly 1990, 18–23.
6. ibid., 23–9.
7. *Epitome of Cassius Dio* LXXVI, 15.
8. RIB 1, *2274*.
9. RIB 1, *618*.
10. Tomlin 1986; RIB III, *3195*.
11. *Eburacum*; RIB III, *3201–3*.
12. RIB I, *720*.
13. Wenham 1960, 298–306; RIB III, *3209*.
14. *Eburacum*, 124, *82*; RIB I, *688*.
15. *Eburacum*, 122, *75*; Rinaldi Tufi 1983, 29, *44*.
16. Neal 1996, 45, fig.31, 1.
17. Morris 1998, 335–7, fig.152, 1–3.
18. Allason-Jones 2006, 238, illus. 10.7, *211–12*.
19. Bowman 1994.
20. Inventory nos 575, 1220, Birley 2002, 38.
21. *Tab. Vindol. II*, 185.
22. *Tab. Vindol. II*, 185; *Tab. Vindol. II*, 343.
23. RIB II, 1, *2401.6*.
24. Tomlin 2008, 381–4.
25. Wright 1976; 1978.
26. RIB II, 1, *2404.61–4*.
27. RIB II, 1, *2411.97*.
28. RIB II, 1, *2411.35*.
29. Kitson Clark 1935, 129; RIB II, 1,

2415.4 and *2415.19*.
30. *Eburacum*, 134, *147*.
31. Buckland et al. 1980, 154–5.
32. RIB II, 1, *2419.131*.
33. *Eburacum*, 133, *143*.
34. Hassall and Tomlin 1987, 373–4.
35. Robertson 2000.
36. Jones 2007, 47–8.
37. Ling 1992.
38. Stead 1979.
39. James 1993, 1–17; Collis 2003.
40. *De Bello Gallico* V, 2.
41. Birley 1979, 121–2.
42. Richmond 1925, 57–9; Purdy and Manby 1973, 96.
43. RIB I, *627*.
44. RIB I, *725*, *727*.
45. Gilyard-Beer 1951, 72.
46. Roy 1793.
47. Faull 1981a, 143–5.
48. MacGregor 1962.
49. *Eburacum*, 119, *54*; Rinaldi Tufi 1983, 11, *21*.
50. Ecroyd Smith 1852.
51. Kitson Clark 1935, 121–2.
52. Fitts 2009.
53. Kitson Clark 1935, 99–100, map after p.59.
54. RAI 1846.
55. MacLauchlan 1849.
56. Barber 1870; Dodd and Woodward 1922, 8.
57. May 1922, 14.
58. Procter 1855.

59. Lukis 1875.
60. Corder and Kirk 1932.
61. Kitson Clark 1935, 104–5.
62. *Eburacum*, 80–92.
63. May 1922.
64. Miller 1925; 1928.
65. Corder 1930a.
66. Corder and Richmond 1942.
67. Droop 1929; 1930; 1932.
68. Woodward 1925.
69. Simpson 1926; Richmond 1933.
70. Collingwood 1931.
71. Hildyard and Wade 1950.
72. Myres et al. 1959.
73. Corder and Kirk 1932.
74. Congreve 1937; 1938; Corder 1940.
75. Corder 1930b.
76. Wright 1946, 383.
77. Slack 1951.
78. Phillips and Heywood 1995.
79. Wade 1952; Hartley 1960.
80. Frere and Hartley 2009.
81. Rosser 1958; Thompson 1974.
82. Buckland 1978; 1986, 12–18.
83. Frere and Fitts 2009.
84. Hunter et al. 1967.
85. Wacher 1969.
86. Wilson 2002a, 46–121.
87. Mitchelson 1964; Wenham and Heywood 1997.
88. Frere and St Joseph 1983; Riley 1980.
89. Brewster 1980; Dent 1983.

90. Hayes 1988.
91. Stead 1980.
92. Neal 1996.
93. Wrathmell and Nicholson 1990.
94. Hartley and Fitts 1988, 75–84.
95. Loughlin and Miller 1979; Faull and Moorhouse 1981.
96. Haselgrove et al. 1990a; 1990b; Welfare et al. 1990; Frere 1989, 277–8; Frere 1990, 323–5.
97. Abramson et al. 1999.
98. Redhead et al. 1989.
99. Johnson 1978.
100. Fitts 2009, 205.
101. Lee 1997; Wilson et al. 2003.
102. Goodburn 1978, 429, pl. 23A; Buckland 1986, 8–9, 11.
103. Bewley and Macleod 1993.
104. Bishop 2005.
105. White 1997, 36, pl. 23.
106. Whitwell 1976.
107. Ottaway 1996.
108. Carver et al. 1978; Ottaway 2004.
109. Ottaway 2011.
110. Roberts et al. 2001.
111. Brown et al. 2007.
112. Beresford and Hurst 1990, 69–76; Rahtz and Watts 2004.
113. Powlesland 1988; 2003.
114. Halkon 1989; 1990; 1999a; 1999b; 2003; 2008; Halkon and Millett 1999.
115. Margary 1973.

Chapter 4

1. Buckland 1986, 8, fig.6.
2. *Annals* XII, 36, 40.
3. *Agricola* 17.
4. Rivet and Smith 1979, 278–80.
5. Hartley and Fitts 1988, 4–6.
6. Ramm 1978, 21; Spratt 1993, 152.
7. Evans 1995; Rigby 2004.
8. Rigby 1993.
9. *Annals* XII, 31–7.
10. Riley 1980; Stoertz 1997; Horne 2003; Taylor 2007; Roberts 2010, 20–35.
11. Fleming 1998, 133–42; Laurie 2011.
12. Raistrick 1939.
13. Raistrick 1935.
14. Martlew 2011.
15. Johnson 2004.
16. King 1978; 1986, 183; 2011.
17. King 1970a, 61; 1986, 182.
18. Moorhouse 2003.
19. Beswick and Merrills 1983.

20. Dolby 1981; Latham 1993; ASWYAS 2005a.
21. Northamptonshire Archaeology 2001.
22. ASWYAS 2002; 2003.
23. Roberts and Richardson 2002.
24. Timms 2005.
25. Howell 2001.
26. Roberts 2010.
27. WYAS 1991; Martin et al. forthcoming.
28. Roberts et al. 2001.
29. Richardson 2005.
30. Dearne and Parsons 1997, 84–5.
31. Still and Vyner 1986, 13, 16; Still et al. 1989, 4.
32. Harding 1984; Cool and Mason 2008, 295.
33. Carne 2001; ASDU 2008.
34. Inman 1988.
35. Sherlock 2012.
36. NAA 2002a.
37. Whyman and Howard 2005, 22–5.
38. Horne 2003.
39. Jones 1988; 1990.
40. http://www.york.ac.uk/campus-development/expansion/archaeology/.
41. Pearson 1996.
42. Halkon and Millett 1999; Halkon 2003; 2008.
43. Roberts 2003.
44. Riley 1980, 12; Roberts 2010, 20–2.
45. Riley 1976, 16.
46. Atkinson 1993–94.
47. Richardson 2008.
48. Magilton 1978.
49. ASWYAS 2006a.
50. ASWYAS 2005b.
51. Jones et al. 2007.
52. Inman et al. 1985.
53. Hayes 1966; Close et al. 1975.
54. Hayes 1983.
55. ASWYAS 2006b.
56. Stoertz 1997, 51–3.
57. Brewster 1980; Dent 1983.
58. Ramm 1978, 18–19; Stoertz 1997, 73, fig.37.
59. Powlesland 1988, 140–1; 2003, 282, fig.88.
60. Roberts 2009.
61. Fenton-Thomas 2009.
62. Fenton-Thomas 2011.
63. Didsbury 1999, 45–6.
64. Tibbles 2002; 2003.
65. Didsbury 1988, 24; 1989.
66. Evans and Atkinson 2009, 249–51.
67. Harding 2009, Chapter 8.
68. Wrathmell and Nicholson 1990, 276–9.
69. Inman et al. 1985.
70. King 1986, 182.
71. Haselgrove et al. 1990a; 1990b; Welfare et al. 1990.
72. Wheeler 1954.
73. Frere 1989, 277–8; Frere 1990, 323–5.
74. Evans 1995, 54–5; Willis 1996, 202–3.
75. *Histories* III, 45.
76. MacGregor 1962.
77. Fitts et al. 1999.
78. Abramson 1995.
79. *De Bello Gallico* I, 1.
80. Thompson 1993.
81. Wheeler 1954, 19.
82. Rees 1979, 79–91.
83. King 1986, 187.
84. Huntley 2002, 439.
85. Murray 1990; Reynolds 1979.
86. O'Connor and van der Veen 1998, 130.
87. Reynolds 1979.
88. Cool 2009, 17.
89. Hillman 1981.
90. Heslop 2009, 48.
91. Berg 1990, 175.
92. Stead 1991, Chapter 4.
93. Tylecote 1986, 142–52.
94. Halkon and Millett 1999, 75–81; Clogg 1999; Halkon 2012.
95. Inman et al. 1985, 198, 204.
96. Hayes 1983, 22.
97. Evans 1995, 53.

98. Leary 2009.
99. MAP 2001.
100. Heslop 2009, 37.
101. Gwilt and Heslop 1995; Heslop 2009, Chapter 6.
102. Bohannon and Dalton 1962.
103. Corder and Pryce 1938; Crowther et al. 1989; 1990.
104. May 1992.
105. Evans 2005.
106. Richmond 1925, 14; May 1992, 95–6.
107. Corder and Hawkes 1940.
108. King 1970b, 411, fig.1a; www.britishmuseum.org/research/search-the-collection-database.
109. Bishop 1996, 6, fig.3, *3*.
110. Richmond 1954, 50.
111. Stead 1988.
112. Lane Fox 1986, 30.
113. *De Bello Gallico* I, 1.
114. *Germania* IX.
115. Green 1986, 14–17.
116. *Natural History* XXX, 13.
117. Green 2001, 87–9.
118. Evans 2006; Marchant and Halkon 2008.
119. Legge 1991.
120. Stead 1991.
121. Brewster 1980; Dent 1983.
122. Raistrick 1939, 126–8.
123. ASWYAS 2004.
124. Haselgrove et al. 1990b, 63–4.
125. Brown et al. 2007, 99–103.
126. Sumpter and Marriott 2005, 5–12.
127. Richardson 2005.
128. Stead 1965, 22–3.
129. Crowther et al. 1989, 8.
130. ASWYAS 2005c.
131. Roe 2009.
132. Cunliffe 2005, 593.

Chapter 5

1. *Histories* III, 45.
2. Birley 1981, 66–8.
3. Wright and Tomlin 1995, 246; RIB III, *3201*.
4. RIB 1, *638*.
5. RIB 1, *649*.
6. *Eburacum*, 122, *75*; Rinaldi Tufi 1983, 29, *44*.
7. Feugère 2002, 140–2.
8. Bishop 1998, 64–6, fig.20.
9. Buckland 1978.
10. Bishop 1998, 62–3.
11. King 1970a, 48; 1970b.
12. Scott 1998, 130, fig.45, 3–5.
13. Webster 1971.
14. Berg 1999, 236.
15. King 1970a, 46–7; White 1997, 40.
16. RIB II, 1, 2404.61–2.
17. RIB II, 1, 2404.63–4.
18. *Agricola* 17.
19. *Tab. Vindol.* II 164, Bowman 1994, 106.
20. Wacher 1969, 76–81.
21. Johnson 1978; Ramm 1978, 31–3.
22. White 1964.
23. Buckland and Magilton 1986, 11–12.
24. ASWYAS 2008a; 2008b.
25. Roberts 2010, 37, 67–8, fig.48.
26. Abramson 1999a.
27. Buckland 1986, 8, 11, fig.7.
28. Bewley and Macleod 1993.
29. Alcock 1954; Wheelhouse 2001, 144–8.
30. Boutwood 1996.
31. Bishop 2005.
32. NAA 2006.
33. Wilson 2002a, 447.
34. St Joseph 1955, 82.
35. Brickstock et al. 2007.
36. NAA 2002a.
37. Welfare and Swan 1995, 136.
38. Gates and Ainsworth 2008.
39. Welfare and Swan 1995, 57–60; Vyner 2001, 76–87.
40. Welfare and Swan 1995, 143–5.
41. Horne and Lawton 1998; Burnham et al. 2000, 395.

42. Welfare and Swan 1995, 145.
43. F. Wild 2002.
44. Wilson 2002a.
45. Cool and Mason 2008, 297–301.
46. Frere and Hartley 2009.
47. White 1988, 36, pl. 23.
48. Faull 1981a, 143–5.
49. ASWYAS 2006c.
50. Hartley 1987.
51. May 1911.
52. Dodd and Woodward 1922; Hunter et al. 1967.
53. Lunn et al. 2008.
54. Redhead et al. 1989.
55. Ramm 1978, 31–5.
56. Corder 1930a; Robinson 1978; P. Wilson 2006.
57. Bidwell and Hodgson 2009, 164–5; Wilson forthcoming.
58. Richmond 1933; Lee 1997; Wilson et al. 2003.
59. Hayes and Rutter 1964, 47–54.
60. Fitts 2009, 279.
61. *Histories* I, 2.
62. Hartley 1960.
63. *Eburacum*, 114.
64. Hanson 1978.
65. Wilson 1969.
66. Phillips 1995.
67. May 1922, 36–9.
68. Woodward 1925, fig.11.
69. *Eburacum*, 40–1; Ottaway 1996.
70. Dodd and Woodward 1922, 28–30.
71. Wacher 1969, 18.
72. Johnson 1978, 75.
73. Anderson 1992, Appendix H.
74. Abramson 1999a, 87–9.
75. Kenward and Williams 1979; Hall 1986.

76. Whitwell 1976.
77. Buckland 1976b.
78. Wilson 2002a, 48–50.
79. Abramson 1999a, 28–37.
80. May 1922, 48.
81. Ottaway 1996, 189–91.
82. May 1922, 17.
83. Dodd and Woodward 1922, 11.
84. Wilson et al. 2003.
85. Corder and Richmond 1942, 6, fig.3.
86. Corder 1930a.
87. Ottaway 1996, 286–7.
88. *Eburacum*, 111, 1; RIB I, 665.
89. Hunter-Mann 2009.
90. Adam 1989, 155.
91. Wilson 2002a, 51.
92. *Eburacum*, xxxiv.
93. Hunter et al. 1967; Wilson 1969, 207; ASWYAS 1997.
94. Wilson 2002a; Brickstock et al. 2007.
95. Bishop 2005.
96. Abramson 1999b.
97. ASWYAS 2008b.
98. Wenham and Heywood 1997, 7–9.
99. Riley 1980, 25; Roberts 2010, 70–1.
100. Wilson 2002a, 217–19; NAA 2004.
101. Fitzpatrick and Scott 1999, 115; Cool and Mason 2008, 96.
102. Ottaway 2004, 50–1.
103. Millett and Taylor 2006, 42.
104. Wroe 1982, 67.
105. Thackrah 1967; O'Neill 2001.
106. van de Noort 2004, 112.
107. Lunn et al. 2008.
108. Fitzpatrick and Scott 1999.
109. White 1964.

Chapter 6

1. Millett 1990, 181–6.
2. Fitts et al. 1994.
3. Hall and Kenward 1990.
4. Jones 1998; 1990.
5. Mason 1988, 163–6, 184–9.
6. Ramm 1976a.

7. Martin 2005.
8. Corder and Kirk 1932; Ramm 1978, 73–4.
9. Ramm 1978, 74–5.
10. Brewster 1957.
11. Mitchelson 1950; Rutter and Duke

1958; Pye 1976.

12. MAP 1999; Stephens 2000.
13. Mackey 1999.
14. Fenton-Thomas 2011.
15. NAA 2002b.
16. Reece 2002, 115.
17. Kenward and Williams 1979.
18. Johnson 2005.
19. Bastow 1999, 175.
20. Mabey 1972.
21. Rees 1979, 473–9.
22. Berg 1999.
23. Monk 1978.
24. Monaghan 1997, 869–70; Swan and McBride 2002, 193.
25. Purdy and Manby 1973; Swan 1984, 89.
26. Evans 2002, 248.
27. Jones 1971, 59–60; Swan 2002, 35.
28. Dungworth 2002.
29. Bayley and Budd 1998, 203–22.
30. May 1922, 57.
31. van Driel-Murray 1998.
32. Hooley 2002.
33. *Tab. Vindol. II* 343; Birley 2002, 92–3.
34. Morris 1998.
35. J. Wild 2002, 5.
36. Greep 1997, 144–5.
37. Turner et al. 1991.
38. Sitch 1989; 1990.
39. Dickinson and Hartley 1993.
40. Cool and Price 1998.
41. Williams 1990.
42. Hopkins 1980, 102.
43. Mould 1998, 122, fig.43, *13*.
44. Lentowicz 2002, 69, fig.262, *9*.

45. Rinaldi Tufi 1983, 62–3, *105*, Mattern 1989, 719.
46. Jackson 1973.
47. Henig 1976; 1995.
48. Cool 1998, 31, fig.10.
49. Johns 1996, 151–3, 183–4.
50. Beswick et al. 1990.
51. RIB I, *623, 627–8, 630*.
52. RIB I, *635*.
53. *Eburacum*, 116, 32; RIB I, *659*.
54. *Eburacum*, 114–15, *29*; Rinaldi Tufi 1983, 3, *6*.
55. Rinaldi Tufi 1983, 21, *35*.
56. *Eburacum*, 133, *142*.
57. RIB I, *708*.
58. *Eburacum*, 115–16, *30–1*; RIB I, *650–1*.
59. RIB I, *622*.
60. RIB I, *730*.
61. Barber 1870; RIB I, *624*.
62. Rinaldi Tufi 1983, 62–3, *105*.
63. Turcan 1996, 37ff.
64. Mortimer 1905, 194–8.
65. Kitson Clark 1935.
66. Moore 2008, 36–7.
67. Ottaway 2011, 351.
68. *Eburacum*, 69; Spall and Toop 2005.
69. *Eburacum*, 72.
70. Wenham 1965, 531.
71. Barber 1870, 2; Richmond 1925, 44–5.
72. Bishop 2005, 158.
73. RIB I, *680*; *Eburacum*, 126, *91*.
74. RIB I, *621*; Rinaldi Tufi 1983, 62, *104*.
75. Mattingly 2006, 3.

Chapter 7

1. *Eburacum*, 47; Welfare and Swan 1995, 135–6.
2. Johnson 2005.
3. Frere and Hartley 2009, 49–53; RIB I, *739*.
4. *Epitome of Cassius Dio* LXXII, 8.
5. Philips 1995; Hall 1997, 331–55.
6. *Eburacum*, 8–12; Ottaway 1996,

197–9.
7. RIB I, *283*.
8. RIB I, *636*.
9. Hartley 1963, 32.
10. May 1911, 144; Bidwell and Hodgson 2009, 27, 104–5.
11. Hartley 1960; Bidwell and Hodgson 2009, 108–9.

12. Wilson 2002a, 58, 76.
13. RIB I, *725–6*.
14. Buckland 1978, 247.
15. May 1922; McCoy 2008.
16. Corder 1930a; Bidwell and Hodgson 2009, 165.
17. Wenham and Heywood 1997, 39; RIB III, *3207*.
18. Fitzpatrick and Scott 1999.
19. Bishop and Coulston 1989, 50–3, Feugère 2002, 115–22.
20. RIB II, 3, *2429.6*; Bishop 1996, 67–8, fig. 37, *422–7*.
21. *Eburacum*, 58–61; Brinklow et al. 1986.
22. *Eburacum*, 119, *52*; RIB I, *656*.
23. *Eburacum*, 61.
24. Ottaway 2004, 90–4.
25. Cool 2002.
26. Hall and Kenward 1990.
27. *Eburacum*, 53, 116, *35*.
28. Ottaway 2004, 110–11.
29. Ramm 1976; Carver and Sumpter 1978.
30. Brinklow and Donaghey 1986.
31. *Eburacum*, 49.
32. Ottaway 2011, 279–90.
33. *Eburacum*, 49.
34. Ottaway 2011, 370–3ff.
35. *Eburacum*, 128, *96*, Rinaldi Tufi 1983, 37–8, *56*.
36. McComish 2011; Ottaway 2011, 352.
37. Breeze 2005.
38. Myres et al. 1959; Charlesworth 1971; Jones 1971; Snape et al. 2002.
39. Dobinson 1987–88; 1988–89.
40. Myres et al. 1959, 11, 14, 17.
41. Neal and Cosh 2002, 311–14, *123. 13–14*.
42. Snape et al. 2002, 59.
43. Myres et al. 1959, 55–8.
44. Ferraby and Millett 2012.
45. Wacher 1969, 27.
46. RIB I, *707*; Corder and Richmond 1942, 37.
47. Halkon 2008, 192.
48. Corder and Romans 1939; Corder and Richmond 1942, 18–19; Wacher 1969, 59–71.
49. Hunter-Mann 2000; Evans and Steedman 2001, 77–9.
50. Fraser and Brigham 2009.
51. Goodburn 1978, 427; 1979, 287.
52. Carlton 2008; Frere and Fitts 2009.
53. Casey and Hoffman 1998.
54. Hartley 1987, 24–34.
55. Faul 1981a, 144; JRS 1958, 136.
56. Wilson 2002a, 122–37.
57. NAA 2004.
58. Blagg 2002, 297–9.
59. Abramson 1999b, 132–4; Hartley 2000.
60. Frere 1989, 278; Cool 2005.
61. Buckland and Magilton 1986.
62. Wenham and Heywood 1997, 9; P. Wilson 2006.
63. Dean 2001.
64. Robinson 1978, 7, 28, *119*; Wenham and Heywood 1997, 11–13.
65. MAP 1994, 28–9.
66. Robinson 1978, 7–8; Hayes 1988, 66–89.
67. Cool and Mason 2008, 302.
68. Scott and Large 2008, 124.
69. NAA 2006; Ross and Ambry 2010.
70. Lawton 1994a; 1994b; 1997.
71. NAA 2005.
72. Adams 2007.
73. Lawton 2005.
74. Fraser et al. 2000.
75. Evans and Steedman 2001, 81–2.
76. MAP 2004.
77. Burnham et al. 2001, 341, fig.14; Evans and Steedman 2001, 82–3; Easthaugh et al. in prep.
78. Millett and Taylor 2006.
79. Fleming 1998, 141.
80. Thorp 1974, 145; White 1997, 41.
81. Hartley and Fitts 1988, 74–85.
82. Dearne and Lord 1998.
83. Beswick and Merrills 1983.
84. Makepeace 1984.
85. Dolby 1981, 60.

86. WYAS 1995; Howell 2001.
87. Burgess and Roberts 2004.
88. Lukis 1875; Branigan 1980, 22–3.
89. Gilyard-Beer 1951.
90. Wrathmell and Nicholson 1990.
91. WYAS 1991; Martin et al. forthcoming.
92. Holbrey and Burgess 2001.
93. Brown et al. 2007.
94. Roberts 2005.
95. Sumpter 1973; Ramm 1980.
96. Radley and Plant 1969.
97. Annis 1996; Sherlock 2012, 167.
98. Annis 1992–93.
99. ASDU 2008a.
100. Harding 1984; 2008; 2009, 162–5.
101. NAA 1994.
102. Roberts 2003.
103. Richardson 2008.
104. Atkinson 1993–94; Chadwick and Cumberpatch 1994–95.
105. NAA 2007a.
106. Close et al. 1975, 64–5.
107. Neal 1996, 13.
108. Ramm 1978, 76–7.
109. Corder and Kirk 1932, 57–8.
110. Ramm 1978, 80–6.
111. Brewster 1980.
112. Stoertz 1997, map 2.
113. Stead 1980, 17–19.
114. Mackey 1999.
115. Roberts 2009.
116. Fenton-Thomas 2009.
117. Westwood 2009.
118. Evans and Atkinson 2009, 249–51.
119. Didsbury 1988; 1989; 1990.
120. Crowther and Didsbury 1985.
121. Evans 2000.
122. Hall and Kenward 1990, 410–11.
123. Aldritt 2005.
124. Huntley 2002, 439.
125. Hall and Kenward 1990, 404.
126. Manning 1964; 1984, 143–4.
127. Tweddle 1986, 195–7.
128. Manning 1964, 56–7.
129. Wenham 1966; Wilson 1989, 99–103.
130. Martin 2005, 117–21.
131. Fenton-Thomas 2009, 232–7.
132. Reynolds and Langley 1979.
133. van der Veen 1989, 313.
134. O'Connor 1988.
135. Berg 1999.
136. Meddens 2002a; 2002b.
137. Bates et al. 2007.
138. Gidney 2008.
139. O'Connor 1988, 83.
140. Hall and Kenward 1990, 409.
141. *Eburacum*, 114, *19*.
142. PRS 2011.
143. Stallibrass 2002, 409.
144. Berg 1999, 236.
145. Lawton 1992–93; Monaghan 1997, 870–1.
146. Swan 2002, 49; Swan and McBride 2002, 193.
147. Annable 1954; Gilmour 1954; Cregeen 1957; Buckland 1976c; Buckland et al. 1980; Swan 1984, 105–8.
148. Corder 1958.
149. Corder 1930b; Halkon 1983; Halkon and Milllett 1999; Swan 2002, 63.
150. Swan 2002, 63.
151. Cool 2002.
152. Wilson 2002a, 151.
153. Cregeen 1957, 36–41.
154. RIB I, *712*.
155. Cool et al. 1999.
156. Sumpter 1976, 45.
157. Neal and Cosh 2002, 311–14, *123.13–14*, 335–7, *131.1*, 346, *138.1–3*, 365, *146.1*.
158. Hooley 1988–89.
159. Dearne and Lord 1998, 97, figs 25–6, *13.24–35*; Greep 1998, 275–7, fig.120, *128–35*.
160. Allason-Jones 1996; 2002.
161. *Natural History* XXXVI.
162. Todd 1992.
163. Monaghan 1997, 1113–15, table 211.
164. Tomlin 1986; RIB III, *3195*.

165. Leary 2008, 29.
166. Harden 1962.
167. Hall and Kenward 1990, 407–9.
168. Williams 1990.
169. Gwilt 2006, 206.
170. Buckley and Major 2005, 117.
171. *Natural History* XXXIII.
172. Hedges 1976.
173. Fraser and Steedman 2001, 21; Long 2001, 46.
174. Walker 1988, 304; Reece 2002, 115.
175. *Eburacum*, 120, *60*.
176. *Eburacum*, 120, *59*.
177. Turnbull 1982.
178. Rinaldi Tufi 1983, 8–9, *16–17*.
179. Halkon 1998.
180. *Eburacum*, 121, *70*.
181. Rinaldi Tufi 1983, 57–8, *98*.
182. ibid., 9–10, *19*.
183. Tomlin 1998.
184. Bishop 1996, 10.
185. *Eburacum*, 142–3; Allason-Jones 1996, 15.
186. Henig 2002.
187. Green 1986, 178–9.
188. *Eburacum*, 128, *95*.
189. Butcher 2002, 159, fig.307, *12*; Thompson 2002, 161, fig.308, *2*.
190. *Eburacum*, 132, *129*.
191. Rinaldi Tufi 1983, 56–7, *95–6*; Blagg 2002, 287, fig.362, *4*.
192. Mackreth 2002, 156–7, fig, 305, *31*.
193. *Eburacum*, 114, *14–15*; Rinaldi Tufi 1983, 75, 51–2, *130* and *83*.
194. Lloyd-Morgan 1995, 384, fig.155, *44*.
195. Cool et al. 1995, 1550, fig.727, *6341*.
196. Hassall and Tomlin 1983, 337, fig.39.
197. Henig 1998, plate 6.
198. Davey et al. 2002.
199. Ling 1990.
200. White 1997, 43; Dearne and Lord 1998.
201. Casey 1984; Walton 2008.
202. *Eburacum*, 118, *40*; RIB I, *640*, Rinaldi Tufi 1983, 14, *24*.
203. RIB I, *711*.
204. RIB I, *742*.
205. Green 1986, 72–83.
206. *Eburacum*, 118, *42*; Rinaldi Tufi 1983, 15, *6*.
207. *Eburacum*, 116, *36*; RIB I, *653*.
208. RIB I, *629*.
209. RIB I, *618*.
210. RIB III, *3210*.
211. RIB I, *708*.
212. Dent 1988.
213. Ramm 1978, 101–2; 1989–90; Halkon 2008, 198–200.
214. *Eburacum*, 131, *110*; RIB I, *678*.
215. *Eburacum*, xxxvi.
216. Henig 1984, 97ff, Turcan 1996, 197–247.
217. *Eburacum*, 120, *67*; Rinaldi Tufi 1983, 12–13, *23*.
218. *Eburacum*, 120, *58*; RIB I, *641*; Rinaldi Tufi 1983, 11–12, *22*.
219. *Eburacum*, 119, *54*; RIB I, *658*, Rinaldi Tufi 1983, 11, *21*.
220. *Eburacum*, 122, *73*; RIB I, *684*.
221. *Eburacum*, 67–109; Jones 1984.
222. Wenham 1968, 26–32.
223. RIB I, *710*.
224. Chapman et al. 2009, 236.
225. Wilson 2002a, 165–6.
226. Buckland and Magilton 1986, 31, 60.
227. Atkinson and Cumberpatch 1994–95.
228. Dolby 1969.
229. Kitson Clark 1935, 104–5.
230. MAP 1994, 28–9.
231. RIB I, *714*.
232. RIB I, *720*.
233. Wenham 1960, 298–306; RIB III, *3209*.
234. Wenham 1967.
235. Easthaugh et al. in prep.
236. Brown et al. 2007, 76–7.
237. Fenton Thomas 2009, 240–1.
238. Ottaway 2011, 291–308.

239. *Eburacum*, 95–6.
240. Barber 1870.
241. Wenham 1968, 21–6.
242. NAA 2005, 13.
243. Ottaway 2005; Hunter-Mann 2006.
244. *Eburacum*, 106–8; Ottaway 2011, 260.
245. Faull 1981a, 144.
246. Philpott 1991 90–4.
247. Wenham 1968, 41; Spall and Toop 2005, 42.
248. *Eburacum*, 70; Allason-Jones 1996, 20–1, fig.15.
249. *Eburacum*, 82.
250. *Eburacum*, 71.
251. Wilson 2002a, 74; Lentowicz 2002, 68, fig.260.
252. Corder 1930a, 32; 1948, 173.
253. Corder and Richmond 1938.
254. Warwick 1968.
255. RIB I, *748*.
256. Wright and Tomlin 1995, 246.
257. RIB I, *690*; *Eburacum*, 130, *108*.
258. RIB I, *750*.
259. RIB I, *678*, *687*; *Eburacum*, 130–1, *106*, *110*.
260. RIB I, *639*.
261. RIB I, *621*.

Chapter 8

1. *Herodian* III, 14, 2–3.
2. *Epitome of Cassius Dio* LXXVI, 15, 1–2.
3. *Epitome of Cassius Dio* LXXVI, 5, 4.
4. Frere and Fitts 2009.
5. RIB I, *730*.
6. RIB I, *637*.
7. Hartley 1963, 35.
8. *Herodian* III, 14, 1.
9. RIB III, *3445*.
10. Cool and Mason 2008, 302.
11. RIB I, *1143*.
12. RIB I, *740*.
13. RIB I, *746*.
14. RIB III, *3215*.
15. RIB I, *723*; Wade 1952, 12–13; Wilson 1969, 207.
16. RIB I, *722*.
17. RIB II, 1, *2411.97*.
18. Swan and Monaghan 1993; Monaghan 1997, 914–21.
19. Swan 1994, 8–9; 2002, 62.
20. Swan and McBride 2002, 195–203.
21. RIB I, *627*.
22. Wright 1946; Richmond and Wright 1948.
23. *Epitome of Cassius Dio* LXXVII, 15, 3–4.
24. *Eburacum*, 124–6, *84*; Rinaldi Tufi 1983, 27–8, *43*; RIB 1, *688*.
25. RIB III, *3208*.
26. *Eburacum*, 128–30, *104*; RIB I, *670*.
27. Tomlin 1986; RIB III, *3195*.
28. *Eburacum*, 128, *103*; RIB I, *683*.
29. *Eburacum*, 120, *57*; RIB I, *643*.
30. Wright and Tomlin 1995, 247, RIB III, *3202*.

Chapter 9

1. Brown 1971, 22.
2. Swan 1984, 111; 2002, 72; Evans 1989.
3. *Eutropius* X, 1, 3.
4. *Zosimus* II, 8, 2 and 9, 1.
5. Wood 2006; Drinkwater 2009.
6. *Eburacum*, 112, *8*; Rinaldi Tufi 2006.
7. Wenham 1962, 519–21, 525–9.
8. Phillips 1995, 63–4; Weatherhead 1995, 251–4.
9. Frere and Hartley 2009, 10, 52–4ff.
10. Hawkes 1974.
11. Hartley 1960, 110.
12. Hartley 1963, 38.
13. Woodward 1925, 172–6.
14. May 1911, 130–1; Bidwell and Hodgson 2009, 27.

15. Simpson 1981; Ramm 1976a; Boutwood 1996.
16. Crockett and Fitzpatrick 1998; Abramson 1999c, 305.
17. Buckland 1986, 32.
18. Corder 1930a, 47.
19. Hall et al. 2011.
20. *Eburacum*, 59.
21. Magilton 1986.
22. Ramm 1976.
23. Wenham and Hall 1987, 76–80.
24. *Eburacum*, 57–8.
25. *Eburacum*, 53; Ling 1991, 153–4.
26. Brinklow and Donaghey 1986.
27. Smith 1986a.
28. Myres et al. 1959, 7, 12, 25–6, 32–4, 46–7; Jones 1971, 44–5.
29. Neal and Cosh 2002, 305–22.
30. Johnson and Neal 2002.
31. Wacher 1969, 34–6.
32. Corder and Romans 1939, 38; Wacher 1969, 61–2, 67.
33. Evans and Steedman 2001, 76.
34. Fraser 2004a, 18.
35. Hildyard 1957; Wilson 2002a, 98.
36. Wilson 2002a, 168–72.
37. Mitchelson 1964, 215–20.
38. Neal and Cosh 2002, 344–6, *137.1*.
39. Wenham and Heywood 1997, 20–4.
40. Casey and Hoffmann 1998.
41. Burnham et al. 2001, 341.
42. Millett 2006.
43. Millett and Taylor 2006, 56–7, 311–13.
44. King and Simpson 2011, 33–4.
45. White 1997, 41; Maude 1998.
46. Hartley and Fitts 1988, 79.
47. Kitson Clark 1941; JRS 1957, 208, fig.19.
48. Paul Buckland pers. comm.
49. Neal and Fraser 2004.
50. Gilyard-Beer 1951, 24–5.
51. Lukis 1875.
52. Tindall 1990, 35.
53. Ramm 1976b, 3.
54. Brown et al. 2007, 112.
55. Saitch and Matthews 2001–03; Bevan 2007, 6–8, fig.2.
56. Whiting 1941.
57. Holbrey and Burgess 2001.
58. Martin 2005.
59. ASDU 2008a.
60. Brown 1999.
61. Lawton 2002–03.
62. OSA 2000; Hopkinson 2001.
63. Robinson 2009.
64. van de Noort 2004, 119.
65. Roe 2009, 77–9.
66. Burnham et al. 1999, 342; Halkon 2008, 195–7.
67. Wilson 1966.
68. ASDU 2008b; Buckland and Magilton 1987.
69. Buckland and Dolby 1987.
70. Richardson 2008.
71. Hayes 1968.
72. Hayes 1966a.
73. Whitaker 1967.
74. Hayes 1980.
75. Hayes 1988, 57–65.
76. Watts et al. 2003.
77. Neal 1996.
78. Neal and Cosh 2002, 322–3, *124.1*.
79. McDonnell 1963.
80. Kitson Clark 1935, 111.
81. Kitson Clark 1935, 88–92.
82. Corder and Kirk 1932; Ramm 1978, 85–7.
83. Slack 1951; Liversidge et al. 1973.
84. Corder 1941; Ramm 1978, 100.
85. Rahtz and Watts 2004.
86. Rahtz et al. 1986.
87. Brewster 1980.
88. Stead 1980.
89. Collier 1907; Mellor 1952.
90. Neal and Cosh 2002, 338, *132.1–7*.
91. Mackey 1999 and pers. comm.
92. Kitson Clark 1935, 67 (quoting T. Gent, *History of Ripon* 1733).
93. Corder 1940.
94. van de Noort 2004, 110.
95. Evans 2000, 208–9.
96. Berg 1999.

97. Meddens 2002b.
98. Meddens 2002a.
99. Mainland 2006.
100. Richardson 2004.
101. Halkon 2002.
102. Corder 1930b.
103. Hicks and Wilson 1975.
104. Halkon and Millett 1999, 103–28.
105. Evans and Steedman 2001, 84–5.
106. Hayes and Whitley 1950; Robinson 1978, 7; Swan 1984, 109–11; 2002, 63; Hayes 1988, 72–7; Stephens and Ware 2012.
107. Corder 1928; Evans 1989.
108. Swan 2002, 72.
109. Busby et al. 1996; Evans 2002.
110. Buckland 1976c; Swan 1984, 108; Buckland and Magilton 2005.
111. Bayley and Budd 1998, 196–203.
112. Wilson 2002a.
113. Johns 1996, 166–70.
114. Blagg 2002, 300, 303, fig.372, 57–60; Goodall 1972.
115. Mould 2002, 95, fig.276, 201; Starley 2002.
116. Neal and Cosh 2002.
117. Wilson 1995.
118. Evans 1989; Halkon 2002, 29.
119. Williams 1995, 295.
120. Williams 1990, 347.
121. Price 1995.
122. Hopkins 1980, 120.
123. Magilton 1986, 39–40; MAP 2004, 20.
124. RAI 1846.
125. Depeyrot 2006, 237.
126. Robertson 2000.
127. Kitson Clark 1935, 76.
128. Neal and Cosh 2002, 314–18, 123.15; Johnson and Neal 2002; Ling 2007, 71–4.
129. Witts 1996; Neal and Cosh 2002, 320–1, 123.19.
130. Liversidge et al. 1973; Smith 1976; Ling 1991; 1997; Neal and Cosh 2002, 327–9, 126.3.
131. Cookson 1990; Neal and Cosh 2002, 333, 130.1.
132. Mitchelson 1964; Smith 2000; Neal and Cosh 2002, 344–6, 137.1.
133. Neal and Cosh 2002, 348–50, 141.1.
134. Smith 1976; 1980; Ling 1997, 281; 2007, 74–6; Neal and Cosh 2002, 353–6, 143.2; Wilson 2003.
135. Smith 1976; 1980; Neal and Cosh 2002, 357, 143.5.
136. Smith 1976; 1980; Neal and Cosh 2002, 358–62, 143.7.
137. Magilton 1986; Smith 1986b; Neal and Cosh 2002, 376–7, 149.9.
138. Eburacum, 54; Neal and Cosh 2002, 372–3, 149.4; Henig 2006.
139. Eburacum, 57–8; Neal and Cosh 2002, 373–5, 149.5.
140. Eburacum, 53; Ling 1991, 153–4; 1997, 278.
141. Ling 1983.
142. Croom 2000, 34.
143. R. Wilson 2006, 302–6.
144. Neal and Cosh 2002, 23.
145. Smith 2000.
146. Liversidge 1973.
147. Liversidge 1980.
148. Bidwell and Croom 1997, 98.
149. Berg and Major 2006; Roberts 2010, 77.
150. Wright 1975.
151. Thomas 1981, 106; RIB III, 3214.
152. Henig 2011.
153. Ramm 1958; Eburacum, 67–9.
154. Ottaway 2011, 305–8.
155. Thomas 1981, 232.
156. Hunter-Mann 2006.
157. Foster and Jacques 2012.
158. Ross 1967, 322–3.
159. Eburacum, 83; Allason-Jones 1996, 16.
160. YPS 1832.
161. Wilson 2002a, 176.
162. Daily Telegraph and Daily Mail, 22 May 2002.
163. Corder 1930a, 26; Robinson 1978, 26, 69.

164. Hayes 1988.
165. Robinson 1978, 39.
166. Mitchelson 1964, 229.

167. Holbrey and Burgess 2001, 96–8.
168. ASDU 2008a.

Chapter 10

1. Corder 1928; Evans 1989.
2. Braithwaite 1997; Monaghan 1997, 906–7.
3. *Ammianus Marcellinus* XIV, 5.
4. *Ammianus Marcellinus* XX,1.
5. *Ammianus Marcellinus* XXVI, 4–5.
6. *Ammianus Marcellinus* XXVII, 8.
7. Wilson 1966, 686.
8. Ramm 1978, 130.
9. Curle 1923.
10. Hornsby and Stanton 1912.
11. Hornsby and Laverick 1932.
12. Kitson Clark 1935, 121–2.
13. Collingwood 1931.
14. Ottaway 2000.
15. RIB I, *721*.
16. Casey 1980.
17. Wilson 1989.
18. Vyner 2001.
19. Radley 1972; Buckland 1984; Ottaway 1996.
20. Hall 1997, 327, 349–50.
21. Philips 1995, 56–61.
22. ibid., 65–6; Carver 1995, 187–90.
23. Frere and Hartley 2009, 12–13.
24. Hartley 1960, 115–16.
25. Woodward 1925; Hartley 1963.
26. Todd 1973, 135.
27. Corder 1930a, 49.
28. Ottaway 2004, 140–9.
29. Johnson and Neal 2002.
30. Wacher 1969, 54; Halkon 2008, 205.
31. Wilson 2002a, 100–18.
32. Hildyard 1957.
33. Mould 2002, 82–3, fig. 270, *3, 6, 8–9, 11*, fig.271, *18*.
34. NAA 2004.
35. Mitchelson 1964, 219.
36. Wenham and Heywood 1997, 24.
37. ibid., 28.
38. Hayes 1988, 66–72, 89.

39. Millett and Taylor 2006, 74.
40. Lawton 1994a; 1994b.
41. Fraser et al. 2000.
42. Hartley and Fitts 1988, 114.
43. Howell 2001, 65.
44. Burnham et al. 2008, 289–90; Martin et al. forthcoming.
45. Wrathmell 1990.
46. Gilyard-Beer 1951, 24–5.
47. ASDU 2008a.
48. OSA 2000; Hopkinson 2001.
49. Sitch 1989; 1990.
50. Wilson 1966.
51. van de Noort and Ellis 1997, 460.
52. Samuels and Buckland 1978b, 72.
53. Neal 1996, 43–4.
54. Mitchelson 1950.
55. Rutter and Duke 1958, 15–20.
56. Lee 1997.
57. Corder and Kirk 1932, 60.
58. Rahtz and Watts 2004.
59. Rahtz et al. 1986.
60. Stead 1980, 40.
61. Buckland 1980.
62. Mackey 1999 and pers. comm.
63. Corder 1940.
64. Mellor 1951.
65. Evans and Steedman 1997.
66. Evans 2000, 209.
67. Dobney et al. 2000.
68. Hornsby and Laverick 1932, 213.
69. Phillips 1995, 65–9; Rackham 1995.
70. Hull 1932; Monaghan 2000.
71. Neal 1996, 18, 52–60.
72. ASDU 2008a.
73. Hildyard 1957; Johns 1996, 119–20.
74. Neal 1996, 50, fig.33, *26*.
75. *Ammianus Marcellinus* XVIII.
76. Evans 1989.
77. Monaghan 1997, 902.
78. Price 2008.

79. Brickstock 2000a.
80. Carson and Kent 1971.
81. Brickstock 2000b.
82. Chapman et al. 2009, 236.
83. Kitson Clark 1935, 139; Johns and Burnett 1979.
84. Neal 1996, 35–6.
85. Millett and Taylor 2006, 62; Millett 2006, 314.
86. Corder and Kirk 1932, 51, 68.
87. Stead 1980, 29.
88. Brewster 1976, 116; 1980, 259.
89. *Ammianus Marcellinus* XXV, 10.
90. Hall et al. 2011.
91. *Eburacum* 73; Cool 2006, 155–7.
92. Wilson 2002a, 178.
93. Bell and Thompson 2002, 303.
94. Kent and Kitson Clark 1934.
95. Corder 1928; 1989, 8–9.
96. Corder 1928; 1989, 4.
97. Wenham 1960.
98. Johnson and Neal 2002, 113.
99. Faull 1981a, 157.
100. Neal 1986, 21.
101. Lukis 1875, 144–5.
102. Hornsby and Laverick 1932.
103. Hornsby and Stanton 1912, 222.
104. Dobney et al. 2000, 170, 176.

Chapter 11

1. *Zosimus* VI, 5, 2–3.
2. Faull 1981b, 171–2.
3. Loveluck 2003, 156–8.
4. Wood 1996.
5. Richardson 2005, 70.
6. Holbrey and Burgess 2001, 101–2.
7. Myres and Southern 1973; Timby 1993.
8. Haughton and Powlesland 1999.
9. Head 1997.
10. Tweddle et al. 1999, 167–70, 235–6.
11. Ottaway 2004, 148.
12. Breeze 2005.
13. NAA 2007b.
14. Wilson et al. 1996.
15. Rutter and Duke 1958.
16. Powlesland 2003, 288–91.
17. Abramson 1996, 25.
18. Hunter-Mann 2002.
19. Rahtz 1988, 129–30.
20. Corder 1940, 35.

Bibliography

Abbreviations

ASDU   Archaeological Services, Durham University
ASWYAS   Archaeological Services, West Yorkshire Archaeological Service
Forum   Annual Newsletter of Council for British Archaeology, Yorkshire
                Group
HER   Historic Environment Record
NAA   Northern Archaeological Associates
OSA   On Site Archaeology
RASB   *Yorkshire Archaeological Society, Roman Antiquities Section Bulletin*
YAJ   *Yorkshire Archaeological Journal*
YAT   York Archaeological Trust
YAS   Yorkshire Archaeological Society

Abramson, P. 1995. A late Iron Age settlement at Scotch Corner, North Yorkshire,
    Durham Archaeol. J. 11, 7–18
Abramson, P. 1996. Excavation along the Caythorpe Gas Pipeline, North
    Humberside, *YAJ* 68, 1–88
Abramson, P. 1999a. The major trenches: excavations of the fort and annexe, 1977–
    85, in Abramson et al. 1999, 21–126
Abramson, P. 1999b. Excavations of the vicus, 1974 and 1980–82, in Abramson et al.
    1999, 126–51
Abramson, P. 1999c. The Roman occupation of Castleford, in Abramson et al. 1999,
    285–307
Abramson, P., Berg, D. S. and Fossick, M. R. 1999. *Roman Castleford Excavations
    1974–85, 2: The Structural and Environmental Evidence*, Yorkshire Archaeol. 5
Adam, J-P. 1989, *La Construction Romaine* (2nd edn)
Adams, K. 2007. *Archaeological Trial Excavation on Land off High Catton Road,
    Stamford Bridge, East Riding of Yorkshire*, Humber Archaeol. Rep. 226
Addyman, P. V. and Black, V. E. (eds), 1984. *Archaeological Papers from York
    Presented to M. W. Barley*
Alcock, L.1954. Aberford Dykes: the first defence of the Brigantes? *Antiquity* 28,
    147–54

Aldritt, D. 2005. Carbonised plant macrofossils and charcoal, in Roberts 2005, 184–7

Allason-Jones, L. 1996. *Roman Jet in the Yorkshire Museum*

Allason-Jones, L. 2006. The small finds, in Millett 2006, 220–48

Anderson, J. D. 1992. *Roman Military Supply in North-East England*, Brit. Archaeol. Rep. Brit. Ser. **224**

Annable, F. K. 1954. The Roman Pottery at Cantley Housing Estate, Doncaster: Kilns 1–8, *YAJ* **38**, 403–6

Annis, R. 1992–93. Two Romano-British settlement sites at Coulby Newham, Cleveland, *YAS Roman Antiq. Sect. Bull.* **10**, 9–16

Annis, R. 1996. Bonny Grove Farm and Dixon's Bank: two Romano-British settlement sites in Cleveland, *Durham Archaeol. J.* **12**, 41–60

ASDU. 2008a. *A Romano-British Villa and Settlement at Ingleby Barwick Stockton on Tees*, Rep. **1709**

ASDU. 2008b. *Gale Common Ash Disposal Site, Phase 3, Womersley North Yorkshire, Archaeological Assessment Report and UPD*, Rep. **2112**

ASWYAS. 1997. *Slack Roman Fort, Outlane Golf Club: Archaeological Watching Brief and Excavation*

ASWYAS. 2002. *High Street, Shafton, South Yorkshire: Archaeological Excavation*, Rep. **993**

ASWYAS. 2003. *Shafton Bypass, Shafton, Barnsley, South Yorkshire*, Rep. **1104**

ASWYAS. 2004. *Land at High Street, Gargrave, North Yorkshire: Archaeological Evaluation and Excavation*, Rep. **1234**

ASWYAS. 2005a. *Grange Park Woods, Canklow Wood and Treeton Wood, Rotherham, South Yorkshire, Archaeological Level III Topographic Survey*, Rep. **1373**

ASWYAS. 2005b. *Balby Carr, Doncaster, South Yorkshire: Archaeological Assessment Report*, Rep. **1345**

ASWYAS. 2005c. *Natural Gas Terminal, Easington, East Yorkshire: Assessment and Updated Project Design*, Rep. **1435**

ASWYAS. 2006a. *First Point, Balby Carr (Zone D1), Doncaster, South Yorkshire: Archaeological Excavation*, Rep. **1556**

ASWYAS. 2006b. *Newbridge Quarry, Newbridge, Pickering, North Yorkshire*, Rep. **1627**

ASWYAS. 2006c. *Adel Roman Road, Adel, West Yorkshire, Archaeological Evaluation*, Rep. **1468**

ASWYAS. 2008a. *10–14A Hall Gate, Doncaster, South Yorkshire*, Rep. **1767**

ASWYAS. 2008b. *8–10 High Street, Doncaster, South Yorkshire: Archaeological Post-excavation Report*, Rep. **1822**

ASWYAS. 2010. *Newbridge Quarry Extension, Pickering, North Yorkshire: Archaeological Excavation Phase 1*, Rep. **2105**

Atkinson, S. 1993–94. An archaeological evaluation at Far Fields Road, Edenthorpe, *Archaeol. in South Yorkshire*, 1993–94, 19–21

Atkinson, S. and Cumberpatch, C. G. 1994–95. Recent excavations in Hallgate and Wood Street, Doncaster, *Archaeol. in South Yorkshire*, 1994–95, 19–25

Barber, F. 1870. On the Roman station at Slack, *YAJ* **1**, 1–12

Bastow, M. E. 1999. The botanical material, in Abramson et al. 1999, 163–222

Bastow, M. and Murray, J. 1990. Botanical remains, in Wrathmell and Nicholson 1990, 259–71

Bates, A., Jones, G. and Orton, D. 2007. Animal bones from the Ferry Fryston chariot burial, in Brown et al. 2007, 326–337

Bayley, J. and Budd, P. 1998. The clay moulds, in Cool and Philo 1998, 195–222

Bell, A. and Thompson, A. 2002. Stone objects from the Cfa excavations, in Wilson 2002b, 303–6

Beresford, M. W. and Hurst, J. 1990. *Wharram Percy Deserted Medieval Village*

Berg, D. 1990. The mammal bones, in Wrathmell and Nicholson 1990, 174–189

Berg, D. 1999. The mammal bones, in Abramson et al. 1999, 223–79

Berg, D. 2001. The physical environment, in Roberts 2001, 3–9

Berg, D. and Major, P. 2006. *River Idle Washlands, Bawtry, South Yorks: Archaeological Watching Brief*, ASWYAS Rep. **1559**

Beswick, P. and Merrills, D. 1983. L. H. Butcher's survey of early settlement and fields in the south Pennines, *Trans Hunter Archaeol. Soc.* **12**, 16–50

Beswick, P., Megaw, M. R., Megaw, J. V. S. and Northover, P. 1990. A decorated Late Iron Age torc from Dinnington, South Yorkshire, *Antiq. J.* **70**, 16–33

Bevan, B. 2007. Romans on the Don, *RASB* **23**, 6–9

Bewley, R. H. and Macleod, D. 1993. The discovery of a Roman fort at Roall Manor Farm, North Yorkshire, *Britannia* **24**, 243–7

Bidwell, P. T. and Croom, A. T. 1997. Coarse wares, in Wenham and Heywood 1997, 61–103

Bidwell, P. T. and Hodgson, N. 2009. *The Roman Army in Northern England*

Birley, A. 1979. *The People of Roman Britain*

Birley, A. 1981. *The Fasti of Roman Britain*

Birley, A. 2002. *Garrison Life at Vindolanda: A Band of Brothers*

Bishop, M. C. 1996. *Finds from Roman Aldborough*, Oxbow Monogr. **65**

Bishop, M. C., 1998. Military equipment, in Cool and Philo 1998, 61–83

Bishop, M. C. 2005. A new Flavian military site at Roecliffe, North Yorkshire, *Britannia* **36**, 135–223

Bishop, M. C. and Coulston. J. C. 1989. *Roman Military Equipment*, Shire Archaeology **59**

Blagg, T. F. C. 2002. Architectural and other stonework from the 1958–9 bypass excavations and the 1972 excavations (Sites 433 and 434), in Wilson 2002b, 286–303

Bohannan, P. and Dalton, G. 1962. Introduction, in P. Bohannan and G. Dalton (eds) *Markets in Africa*, 1–26

Boutwood, Y. 1996. Roman fort and *vicus*, Newton Kyme, North Yorkshire, *Britannia* **27**, 340–4

Bowman, A. K. 1994. *Life and Letters on the Roman Frontier*

Braithwaite, G. 1997. The face fragments from the Malton vicus, in Wenham and Heywood 1997, 103–6

Branigan, K. 1980. Villas in the north: change in the rural landscape? in K. Branigan (ed.) *Rome and the Brigantes: the Impact of Rome on Northern England*, 18–27

Breeze, A. 2005. Celtic boundaries and *Isurium Brigantum*, *Northern Hist.* **42** (**2**), 349–51

Brewster, T. C. M. 1957. Excavations at Newham's Pit, Staxton, 1947–48, *YAJ* **39**, 193–223

Brewster, T. C. M. 1976. Garton Slack, *Current Archaeol.* **51**, 104–16

Brewster, T. C. M. 1980. *The Excavation of Garton and Wetwang Slacks* (published as microfiche by Royal Commission on Historical Monuments for England)

Brickstock, R. J. 2000a. Coin supply in the late Roman period, in T. Wilmott and P. Wilson, *The Late Roman Transition in the* North, Brit. Archaeol. Rep. Brit. Ser. **299**, 33–7

Brickstock, R. J. 2000b. The coins, in Ottaway 2000, 131–40

Brickstock, R.J., Cardwell, P. A., Busby, P. A., Cool, H. E. M., Huntley, J., Evans, J., Makey, P., Ronan, D. and Wilson, P. R. 2007. Catterick metal detecting project 1997–1999, *YAJ*, **79**, 65–153

Bridgland, D., Innes, J., Long, A. and Mitchell, W. 2011. *Late Quaternary Landscape Evolution of the Swale-Ure Washlands, North Yorkshire*

Brinklow, D. and Donaghey, S. 1986. A Roman building in Clementhorpe, in Brinklow et al. 1986, 54–73

Brinklow, D., Hall, R., Magilton, J. and Donaghey, S. 1986. *Coney Street, Aldwark and Clementhorpe, Minor Sites and Roman Roads*, Archaeol. York **6/1**

Brown, P. 1971. *The World of Late Antiquity*

Brown, J. 1999. Romano-British villa complex at Chapel House Farm, Dalton on Tees, North Yorkshire, *RASB* **16**, 19–27

Brown, F., Howard-Davis, C., Brennand, M., Boyle, A., Evans, T., O'Connor, S., Spence, A., Heawood, R. and Lupton, A. 2007. *The Archaeology of the A1 (M) Darrington to Dishforth DBFO Road Scheme*, Lancaster Imprints **12**

Buckland, P. C. 1976a. Geological and archaeological notes on the rocks used in the construction of the sewer, in Whitwell 1976, 32–7

Buckland, P. C. 1976b. *The Environmental Evidence from the Church Street Roman Sewer System*, Archaeol. York, **14/1**

Buckland, P. C. 1976c. A Romano-British pottery kiln site at Branton, near Doncaster, *YAJ* **48**, 69–82

Buckland, P. C. 1978. A first-century shield from Doncaster, *Britannia* **9**, 247–69

Buckland, P. C. 1980. Insect remains from the well, in Stead 1980, 162–7

Buckland, P. C. 1984. The 'Anglian' Tower and the use of Jurassic limestone in York, in Addyman and Black 1984, 51–7

Buckland, P. C. 1986. *Roman South Yorkshire: a Source Book*

Buckland, P. C. 1988. The stones of York: building materials in Roman Yorkshire, in Price and Wilson 1988, 237–87

Buckland, P. C., Magilton, J. R. and Dolby, M. J. 1980. The Roman pottery industries of south Yorkshire: a review, *Britannia* **11**, 145–64

Buckland, P. C. and Magilton, J. R. 1986. *The Archaeology of Doncaster, 1: The Roman Civil Settlement*, Brit. Archaeol. Rep. Brit. Ser. **148**

Buckland, P. C. and Dolby, M. J. 1987. A Roman site at Womersley, North Yorkshire, *YAJ* **59**, 1–8

Buckland, P. C. and Magilton, J. R. 2005. Late Roman pottery kilns at Goodison Boulevard, Cantley, Doncaster: excavations by J.R. Lidster in 1957 and 1962, *J. Roman Pottery Stud.* **12**, 35–53

Buckland, P. C. and Gaunt, G. 2003. The geological background to Yorkshire's archaeology, in Manby et al. 2003, 17–23

Buckley, D. and Major, H. 1990. Quernstones, in Wrathmell and Nicholson 1990, 105–20

Burgess, A. and Roberts, I. 2004. *Two Late Iron Age / Romano-British Settlement Sites near Whitwood, West Yorkshire*, ASWYAS Publ. **6**

Burnham, B. C., Keppie, L. J. F. and Esmonde Cleary, A. S. 1999. Roman Britain in 1998, I, sites explored, *Britannia* **30**, 318–74

Burnham, B. C., Keppie, L. J. F. and Esmonde Cleary, A. S. 2000. Roman Britain in 1999, I, sites explored, *Britannia* **31**, 371–431

Burnham, B. C., Keppie, L. J. F. and Fitzpatrick, A. P. 2001. Roman Britain in 2000, I, sites explored, *Britannia* **32**, 312–85

Burnham, B. C., Hunter, F. and Booth, P. 2008. Roman Britain in 2007, I, sites explored, *Britannia* **39**, 263–336

Busby, P. A., Evans, J., Huntley, J. P. and Wilson, P. R. 1996. A pottery kiln at Catterick, *Britannia* **27**, 283–98

Butcher, S. 2002. Brooches from Bainesse, Catterick Bridge and Catterick Racecourse, in Wilson 2002b, 157–61

Butler, R. M. (ed.) 1971. *Soldier and Civilian in Roman Yorkshire*

Carlton, R. 2008. *Archaeological Evaluation at Holme Lea, Bowes* (unpublished report in Co. Durham HER)

Carne, P. 2001. A Roman villa and settlement at Ingleby Barwick, *RASB* **18**, 12–16

Carson, R. and Kent, J. 1971. A hoard of Roman 4th century bronze coins from Heslington, Yorks., *Numismatic Chron.* **11**, 207–25

Carver, M. O. H. 1995. Roman to Norman at York Minster, in Phillips and Heywood 1995, 177–222

Carver, M. O. H. and Sumpter, A. 1978. Buildings in Bishophill, in Carver et al. 1978, 29–40

Carver, M. O. H., Donaghey, S. and Sumpter, A. 1978. *Riverside Structures and a Well in Skeldergate and Buildings in Bishophill*, Archaeol. York **4/1**

Casey, P. J. 1980. Magnus Maximus in Britain: a reappraisal, in P. J. Casey (ed.) *The End of Roman Britain*, Brit. Archaeol. Rep. Brit. Ser. **71**, 66–79

Casey, P. J. 1984. A votive deposit from the River Tees at Piercebridge, Co. Durham, *Durham Archaeol. J.* **5**, 37–42

Casey, P. J. and Hoffmann, B. 1998. Rescue excavations in the *vicus* of the fort at Greta Bridge, Co. Durham, 1972–4, *Britannia* **29**, 111–84

Chadwick, A. M. and Cumberpatch, C. G. 1994–95. Further work on the Iron Age and Romano-British landscape at Edenthorpe, *Archaeol. in South Yorkshire* 1994–95, 41–9

Chapman, E. M., Hunter, F., Booth, P. and Wilson, P. 2009. Roman Britain in 2008, I, sites explored, *Britannia* **40**, 219–79

Charlesworth, D. 1971. The defences of *Isurium Brigantum*, in Butler 1971, 155–64

Clogg, P. 1999. The Welham Bridge slag, in Halkon and Millett 1999, 81–95

Close, R. S., Hayes, R. H. and Spratt, D. A. 1975. Romano-British settlements at Crag Bank and Lonsdale, near Kildale, North Riding, *YAJ* **47**, 61–8

Collier, C. V. 1907. The Roman remains at Harpham, *Trans E. Riding Antiq. Soc.* **13**, 141–52

Collingwood, R. G. 1931. The Roman signal station, in A. Rowntree (ed.) *The History of Scarborough*, 40–50

Collis, J. 2003. *The Celts: Origins, Myths, Inventions*

Congreve, A. L. 1937. *A Roman and Saxon Site at Elmswell, East Yorkshire, 1935–1936*, Hull Mus. Publ. **193**

Congreve, A. L. 1938. *A Roman and Saxon Site at Elmswell, East Yorkshire, 1937*, Hull Mus. Publ. **198**

Cookson, N. 1990. The mosaic remains, in Wrathmell and Nicholson 1990, 146–50

Cool, H. E. M. 1998. The brooches, in Cool and Philo 1998, 29–57

Cool, H. E. M. 2002. Craft and industry in Roman York, in Wilson and Price 2002, 13–20

Cool, H. E. M. 2005. *Review of the Evidence for the Excavations at Castleford, 1987–88* (unpublished report in South Yorks HER)

Cool, H. E. M. 2006. in Hartley et al. 2006, 155–7

Cool, H. E. M. 2009. Fish knives, silver spoons and red dishes, in S. Baker, A. Gray, K. Lakin, R. Madgwick, K. Poole and M. Sandias (eds) 2009, *Food and Drink in Archaeology* **2**, 11–20

Cool, H. E. M., Lloyd-Morgan, G. and Hooley, A. D. 1995. *Finds from the Fortress*, Archaeol. York **17/10**

Cool, H. E. M. and Price, J. 1998. The vessel glass, in Cool and Philo 1998, 141–81

Cool, H. E. M., Jackson, C. M. and Monaghan. J. 1999. Glass-making and the Sixth Legion at York, *Britannia* **30**, 147–62

Cool, H. E. M. and Mason, D. J. P. 2008. Piercebridge: the current state of knowledge, in Cool and Mason 2008, 295–312

Cool, H. E. M. and Mason, D. J. P. (eds) 2008. *Roman Piercebridge. Excavations by D.W. Harding and Peter Scott 1969–1981*, Architect. Archaeol. Soc. Durham and Northumberland Res. Rep. **7**

Cool, H. E. M. and Philo, C. (eds) 1998. *Roman Castleford Excavations 1974–85, 1: The Small Finds*, Yorkshire Archaeol. **4**

Corder, P. 1928. *The Roman Pottery at Crambeck, Castle Howard*, Roman Malton and Dist. Rep. **1**, reprinted in Wilson 1989, 3–24

Corder, P. 1930a. *The Defences of the Roman Fort at Malton*, Roman Malton and Dist. Rep. **2**

Corder, P. 1930b. *The Roman Pottery at Throlam, Holme-on-Spalding Moor, East Yorkshire*, Roman Malton and Dist. Rep. **3**

Corder, P. 1940. *Excavations at Elmswell, East Yorkshire, 1938*, Hull Mus. Publ. **207**

Corder, P. 1941. Roman site at North Newbald, East Yorkshire, *Proc. Leeds Phil. Lit. Soc. (Lit. and Hist. Sect.)* **5**, 231–8

Corder, P. 1948. Miscellaneous small objects from the Roman fort at Malton, *Antiq. J.* **28**, 173–6

Corder, P. 1958. Parisian ware, *YAJ* **39**, 48–52

Corder, P. and Kirk, J. L. 1932. *A Roman Villa at Langton, near Malton, East Yorkshire*, Roman Malton and Dist. Rep. **4**

Corder, P. and Pryce, T. D. 1938. Belgic and other early pottery found at North Ferriby, Yorks, *Antiq. J.* **18**, 262–77

Corder, P. and Richmond, I. A. 1938. A Romano-British interment with bucket and sceptre from Brough, East Yorkshire, *Antiq. J.* **18**, 68–74

Corder, P. and Romans, T. 1939. Excavations at Brough-*Petuaria*, East Yorkshire, 1937, fifth interim report, *Trans E. Riding Antiq. Soc.* **28**, 173–234

Corder, P. and Hawkes, C. F. C. 1940. A panel of Celtic ornament from Elmswell, East Yorkshire, *Antiq. J.* **20**, 338–57

Corder, P. and Richmond, I. A. 1942. Petuaria, *J. Brit. Archaeol. Assoc.*, third ser. 7, 1–30

Cregeen, S. M. 1957. The Romano-British excavations at Cantley Estate, Doncaster, the pottery from kilns 9–25, *YAJ* **39**, 362–88

Creighton, J. 1988. The place names of east Yorkshire in the Roman period, in Price and Wilson, 1988, 387–406

Crockett, A. and Fitzpatrick, A. P. 1998. Archaeological mitigation in the Flavian fort annexe and later Roman settlement at Bradley Street, Castleford, West Yorkshire 1991–93, *YAJ* **70**, 35–60

Croom, A. 2000. *Roman Clothing and Fashion*

Crowther, D. and Didsbury, P. 1985. Excavation of a Romano-British ditch at Greylees Avenue, Hull, *Forum* 1984–5, 11–16

Crowther, D., Willis, S. and Creighton, J. 1989. Excavations at Redcliff, in Halkon 1989, 6–9

Crowther, D., Willis, S. and Creighton, J. 1990. The topography and archaeology of Redcliffe, in Crowther and Willis 1990, 172–81

Crowther, D. and Willis, S. (eds) 1990. *Humber Perspectives: a Region through the Ages*

Cunliffe, B. 2005. *Iron Age Communities in Britain* (4th edn)

Curle, A. O. 1923. *The Traprain Treasure*

Davey, N., Long, C. A. and Thompson, A. 2002. Painted plaster from Catterick bypass, in Wilson 2002b, 308–16

Dean, G. 2001. *A Survey of the Fort and Vicus at Malton*, MA Diss. Dept Archaeology, University of York

Dearne, M. J. and Parsons, J. 1997. Recent Romano-British metal detector finds in the Sheffield and Rotherham museum collections and rural settlement patterns in South Yorkshire, *YAJ* **69**, 39–92

Dearne, M. J. and Lord, T. C., 1998. *The Romano-British Archaeology of Victoria Cave, Settle, Researches into the Site and its Artefacts*, Brit. Archaeol. Rep. Brit. Ser. **273**

Dent, J. S. 1983. A summary of the excavations carried out in Garton and Wetwang Slack 1964–80, *E. Riding Archaeol.* **7**, 1–14

Dent, J. S. 1988. Roman religious remains from Elmswell, in Price and Wilson 1988, 89–98

Depeyrot, G. 2006. Economy and society, in N. Lenski, *The Cambridge Companion to the Age of Constantine*, 226–52

Dickinson, B. M. and Hartley, K. F. 1971. The evidence of potters stamps on samian ware and on mortaria for the trading connections of York, in Butler 1971, 127–42

Dickinson, B. M. and Hartley, B. R. 1993. Samian ware, in Monaghan 1993, 722–5

Didsbury, P. 1988. Evidence for Romano-British settlement in Hull and the lower Hull valley, in Price and Wilson 1988, 21–36

Didsbury, P. 1989. Recent discoveries in Hull and district, in Halkon 1989, 23–5

Didsbury, P. 1990. Exploitation of the alluvium in the lower Hull valley in the Roman period, in Ellis and Crowther 1990, 199–210

Didsbury, P. 1999. The pottery, in Bishop 1999, 44–50

Dobinson, C. 1987–8. Excavations at Aldborough 1987: interim report, *RASB* **5**, 3–7

Dobinson, C. 1988–9. Roman Aldborough, *RASB* **6**, 3–9

Dobney, K., Jaques, D., Carrott, J., Hall, A., Issitt, M. and Large, F. 2000. Biological remains, in Ottaway 2000, 148–82

Dodd, P. W. and Woodward, A. M. 1922. Excavations at Slack, 1913–15, *YAJ* **26**, 1–92

Dolby, B. 1981. A review of the earthworks in Canklow Woods, Rotherham, *Trans Hunter Archaeol. Soc.* **11**, 59–64

Dolby, M. J. 1969. Roman remains from Adwick-le-Street, West Riding, *YAJ* **42**, 252–3

Drinkwater, J. F. 2009. Crocus, king of the Alemanni, *Britannia* **40**, 185–95

Droop, J. P. 1929. Excavations at Brough-by-Bainbridge: 1st interim report 1928, *Proc. Leeds Phil. Lit. Soc.* **2**, 77–85

Droop, J. P. 1930. Excavations at Brough-by-Bainbridge: 2nd interim report 1929, *Proc. Leeds Phil. Lit. Soc.* **2**, 234–45

Droop, J. P. 1932. Excavations at Brough-by-Bainbridge in 1931 and remarks on the Bainbridge finds 1928, 1929, 1931, *Proc. Leeds Phil. Lit. Soc.* **3**, 16–38

Dungworth, D. 2002. Copper alloys in Roman Yorkshire, in Wilson and Price 2002, 95–9

Easthaugh, E., Halkon, P., Millett, M. and Woodhouse, H. in prep. *Excavations at Hayton*

Ecroyd Smith, H. 1852. Reliquiae Isurianae: *The Remains of the Roman Isurium, now Aldborough near Boroughbridge, Yorkshire*

Evans, D. H. 2000. Archaeology in the modern city of Kingston upon Hull, and recent research at Kingswood, in van de Noort and Ellis 2000, 193–216

Evans, D. 2006. Celtic art revealed. The South Cave weapons hoard, *Current Archaeol.* **203**, 572–77

Evans, D. H. and Steedman, K. 1997. Recent archaeological work in the East Riding, *E. Riding Archaeol.* **9**, 116–71

Evans, D. H. and Steedman, K. 2001. Recent archaeological work in the East Riding, *E. Riding Archaeol.* **10**, 67–156

Evans, D. H. and Atkinson, R. 2009. Recent archaeological work in the East Riding, *E. Riding Archaeol.* **12**, 249–403

Evans, J. 1989. Crambeck; the development of a major northern pottery industry, in Wilson 1989, 43–90

Evans, J. 1995. Later Iron Age and 'native' pottery in the north-east, in Vyner 1995, 46–68

Evans, J. 2002. Synthesis of the Catterick pottery, in Wilson 2002a, 246–9

Evans, J. 2005. Late Iron Age and Roman pottery, in Roberts 2005, 130–43

Faull, M. L. 1981a. The Roman period, in Faull and Moorhouse 1981, 141–70

Faull, M. L. 1981b. The post-Roman period, in Faull and Moorhouse 1981, 171–8.

Faull, M. L. and Moorhouse, S. A. (eds) 1981. *West Yorkshire: an Archaeological Survey to A.D. 1500* (4 vols)

Fenton-Thomas, C. 2009. *A Place by Sea: Excavations at Sewerby Cottage Farm, Bridlington*, OSA Monogr. **1**

Fenton-Thomas, C. 2011. *Where Sky and Yorkshire and Water Meet: The Story of the Melton Landscape from Prehistory to the Present*, OSA Monogr. **2**

Ferraby, R. and Millett, M. 2012. Seeing Roman Aldborough beneath the ground, *British Archaeol.* May – June 2012, 28–33

Feugère, M. 2002. *Weapons of the Romans* (English trans.)

Fitts, R. L., Haselgrove, C. C., Lowther, P. C. and Turnbull, P. 1994. An Iron Age farmstead at Rock Castle, Gilling West, North Yorkshire, *Durham Archaeol. J.* **10**, 13–42

Fitts, R. L., Haselgrove, C. C., Lowther, P. C. and Willis, S. H. 1999. Melsonby revisited: survey and excavation 1992–95 at the site of the discovery of the 'Stanwick', North Yorkshire, hoard of 1843, *Durham Archaeol. J.* **14–15**, 1–52

Fitts, R. L. 2009. Lease Rigg Roman fort, in Frere and Fitts 2009, 205–84

Fitzpatrick, A. P. and Scott, P. R. 1999. The Roman bridge at Piercebridge, North Yorkshire-County Durham, *Britannia* **30**, 111–32

Fleming, A. 1998. *Swaledale. Valley of the Wild River*

Foster, A. and Jacques, D. 2012. *6 Driffield Terrace: Vertebrate Remains Analysis*, Unearthed **3**, www.yorkarchaeology.co.uk/resources/unearthed.htm

Fraser, J. 2004a. *An Archaeological Evaluation on Land at 66 Station Road, Brough, East Riding of Yorkshire*, Humber Archaeol. Rep. **168**

Fraser, J., George, R. and Steedman, K. 2000. *BP Teeside to Saltend Ethylene Pipeline: Assessment of Results of Archaeological Excavations in the East Riding of Yorkshire, Report 6 – Sites 218, 222 and 908*, Humber Archaeol. Rep. **66**

Fraser, J. and Steedman, K. 2001. *BP Teeside to Saltend Ethylene Pipeline: Assessment of Results of Archaeological Excavations in the East Riding of Yorkshire, Report 8 – Site 907*, Humber Archaeol. Rep. **68**

Fraser, J. and Brigham, T. 2009. A Romano-British and medieval haven at Brough, *East Riding Archaeol.* **12**, 115–26

Frere, S. S. 1989. Roman Britain in 1988, 1: sites explored, *Britannia* **20**, 258–326

Frere, S. S. 1990. Roman Britain in 1989, 1: sites explored, *Britannia* **21**, 304–64

Frere, S. S. and St Joseph, J. K. S. 1983. *Roman Britain from the Air*

Frere, S. S. and Fitts, R. L. 2009. *Excavations at Bowes and Lease Rigg Roman Forts*, Yorkshire Archaeol. Rep. **6**

Frere, S. S. and Hartley, B. 2009. Excavations at the Roman fort at Bowes in 1966–67 and 1970, in Frere and Fitts 2009, 1–203

Gates, T. and Ainsworth, S. 2008. A newly identified Roman temporary camp at Cow Close, near Bowes, Co. Durham, *Britannia* **39**, 240–5

Gidney, L. J. 2008. The animal bone, in Cool and Mason 2008, 148–56

Gilyard-Beer, R. 1951. *The Romano-British Baths at Well*, Yorkshire Roman Antiq. Comm. Res. Rep. **1**

Gilmour, E. F. 1954. The Roman pottery kilns at Cantley housing estate, Doncaster: kilns 9–15, *YAJ* **38**, 408–12

Goodall, I. H. 1972. Industrial evidence from the villa at Langton, East Yorkshire, *YAJ* **54**, 32–7

Goodburn, R. 1978. Roman Britain in 1977, 1: sites explored, *Britannia* **9**, 404–72

Goodburn, R. 1979. Roman Britain in 1978, 1: sites explored, *Britannia* **10**, 268–338

Green, M. 1986. *The Gods of the Celts*

Green, M. A. 2001. *Dying for the Gods: Human Sacrifice in Iron Age and Roman Europe*

Greep, S. J. 1997. Objects of bone, antler and ivory, in Wenham and Heywood 1997, 144–8

Greep, S. J. 1998. The bone, antler and ivory artefacts, in Cool and Philo 1998, 267–85

Gwilt, A. 2006. The quernstones, in Millett 2006, 206–19

Gwilt, A. and Heslop, D. 1995. Iron Age and Roman querns in the Tees Valley, in Vyner 1995, 38–45

Halkon, P. 1983. Investigations into the Romano-British industries of Holme-on-Spalding Moor, *E. Riding Archaeol.* 7, 15–24

Halkon, P. 1989. Iron Age and Romano-British settlement and industry around Holme-on-Spalding Moor, in Halkon 1989, 15–22

Halkon, P. 1990. The Holme-on-Spalding Moor landscape, in Ellis and Crowther 1990, 147–57

Halkon, P. 1998. A Roman relief depicting Victory from Bolton, East Yorkshire, *Britannia* **29**, 322–5

Halkon, P. 1999a. The Foulness Valley in the Iron Age and Roman periods, in Halkon 1999, 14–22

Halkon, P. 1999b. The early landscape of the Foulness valley, East Yorkshire, in Bridgland et al. 1999, 173–5

Halkon, P. 2002. The Roman pottery industry at Holme-on-Spalding Moor in its landscape, in Wilson and Price 2002, 21–33

Halkon, P. 2003. Researching an ancient landscape: the Foulness Valley, East Yorkshire, in Manby et al. 2003, 261–74

Halkon, P. 2008. *Archaeology and Environment in a Changing East Yorkshire Landscape, The Foulness Valley, c.800BC – c.AD 400*, Brit. Archaeol. Rep. Brit. Ser. **472**

Halkon, P. 2012. Iron, landscape and power in Iron Age East Yorkshire, *Archaeol. J.* **168**, 133–65

Halkon, P. (ed.) 1999. *Recent Research in Iron Age and Roman Yorkshire*

Halkon, P. and Millett, M. (eds) 1999. *Rural Settlement and Industry: Studies in the Iron Age and Roman Archaeology of Lowland East Yorkshire*, Yorkshire Archaeol. Rep. **4**

Hall, R. A. 1986. Roman warehouses and other riverside structures in Coney Street, in Brinklow et al. 1986, 5–20

Hall, R. A. 1997. *Excavations in the* Praetentura: *9 Blake Street*, Archaeol. York **3/4**

Hall, R. A., Evans, D. T. and Ottaway, P. 16–22 Coppergate, in Ottaway 2011, 199–221

Hall, A. R. and Kenward, H. K. 1990. *Environmental Evidence from the* Colonia: *Tanner Row and Rougier Street*, Archaeol. York **14/6**

Hanson, W. 1978. The Roman military timber supply, *Britannia* **9**, 293–305

Harden, D. B. 1962. Glass in Roman York, in *Eburacum*, 136–41

Harding, D. W. 1984. *Holme House, Piercebridge: Excavations 1969–70. A Summary Report*, Univ. Edinburgh, Dept. Archaeol. Project Pap. **2**

Harding, D. W. 2008. The Holme House villa, in Cool and Mason 2008, 127–56

Harding, D. W. 2009. *The Iron-Age Roundhouse: Later Prehistoric Building in Britain and Beyond*

Hartley, B. R. 1960. The Roman fort at Bainbridge: excavations of 1957–59, *Proc. Leeds Phil. Lit. Soc.* **9**, 107–31

Hartley, B. R. 1963. The Roman fort at Ilkley: excavations of 1962, *Proc. Leeds Phil. Lit. Soc.* **12**, 23–72

Hartley, B. R. 1987. *Roman Ilkley*

Hartley, B. R. and Fitts, L. 1988. *The Brigantes*

Hartley, E., Hawkes, J., Henig, M. and Mee, F. (eds), 2006. *Constantine the Great: York's Roman Emperor*

Hartley, K. F. 2000. The 'pottery shop' mortaria, in Rush et al. 2000, 183–6

Haselgrove, C., Turnbull, P. and Fitts, R. L. 1990a. Stanwick, North Yorkshire, 1: recent research and previous archaeological investigations, *Archaeol. J.* **147**, 1–15

Haselgrove, C., Lowther, P. C. and Turnbull, P. 1990b. Stanwick, North Yorkshire, 3: excavations on earthwork sites 1981–6, *Archaeol. J.* **147**, 37–90

Hassall, M. W. C. and Tomlin, R. S. O. 1983. Roman Britain in 1982, II, Inscriptions, *Britannia* **14**, 336–56

Hassall, M. W. C. and Tomlin, R. S. O. 1987. Roman Britain in 1986, II, Inscriptions, *Britannia* **18**, 361–77

Haughton, C. and Powlesland, D. 1999. *The Anglian Cemetery: The Excavation and Discussion of the Evidence*, **1**

Hawkes, S. 1974. Some recent finds of late Roman buckles, *Britannia* **5**, 386–93

Hayes, R. H. 1966a. A Romano-British site near Hutton-le-Hole, *Rydedale Hist.* **2**, 12–19

Hayes, R. H. 1966. A Romano-British site at Pale End, Kildale, *YAJ* **41**, 687–700

Hayes, R. H. 1968. A Romano-British site north-west of Newbiggin Hall, Grosmont near Whitby, *YAJ* **42**, 120–5

Hayes, R. H. 1980. A Romano-British site near Sinnington Moor, North Yorkshire, *Trans Scarborough Archaeol. Hist. Soc.* **23**, 3–7

Hayes, R. H. 1983. *Levisham Moor Archaeological Investigations 1957–78*

Hayes, R. H. 1988. *North-East Yorkshire Studies: Archaeological Papers*

Hayes, R. H. and Whitley, E. 1950. *The Roman Pottery Kilns at Norton, East Yorkshire*, Roman Malton and District Rep. 7

Hayes, R. H. and Rutter, J. G. 1964. *Wade's Causeway, a Roman Road in North-East Yorkshire*, Scarborough Dist. Archaeol. Hist. Soc. Res. Rep. **4**

Head, R. 1997. An Anglo-Saxon cemetery at Hornsea, East Riding of Yorkshire, *East Riding Archaeol.* **9**, 10–59

Hedges, J. 1976. Textile, in MacGregor 1976, 14–15

Henig, M. 1976. Intagli, in MacGregor 1976, 6–10

Henig, M. 1984. *Religion in Roman Britain*

Henig, M. 1995. Roman intaglios, in Philips and Heywood 1995, 372–3

Henig, M. 1998. The intaglios and gold jewellery, in Cool and Philo 1998, 23–6

Henig, M. 2002. Vulcan figurine from Bainesse, in Wilson 2002b, 115–6

Henig, M. 2006. Mosaic, in Hartley et al. 2006, 170

Henig, M. 2011. Sealed in stone: Roman gem stones excavated in York by YAT, *Yorkshire Archaeology Today* **20**, 7–9

Heslop, D. H. 2009. *Patterns of Quern Production, Acquisition and Deposition: A Corpus of Beehive Querns from Northern Yorkshire and Southern Durham*, Yorkshire Archaeol. Soc. Occas. Pap. **5**

Hicks, J. D. and Wilson, J. A., 1975. The Romano-British kilns at Hasholme, East Yorkshire, *E. Riding Archaeol.* **2**, 49–70

Hildyard, E. J. W. 1957. *Cataractonium* fort and town, *YAJ* **39**, 224–65

Hildyard, E. J. W. and Wade, W. V. 1950. Trial excavations of 1939 at Catterick Bridge, *Yorkshire Archaeol. J.* **37**, 402–19

Hillman, G. 1981. Reconstructing crop husbandry practices from charred remains of crops, in R. Mercer (ed.) *Farming Production in British Prehistory*, 123–62

Holbrey, R. and Burgess, A. 2001. Parlington Hollins, in Roberts et al. 2001, 83–105

Hooley, A. D. 1988–9. Roman leatherwork from the General Accident site, York and Catterick, North Yorkshire, *RASB* **6**, 16–26

Hooley, A. D. 2002. Leather from Catterick bypass (Site 433), in Wilson 2002b, 318–49

Hopkins, K. 1980. Taxes and trade in the Roman Empire, *J. Roman Stud.* **70**, 101–25

Hopkinson, G. 2001. Recent archaeological investigations at West Lilling, North Yorkshire, *RASB* **18**, 19–21

Horn, H. G. 1987. *Die Römer in Nordrhein-Westphalen*

Horne, P. D. 2003. Case Study 2: Rural settlement in Roman North Yorkshire, an aerial view, in R. A. Butlin (ed.) *Historical Atlas of North Yorkshire*, 58–61

Horne, P. D. and Lawton, I. 1998. Buttercrambe Moor Roman Camp, Buttercrambe with Bossall, North Yorkshire, *Britannia* **29**, 327–9

Hornsby, W. H. and Stanton, R. 1912. The Roman fort at Huntcliff near Saltburn, *J. Roman Stud.* **2**, 215–32

Hornsby, W. and Laverick, J. D. 1932. The Roman signal station at Goldsborough near Whitby, *Archaeol. J.* **89**, 203–19

Howell, J. K. 2001. Swillington Common, in Roberts et al. 2001, 47–68

Hull, M. R. 1932. The pottery from the Roman signal stations on the Yorkshire coast, *Archaeol. J.* **89**, 220–53

Hunter, J. K. T., Manby, T. G. and Spaul, J. E. H. 1967. Recent excavations at the Slack Roman fort, near Huddersfield, *YAJ* **42**, 74–97

Hunter-Mann, K. 2000. Excavations on a Roman extra-mural site at Brough-on-Humber, East Yorkshire, UK, *Internet Archaeol.* **9** http://intarch.ac.uk/journal/issue9/brough_index.html

Hunter-Mann, K. 2002. The view from the Wolds, *Yorkshire Archaeology Today*, **3**, 2–3

Hunter-Mann, K. 2006. *An Unusual Roman Cemetery in York*, Archaeol. York, Web Publ. **6**

Hunter-Mann, K. 2009. New light on the Roman fortress defences, *Yorkshire Archaeology Today*, **17**, 1–4

Huntley, J. P. 2002. Charred and waterlogged plant remains from Thornborough Farm (Sites 452 and 482), in Wilson 2002b, 439–43

Inman, R. 1988. Romano-British settlement in the south Tees basin, in Price and Wilson 1988, 219–36

Inman, R., Brown, D. R., Goddard, R. E. and Spratt, D. A. 1985. Roxby Iron Age settlement and the Iron Age in north-east Yorkshire, *Proc. Prehist. Soc.* **51**, 181–213

Jackson, S. 1973. *Celtic and Other Stone Heads*

James, S. 1993. *Exploring the World of the Celts*

Johns, C. 1996. *The Jewellery of Roman Britain: Celtic and Classical Traditions*

Johns, C. and Burnett A. M. 1979. The Whorlton (Yorkshire) Hoard (1810), in R.

A. G. Carson and A. M. Burnett, *Recent Coin Hoards from Roman Britain*, British Museum Occas. Pap. **5**, 110–118.

Johnson, D. (ed.) 2004. *Excavation of Broadwood Enclosure, Thornton in Lonsdale, North Yorkshire*, Ingleborough Archaeology Group Publ.

Johnson, P. 2005. Millstones, in NAA 2005, 138–40

Johnson, S. 1978. Excavations at Hayton Roman fort, 1975, *Britannia* **9**, 57–114

Johnson, S. and Neal, D. S. 2002. The re-excavation and study of the Helicon mosaic, Aldborough Roman town, *YAJ* **74**, 113–134

Jones, B. and Mattingly, D. 1990. *An Atlas of Roman Britain*

Jones, L. 2007. Archaeological excavation of a brickwork plan field system at Catesby Business Park, Balby Carr, Doncaster, South Yorkshire, 2002, *YAJ* **79**, 17–53

Jones, M. U. 1971. Aldborough, West Riding 1964: excavations at the south gate and bastion and at extra-mural sites, *YAJ* **43**, 39–78

Jones, R. F. J. 1984. The cemeteries of Roman York, in Addyman and Black 1984, 34–42

Jones, R. F. J. 1988. The hinterland of Roman York, in Price and Wilson 1988, 161–70

Jones, R. F. J. 1990. Natives and the Roman army: three model relationships, in H. Vetters, and M. Kandler, *Akten des 14 Internationalen Limeskongress 1986 in Carnuntum* (Vienna), 99–110

JRS 1957. Roman Britain in 1956, 1, sites explored, *J. Roman Stud.* **47**, 198–226

JRS 1958. Roman Britain in 1957, 1, sites explored, *J. Roman Stud.* **48**, 130–49

Kent, B. J. W. and Kitson Clark, M. 1934. A Roman settlement at Wetherby, *YAJ* **31**, 170–84

Kenward, H. K. and Williams, D. 1979. *Biological Evidence from the Roman Warehouses in Coney Street*, Archaeol. York **14/2**

Kenward, H. K., Hall, A. R. and Jones, A. K. G. 1986. *Environmental Evidence from a Roman Well and Anglian Pits in the Legionary Fortress*, Archaeol. York **14/5**

Kent, B. J. W. and Kitson Clark, M. 1934. A Roman settlement at Wetherby, *YAJ* **31**, 170–84

King, A. 1970a. *Early Pennine Settlement: A Field Study*

King, A. 1970b. Romano-British metalwork from the Settle district of West Yorkshire, *YAJ* **42**, 410–7

King, A. 1974. A review of archaeological work in the caves of north-west England, in A. C. Waltham and M. M. Sweeting (eds) *The Limestone Caves of North-west England*, 182–200

King, A. 1978. Early Agriculture in Craven, North Yorkshire, in H. C. Bowen and P. J. Fowler (eds) *Early Land Allotment in the British Isles*, Brit. Archaeol. Rep. Brit. Ser. **48**, 109–14

King, A. 1986. Romano-British farms and farmers in Craven, North Yorkshire, in T. G. Manby and P. Turnbull (eds) *Archaeology in the Pennines: Studies in Honour of Arthur Raistrick*, Brit. Archaeol. Rep. Brit. Ser. **158**, 181–93

King, A. 2011. A review of the land use and settlement of the Ingleborough massif throughout the prehistoric and Romano-British periods, in Martlew 2011, 22–36

Kitson Clark, M. 1935. *A Gazetteer of Roman Remains in East Yorkshire*, Roman Malton and Dist. Rep. **5**

Kitson Clark, M. (ed.), 1941. Roman Yorkshire, 1940, *YAJ* **35**, 222–7

Lamb, H. H. 1981. Climate from 1000BC – 1000AD, in M. Jones and G. Dimbleby (eds) *The Environment of Man in the Iron Age to the Anglo-Saxon Period*, Brit. Archaeol. Rep. Brit. Ser. **87**, 53–63

Lane Fox, R. 1986. *Pagans and Christians*

Latham, I. D. 1993. Archaeological survey in Canklow Woods, Rotherham, *Trans Hunter Archaeol. Soc.* **17**, 1–8

Laurie, T. C. 2011. Co-axial field systems in Swaledale: a reassessment following recent fieldwork, in Martlew 2011, 37–53

Lawton, I. G. 1992–3. Apple Tree Farm 1987–1992: an Ebor Ware kiln site, *RASB* **10**, 4–8

Lawton, I. G. 1994a. *Derventio*: a Roman settlement at North Farm, Stamford Bridge, *Forum* 1994, 8–13

Lawton, I. G. 1994b. *Derventio*: a Roman settlement at North Farm, Scoreby, Stamford Bridge, *RASB* **11**, 3–9

Lawton, I. G. 1997. The Roman roads around Stamford Bridge, *Forum* 1997, 23–9

Lawton, I. G. 2002–3. Wilstrop Hall, Green Hammerton: a Roman villa site, *RASB* **19**, 6–8

Lawton, I. G. 2005. A Roman heated building at *Derventio*, Stamford Bridge, *RASB* **21**, 14–15

Leary, R. 2008. The Iron Age and Romano-British pottery, in Richardson 2008, 25–45

Leary, R. 2009. Pot, Appendix 5 in ASWYAS 2009

Leak, J. M. and Leak, D. 1970. Note on an earthwork at Arncliffe, W.R., *YAJ* **42**, 402–5

Lee, G. 1997. Cawthorn Roman military complex, *Archaeol. J.* **154**, 260–7

Legge, A. J. 1991. Animal bones in Stead 1991, 140–7

Lentowicz, I. J. 2002. Copper-alloy objects from Catterick Bypass and Catterick 1972 (Sites 433 and 434), in Wilson 2002b, 46–78

Ling, R. 1983. Seasons in Romano-British mosaic pavements, *Britannia* **14**, 13–22

Ling, R. 1990. Painted plaster from Structure B, in Wrathmell and Nicholson 1990, 151–6

Ling, R. 1991. Brading, Brantingham and York: a new look at some fourth century mosaics, *Britannia* **22**, 147–57

Ling, R. 1992. A collapsed building facade at Carsington, Derbyshire, *Britannia* **23**, 233–6

Ling, R. 1997. Mosaics in Roman Britain: discoveries and research since 1945, *Britannia* **28**, 259–95

Ling, R. 2007. Inscriptions on Romano-British mosaics and wall paintings, *Britannia* **38**, 63–91

Lloyd-Morgan, G. 1995. Roman non-ferrous metalwork, in Philips and Heywood 1995, 378–90

Liversidge, J. 1973. The wall-paintings, in Liversidge et al. 1973, 99–103

Liversidge, J. 1980. Wall-paintings, in Stead 1980, 139–45

Liversidge, J., Smith, D. and Stead, I. M. 1973. Brantingham Roman Villa: discoveries in 1962, *Britannia* **4**, 84–106

Long, D. A. 2001. The woodworking plane, in Fraser and Steedman 2001, 46

Loughlin, N. and Miller, K. R. 1979. *A Survey of Archaeological Sites in Humberside*

Loveluck, C. P. 2003. The archaeology of post-Roman Yorkshire AD 400–700: overview and future directions for research, in Manby et al. 2003, 151–70

Lukis, W. C. 1875. Castle Dykes, *Archaeol. J.* **32**, 135–54

Lunn, N., Crosland, W., Spence, B. and Clay, G. 2008. *The Romans Came This Way: The Story of the Discovery and Excavation of a Roman Military Way across the Pennines*

Mabey, R. 1972. *Food for Free*

MacGregor, A. 1976. *Finds from a Roman Sewer System and an Adjacent Building in Church Street*, Archaeol. York **17/1**

MacGregor, M. 1962. The Iron Age metalwork hoard from Stanwick, North Riding of Yorkshire, *Proc. Prehist. Soc.* **28**, 17–57

Mackey, R. 1999. The Welton villa: a view of social and economic change during the Roman period in East Yorkshire, in Halkon 1999b, 23–35

Mackreth, D. 2002. Brooches from Catterick Bypass and Catterick 1972 in Wilson 2002b, 149–57

MacLauchlan, H.H. 1849. On the Roman roads, camps and other earthworks between the Tees and the Swale, in the North Riding of the county of York, *Archaeol. J.* **6**, 213–35, 335–51

Magilton, J. R. 1978. Excavations at Lings Farm, Dunsville, Hatfield, *YAJ* **50**, 57–64

Magilton, J. R. 1986. A Roman building and Roman roads in Aldwark, in Brinklow et al. 1986, 32–47

Mainland, I. 2006. The mammal and bird bone, in Millett 2006, 258–79

Makepeace, G. A. 1984. Report of the Romano-British settlement at Whitley, Wharncliffe, excavated by the late L. H. Butcher, *Trans Hunter Archaeol. Soc.* **13**, 34–41

Manby, T. G., Moorhouse, S. and Ottaway, P. (eds) 2003. *The Archaeology of Yorkshire: An Assessment at the Beginning of the 21st Century*, Yorkshire Archaeol. Soc. Occ, Pap. **3**

Manning, W. H. 1964. The plough in Roman Britain, *J. Roman Stud.* **54**, 54–65

Manning, W. H. 1984. Objects of iron, in S. S. Frere, Excavations at Dorchester on Thames, *Archaeol. J.* **141**, 139–52

MAP Archaeological Consultancy. 1994. Recent work by MAP Archaeological Consultancy Ltd, *Forum* 1994, 28–38

MAP Archaeological Consultancy. 1999. *Crossgates Farm Phases II and III, Seamer, North Yorkshire, Interim Report*

MAP Archaeological Consultancy. 2001. *Crossgates Phase III, Crab Lane, Seamer, North Yorks, Archaeological Excavations*

MAP Archaeological Consultancy. 2004. *Land South of Glen Garth, Town Street, Hayton, East Riding of Yorkshire: Archaeological Excavations Assessment Report*

Marchant, D. and Halkon, P. 2008. *Heavy Metal in the Iron Age: the South Cave Weapons Cache and Other Treasures*

Margary, I. D. 1973. *Roman Roads in Britain* (3rd edn)

Martin, L. 2005. The Iron Age and Romano-British enclosures, in Roberts 2005, 89–124

Martin, L., Richardson, J. and Roberts, I. forthcoming (2013). *Iron Age and Roman Settlements at Wattle Syke*, Yorkshire Archaeology, **11**

Martlew, R. D. 2011. Late prehistory and the Roman Iron Age in Upper Wharfedale: problems, potential and progress, in Martlew 2011, 60–72

Martlew, R. D. (ed.) 2011. *Prehistory in the Yorkshire Dales: Recent Research and Future Prospects*

Mason, D. J. P. 1988. '*Prata Legionis*' in Britain, *Britannia* **19**, 163–90

Mattern, M. 1989. Die reliefverzierten Römischen Grabstelen der Provinz Britannia, Themen und Typen, *Kölner Jahrbuch für Vor- und Frühgeschichte* **22**, 707–801

Mattingly, D. 2006. *An Imperial Possession: Britain in the Roman Empire*

Maude, K. 1998. The very edge: reappraising Romano-British settlement in the Central Pennines: the Littondale experience, in M. Nevell (ed.) *Living on the Edge of Empire: Models, Methodology and Marginality. Late Prehistoric and Romano-British Rural Settlement in North-west England*, Archaeology North-west **3**, 42–6

May, J. 1992. Iron Age coins in Yorkshire, in M. Mays (ed.) *Celtic Coinage: Britain and Beyond*, Brit. Archaeol. Rep. Brit. Ser. **222**, 93–111

May, T. 1911. The Roman forts at Elslack, *YAJ* **21**, 113–67

May, T. 1922. *The Roman Forts at Templeborough near Rotherham*

McComish, J. 2011. *The Former Starting Gate Public House, 42–50 Tadcaster Road, Dringhouses, York*, Archaeol. York Web Publ. **8**

McCoy, M. 2008. *Archaeological Mitigation at Templeborough Rolling Mill near Rotherham, South Yorkshire*, ARCUS Rep. **1023b.2(1)**

McDonnell, J. (ed.) 1963. *A History of Helmsley, Rievaulx and District*

Meddens, B. 2002a. Animal bones from Bainesse (Site 46), in Wilson 2002b, 419–425

Meddens, B. 2002b. Animal bones from Catterick Bridge (Site 240), in Wilson 2002b, 425–31

Mellor, E. 1951. A Romano-British settlement, *YAJ* **37**, 438–40

Mellor, E. 1952. The Harpham villa, *YAJ* **38**, 117–18

Miller, S. 1925. Roman York: excavations of 1925, *J. Roman Stud.* **15**, 176–94

Miller, S. 1928. Roman York: excavations of 1926–27, *J. Roman Stud.* **18**, 61–99

Millett, M. 1990. *The Romanization of Britain*

Millett, M. 2006. Stile of a cupboard door, in Hartley et al. 2006, 156–7

Millett, M. and Taylor, J. 2006. Part 3: the excavated sequences, in Millett 2006, 38–89

Millett, M. (ed.) 2006. *Shiptonthorpe, East Yorkshire: Archaeological Studies of a Romano-British Roadside Settlement*, Yorkshire Archaeol. Rep. **5**

Mitchelson, N. 1950. A late 4th-century occupation site at Seamer near Scarborough, *YAJ* **37**, 420–9

Mitchelson, N. 1964. Roman Malton; the civilian settlement, *YAJ* **41**, 209–61

Monaghan, J. 1993. *Roman Pottery from the Fortress*, Archaeol. York **16/7**

Monaghan, J. 1997. *Roman Pottery from York*, Archaeol. York **16/8**

Monaghan, J. 2000. The pottery, in Ottaway 2000, 140–7

Monk, J. 1978. The animal bone, in Johnson 1978, 99–103

Moore, R. 2008. Village, cemetery and dyke: the archaeology of a northern pipeline, *Current Archaeol.* **222**, 33–9

Moorhouse, S. 2003. Anatomy of the Yorkshire Dales: decoding the medieval landscape, in Manby et al. 2003, 293–362

Morris, C. A. 1998. The wooden artefacts, in Cool and Philo 1998, 335–346

Mortimer, J. R. 1905. *Forty Years Researches in British and Saxon Burial Mounds of East Yorkshire*

Mould, Q. 1998. The lead-alloy artefacts, in Cool and Philo 1998, 121–8

Murray, J. 1990. The carbonised plant remains from selected Roman deposits, in Wrathmell and Nicholson 1990, 189–94

Myres, J. N. L. Steer, K. A. and Chitty, A. M. H. 1959. The defences of *Isurium Brigantum* (Aldborough), *YAJ* **40**, 1–77

Myres, J. N. L. and Southern, W. H. 1973. *The Anglo-Saxon Cemetery at Sancton, East Yorkshire*, Hull Museum Publ. **218**

NAA 1994. *An Archaeological Evaluation of Iron Age and Late Romano-British Settlement with Associated Field System near Flaxby, North Yorkshire*, NAA94/17

NAA 2002a. *Hollow Banks Quarry, Scorton, North Yorkshire, Archaeological Post-Excavation Assessment*, NAA02/121

NAA 2002b. *Melton near Brough, East Yorkshire, Proposed Waste Water Treatment Works, Archaeological Trial Trenching, Final Report*, NAA02/109

NAA 2004. *Bridge Road, Brompton on Swale, North Yorkshire, Archaeological Post-Excavation Assessment, Vol.1*, NAA03/141

NAA 2005. *Stamford Bridge, Water Pipeline, Archaeological Watching Brief and Excavation: Post-Excavation Assessment Report*, NAA05/05

NAA 2006. *A1 Dishforth – Barton, Healam Bridge, Pickhill with Roxby, North Yorkshire: Archaeological Evaluation Trenching, Post-Excavation Assessment Report*, NAA06/03

NAA 2007a. *Teesside to Saltend Ethylene Pipeline Sites 718 and 721, Sike Spa, Crayke, North Yorkshire, Post-Excavation Assessment Report*, NAA06/75

NAA 2007b. *A1 Dishforth – Barton, Phase 2 Evaluation Trenching Post-Excavation Report*, NAA06/155

Neal, D. S. 1996. *Excavations on the Roman Villa at Beadlam, Yorkshire*, Yorkshire Archaeol. Rep. **2**

Neal, D. S. and Cosh, S. R. 2002. *Roman Mosaics of Britain, 1, Northern Britain incorporating the Midlands and East Anglia*

Neal, P. G. E. and Fraser, R. 2004. A Romano-British enclosed farmstead at Billingley Drive, Thurnscoe, South Yorkshire, *YAJ* **76**, 7–92

Northamptonshire Archaeology, 2001. *Wombwell Open Cast Site, Wombwell Woods, Barnsley, South Yorkshire, Archaeological Evaluation*

O'Connor, T. P. 1988. *Bones from the General Accident Site, Tanner Row*, Archaeol. York **15/2**

O'Connor, T. P. and van der Veen, M. 1998. *The Expansion of Agricultural Production in Late Iron Age and Roman Britain*

O'Neill, R. 2001. Roman ridge, in Roberts et al. 2001, 118–23

OSA 2000. *BPTSEP169, West Lilling: An Archaeological Evaluation and Excavation Assessment Report*, OSA Rep. EV02/99EX03

Ottaway, P. 1996. *Excavations and Observations on the Defences and Adjacent Sites 1971–90*, Archaeol. York **3/3**

Ottaway, P. 2000. Excavations on the site of the Roman signal station at Carr Naze, Filey, 1993–4, *Archaeol. J.* 157, 79–199

Ottaway, P. 2004. *Roman York* (2nd edn)

Ottaway, P. 2005. *1–3 Driffield Terrace, York: Assessment Report on an Archaeological Excavation*, YAT Field Rep. **1213**

Ottaway, P. 2011. *Archaeology in the Environs of Roman York, Excavations 1976–2005*, Archaeol. York **6/2**

Pearson, N. 1996. *Archaeological Assessment: a Report on the Yorkshire Water Pipeline – Moor Monkton to Elvington*, YAT Rep.**15**

Phillips, A. D. 1995. The excavations, in Phillips and Heywood 1995, 33–170

Phillips, A. D. and Heywood, B. 1995. *Excavations at York Minster, 1, From Roman Fortress to Norman Cathedral*

Philpott, R. 1991. *Burial Practices in Roman Britain*, Brit. Archaeol. Rep. Brit. Ser. **219**

Powlesland, D. 1988, Approaches to the excavation and interpretation of the Romano-British landscape in the Vale of Pickering, in Price and Wilson 1988, 139–52

Powlesland, D. 2003. The Heslerton parish project, in Manby et al. 2003, 275–91

Price, J. 1995. Roman glass, in Philips and Heywood 1995, 346–71

Price, J. 2008. Glass in ASDU 2008a, 71–6

Procter, W. 1855. An account of the excavation of the remains of a Roman villa near Collingham, *Proc. Yorkshire Phil. Soc.* **1**, 270–81

PRS (Palaeoecological Research Services) 2011. The animal bones, in McComish 2011

Purdy, J. G. and Manby, T. G. 1973. The Roman tilery at Grimescar, Huddersfield, *YAJ* **45**, 96–107

Pye, G. R. 1976. Excavations at Crossgates, near Scarborough in 1957–65, *Trans Scarborough Archaeol. Hist. Soc.* **3** (**19**), 1–22

Rackham, D. J. 1995. Animal bone from post-Roman contexts, in Philips and Heywood 1995, 533–58

Radley, J. 1972. Excavations on the defences of the city of York: an early medieval stone tower and the successive earth ramparts, *YAJ* **44**, 38–64

Radley, J. and Plant, M. 1969. Roman remains from south Yorkshire and north-east Derbyshire, *Trans Hunter Archaeol. Soc.* **9**, 158–69

Rahtz, P. A. 1988. From Roman to Saxon at Wharram Percy, in Price and Wilson 1988, 123–38

Rahtz, P. A., Hayfield, C. and Bateman, J. 1986. *Two Roman Villas at Wharram-le-Street*, York Univ. Archaeol. Publ. **2**

Rahtz, P. A. and Watts, L. 2004. *Wharram, A Study of Settlement on the Yorkshire Wolds, 9, The North Manor Area and North-west Enclosure*, York University Archaeol. Publ. **11**

RAI (Royal Archaeological Institute) 1846. *Memoirs Illustrative of the Historic Antiquities of the County and City of York communicated to the Annual Meeting of the Archaeological Institute of Great Britain and Ireland, July 1846*

Raistrick, A. 1935. Prehistoric cultivations at Grassington, West Yorkshire, *YAJ* **33**, 166–74

Raistrick, A. 1939. Iron Age settlements in West Yorkshire, *YAJ* **34**, 115–50

Ramm, H. G. 1958. Roman burials from Castle Yard, York, *YAJ* **39**, 400–18

Ramm, H. G. 1976a. The Roman roads west of Tadcaster, *York Hist.* **1**, 3–12

Ramm, H. G. 1976b. Excavations on the site of the church of St Mary Bishophill Senior, York, *YAJ* **48**, 35–68

Ramm, H. G. 1978. *The Parisi*

Ramm, H. G. 1980. Native settlements east of the Pennines, in Branigan 1980, 28–40

Ramm, H. G. 1989–90. The Millington Roman temple and Haynes' map, *RASB* 7, 8–15

Redhead, N., Roberts, J., Start, D., Walker, J. and McNeil, R. 1989. *Castleshaw, The Archaeology of a Roman Fortlet*, Archaeol. Greater Manchester 4

Reece, R. 2002. *Coinage in Roman Britain*

Rees, S. 1979. *Agricultural Implements in Prehistoric and Roman Britain*, Brit. Archaeol. Rep. Brit. Ser. 69

Reynolds, P. J. 1979. *Iron Age Farm, The Butser Experiment*

Reynolds, P. J. and Langley, J. K. 1979. Romano-British corn-drying oven: an experiment, *Archaeol. J.* 136, 27–42

Richardson, J. 2004. The animal remains, in Rahtz and Watts 2004, 257–72, 332–9

Richardson, J. 2005. The Iron Age and Romano-British field system, in Roberts 2005, 72–89

Richardson, J. 2008. *The Late Iron Age and Romano-British Rural Landscape of Gunhills, Armthorpe, South Yorkshire*, ASWYAS Publ. 10

Richmond, I. A. 1925. *Huddersfield in Roman Times*

Richmond, I. A. 1933. The four Roman camps at Cawthorn in the North Riding of Yorkshire, *Archaeol. J.* 89, 17–78

Richmond, I. A. 1954. Queen Cartimandua, *J. Roman Stud.* 44, 43–52

Richmond, I. A. and Wright, R. P. 1948. Two Roman shrines to *Vinotonus* on Scargill Moor near Bowes, *YAJ* 37, 107–16

Rigby, V. 1993. Early Gaulish imports, in Monaghan 1993, 725–8

Rigby, V. 2004. *Pots in Pits: The British Museum Yorkshire Settlements Project 1988–92*, East Riding Archaeol. 11

Riley, D. N. 1976. Air reconnaissance of west and south Yorkshire in 1975, *YAJ* 48, 13–17

Riley, D. N. 1980. *Early Landscapes from the Air*

Rinaldi Tufi, S. 1983. Corpus Signorum Imperii Romani (*Corpus of Sculpture of the Roman World*) Great Britain, *1*, fasc. *3*, Yorkshire

Rinaldi Tufi, S. 2006. Head of Constantine, in Hartley et al. 2006, 120

Rivet, A. and Smith, C. 1979. *The Place-Names of Roman Britain*

Roberts, I. 2003. *Excavations at Topham Farm, Sykehouse, South Yorkshire: A Late Iron Age and Romano-British Settlement in the Humberhead Levels*, ASWYAS Publ. 5

Roberts, I. 2009. A Late Iron-Age and Romano-British Settlement at High Wold, Bempton Lane, Bridlington, East Yorkshire, *YAJ* 81, 47–137

Roberts, I. 2010. *Understanding the Cropmark Landscapes of the Magnesian Limestone*

Roberts, I., Burgess, A. and Berg, D. (eds) 2001. *A New Link to the Past: the Archaeological Landscape of the M1 – A1 Link Road*, Yorkshire Archaeol. 7

Roberts, I. and Richardson, J. 2002. *Iron Age and Romano-British Settlement Enclosures at Moss Carr, Methley, West Yorkshire*, Archaeological Services ASWYAS Publ. 2

Roberts, I. (ed.) 2005. *Ferrybridge Henge: the Ritual Landscape*, Yorkshire Archaeol. 10

Robertson, A. S. 2000. *An Inventory of Romano-British Coin Hoards*, Royal Numismatic Society, Spec. Publ. 20

Robinson, G. 2009. A Romano-British Settlement at Millfield Farm, Wheldrake, near York, *YAJ* **81**, 139–77

Robinson, J. F. 1978. *The Archaeology of Malton and Norton*

Roe, A. 2009. A Roman landscape at Moor Lane, Stamford Bridge, *East Riding Archaeol.* **12**, 70–85

Ross, A. 1967. *Pagan Celtic Britain*

Ross, S. and Ambry, C. 2010. *A1 Dishforth-Barton Improvement, Healam North, Fields 63 and 64, Summary Archaeological Report*

Rosser, C. E. P. 1958. Interim report on the excavations at Castleshaw, *Trans Lancashire Cheshire Antiq. Soc.* **67**, 118–19

Roy, W. 1793. *The Military Antiquities of the Romans in Britain*

Rutter, J. G. and Duke, G. 1958. *Excavations at Crossgates, near Scarborough 1947–56*, Scarborough Dist. Archaeol. Soc. Res. Rep. **1**

St Joseph, J. K. 1955. Aerial reconnaissance in Britain, 1951–55, *J. Roman Stud.* **45**, 82–91

Saitch, D. and Matthews, L. (eds) 2001–3. Hazel Lane Quarry, Hampole, Doncaster, *Archaeology in South Yorkshire* **11**, 70–3

Samuels, J. and Buckland, P.C., 1978. A Romano-British settlement at Sandtoft, South Humberside, *YAJ* **50**, 65–75

Scott, I. R. 1998. The iron artefacts, in Cool and Philo 1998, 128–39

Scott, P. and Large, S. 2008. The southern vicus, in Cool and Mason 2008, 123–6

Sherlock, S. 2012. *Late Prehistoric Settlement in the Tees Valley and North-east England*, Tees Archaeol. Monogr. 5

Simmons, I. G., Atherden, M. A., Cloutman, E. W., Cundill, P. R., Innes, J. B. and Jones, R. L. 1982. Prehistoric environments in Spratt 1982, 15–50

Simpson, F. G. 1926. The Roman camps at Cawthorn, near Pickering: preliminary report, 1923, *YAJ* **28**, 17–78

Simpson, G. 1981. Trial excavations at Newton Kyme Roman fort in 1908 and 1909 by F. Gerald Simpson, *YAJ* **53**, 120–1

Sitch, B. J. 1989. A small Roman port at Faxfleet near Broomfleet, in Halkon 1989, 10–14

Sitch, B. J. 1990. Faxfleet B a Romano-British site near Broomfleet, in Ellis and Crowther 1990, 158–71

Slack, P. E. 1951. Report on a Roman villa at Brantingham, East Yorkshire, *YAJ* **37**, 514–9

Smith, D. J. 1976. *The Roman Mosaics from Rudston, Brantingham and Horkstow*

Smith, D. J. 1980. Mosaics, in Stead 1980, 131–8

Smith, D. J. 1986a. untitled, in Brinklow and Donaghey 1986, 59–60

Smith, D. J. 1986b. untitled, in Magilton 1986, 41

Smith, D. 2000. The wall-paintings of the town-house in the vicus outside the Roman fort of Malton, North Yorkshire, *YAJ* **72**, 7–15

Snape, M., Bidwell, P. and Croom, A. 2002. Aldborough Roman town: excavations by Miss D. Charlesworth, 1961–73, and by RCHME, 1959–60, *YAJ* **74**, 29 – 111

Spall, C. A. and Toop, N. J. 2005. *Blue Bridge House and Fishergate House, York., Report on Excavations: July 2000 – July 2002*, published on-line at http://www. archaeologicalplanningconsultancy.co.uk/mono/001/index.html

Spratt, D. A. (ed.), 1982. *Prehistoric and Roman Archaeology of North-east Yorkshire*, Brit. Archaeol. Rep. Brit. Ser. **104**. Reprinted as Spratt, D. A. (ed.) 1993. *Prehistoric and Roman Archaeology of North-East Yorkshire*, Counc. Brit. Archaeol. Res. Rep. **87**

Stallibrass, S. 2002. An overview of the animal bones, in Wilson 2002b, 392–419

Starley, D. 2002. Metallurgical study of an iron beam from Catterick Bypass (Site 433), in Wilson 2002b, 166–71

Stead, I. M. 1979. *The Arras Culture*

Stead, I. M. 1980. *Rudston Roman Villa*

Stead, I. M. 1991. *Iron Age Cemeteries in East Yorkshire*, English Heritage Archaeol. Rep. **22**

Stephens, M. 2000. A Roman site at Crab Lane, Crossgates, North Yorkshire, *RASB* **17**, 11–14

Stephens, M. and Ware, P. 2012. *A Roman Pottery Kiln from the Community Primary School, Norton-on-Derwent, North Yorkshire*, MAP Ltd Publ. **1**

Still, L. and Vyner, B. E. 1986. Air photography evidence for later prehistoric settlement in the Tees Valley, *Durham Archaeol. J.* **1**, 11–23

Still, L., Vyner, B. E. and Bewley, R. 1989. A decade of air survey in Cleveland and the Tees Valley hinterland, *Durham Archaeol. J.* **5**, 1–10

Stoertz, C. 1997. *Ancient Landscapes of the Yorkshire Wolds*

Sudell, T. 1990. The insects from Well 1, in Wrathmell and Nicholson 1990, 267–71

Sumpter, A. B. 1973. Excavations on a Romano-British enclosure site in Edlington Wood (site 8), an interim report, in M. J. Dolby, Archaeology, in H. Phillips (ed.), *Edlington Wood (Doncaster)*, 5–41

Sumpter, A. B. 1976. The pottery, in Whitwell 1976, 37–46

Sumpter, A. B. and Marriott, J. J. 2005. The 1976 excavation, in I. Roberts (ed.) *The Iron Age Settlement at Ledston: A Report on the Excavations of 1976 and 1996*, ASWYAS Publ. **7**

Swan, V. G. 1984. *The Pottery Kilns of Roman Britain*, RCHME Suppl. Ser. **5**

Swan, V. G. 1994. Legio VI and its men: African legionaries in Britain, *J. Roman Pottery Stud.* **5**, 1–34

Swan, V. G. 2002. The Roman pottery of Yorkshire in its wider context, in Wilson and Price 2002, 35–79

Swan, V. G. and McBride, R. M. 2002. A Rhineland potter at the legionary fortress of York, in M. Aldhouse-Green and P. Webster, *Artefacts and Archaeology: Aspects of the Celtic and Roman World*, 190 – 234

Swan, V. G. and Monaghan, J. 1993. Head pots: a North African tradition in Roman York, *YAJ* **65**, 21–38

Taylor, J. 2007. *An Atlas of Roman Rural Settlement in England*, Counc. Brit. Archaeol. Res. Rep. **151**

Thackrah, M. 1967. Excavation of the Roman ridge, Nut Hill, Hazlewood, near Aberford, *YAJ* **42**, 10–12

Thomas, A. C. 1981. *Christianity in Roman Britain*

Thompson, A. 2002. Brooches from other sites and find spots, in Wilson 2002b, 161–3

Thompson, F. H. 1974. The Roman fort at Castleshaw, Yorkshire (West Riding), excavations 1957–64, *Trans Lancashire Cheshire Antiq. Soc.* **77**, 1–13

Thompson, H. 1993. Iron Age and Roman slave shackles, *Archaeol. J.* **150**, 57–168

Thorp, F. 1974. The Yorkshire Archaeological Register, *YAJ* **46**, 141–51

Tibbles, J. 2002. *An Archaeological Evaluation on Land at Low Farm, Cottingham, East Riding of Yorkshire*, Humber Archaeol. Rep. **109**

Tibbles, J. 2003. *An Archaeological Excavation on Land at Low Farm, Cottingham, East Riding of Yorkshire*, Humber Archaeol. Rep. **126**

Timby, J. 1993. Sancton I Anglo-Saxon cemetery excavations carried out between 1976 and 1980, *Archaeol. J.* 150, 243–365.

Timms, S. 2005. *Normanton Golf Course, Normanton, West Yorkshire, Excavation and Evaluation Report* (in South Yorks HER)

Tindall, A.1990. The Roman structures, in Wrathmell and Nicholson 1990, 33–74

Todd, M. 1973. *The Coritani*

Todd, M. 1992. Jet in northern Gaul, *Britannia* **23**, 246–8

Tomlin, R. S. O. 1986. untitled in Brinklow et al. 1986, 63–7

Tomlin, R. S. O. 1998. The graffiti and inscriptions, in Cool and Philo 1998, 349–53

Tomlin, R. S. O. 2008. in Burnham et al., III, Inscriptions, 369–89

Turcan, R. 1996. *The Cults of the Roman Empire* (English trans.)

Turnbull, P. 1982. A Romano-British sculpture from Well, North Yorkshire, *Britannia* **13**, 324–5

Turner, R. C., Rhodes, M. and Wild, J. P. 1991. The Roman body found on Grewelthorpe Moor in 1850: a reappraisal, *Britannia* **22**, 191–202

Tweddle, D. 1986. *Finds from Parliament Street and Other Sites in the City Centre*, Archaeol. York **17/4**

Tweddle, D., Moulden, J. and Logan, E. 1999. *Anglian York: A Survey of the Evidence*, Archaeol. York **7/1**

Tylecote, R. F. 1986. *The Prehistory of Metallurgy in the British Isles*

van de Noort, R. 2004. *Humber Wetlands: the Archaeology of a Dynamic Landscape*

van de Noort, R. and Ellis, S. (eds) 1997. *Wetland Heritage of the Humberhead Levels: an Archaeological Survey*

van der Veen, M. 1989. Charred grain assemblages from Roman-period corn driers in Britain, *Archaeol. J.* **146**, 302–19

van Driel Murray, C. 1998. The leatherwork from the fort, in Cool and Philo 1998, 285–334

Vyner, B. E. 2001. *Stainmore: the Archaeology of a North Pennine Pass*, Tees Archaeol. Monogr. **1**

Wacher, J. S. 1969. *Excavations at Brough-on-Humber 1958–61*, Rep. Res. Comm. Soc. Antiq. London **25**

Wade, W. V. 1952. The Roman fort at Bainbridge, Wensleydale, *Proc. Leeds Philos. Lit. Soc.* **7(1)**, 1–19

Walker, D. R. 1988. The Roman coins, in B. Cunliffe (ed.) *The Temple of Sulis Minerva at Bath, 2, The Finds from the Sacred Spring*, 281–358

Walton, P. 2008. Piercebridge: Roman votives from the waters of the Tees, *Current Archaeol.* **221**, 36–41

Warwick, R. 1968. The skeletal remains, in Wenham 1968, 113–216

Watts, L., Jones, A. and Rahtz, P. 2003. The Roman villa at Blansby Park, Pickering: Excavations at the Park Gate Roman site in 2000, *YAJ* **75**, 15–56

Weatherhead, F. J. 1995. Roman wall-plaster from York Minster, in Phillips and
    Heywood 1995, 248–64

Webster, G. A. 1971. A hoard of military equipment from Fremington Hagg, in
    Butler 1971, 107–25

Welfare, H., Topping, P., Blood, K. and Ramm, H. 1990. Stanwick, North
    Yorkshire, Part 2: a summary description of the earthworks, *Archaeol. J.* **147**,
    16–36

Welfare, H. and Swan, V. 1995. *Roman Camps in England: The Field Archaeology*

Wellbeloved, C. 1842. *Eburacum, or York under the Romans*

Wenham, L. P. 1960. Seven archaeological discoveries in Yorkshire, *YAJ* **40**, 298–328

Wenham, L. P. 1962. Excavations and discoveries within the legionary fortress in
    Davygate, York, 1955–58, *YAJ* **40**, 507–87

Wenham, L. P. 1965. Blossom Street excavations, 1953–5, *YAJ* **41**, 524–90

Wenham, L. P. 1966. Five archaeological discoveries in Yorkshire, *Yorkshire Phil.
    Soc. Ann. Rep. Trans*, 20–30

Wenham, L. P. 1967. Two excavations, *Yorkshire Phil. Soc. Ann. Rep. Trans*, 1967,
    41–60

Wenham, L. P. 1968. *The Romano-British Cemetery at Trentholme Drive York*,
    Ministry of Public Buildings and Works Archaeol. Rep. **5**

Wenham, L. P. 1989. Cliff House Farm near Crambe, North Riding 1960–65, in P.
    Wilson (ed.) 1989, 99–103

Wenham, L. P. and Hall, R. A. 1987. St Mary Bishophill Junior: Excavation to the
    north of the church, in L. P. Wenham, R. A. Hall, C. M. Briden and D. A.
    Stocker, *St Mary Bishophill Junior and St Mary Castlegate*, Archaeol. York **8/2**,
    75–83

Wenham. L. P. and Heywood, B. 1997. *The 1968–1970 Excavations in the* Vicus *at
    Malton, North Yorkshire*, Yorkshire Archaeol. Rep. **3**

Westwood, B. 2009. Romano-British remains at Wansford, in Evans 2009, 97–114

Wheeler, R. E. M. 1954. *The Stanwick Fortifications, North Riding of Yorkshire*, Rep.
    Res. Comm. Soc. Antiq. London **17**

Wheelhouse, P. 2001. Bullerthorpe Lane in Roberts et al. 2001, 37–47

Whitaker, A. H. 1967. The excavation of a Romano-British farmstead at Spaunton,
    Ryedale Hist. **3**, 12–35

White, D. A. 1964. Roman road from Bawtry to Doncaster, *YAJ* **41**, 20–4

White, R. F. 1988. A Pennine gap? The Roman period in the North Yorkshire
    Dales, in Price and Wilson 1988, 197–218

White, R. 1997. *Yorkshire Dales, Landscapes Through Time*

Whiting, C. E. 1941. Excavations at Stancil 1938–9, *YAJ* **35**, 261–9

Whitwell, J. B. 1976. *The Church Street Sewer and an Adjacent Building*, Archaeol.
    York **3/1**

Whyman, M. and Howard, A. J. 2005. *Archaeology and Landscape in the Vale of York*

Wild, F. 2002. The development of the Roman road system in the north-west: the
    evidence of the samian ware, *Britannia* **33**, 268–74

Wild, J. P. 2002. The textile industries of Roman Britain, *Britannia* **33**, 1–42

Williams, D. 1979. The plant remains, in Kenward and Williams 1979, 52–62

Williams, D. F. 1990. Amphorae from York in J. R. Perrin, *Roman Pottery from the
    Colonia*, 2, Archaeol. York **16/4**, 342–62

Williams, D. F. 1995. Amphorae, in Phillips and Heywood 1995, 291–303

Willis, S. 1996. The Romanisation of pottery assemblages in the east and north-east of England during the first century A.D.: a comparative analysis, *Britannia* 27, 179–222

Wilson, D. R. 1969. Roman Britain in 1968: 1, sites explored, *J. Roman Stud.* 59, 198–234

Wilson, K. 1966. A survey and excavation within the area of Scurff Hall Farm, Drax near Selby, Yorks, *YAJ* 41, 670–86

Wilson, P. R. 1989. Aspects of the Yorkshire signal stations, in V. A. Maxfield and M. J. Dobson (eds) *Roman Frontier Studies 1989, Proc. 15th International Congress of Roman Frontier Studies*, 142–7

Wilson, P. R. 1995. The Yorkshire Moors in the Roman period: developments and directions, in Vyner 1995, 69–78

Wilson, P. R. 2002a-b. Cataractonium: *Roman Catterick and its Hinterland. Excavations and Research 1958–1997*, Parts 1–2, Counc. Brit. Archaeol. Res. Rep. 128–9

Wilson, P. R. 2006. A Yorkshire fort and 'small town': Roman Malton and Norton reviewed, *YAJ* 78, 35–60

Wilson, P. R. 2009 The Roman expansion into Yorkshire reconsidered, in A. Morillo, N. Hanel and E. Martín, *XX International Congress of Frontier Studies*, Anejos de Gladius 13, 103–12

Wilson, P. R. forthcoming. Proceedings of the 2009 International Congress of Frontier Studies at Newcastle upon Tyne

Wilson, P. R., Cardwell, P., Cramp R. J., Evans, J., Taylor-Wilson, R. H., Thompson, A., Wacher, J. S. 1996. Early Anglian Catterick and *Catraeth*, *Medieval Archaeol.* 40, 1–61

Wilson, P., Cromwell, T., Evans, J., Hall, A., Hembrey, N., Makey, P. and Usai, R. 2003. *Excavations at Cawthorn Camps, North Yorkshire 1999–2000: Summary Report at Site Archive Completion*, English Heritage Centre for Archaeology Rep. 17/2003

Wilson, P. R. (ed.) 1989. *The Crambeck Roman Pottery Industry*

Wilson, P.R. and Price, J. (eds), 2002. *Aspects of Industry in Roman Yorkshire and the North*

Wilson, R. J. A. 2003. The Rudston Venus mosaic revisited: a spear-bearing lion? *Britannia* 34, 288–91

Wilson, R. J. A. 2006. Aspects of iconography in Romano-British mosaics: the Rudston 'aquatic' scene and the Brading astronomer revisited, *Britannia* 37, 295–336

Witts, P. 1996. The Aldborough Wolf and Twins mosaic: Roman or Victorian? *RASB* 13, 18–21

Wood, I. 2006. The Crocus conundrum, in Hartley et al. 2006, 77–82

Wood, P. N. 1996. On the little British kingdom of Craven, *Northern Hist.* 32, 1–20

Woodward, A. M. 1925. The Roman fort at Ilkley, *YAJ* 28, 139–321

Wrathmell, S. 1990. Discussion of Well 1 and its contents, in Wrathmell and Nicholson 1990, 271–2

Wrathmell, S. and Nicholson, A. 1990. *Dalton Parlours. Iron Age Settlement and Roman Villa*, Yorkshire Archaeol. 3

Wright, R. P. 1946. A Roman shrine to Silvanus on Scargill Moor, *YAJ* **36**, 383–6

Wright, R. P. 1975. A Roman-Christian monogram from York Minster, *Antiq. J.* **55**, 129–30

Wright, R. P. 1976. Tile-stamps of the Sixth Legion found in Britain, *Britannia* **7**, 224–35

Wright, R. P. 1978. Tile stamps of the Ninth Legion found in Britain, *Britannia* **9**, 379–82

Wright, R. P. and Tomlin, R. S. O. 1995. Roman inscribed stones, in Phillips and Heywood 1995, 246–7

Wroe, P. 1982. Roman roads in the Peak District, *Derbyshire Archaeol. J.* **102**, 49–73

WYAS. 1991. *Wattle Syke, West Yorkshire, Report Synopsis* (in West Yorks HER)

WYAS. 1995 *Stile Hill, Colton, Research Archive Vol.1* (in West Yorks HER)

Yarwood, R. E. 1981. The environmental background, in Faull and Moorhouse 1981, 33–72

YPS (Yorkshire Philosophical Society), 1832. *Yorkshire Philosophical Society: Annual Report*

Index